LADYBIRD

# LADYBIRD

My house burnt down
my head is on fire!

## Janita Sakoscheck

UMUZI

Published in 2010 by Umuzi
an imprint of Random House Struik (Pty) Ltd
Company Reg No 1966/003153/07
80 McKenzie Street, Cape Town 8001, South Africa
PO Box 1144, Cape Town 8000, South Africa
umuzi@randomstruik.co.za
www.umuzi-randomhouse.co.za

The lyrics transcribed on p. 160 are from "Jeans on",
originally released by Lord David Dundas in 1976 and
performed by Keith Urban on the album *Golden Road* (2002).
The *Star Wars* quotation on p. 215 is taken from Episode IV,
"A New Hope" (1977). The Shakespeare quotation on p. 218
is from *Macbeth* Act 5 Scene 5.

First edition, first printing 2010
9 8 7 6 5 4 3 2 1

ISBN 978-1-4152-0133-6

Cover design by Michiel Botha
Text design by Guineafolio
Set in Minion 10.5 on 13.5 pt
Printed and bound by Interpak Books, Pietermaritzburg

# PROLOGUE

I have sat on my building-sites with concrete between my teeth, scribbling notes about these events. The proposed penning of my story boiled in me and, quite frankly, it consumed me. I had thought and talked about it for far too long. So, writing it was quick. Everything that happened is written exactly as I recall it.

So, yes, as much as it has embarrassed me to write it, this is a true story. If anyone asked what I was writing, I would say my story is about the brain, told by a stupid young girl. This is half the truth, but it disguises my indignity.

I have changed the names and characteristics of people and places to protect pharmaceutical companies, hospitals, sanatoriums, psychologists, psychiatrists, alternative healers, drug-addicts, and the insane. If you recognise yourself or people or places in the story, and are offended in any way, I am sorry. No harm is intended. And know that I thank you, because I could not have written the story without you.

The only names I haven't changed are Mouse's, Mackie's and Stef's, because they've insisted on being recognised; and Lucky's, because she's a dog. I also haven't changed the names of Oma, Uncle Gerhard and Pooki, because they are dead. This story honours them.

My story begins in May 2002. I was thirty-eight.

# THE SHITTY-COUCH

I fart into the cushion without shifting my bottom. I must look like hell, but I don't care. All I care about is my next cigarette. I have made two lunch-boxes, attached them to two children, who have followed a husband who will take them to school.

I'm on the shitty-couch in the shitty-townhouse and smoking. I don't know where the couch has come from. It could've fallen off the back of a bus for all I care. But I want to sit on it forever, as long as no-one bothers me and as long as I have my cigarettes. I don't give a damn about my health, or what I look like, or anything really. I know I shouldn't kill myself because that would be selfish. I want to kill myself. I recognise this feeling because I've felt like killing myself since I can remember.

I'm sad for my kids and my husband because I've robbed them of me. The love I have for them must be somewhere inside me. I know it is. But I can't feel it. I feel nothing.

The nothingness I feel becomes too extreme, so I get up and crawl up the stairs to the bathroom. I lock the door behind me. I'm a very private person and used to locking myself in. It's ludicrous to lock the door – no-one's here, and no-one would give a damn anyway. I sit on the closed toilet-seat and bash my wrists against the wall, over and over, and scream blue-murder. Now my throat hurts from screaming as well as smoking.

I'm not very inventive finding methods to hurt myself, but the pain does the trick. I look at the redness of my wrists and I'm satisfied. I clutch my head and wail, "No. No. No."

I press my fists into my eye-sockets, but I can't find wetness in them. I don't have tears. I'm the child who's crying crocodile tears. I find this comical. I unlock the bathroom door and crawl downstairs to the shitty-couch.

I can sit on the other couch that faces the tiny piece of north-facing lawn, but I sit on the opposite one, with my back facing the sunshine. It dawns on me that I've been sitting here like this for three weeks since I threw my body under the blazing palm tree.

I brood over my dismal morning routine and feel a tinge of guilt in spite of my lunacy, because I'm being a bad mom to my kids and a shitty wife to my husband:

*I wake up in hell, just like I have done since I can remember. The only difference is that this hell is worse. Stef brings me coffee, just like he has done since we were married. He must love me. I sip the too-sweet coffee with my eyes closed, like a dead person. I go to the loo and slouch over my knees as I consider how little I urinate because of my inadequate intake of water over wine. My eyes remain closed and I'm sure I'm still grinding my teeth, because I've been working them all night and my jaw is still clenched. The drool at my mouth and the grit in my eyes are sticking my face together.*

*I go back to bed to attempt my death-sleep: I get into my foetal position under the sheets. I bend my hands inwards and feel the stretch of my wrist muscles. I like this feeling because I'm all wound up. I'm doing my stretches inwardly and this locks me in. The only way I can fall asleep is if I fidget my feet to the beat of my lullaby, until my tendons ache. This is why I have good ankles. I've managed to sleep like this since I can remember.*

*My children appear next to me and say, "Good morning, Mom." I smile and kiss them like I always have. They must not see my pain. I mask all that I feel, or don't feel, like I always have. Lately it's more difficult to put on my mask because a cigarette hangs from my mouth as if it were glued there, and now the ash is greying the sheets. I don't think my charade is very effective, because my eyes are sunken in, and I move slowly. Also, someone has given me ten green bottles of herbal calming remedy, which I keep gulping down in inconsistent quantities. The kids linger above me for a few seconds while I wish their staring eyes away. Then they escape my dungeon to the safety of their father.*

*When Stef has taken the kids to school and the house is quiet, I can't fall asleep again because my chest gets too sore as I'm about to doze off. So I go downstairs in my bedroom garb and sit on the shitty-couch staring at nothing. My morning routine is always the same and ends with me slouching on the shitty-couch.*

There's a clawing scratch from a presence on the cushion next to me. I'm familiar with this. It has stuck to me for sixteen years. It's Pooki, my other child. I notice that her little feet are still blistered from the hot coals. She's been in a nervous and fretful state since I can remember. I feel her worry. I realise that, although I can't feel emotion now, I can still sense the feelings of others. I know Pooki senses mine, like she always has.

Her eyes tear under her twitching ears; she must be sad too. But she doesn't know she's famous, because she's dumb. I picture her name on the front page of the newspaper: "House Burns Down due to Pooki's Heated Blanket".

I reach across and fiddle with Pooki's ears, thinking of Pilly. Memories of my Pilly intoxicate me, and I'm in a daze:

*I'm wearing my pigtails and holding my pillow. I always have it with me because it's very important. I think I would kill for it. I call it "my Pilly". I hold it in my right fist, and suck my pointer finger while I crack its feathers. Drool runs from my mouth while I stare into nothing. While I slide Pilly along the wall, I not only feel the feathers cracking, but hear the material catching on the rough plaster. The sensation is infatuating. My mouth, ear and finger are prickling simultaneously. This is when my Pilly-passion is at its greatest.*

*The feathers in my Pilly have turned to powder because I've been cracking them constantly for eleven years. I'm throwing my Pilly into the dustbin. I'm filled with anxiety and my heart aches with the pain of loss, like death. But my fear is stronger than my heartache. My aunt has told me that if I suck my finger any longer, two worms will grow out of the little holes dented-in by my teeth, and bite me in the face. Pilly-fiddling goes with finger-sucking, so Pilly has to go.*

I hold onto Pooki's ears as she lies next to me on the shitty-couch. Pooki's ears are my Pilly now. I fiddle with them because they're cool. I wish I could put them into the fridge when they are too warm, but that would be difficult because Pooki wouldn't like that. I squeeze her cool ears onto my nose and they smell like treacle. The coolness and the smell of them entrance me. If she died, I would cut off one of her ears and keep it in my pocket forever.

I do my favourite things as I stare into nothingness: I press Pooki's cool ears between my right pointer and index finger and chew the skin on my left thumb until it's bleeding. I suck the iron taste from my thumb. My cigarette is poised between the other fingers on my left hand. I look at my poor hands with the two teeth-marks on the pointer, and the raw thumbs. I must be mad to bugger them up so badly, but I can't help myself. I snigger at the lovely sight I must be: ear-fiddling, thumb-chewing, drooling, and all this with bruised wrists, and a cigarette attached to my lips.

# CALL FROM BABS

I've kept my cellphone on because I have children, and their school may call in case of an emergency. I'm a good mother. It rings. The ring-tone is "The Blue Danube", our wedding waltz. I check the caller identity and prepare to answer: I suck in my drool, put my cigarette in the ashtray and, taking my thumb out of my mouth but keeping my other fingers around Pooki's ear, grasp the phone, saying in my usual fantastic and upbeat manner, "Hello, Babs, what's up?"

She's wearing her husky voice. "My love, I made the appointment for you, and you didn't pitch." I hate it when she calls me "my love" because I reserve this term of endearment for Stef and me only.

I squirm and manage, "I'm not going because I can't smoke there."

The "can't smoke" response is instinctive because I'm dazed. But I remember that Babs told me she asked her psychologist to call me, and her psychologist did. I cringe as I remember our conversation.

I told this Tulula-shrink that I'm not the kind of person who would ever see a psychologist, and was certainly not going to entertain any psychological mumbo-jumbo. I told Tulula that I was a professional and very much in tune with the ins and outs of my brain, and on no uncertain terms was I going to have anyone ask me what my first memory was, or how I got on with my father. I told her that I hated depressed people who needed psychologists. I told her that people who were depressed were bored, and paid for conversations with people who really didn't give a shit about them and were only financially interested in the number of patients they could see in a day. I told her that it was only Hollywood actors and bored housewives who needed shrinks, because they didn't live in the real world, and needed some hocus-pocus to make them feel that they did.

In my more exhaustive hypothesising with Tulula, I compared this parody to a doctor's Hippocratic Oath. I told her that it was despicable that shrinks could sympathise with depressed people, when they actually felt nothing for them. I even went as far as pointing out the correct pronunciation of the oath, and said with a sarcastic laugh, "It should be 'hypocritical' and not 'Hippocratic'!"

Tulula didn't utter a word while I talked, so I felt a little embarrassed by this outburst because I knew I was treading on dangerous ground. She was *sort-of* a doctor, and this insult would have dug deep. But I persisted with my insults, telling her that psycho-babble was a very sad situation because all patients really wanted was to talk to someone other than themselves, and that they would probably kill themselves anyway.

I think I went overboard with Tulula, but when I finally stopped talking, she very calmly said that analysis wasn't like that, and that we definitely should have a nice chat. Then I felt that I had wasted her phone-call money, because she had called me and I had spent a long time bending her ear. I felt she probably wanted to tell me to bugger off, but that she had a fiduciary duty to endure my ranting. I wanted to tell her that I would call her back so as not to waste her professionally earned money and, more importantly, that is the way I am. Even if I didn't have a penny to my name, I would be generous. I can't bear anyone spending money on me.

I also admit that I was desperate to force my point across and was unwittingly enjoying the conversation. After all, I was a Bachelor of Science graduate, with tons of adult experience under my belt, who could stand up to a psychologist whose education specification was not nearly as difficult as mine. I could have talked to her about this, and my adverse impressions of psycho-mumbo-jumbo, for hours.

Unexpectedly, Tulula was quite composed and I respected this. I inadvertently believed that she had sincerely tried to convince me to consult with her, so I finally said OK, and asked her if I could smoke in her rooms. She said no, and that I could manage an hour without one. I said no thanks and goodbye. I smoke ten cigarettes per hour. She's got to be joking!

Babs sighs and says, "Oh, my love, what are we going to do with you?"

I sigh and say, "Babs, I'm fine … really. I'm busy with something. I'll call you back."

She sighs. "OK, my love, I'm here for you. Bye, my love."

Babs is a professional consultant who makes lots of money and lives in the real world. Why the hell would she give a fat shit about a boring waste-case like me?

# CALL FROM MOM

Pooki is standing at the front door so I say, "Let's go outside and make clevers. Let's go and make pees and poohs."

It dawns on me that going outside for a clever is the only time Pooki and I actually move in the morning. I unlock the front door and stand outside in my pyjamas like a zombie. I always keep the front door locked because, even though we're in a secure townhouse complex, this is South Africa, and people are getting attacked left, right and centre.

It's "The Blue Danube" again. It's my mom. I have to answer my mom.

She says without introduction, "I'm very concerned about the children. I want to know who is looking after them and if they are eating properly."

I sense panic in her voice and I feel sad for her. I sigh. "Mom, they're fine. All is i n order. I'm here. Nothing has changed. They are doing well under the circumstances. Shame, they have just lost their home, their bedrooms, their toys …"

*… their mother.*

I don't want to talk about any of this, so I say, "I'm very busy and I have to go. I'll call you later."

It seems she's having none of my escape, but her voice softens, "How are you doing?" This isn't a typical question for her under strenuous circumstances like these, but the question jolts my chest. I can't answer, so I let a few seconds slip by in silence.

Here comes the more customary stuff I need and expect from my mom: "Darling, I think you should pull yourself together and get on with it. These little hardships in life are here to test you. You cannot let them get the better of you. You must put your chin up and get on with your life. God! Don't I know how to do that! Can you imagine what would have happened to me if I had been weak and weepy during the hardships in my life? I have never let anything, or anyone, get the better of me."

I've heard these sentences so many times that I can mouth them. But it's difficult to move my mouth now. It's difficult to talk, so I mumble, "I'm fine, Mom. Nothing's changed. Life goes on."

I'm being brave for her like I always am. But I hate these pull-yourself-together conversations! I've always been able to pull myself together, especially when I needed to, during the bad times in my life, and there have been many. What's great about the pulling-myself-together business is that I've become a master at it.

I'm sure pulling myself together has a lot to do with needing to work late into the night, or going berserk, or being the soul of the party, or dancing on tables, or having lots of car accidents, or having to vomit a lot from alcohol poisoning and never learning my lesson. This all happening, of course, when I'm not thinking about killing myself. Feeling like dying because I feel sick from alcohol is a lot better than feeling like dying because I feel sick in the head. Feeling sick because of alcohol is a lot more fun.

I need a drink, especially when I'm about to attempt to pull myself together. I light a cigarette.

She says, "Who have you rented the townhouse from, and for how long?" This is my chance to show my parents up, because we're no longer staying with them, and the reasons for this hurt. The sparks of the stringent flames flash through my mind:

*On this dreadful night, six of us, including Pooki and Beauty, the domestic, move to my parents' farm on a force majeure basis.*

*We leave the farm two days after the fire-force-majeure because of five things:*
- *Our neighbours keep calling Stef to tell him the thatch is re-igniting. But he has to travel too far at night to get there, because the farm is far from our house.*
- *No-one has lifted a finger to help Stef tackle the burning debris.*
- *My father tells me not to stuff my mother around because I arrive late for dinner after a meeting with the insurance agent, while my mother spends hours preparing the meal.*
- *My father tells me to get rid of my bloody dog that's snapping at their dachshunds.*
- *And lastly, my mother keeps telling me to pull myself together.*

The deep love I have for my parents throbs somewhere behind my aching heart and I'm sad for them. I'm aware that they are also traumatised and are behaving badly, but I'm forced to retort to my mother, "Oh, Babs knows this lady, Gill, who was looking for a tenant. Babs organised everything." I cringe at the unfortunate location of the townhouse. It's two blocks away from my burnt-down house. If I walk to the far corner of the complex, I can smell the cinders across the urban valley.

Gill hasn't insisted that I pull myself together. She's come over to visit during the last three weeks to sit with me on the shitty-couch and join me in staring out of the window.

I push these thoughts from my mind and instead, I chance an altercation with her. "Babs and Gill are trying to get me to see a psychologist."

I leave her to ponder this until I hear her catch her breath, "Goodness gracious! What a load of nonsense!"

I decide to leave the psycho-conversation to the dogs. "Gill came over yesterday and tried to drag me out to buy some curtains for the townhouse. I didn't go, but she said we should go shopping for stuff to make it more liveable."

The thought of shopping and material things is making me feel sick. The dreadful day we moved into the unfurnished townhouse with nothing but our sadness is still with me.

*Babs has dragged me from the townhouse floor to shop for a bed. I'm lying in my foetal position on the demo bed, throwing my credit card at her to pay. I know this is a very public display of bad manners, but I don't give a continental shit what people think, even if I'm still wearing my pyjamas. I hear Babs whispering to the salesman, "Fire, two days ago. Lost everything ..." And him, "Shame, now this one is my most expensive, but the best quality ..." And Babs, "We'll take it."*

My mom says, "Oh, for heaven's sake, you know I hate shopping. And anyway, I can't leave the farm."

This is a usual retort, and I feel sad for her. But I don't have any more energy to talk, so I sigh loudly, with my mouth turned away from the phone. This conversation is going nowhere. But I begin to feel something at least. The burning acid creeps into my chest, and it feels bad. Not only is it difficult to breathe, but the clamp begins to tighten around my forehead.

"Mom, I've got to go to the toilet." She must be expecting this response from me, and we're disconnected.

# CALL FROM STEF

There's been that background beeping on my cellphone while I've been talking to my mom. It's Stef. I press the green button.

"Hello, my love."

"Hello, my love."

Short sentences are all we're managing right now because I'm a dead person and Stef is facing a lot of crap. I feel so sorry for him:

- He's getting flack from the fire department because he punched a fireman. He grabbed, as he puts it, an inactive firefighter's neck because he was sitting on the curb watching the active firefighters trying to stop the flames while taking his hour's break.
- He's thinking of suing the fire department because it took them two hours to get to the fire, even after being called repetitively by us, our neighbours, our staff and our security company.
- He's pissed off because he suspects the inactive firefighters stole the last remaining items we owned from the garage, which was the last to burn down. The only items Stef really misses are the things that didn't burn and were stolen, like his power tools.
- He's having problems getting a copy of the recorded fire-alert message sent to Fee, the fire call-centre operator, without which the insurance company won't begin to entertain a claim.
- He's started a new business on a big risk, and is trying to secure his first clients.
- He went to the burnt-down house again last night because squatters had moved there after the fire. He's used his own means to evict them, like firecrackers and insect-repellent flame throwers, because the police don't give a shit about something as menial as squatters and petty crime, and the few who are working are dealing with serious crimes like rape and murder.
- He's very tired.
- His wife is behaving strangely.
- And lastly, we generally both feel pretty crap right now.

This is why we aren't talking in big sentences. He says, "My love, Babs called and said you need to be at this Tulula-lady at four today."

"Oh, crap! I'll call you back, my love."

# CALL FROM TRIXIE

I've got another call beeping on my cellphone which signals "Trixie". Trixie is the insurance-lady, and this one I need to answer. The financial prospect of a possible insurance claim bears down on my survival instinct.

I'm very alert and ready for "financial survival action". "Hi, Trixie. How are you?"

"Hello there. I just wanted to update you on the insurance claim for the fire-destruction of your property."

I like Trixie a lot. Trixie and I have become pretty cushy, because she has an amazing ability to make me feel as though she really cares for us, and that the insurance company she represents cares for us too. Shit, even though I don't trust a soul, she's got me into her swing, and it feels like the two of us are one against the huge conglomerate world of insurers. We've spent the best part of the previous week listing and pricing items that burnt in the fire. As sick as I felt about our loss, it was a small consolation to write down the name of a burnt item like "Eighteenth-century French armoire" – value huge; "German crystal chandelier" – value huge. I told her that I had collected antiques since I was sixteen and our house was filled with the stuff, its walls adorned with expensive paintings. Two particular items come to mind and my heart skips a beat: "Eighteen years of diaries" – value nil; "Thirty-five chronologically ordered photo albums" – value nil.

Trixie's voice is different from the one she used on me while we worked on our lists of burnt items. Her voice sounds practised and high-pitched, as if recorded: "I have collated the replacement cost of all the items you have given me, and the total value lost exceeds the actual value insured."

*Shit!*

I'm not stupid. It dawns on me that I've been set up for yet another one of those you-are-getting-nicely-screwed life-experiences. So I don't say a word. I recoil to the back of my cage and wait for my rival to strike.

"This means that you are under-insured and the insurance company can only pay you out the percentage of the under-insurance of your actual insurance figure. This turns out to be a very small sum, but I am trying to get them to be reasonable and pay you out a little more to cover some of your existing bond-liability. Also, if we cannot get the confirmation of the fire-alert call to the fire department, we cannot pay out anything." She used to refer to the insurance company as "the", but now she's saying "we".

*Oh, Trixie! How can you be such a cold bitch?*

She's sat with me for days, seemingly drooling over my lists. And all the while she was probably rubbing her hands in glee at the prospect of my pricing items which did not appear on their list of insurable items! The no-money realisation hits me like a freight-train. I pull myself together.

"OK, thanks, Trixie. I've got Stef on the other line. I'll call you back."

# SECOND CALL FROM STEF

"Hello, my love."

"Hello, my love."

Stef's voice is kind. "Listen, my love, Babs called again about this Tululawoman. Maybe you need to see her, just to get Babs off our backs."

We've always been flippant with one another, and I know we both sense the ludicrousness of this situation, but we can't laugh. I feel sad for both of us, because we can't laugh now.

Last night pops out of nowhere, and I think of sex. The thought of any human being wanting to have sex with me looking the way I do right now is a dreadful one. I see Stef in the chair at his desk, dealing with all this fire and business-on-his-own stuff. I see the Stef of last night, vulnerable and desperate for physical connection with the woman he's lost, his ex-lover. I feel tremendous guilt as I hold the phone to my ear, because I rejected him, and I know he's hurt. But there's nothing I can do about it.

His strength oozes through the phone into my weakness. He says, "Hang on a minute."

I hear another voice in the background and muted conversation about business-stuff. I don't listen because the Venus–Mars thing consumes me. Stef is so very different from me. When I'm stressed, I can't be physical. When he's stressed, he needs to be. My reaction to the fire was frigidity. His reaction to the fire was intimacy. But I need to keep the physical inside. When I feel morose, I like to dwell in it, particularly when I don't have to wake up in the morning to go to work to keep the family fed.

My self-pity must've brushed off on my family, because the evening routine of the past three weeks has been dismal.

*Stef gets home from the office and is cooking supper for me and the kids, while I sit on the shitty-couch. I know that sitting around like a lazy cow is bad, and I feel guilty that Stef is doing everything to keep things together. But I accept that he is stronger and, anyway, I just can't help myself. I'd rather have someone shoot me than have to get up and do anything. I'm stuck to the shitty-couch like old chewing gum. I can only concentrate on keeping on my happy-mommy mask for the kids, so I pretend to be engrossed in* The Weakest Link *on television.*

*I pretend to eat at the table. Eating at the table with Stef and the kids is the most essential thing we do as a family. I do my best to sit up and eat and chat to the kids about their school day. The nausea of talking and swallowing becomes too much. The kids look at me with big eyes and full mouths, and it seems they just accept the way I've become. I say that I'm very tired, and crawl up the stairs to bed. I don't brush my teeth, or put on a nightdress. I get into my foetal position fully dressed, and grind my teeth. I know I should take off my shoes, so I kick them off and leave them between the sheets. Sleeping is impossible, so I swig the herb-drug.*

*Later Stef is beside me. He's shaking and breathing strangely. I'm not sure if it's in passion or tears. I don't really care what it is because I want to be alone. He puts his arms around me and twists me into a ball and holds me. I'm rigid, but he's managed to get me into his vice and I feel his muscles. I imagine him when he was a boxer. Suddenly I can't breathe. I moan and wriggle and push him away. He says he needs me and loves me. He says everything will be OK. I can only shout out loud, "No, I just can't!" This is the first time I cry since the fire, and he turns away.*

I'm ashamed of my poor performance last night and am mute for a while, until Stef says, "My love, I thought I'd lost you. Are you there?"

I remember Trixie's call, and I say, "We've just been screwed over by the insurance company."

Stef is quiet. I know he will take this badly. He has to keep things going. He's the strong, silent type. So I continue, "Trixie just called and, to cut a long story short, we are under-insured and, as usual, I'm the stupid bitch who caused it because I over-valued our loss!"

"OK, from now on let me deal with them."

I whisper, "OK."

His voice is stern, "Now, please call Babs and tell her you are going today at four. She needs to confirm the appointment with this psychologist-woman."

I feel like a cornered rat. I know I have to go and tolerate some psycho-crap and not smoke for one hour.

"OK, I'll call her. What about the kids?"

"All sorted. Clara is collecting them and I'll fetch them after work. I'll get takeaways."

All I can muster is, "Later."

# FIRST SIGHT OF FLAMES

The thought of getting dressed is foremost in my mind. I have to shower and put make-up on. I hate getting dressed under normal circumstances, but when I feel as low as this, getting showered and dressed for a flipping head-bender is more difficult than having my teeth drilled without an injection. My bum is sore and numb but I don't shift to ease it. The physical pain is welcoming.

The complex gate buzzer goes off.

*Oh, please, no, just go away!*

I get off the shitty-couch and crawl to the intercom on my knees. It's Beauty. I know she's come to get her severance pay.

I picture her big white smile as she talks on the upstairs phone while I sit downstairs like a zombie on the shitty-couch. I can almost hear her say to her friends in Zulu, "The fire, it was big. It burnt too long, for many days. Eish, the madam, she is sitting all day. She is not bathing or eating. She is burning the carpet with the cigarette."

I suddenly wonder if she feels good that the madam's house burnt down the day after she told her that she buggered up the Persian carpet by washing it in boiling water. I think of the damaged Persian carpet, and smirk at the irony of the petty water damage to the carpet, and the major fire damage to everything.

I'm also angry because Beauty and her husband, Moses, who were looking after our home while we were away, were there when the fire happened, and might have had a small opportunity to stop it. I picture them standing in the garden and gazing stupefied at the enormous flames, while the glass windows exploded.

I need to deal with Beauty and I swallow hard. She's standing at the front door with her big, beautiful eyes. The beauty of them makes me aware of what I must look like. It must be bad by the look of horror on her face.

"Hau! Sorry."

I try to conjure up some good things so that I can appear normal and talk. But all I can smell is smoke, and it envelops me.

*Stef, my father and I are pressed together in my father's truck. He's trying to make jokes about the horror of the situation, but I don't see the humour. He's talking very loudly to the point of shouting, but he's pale under his bravado. I know he knows that the two of us are not looking forward to dealing with one another over this catastrophe. I've called him for help from the side of the road after a dozen car accidents, but that doesn't make this one any easier for the two of us. Collecting Stef and me from a red-eye flight from Cape Town to introduce us to the new calamity of our life is hard for him, and I feel sorry for him. The closer we get to home, the further I tuck myself into my pull-yourself-together blanket. I wrap it around me and press my head against the vibrating window until it hurts.*

*We're driving up the road towards our house, but the road doesn't look the same because there are barricades everywhere, and it's strange that we're the only car that's let through. Fire engines are screeching nearby and I hear a helicopter above. I cannot believe they're here for us; it must be a coincidence, because this is not happening. My eyes feel full of sand and my limbs are pinned together. I seem to be on my feet and am floating through the broken-down entrance gate in muscle-memory of my usual return home. I hear a male voice apologising for breaking down the gate. I can't go through the front door of my home because it's not there. The man belonging to the voice leads me around the flames, and into the garden.*

*There are a lot of small papers flitting over the grass. I sense their words because they are mine. They are pages from my diaries. They are eighteen years of my life. I can't move my body to collect and hide them. I am rigid. There are many people about. It feels like my home is being used for a morbid garden party. I wish they would bugger off and leave me alone in the smoke until I wake up, or die of smoke inhalation.*

*I hear the man, who must be a fireman, telling Stef that the house has been burning for twelve hours. The look of it is fascinating and frightening at the same time. My house is a three-metre pile of ash held together with bits of wall, like teeth.*

*I hear explosions. The firemen seem to be enjoying the spectacle of bullets heated by fire detonating. They're laughing and jumping around. The fire has reached our bedroom at the end of the house where we hide our gun, like bandits. Not only is my home and heart exposed and naked, but the fact that we harbour a weapon is no longer secret.*

*I collapse on the lawn under the burning palm tree while Trixie holds me in her arms. This lovely lady has appeared out of the flames whispering, "I'm the*

*insurance-lady,"* and I feel her gentleness. *This feels like the beginning of a mor-*
*bid love-affair, because somewhere inside of me I know I'm going to need her.*

*I pull myself from Trixie's arms because, as if out of nowhere, I remember*
*that I hid my wedding ring in a cupboard. Hoping the ash has cooled sufficiently*
*for searching, I ask Moses to go to the far right corner of what once was my bed-*
*room, and bring back spadesful of ash from the piles of debris.*

*I kneel on the lawn under the gigantic smouldering palm tree pawing through*
*the warm, ashy softness. I find it in the first spadeful. The indestructible dia-*
*mond twinkles at me from its blackened band. I have truly found my needle in*
*the haystack. I see Trixie quickly scribbling, "One diamond salvaged from fire."*

I'm sitting on the floor of the townhouse in front of the security gate. I'm very
hot, so I fiddle with Pooki's cool ears. Beauty's eyes look frightened. From my
position on the doormat, I pass her the envelope of cash through the security
gate bars.

She takes it. "Say hello to the kids."

The sound of her clicking tongue fades and I hear her saying, "Hau, eish."

I crawl inside and sit on the shitty-couch. Thank heavens I'm alone again.

# ENTER TULULA

I look at my watch and realise that I have been sitting here for what seems like an eternity since Beauty made her escape. I must have risen only for clevers, or when I needed to bash my wrists, because my bladder feels empty and my wrists look like a hell-raiser's. I light a cigarette and it quivers under the flame.

I have an appointment with Tulula, but how am I going to force myself to stand up, climb up the stairs and get into the shower? Normally I would be figuring out what to wear. But it's easier now because the fire has wiped out any choice of clothing I used to have. The clothes in the small suitcase I packed when we went to Cape Town before the fire are all I have, and it's easy to dress. In fact, these few items of clothing are the only ones I wear regularly anyway. I feel a pang of guilt. The tons of clothes I had in my cupboard were only kept because they were expensive and throwing them out would have been a waste. It's a happy release that they're gone because most of them were bought in a manic shopping frenzy when I couldn't afford them.

But my heart aches for my diaries and my photographs, and the pain almost trips me as Pooki and I climb the stairs to the bathroom. I light another cigarette and remember how fastidious I used to be about not smoking in bedrooms and bathrooms.

I stand in front of the mirror and watch myself smoke. I watch how my lips crease as I draw on the cigarette and blow smoke against my reflection. My skin is yellow and my eyes are deep-set. The blue in them has gone. My face is expressionless, like that of a foetus.

I lean forward to get a better look at the state of my face, and it strikes me that I'm always aware of its changes. I realise that my skin reflects my moods. When I'm empty, like now, it looks grey and smooth. The only expression is in the lines around my mouth when I draw on a cigarette. When I'm anxious, my skin is white and wrinkled. When I'm thinking of killing myself, I look eighty years old. But when I'm happy and wild, I look like a teenager, and my ability to be the world's most fantastic person sends shivers down my spine. Then I pile on lots of shiny make-up, down a vodka and orange, and dance in front of the mirror.

Dancing would be an impossible task now because my body feels lifeless. After studying my face as it works a couple more cigarettes, I realise that I'm now late. I spin into the shower, slap on a bit of mascara, dress in my usual black garb, grab my keys, leave Pooki her food and water, and drive away from her prickling ears towards my first close encounter with Tulula-shrink, the Tulula who won't let me smoke.

Babs has given me directions to Tulula so I know where to go. I realise I've been blanking out, and only come around a few blocks after the turn I was supposed to take. I think I've been sleep-driving. This scares me and my palms begin to sweat. My mouth is burning. I know I've smoked a lot of cigarettes, but I can't remember where I extinguished them. I have to fit a lot of them into this drive-time. I wonder if my car is burning. Maybe there is a fire-devil around me. This scares me and I sweat even more. I'm driving, blanking out, coming around again, and smoking.

The neighbourhood tells me that Tulula probably works from home. There's a stupid electronic gate that's positioned so badly from the intercom that I scratch the side of my car trying to get in. I don't care if my car is scratched. I press the button that says "Rooms", next to the buttons that say "Main House", "Gazebo", "Office", and "Maid's Cottage".

A staccato voice comes from the intercom, "Please sit in the waiting room, which is just off the driveway, while I finish a consult with a patient."

Shit. I thought I was her only patient! My anti-shrink attitude is confirmed. There's just another psycho-head-case sitting with her, pouring his dear little heart out while she looks at her watch until time's-up. I sweat some more and take a few more swigs of the herb-drug, while I sit in my car and wait for the loony to leave.

After a while, I feel a little calmer. I peer at my eyes in the rear-view mirror and see that my lids are full of mascara. This always happens when I pile it over too-swollen eyes. There's nothing I can do about it now, and I don't give a shit anyway, so I go outside for a cigarette while I wait.

I'm thinking about getting back into my car and making a dash for it when my cellphone rings. It's Babs, and she's doing her deep and caring breathing. "Are you there yet?"

"Tulula's late and I'm about to leave."

Babs is insistent. "My love, give her a few minutes. You've got this far. Did you find it alright?"

I won't say anything because I know she's trying to keep me talking to stop me from leaving. She says, "Listen, I've known Tulula for ages and I've sent a lot of people to her. Trust me, she's helped me a lot, and I've only had good reports from my friends about her. I've known her for so long that I've even gone through her divorces with her. Can you imagine that! Shit, she really knows what she's talking about—"

"What the …" I cut her short. But I'm speechless. I have this picture in my mind of Babs taking sadness-commissions from Tulula, while all her screwed-up friends line up for counselling from the greedy divorcee.

Babs must sense she's made a dreadful mistake by telling me that Tulula-shrink has been divorced more than once and is now about to analyse me, and she whines, "My love—"

"Babs, I'm outta here!"

"Shit, my love," she shrieks, "it's just the way you look at it! Having gone through so much has helped her to help me. Try to see it that way."

"I'm sorry, Babs, but I don't give a shit how you see it. She stuffed up her own life and she'll probably stuff up mine—"

"But this is different—"

Tulula appears out of nowhere.

*Oh, shit!*

I push the red button on my phone to cut off Babs. Trying not to be Freudian, I say, "Hi, that was Babs, she was telling me about your husbands. I mean, that you shrink lots of our friends, and—"

*That's it!*

I resign. I'm dead meat. But I actually don't give a shit and feel dead anyway, so I'm pleased our introduction is so messy. Now she has to let me go, so I say, "I forgot to collect my kids, so I'm going. Sorry. Bye."

I inch towards my car. Tulula approaches and takes my hand. I follow her into her rooms like a circus monkey.

# TULULA, SCENE 1: INTRODUCTIONS

We sit opposite each other across an expansive desk in what feels like a cosy little office. I haven't had a chance to scrutinise it, because I'm squirming a lot and praying for my time's-up. I notice though that Tulula has positioned a lot of knick-knacks all over the desk that mingle with what look like very important documents. I wonder if she received all these stupid little mementos as farewell presents from her loonies when they were broke and finally escaped her. I also wonder why the desk is in such a mess, but a messy desk is what I expect from a woman whose mind is obviously confused enough to get involved with the wrong man more than once.

The window behind her faces a grapevine, and she gives me a sour smile in spite of her prettiness. I estimate that she's in her mid-forties. She's very slim and upright and has made up her face well, and that is all I see. I don't care about what she's wearing because material things are eluding me at the moment. The fire has stripped me of their importance. I look into her eyes and they are pretty and very clear. I think of mine and they tear, because my eyes are sensitive and when I think of them, they sting. Or maybe I got mascara in them, or rubbed them unwittingly.

"Are you OK?" she asks, reaching for the tissue box.

I take a tissue and say, "My mascara has got into my eyes," and swipe under my eyes to prove it.

"We need to get to first things first," she says.

*Oh, no!*

Here comes the head-bending question about my first memory or my relationship with my father, but she says, "I'm a small-cash business and I would like to discuss the account before we continue."

I'm in shock. My disdain for her and her ilk is now confirmed. Knowing that I am now in consultation and obliged to be here, I have two choices:

- I fake diarrhoea, don't pay her, and go home to my shitty-couch and be free; or
- I pay her and stay like a lamb to the slaughter.

She hands me an invoice. I'm not sure when I have to pay it but I slump over my purse and place the notes on her desk. I regret it immediately.

She leans back into her chair with a sigh and says, "You were very antagonistic when we first spoke on the phone."

That's a loaded statement that doesn't require an answer, so I don't say anything. I am still antagonistic and hope this will reduce her confidence. I feel I've got the upper-hand already.

Tulula's voice sounds practised. "But I'm used to this when dealing with a patient for the first time. You must just relax. I'm here to help you."

I think of the hypocritical oath and decide to be honest about how I feel about psychology, so I say, "Really, Tulula, I'm absolutely fine. I'm only here because I've been forced to be here by my friends."

I realise she probably couldn't care less how I got here, and needs to get on with her head-shrinking, because she's been paid for it.

"Have you ever seen a psychologist before?" she asks.

I'm incredulous at the suggestion, but feel a sting of guilt, so I say, "Yes, but only for about five minutes, because I walked into the wrong doctor's rooms." This is half a lie, but it's all I'm going to give her.

"I know that your house burnt down," she says quickly, "but I don't want to talk about that for the moment. I want to talk about *you*."

"I don't want to talk about myself."

*And I certainly don't want to talk about the f—*

I don't want to talk about *me*, because talking about oneself is selfish. And I certainly don't want to talk about the f— because I have forbidden myself to mourn material things – I am much better than that. I don't want to talk about *me* and the effing f—, because I'm absolutely fine! Really!

But I abandon these thoughts, and let her get on with it. "Tell me a little about you."

My haughtiness invades me. I remind myself that I am a professional. Public speaking is easy for me. I feel cocky, because I've presented complex financial proposals that I've prepared to important financiers and governments. I've flitted around Africa and Europe, raising lots of money, and putting big development projects together in the sub-Saharan region. I'm a woman of the world, and this chitter-chatter about *me* and what I "feel" is trivial. But I need to capitulate, even though I've been doing far too much capitulating for today. More importantly, I need to get to my time's-up.

She stretches her neck towards me. I cough and prepare myself for very well-spoken English and say, "I'm a qualified Bachelor of Science graduate. I qualified in 1986." I leave her to work out my age. "I have been working in the construction, finance, development and management consultancy industry since then." I feel like I'm in a business interview.

"Are you working now?"

I try to sound flippant, "No, because my husband is getting his own business up and running, so I resigned as a management consultant to be a mom for a while."

I know she won't like this, because I'm sounding normal and balanced. I'm sounding like a true professional who's taken charge of her life and resigned from the fast-lane to spend quality time with her children.

"When did you stop working?" she asks.

I can't remember, but I say, "Hmmm, just after the—"

*Shit! I still can't even say the bloody word out loud!*

My life seems to slot into "before the f—" and "after the f—". I decide that from now on, I will mentally categorise my life as BF and AF.

She nods, and I shift in my chair. She says, "Interesting. So tell me a bit about your kids."

Now this stuff is normally pure bliss for me, and my heart stirs despite its sadness. "I have two kids of four and seven. They are truly the most amazing children in the world. They are fluent in French and English."

The pride I feel for them surfaces above my shame. They surely show me up. I worked for a French company for two years, and Stef and I have been married for almost ten. I haven't had the time, or inclination, to study French grammar. Or maybe it's because I'm a true perfectionist and don't want to sound like an idiot when I try to say the French word "depuis", which is truly the most difficult word for an English person to pronounce. But I have mastered saying "quatre-vingt-douze". I'm convinced it should be a name of a famous restaurant, and not only mean ninety-two, because it sounds so extravagant to an English ear.

"Why French?"

"Because Stef is French. He's actually half-French and half-Austrian, but he speaks perfect English with an American accent."

I like him as an Austrian better, because he's strong and wiry and I like to tease him in public as being "my strong Austrian mountain goat". He has a wondrous sense of humour and takes it well, but I wonder for the first time if this is such a nice analogy. But yes, right now he is the strong goat, and I am the stupid weak pig. My self-loathing surfaces for a second, but I squash it with my surety that I'm a perfect professional and mother.

# TULULA, SCENE 2: PROPOSAL IN THE SKY

Tulula leans forward with her hands in that apex position that some people force their hands into. "Tell me about your marriage."

*Now I've got you, you silly woman!*

I know she would like me to say that we're having problems, or thinking about divorce, so that she can throw her full expertise of divorce-counselling at me.

I need to gloat at this point, because she needs some serious showing-up, so I tease her and say, "I never wanted to get married, or have children. While all my friends were preparing their trousseaus, I was studying and working. All I cared about was my profession and my business. I never entertained marriage or children."

I feel pompous and need to conclude with this dramatic statement, so I put my chin up, as my mother always tells me to do, to show her that this conversation about marriage is over. But she's not surrendering.

"And why is that?" she asks.

I find myself elaborating in spite of my upward chin, "Because out of all the marriages I knew, not one of them worked. Most people I knew were divorced already, or having an affair, or dismally unhappy, or the wife didn't work anymore and was frustrated. I never thought marriage was necessary, particularly for people like me." I feel a tinge of guilt because, given her supposed track record, this is a bit nasty.

But she must agree with this, or she's interested in the "divorce" word, because she raises an eyebrow and asks, "Oh, and how did you meet Stef?"

*Good, now I'm definitely going to show you up!*

In fact, what I'm about to tell her will put her into a downward spiral, creating enough chaos for me to get the hell out of here. But it's going to be difficult to talk, because I feel intensely sad and anxious. I pine for my shitty-couch and Pooki's cool ears. I try to find some energy because, in spite of the hole in my chest, I need to show her up. So I lean forward in my chair and say as casually as I can, "I met him on an aeroplane."

I let the statement hang in the air until she urges, "And?"

"He immediately asked me to get married, and we did."

Again I leave her in the sky, where she must be wondering about mile-high clubs and weddings-on-board, but she presses on, "But you never wanted to marry."

A rhetorical question, but I'm desperate to answer it. The sexy memories whirl around me in spite of myself, and I blabber, "I know I never wanted marriage, but this was right. I just knew it."

Thinking about what Stef and I always say to each other stabs me, because it's difficult to conjure up passion for it now. We say that our meeting was like two people finding one another across timelines, across centuries of reincarnations, across the universe. We say that even if we hadn't met in the aeroplane, our energies would have collided at some point across the seas, like the opposite poles of a magnet.

I drift back into Tulula's head-shrinking dungeon as she says, "How romantic."

"Yes, it was romantic." I feel like being a bit nasty and add, "I tell all my single friends that if you don't find 'The Thunderbolt,' rather live a thousand lifetimes until you do."

She's probably trying to imagine a perfect man, a perfect relationship, a perfect love, and she visibly shudders, perhaps at its impossibility, but she continues, "So did he ask you to marry him on the aeroplane?"

I think it's an ambiguous question, but I just say, "No."

I know I'm being a brat by being so curt, and she must sense it, so she says, "Tell me about it. I would truly love to know."

She's got me into her web, because she's actually being quite nice and probably asked me a genuine question. I take a deep breath to spur me on. "In the days when one could still smoke on aeroplanes, I went to the back row to smoke, because my girlfriend and I were sitting in the non-smoking zone."

I remember that a man in the seat behind us farted, and we blocked up the hole between the seats and laughed ourselves silly. Memories of laugher hurt, but I continue the story that I've told a thousand wannabe brides and chauvinists, as if in a recording: "So I walked down the aisle and sat in the last row where he was sitting."

Stef claimed the entire back row of economy class for himself, and when I first clapped eyes on him, I thought him deliciously handsome. I'm too empty to explain all this stuff to Tulula, so I do my best to give her the bare minimum.

But I'm still on the aeroplane. Memories of travelling first class during my career as the professional-businesswoman-of-the-universe invade me:

*Sue, the air-hostess, who's become a familiar face because of my many trips in first class, whispers, "Can I take your coat, madam? So nice to see you. Veuve Clicquot, caviar as usual? Just sit back and relax, madam."*

I shudder. What an obnoxious bitch I must have been. But my usual intake of far too much champagne left me puking above the sticky floors of the aeroplane toilets and passing out on horizontal seat A1.

Tulula's here, and says, "And then?"

My stomach turns, so I turn my attention back to showing up Tulula in the love-department. "Anyway, we started talking about what we did professionally. Stef was working for the European Economic Community, and I was sourcing a ship for one of our developments on the eastern seafront."

I'm still on my mission to prove to Tulula just how normal and fantastic I am, and that I'm not meant to be here. But the memories of my wondrous meeting with Stef are flitting around me like butterflies I can't ignore:

*The passengers in the plane are like ghosts. The only presence we feel is the heat of our bodies, as we sit close together. We are flashing our success about and impressing each other no end, but underneath it all I know we have both experienced "The Thunderbolt". We are smitten. It's cosmic. There's no turning back. The only turning back I'm going to do is returning to the back row to blow smoke into the face of the man who's stolen my heart.*

"And then?"

Tulula's probably trying to get to the mile-high bit, but she's not going to get it, and anyway, it didn't happen. I pride myself at the person I was then: a ridiculous and old-fashioned prude – even though I was dating a polygamist at the time.

*Where the hell did that come from?*

I feel a spasm of guilt and a bit of bile edges its way up my throat, but I swallow it down and manage, "Well, I was a real prude in those days, because Stef had asked a number of times if he could give me and my girlfriend a lift to our Paris hotel, but I kept saying, no."

"And then?"

I'm still in my recording to wannabe brides. "We were standing at the baggage-reclaim at Charles de Gaulle, and he walked up to us and asked if we were sure we didn't want a lift to our hotel, and my girlfriend said, 'Sure we do!'"

Oh, heavens, what if she hadn't accepted that lift? Would I be sitting here now like a head-patient in the wrong place at the wrong time? My head spins.

*But Stef is swanking towards us at the baggage-reclaim with his sexy, twisted smile and his American accent, and my knees are weak, and I think how lucky I am because my girlfriend says, "Sure we do".*

*We hang under his armpits on the rails of the bus on the way to his car, and I whisper in her ear that she's crazy to have accepted his offer. What if he attacks and rapes us? But she knows I'm the prude, and says that there are two of us to one of him, and if he tries anything, we could jump him and kill him.*

*We giggle all the way to the hotel and I think how manly he is by not reacting to our silliness, as all my previous boyfriends had done. He stares at me in the rear-view mirror with his sexy eyes as I sit in the back seat and tingle all over. Not only is he good-looking and masculine, but there's dog hair all over the car. This is the cherry on top. He loves animals too!*

"And then?"

I'm getting aggravated with all Tulula's "And thens", but I push on. "And then he dropped us at our hotel and the next day he asked me to marry him, and I said yes. And that's it."

I'm getting tired and giddy, and need a cigarette to wake me up. The memories of that wonderful time are bearing down hard on me.

"And then?"

*That's enough!*

I've got to get out of here and my ciggy is calling me, so I say, "Excuse me, I'm just going to the bathroom."

She gestures me to the back of her office where I see a door with a metal lady on it, and she mumbles, "By the way, you can't smoke in there." So I spin out the front door with cigarette-lighter poised.

She doesn't follow me outside, and I stand with my back against her closed door puffing away. I take a few swigs of the herb-drug. With all this nice stuff running through my chest and veins, I'm starting to feel a little more alive, so I chance it and, instead of going home, walk back into her rooms.

She's on the phone, probably talking to her accountant or getting her bank balance, but she puts the receiver down quickly and shifts back into her "fake-caring" position.

"OK, he dropped you at your hotel … and then?"

I wonder why she's still interested in this story. There is no mile-high or first-night sex in it, but I'm feeling a little fresher after my cigarette and try to continue. "And then the next day he collected us early to take us around Paris and show us the sights." I find it hard to talk about these nice things. But I'm back in Paris, and this was a very good time indeed.

*Stef manages to squeeze his car into the tiniest parking space in the Champs-Elysées at high speed, and this show of confidence is very sexy. He's collecting his friend. I am sure the friend is meant as a date for my girlfriend. As much as she is single and I am not, the force of his passion is directed at me. I gloat at this beautiful surety as I sit stupefied in the back of his car.*

A funny thing pops out of nowhere. My girlfriend was not at all charmed with Stef's friend's advances and his chapped lips when he tried to kiss her. Stef told me that his friend wasn't charmed either because he spent a lot of his dwindling student loan on her, and hadn't managed to score a bonk. Tulula's tapping her pen on the desk but I'm too far away to care.

*We're walking to the friend's apartment block in the east end of Paris when Stef stops me short in the street, looks me hard in the face, and asks, "What are you doing for the next fifty years?" I think he's just full of bravado, and giggle into my redness.*

*Later, the four of us are sitting in a pancake shop in Montmartre. My heart is a-flutter with emotion. People are walking by in slow motion in the rain. It's cosy inside. I feel so very, very loved and I don't know why. My friend and his friend seem happy bantering, but I can't hear a word they're saying because Stef is zapping me with his secret passion device.*

*He offers me a cigarette with his eyes burning into me. I open the box to take one. The words written on the flip-cover read "Marry me". He's drawn a face with a pleading smile, in caricature, underneath the writing. I think he's a very good artist. I write back, "Yes, now or never."*

I remember only now, after so many years, that I had kept the cigarette box, and all of his letters, under my bed, and I have forgotten about them. The sadness of their loss burns into my chest. I try to force myself to ignore it and to feel the glorious emotions of our meeting, but they're evading me.

But Tulula is here, and she helps me to pull myself together by saying, "And when did he actually propose?"

"Oh, on the day after we met, at about ten o'clock in the morning, and I said yes, and that was that."

*The past hours are swirling around me like the fumes of whisky. We're standing alone on the dark cobbled streets of Paris. The Seine is twinkling in my perfect screen, like in the movies. We have left the bar, Whisky a Go-Go, where the South African rugby team is celebrating a victory over the French and I'm oh so proud to be South African. Stef gives me a pin from his leather jacket. I take it and say, "I will keep it forever." We finally kiss on the Pont de l'Alma. He slips his hand under my pink polo-neck. I arch my back towards him as his hand creeps up to my breasts. Even though they are small, he makes them feel bigger.*

The passion I felt eludes me, and I feel so sad. My head is sore and misery pumps at my temples.

"So you got married then and there."

*Of course not, you fool!*

I'm incredulous at how she could expect a professional like me to dart off into nowhere and shirk my responsibilities. "Of course not!"

Tulula's eyebrows shoot up, but I can't leave the scene of our parting in Paris outside my hotel.

*Stef arrives the next day with a ticket for me to the Caribbean. He wants me to join him on his next assignment for the European Economic Community. "This is your chance for eternal happiness, just do it," he says. And my girlfriend says, "Just do it!"*

*The concierge is glaring at me from his little desk because he's been kept up all night by frantic calls from South Africa by a crazed and jealous man who has threatened his life. I'm terrified and trapped and breathless because I know I'm right in the middle of one of those split-path life choices. My sense of duty and prudishness is going to be responsible for this decision, and it makes me so very sad I could rip my heart out on the street, and really give the concierge something to worry about.*

I gag at the reasons for my not going with Stef, but I say to Tulula, "No, we didn't get married then and there. I went back to South Africa because I had a business, and people in my employ, and a house and a dog. I went back to resign as a shareholder and director, and to close the doors of my life."

This is a mild way of putting the hell I went through in getting out of South Africa, but I stiffen my shoulders and say casually, "I had a few things to sort out at home. But we were set to marry and that was that."

Tulula looks a tad sad that I didn't go right away, but I can't help her. I have to help myself.

*I'm pressing my nose into Stef's chest-hairs as we slow-dance to "Last Train to London". We have kissed on the Pont de l'Alma and we are dancing in a night-club in a converted section of the Paris catacombs. It's difficult to slow-dance to this song but we don't care because it's our first dance and we can't separate our bodies. I'm sniffing his body odour and he smells of soap. I'm intoxicated.*

"So you didn't go with him right there and then. And then?"

*I've gone back to South Africa and cleared the cobwebs of my private life, but now I am back in Europe. I am waiting for Stef at Schiphol Airport. I'm dizzy with passion and lust and love. Here he comes, wearing the same leather jacket and the same sexy smile. I like the look of his jeans as they crease at the top of his legs, and his cowboy boots, and his shirt, and everything about him. We bash our teeth together when we kiss and our tongues disappear into each other's mouths. We are together again, and we will make love tonight for the first time. And we will be married ... forever.*

*While we're both laughing at the blood on our gums from our violent kiss, he opens his satchel and presents me with a gift. It's a* Tintin *book,* The Shooting Star. *Before I can determine whether I'm dreaming, I give him my gift: a T-shirt imprinted with the cover of the same book. I nearly pass out as we stand here looking at each other for a long time.*

I feel dizzy again. The memories are like fleeting winds blowing over my madness. But I'm here with Tulula and it's ten years later and I am married to Stef, and I am safe.

I don't know why – maybe to punish myself in the face of such happy memories – but I add quickly for shock-effect, "Stef is younger than me, but when I met him I was involved with a man thirty-five years my senior …" I immediately regret saying it.

# TULULA, SCENE 3: THE REVILED ASSOCIATE

Tulula exacerbates my regret over my mentioning "the senior partner" by asking, "Tell me a little about this older man."

I'm mute. I feel the head-clamp tighten around my forehead and the acid creep up my chest and I sweat. I don't want to talk about him. He almost killed me. I hate him, I hate him, I hate him! So I mumble, "I don't want to talk about him."

My head feels fuzzy and I'm confused. Suddenly I'm blurting out words like vomit and the bitterness burns my throat, "I hate myself. I was stupid. He made everybody like him. He showered me with expensive gifts and extravagant trips. He manipulated me, even though I was clever. I made long lists of lies and he would explain them away, and I believed him, and he cried, and he begged me to stay, and I felt sorry, and his secretary told me that different women called claiming to be his wives, and I didn't believe it. I was young, I was stupid, I made a mistake. I wish I could apologise to his wives. I wish they could forgive me. I will never forgive myself ... I hate myself!" I hear my voice, and it's screeching.

Tulula lunges at me across her desk and tries to grab my hand. "Slow down ... Breathe ... It's OK ... We'll get through this ..."

*I can't calm down, you idiot! And I'll get through this now!*

I pull my hand away from hers and suck in as much air as I can, "There were evil spies who recorded hours of my voice and took secret photographs of me and followed me and searched my suitcase when I got back from Paris and found out about Stef and called him in Paris and told him they were going to have him and his family killed so that Stef had to move away from his family to protect them and I signed a surety for the old codger because I was sorry that I was leaving him and the bank gave him the loan by mistake because he was already in debt at another branch and they admitted he was screwing the bank manager but they called up my surety and sold my house for nothing because the sheriff of the auction was in cahoots with the manager and I lost everything and he took me to the cleaners after I told him I was leaving and he was violent—"

I can't breathe! I hear the words coming from my mouth and it sounds like the plot of a bad movie, but the hatred I have for the senior partner overwhelms me.

Tulula looks as confused as I feel, but at least I'm breathing again. I feel my chest heaving. "Anyway, I was conned, I made a bad business mistake just like everybody does and it certainly doesn't warrant discussing here. All of that is old news and I don't want to talk about it. I've had many awful things happen to me in my life, just like everybody has, and I have never let them get the better of me. It's over and I'm fine." I'm sounding like my mother and I know that if she could hear me now, she would be proud.

Tulula says, "We need to book some sessions about this, because you need to revisit all that stuff. It's the only way you can go forward."

*I'm listening to my recorded voice on the hidden tapes that I've just discovered, and I'm looking at black-and-white photos of me doing my daily activities, and I am ashamed, so very ashamed.*

I feel ill. Just the thought of saying one more word about this is choking me, so I insist, "Trust me, I'm fine, it's over and I don't want to talk about it. Really."

She's not hearing me because she says, "I really shouldn't say it before I've got all the facts, but what you've said hints at psychopathic behaviour …" She must be talking about me and I'm impressed – at least I've been diagnosed! I'm not sure what a psychopath is but it sounds exciting.

Tulula's still onto the psychopathic thing. "The people who've been spun into a psychopath's web need more psychological help than the psychopath because the guilt and shame that consumes them can reduce their confidence and affect their behaviour. I'm a little worried about the effects your experience has had on you, so I think we should have a few sessions about it."

I'm certainly never coming back here, but I'm a little disappointed because I thought I was diagnosed and ready for my time's-up.

But Tulula's not conceding. "Do you ever think about him now?"

*Oh, my God!*

"No, not at all. So I'm fine, really."

*I'm in my recurring dream, and I'm shooting him, but the barrel of my gun melts and points downwards and doesn't fire, and he just keeps coming at me with his steely teeth, and I am angry and terrified, and the hatred is consuming me like acid.*

I won't tell her this. I sit up straight, still trying to shoot him with my melting gun. I think my eyes have been rolling because the muscles in my eye-sockets are sore. Tulula must be in heaven.

But memories of the senior partner are flooding over me like tongues of fire on the ceiling:

*It's the senior partner, and he's near me. I'm flitting around London in five-star hotels and presenting big development projects to very important financiers, and having drinks with the boys in Bond Street, and being the only woman invited to exclusive men's clubs, and all the men are hanging on to my every word, and I am the belle of the ball, and oh so clever and pretty and fascinating.*

*I'm washed out and in my hotel room, and alone. I'm putting up the "Do Not Disturb" sign and locking the door and cancelling my flight home, and making excuses to colleagues that I'm ill and need to recover. And I'm trembling because I've been here so many times in my life before. If it's not staring at the grey speckled ceilings of hotel suites, it's mentally tracing the tiny pink roses on the wallpaper of my childhood bedroom until they look like monsters. And I cannot get up and I lie in the hotel bed watching CNN, and take food-trays slid in on the carpet because I can't face anyone, not even the concierge. And I don't take calls, and I bathe ten times a day, and I stay like this for days on end. And then suddenly, as if the sun comes up inside me, I finally open the curtains of my hotel room and book my ticket home as if nothing had happened at all. And I am Miss Wonderful once again, and can't believe that I've been such a baby and done this to myself again.*

I'm probably looking like a crazed animal and I see Tulula glance at my hideous, deformed thumbs. It seems she wants to make this easier for me because she says, "OK, just calm down."
*I am calm, you idiot!*
"Let's leave all that stuff aside for now."
*We'll leave it for good, you silly woman!*
"Go and have a cigarette, and hurry; we don't have much time left."
*Sure!*

I spin out of her room to the open arms of my dear friend, Mr Ciggy. No thought crosses my mind until the smoke is drawing through my lungs and whirling around my head. I'm going to stay outside until my time's-up, and I lean against the wall like the prostitute I am, and puff away. All thoughts of our session are now gone, tucked nicely away under the pull-yourself-together blanket.

She's next to me. "Come inside now."

*What the hell? Let's just say our goodbyes now, you silly cow!*

I toss my cigarette into the bush and say, "Oh, do you mind if I throw it over there?" She doesn't answer and I follow her inside once again. This time I'm a raging tiger, ready for my gladiator.

We're back in our positions and I stare at her with lazy tiger-eyes across the miniature figurines, my tail swishing.

"Well now? You look better. OK, I'm now going to ask you a few questions from my list, so please answer them quickly and truthfully. It won't take long."

She's already asked me enough, so I will just sit here and stare at her. She takes out a yellow folder and poises a pen above it, and nods up and down from my face to the folder and back again.

# TULULA, SCENE 4: 20-QUESTIONS

I know I'm going to need to respond to her questions, because sitting here like an indignant child and not talking to her will lead to another embarrassing situation of failing to get the hell out of here. I need to capitulate to get this over with. I need to draw on my many years of experience in meetings and interviews. I shift my bum so that I'm upright on the chair and prepare myself for Tulula's stupid questions. The questions that don't seem to be her own.

She shifts her bum too and sits upright to meet my haughtiness. "OK, let's go. Babs told me that Stef thinks you are hurting yourself."

My head explodes.

I'm astonished, and blurt out, "Oh, nonsense. What the hell is Babs talking about?"

Tulula looks at my bruised wrists and I feel like a rat in a trap: little paws stretched out and pinned under the snap-bar. I pull my hands into my stomach and look at her with my mouth open.

"Have you ever hurt yourself before?"

I slump into my chair like a raggedy doll and yearn for Pilly, or Pooki's ears, or a bottle of vodka, and I mumble, "Yes."

"These questions are mechanical, so just relax and answer as spontaneously as you can."

I'm very relaxed, and I feel humble, and I want her to hold me and rock me until I die. But of course she won't, so I put my thumb to my mouth and rub the cracked skin against my lips.

"Have you ever pulled out your hair?"

"Only once."

She doesn't twitch. "Have you ever felt like you are moving quickly but everything around you is in slow motion."

"Huh?"

"For example, you may be in a crowded room, or walking in a shopping mall, and everything around you is moving slowly, as if you are viewing a slow-motion picture. Or alternatively, you are moving slowly, and all else around you is moving quickly and whizzing by?"

This is a weird question but I know the feeling and am actually feeling it right now, so I take a little time, and say, "Yes."

"Have you ever experienced strange smells?"

I mumble, "What do you mean?"

"For example, like a smell that comes out of nowhere. You smell it but you don't know where it's coming from."

"What kind of smells?" This is all becoming very weird.

"Oh, like perfume, or fire, or rotting meat, or acid."

*I'm in my nightmare. I'm hiding under my bed and the wolf is after me again. I'm running to my parents' room, but he's gaining on me, and I can't get there. I can smell acid and my nose is burning. I wake up screaming and the smell is still in my room. I know that this is my repeating dream. It's the one I always have at the end of any other dream. It's followed by me being in the sky above the garage of our house, and looking down at my grandmother, who is lying on the floor at the front door with an old blanket around her; she's asking my mother for a room to stay, while my mother peers down at her.*

I think of my grandmother, and her being an alcoholic, and my poor mother having to fetch her off the streets of Johannesburg. I picture Granny being found slouching, dead and alone, over the toilet cistern where she died from liver failure. I am sad. I can see Granny: she's wearing her big sunglasses and smelling our little feet and going, "Eeeuw."

But the acid creeps back into my nose, and I say, "Yes, I think I have experienced strange smells. I've smelt acid, like that stuff you clean toilets with."

Again Tulula scribbles down my response in her yellow folder. "Any other smells?" I think hard about this.

*I'm on the piano stool in my parents' lounge in our haunted house playing "Chopsticks". I smell perfume and I don't know where it's coming from. I ask my brother who's sitting next to me playing "Chopsticks" along with me on the base keys, and he says he can't smell anything and that I am truly crazy. And he says that it's probably the ghost that smells, and we scream and clutch each other closely until we manage to laugh again.*

I'm incredulous at this realisation of something I thought was insignificant, but I say, "Yes, perfume."

"What kind of perfume did you smell? Was it floral or musky?"

That's easy and I'm quick to answer, "It was definitely musky."

"Other than the acidic smell that came about after your recurring nightmare, how often did you smell the perfume?"

"Not often." I try to remember and add, "Maybe once a month."

She scribbles something down, and asks, "Have you ever felt that parts of your body are enormous, or growing in size, compared to the size of other parts?"

*Shit, she's good.*

*I don't like the wallpaper because it's old-fashioned, like my antique headboard. The fabric of the padding on the headboard and the curtains are identical to the wallpaper. The whole bedroom is just roses, roses, roses. My friend Lindy has posters of horses and rock-stars on her wall. I wish I could rip off my pink roses and do the same. I'm being a brat because Mommy's tried so hard to make my room pretty. I can't make out the monsters on my wallpaper anymore because it's dark and I can't see the roses on it. Fear wells up inside me as I lie in my bed and look at my hand. It's gigantic, and I rest it on an imaginary miniature table.*

Dammit! How can anyone know about these things? I feel exposed. So again I have to say, "Yes, but I don't experience it anymore. But what the hell is it?"

She's cool and professional and states, "It's called dysmegalopsia, and don't feel alone, a lot of people experience it." That's a very small consolation because it used to scare the hell out of me.

"Do you experience a lot of déjà vu?"

"Sure, but so does everyone."

"Hmmm."

She ticks her yellow folder.

"Have you ever heard voices in your head?"

"No."

"Have you ever heard buzzing or ringing in your head?"

"Yes."

These questions are creepy, yet pointed. I'm inwardly astonished and even want to add to them, so I say, "I am making things happen at the moment."

She raises a brow. "Really, what do you mean?"

"I just look at a light bulb and it pops, or I think of the vacuum and it stops working. Anything that could go wrong does, if I just think it. And the funniest thing of all is that the only thing we salvaged from the f— was our washing machine, and we had brought it to the townhouse and it was still working perfectly. And I thought to myself that it would be extremely ironic if it broke, and I turned it on to see if it had, and it was broken. Isn't that a laugh?"

Tulula doesn't laugh, but my humour is back, and I'm comforted. And it suddenly startles me that, given enough course-altering power like I have at the moment, the prophecies of soothsayers, fortune-tellers and people like Nostradamus could indeed happen if enough people believed and thought about them long enough. I picture a glass of wine flitting through the air as I will it towards me, and my not even having to get off the shitty-couch to get it. But I caution myself not to believe anything any shrink tells me or makes me feel about myself, because I know that if I thought about it, it would indeed be the case.

My glass of wine is flying towards me again. I try to duck down as the wine bubbles explode in my face, but I feel weak and the hotness of my face burns at my hairline.

*I'm having dinner with Babs the night before we leave our home for the last time. We are drinking a lot and chatting into the night with a candle flickering between us. I'm fiddling with the wax as it drips onto my fingers. I've pulled out a thread of hair from my head and I'm holding it poised above the flame. I need to smell the burn and watch my hair sizzle and snap. Babs is yelling, "Don't do that, you fool! Don't ever burn hair, especially your own! It will invite terrible evil!" She is giving me a shocked witch-like face over glinting eyes.*

*But Babs is into these weirdo things, and has strange people coming to her home to chant, and chuck holy water all over the place to expel bad vibes. I think that's all a crock-of-crap so I laugh in her face and say, "Don't be ridiculous, Babs!" But I'm angry with her, because deep down I know she has evoked some evil, which has nothing to do with the physical hair-burning. The two of us are thinking about it now, and this will energise the air, and invite hell.*

And the devil did visit me the next day, and he burnt my house down with a smile. He also made sure that Fee, the effing call-centre operator, was off-duty at the time! I'm gob-smacked at this realisation, and even more so by how this little conversation with Tulula is opening my eyes to my electricity. I must remind Babs about the hair-burning night – that will surely electrify her.

I know I've made a mistake by telling Tulula about my brain power, because she's looking at me strangely. Thank heavens I only mentioned the light-bulb and washing-machine incidents, and not the hair-burning thing, because that would be too much irony for anyone to cope with, let alone a shrink. This is not psycho-mumbo-jumbo, but pure electrical mind-power, and surely out of her league.

"Very interesting indeed." She nods at her yellow folder again, and asks, "Do you shop a lot?"

The question seems banal. "Huh?"

"For instance," she says with an air to her voice, "I go shopping when I need to, or when I feel the need to treat myself to something special. I shop for luxury goods especially when I've been working hard and need some sort of reward. Now, when and why do you shop?"

My answer is the same as hers, so I say, "The same answer as yours."

She seems to be getting annoyed because she's shifting in her chair and she says, "OK, let's look at it another way. Do you ever buy things that you don't need or want?"

*Shit, of course I do, but so does everyone else.*

"I hate shopping."

Now I'm the one shifting in my chair. I buy a lot of shit I don't need, and always regret it because I know I can't afford the expense. Moreover, when I've bought the bloody thing, I know I'm going to take it back to the shop and change it, or buy something else. But I know that that doesn't help because I don't get my money back, but swap the stupid item for another stupid item, and land up giving it away because this eases a little of my conscience – so many people are starving and have no clothes. And here I am, buying yet another pair of expensive jeans that are torn on purpose, and would look a lot more appropriate on the poor people I'm feeling guilty about.

"Do you buy stuff you don't need?" She's looking down at her yellow folder.

*Hmmm ...*

"Do you buy stuff you can't afford?"

*Hmmm ...*

"Do you ever return stuff because you don't need it?"

*Hmmm ...*

"Are you happy when you shop for stuff you don't need, or can't afford, or when you take stuff back to the shop for a refund?"

*Hmmm ...*

I haven't answered any of these questions because she's probably read my pursed lips. Maybe I'm getting her drift because I realise that I actually feel like shit when I'm shopping for expensive stuff I don't need. And it's only when I'm feeling like shit that I do this. I go from shop to shop paining over each decision, but all the while I know I'm going to buy the stupid thing, and I chew my fingers off while the cashier processes the credit card. I sign the slip with an incognito signature in the stupid silent belief that the bank won't process the credit, but know that when the thing reels out of the machine, the deed is done, and I'm all the poorer for a stupid thing that's going to cause me pain when I need to make excuses to the shop assistant to explain why I'm returning it.

And not only have I got acid in my stomach while I pace the malls like a manic shopping weirdo, but window displays and people are moving around me in slow motion, just like Tulula has described.

*Am I such a freak?*

I chew my finger. I hate myself and need to damage this finger badly, because I don't care about my body ... or anything else.

A bit of spit escapes onto my bleeding appendage and I suck it off with the blood. Tulula looks down on me, and says, "I need to get an understanding of these things in order to make my diagnosis."

*So you need to diagnose me, do you?*

This is the first time in my life that anyone has ever tried to. It makes me feel slightly special, in spite of my overwhelming acid-rush. But it also means that I need to answer the stupid question, so I say, "Well, I can't say anyone would be happy shopping for expensive stuff they neither can afford nor need, especially when they have to take the bloody things back all the time."

"Hmmm," is her only response. "Do you find that you can never make up your mind about anything?"

"What?"

"Well, like you can't decide on anything conclusively. You constantly bargain between the two options and find it difficult to have enough rationale to support either one."

Shit, I can never make up my bloody mind! I hear myself saying to someone, "OK, let's do it. No! Stop! Let's not do it! Wait. OK, let's go for it! No! Stop! Hmmm ... OK, let's do it! What the hell!" And in the middle of doing it, I yell, "Stop! We can't do this!" And the poor person just lies there completely flaked out.

Thinking about my poor decision-making for the first time makes me say out loud, "What a stupid cow I must be. I can never make up my bloody mind. I think this links to the shopping-thing when I always have to take stuff back."

She's looking at me strangely, so I add, "But a lot of people are indecisive. There's nothing wrong with being indecisive. Well, is there?"

I want an answer and think I've thumped my fist on the table, but she peers down at her folder with a little grunt, and without looking up she asks, "Do you drink?"

*Duh.*

"Of course."

"Do you drink alcohol every day?"

"Yes."

"What do you drink? Wine, whisky?"

"Wine mostly, but vodka at parties."

Everyone drinks. Drinking is part of living. If you are a professional, intelligent person, drinking takes the edge off. Otherwise us clever people would truly go insane, and wouldn't Tulula just love that! I wonder why I've never drunk whisky; maybe it's because my mother may have drank it, and breathed it over me as she kissed me goodnight.

"How many glasses of wine do you drink per day?"

"I don't know."

"More than two?"

"Yes."

"More than five?"

"Yes." She scratches in her folder.

But I don't drink alone, so no alcoholic problems for me! I can drink up to two bottles of wine and not get drunk! I feel like a double vodka and orange now because it's the only drink that makes me feel truly fabulous. When I've had my second one, I feel absolutely wild. I dance in the kitchen with the kids, and spin them around until they are delirious with happiness. Kids just love it when I'm a bit tipsy. I generally behave like a kid anyway, and once I've had a few drinks, we all sing and dance while I get them to set the dinner table. But even though I get a little tipsy now and then, I am a truly fantastic mother, and never forget to have dinner on the table by seven. I'm fastidious about routine – I experience terrible panic attacks if my timetable is disrupted.

I cringe a little because, although the kids and I have oodles of fun when I'm tipsy, I am probably being a little irresponsible. But then again, dammit, any fun and happiness derived from any bloody thing is worth every bloody minute and what the bloody hell!

I'm certainly not letting Tulula in on my private alcohol–happiness rationale, but she pushes on, asking, "Have any of your immediate family been diagnosed with alcoholism?"

"Yes, my grandmother." This is a quick, easy answer, because I think of her death a lot. I miss my granny, even if I didn't know her for very long.

Mom had to keep tabs on the toilet cisterns, because Granny would hide her stash in there. Something clicks in my mind – maybe Granny was so busy searching for the bottle that she had a panic attack and died, right there, alone in the toilet, with no-one to find her.

Tulula taps her pen and I'm back on the booze again. Come to think of it, my whole family drinks. We are certainly not boring like other people, and we know how to live. In fact, I was often drinking half a glass of homemade wine diluted with water when I was a child. This is an Italian family tradition, so nothing wrong with it at all.

Out of nowhere, I wonder what it would be like to get drunk with Tulula; if she would go the extra mile, and if we would land up saying and doing things we would regret in the morning. But then again she doesn't smoke, and she probably doesn't drink, and I have this rule that only people who drink or smoke are good people. They are the ones you bump into on the office balcony who are always so nice that you can't stop talking to them as you laugh and cough through the smoke. Their vice is public. I'm convinced that people who don't drink or smoke are weird and do strange things behind closed doors. I resign myself to the fact that Tulula's vice is devouring husbands, even if she's a boring date.

She seems uppity, and any thoughts I had of her and I having a good time quickly vanish. She asks, "Have you ever taken drugs?"

*Of course not!*

I'm disgusted! I've never even taken an aspirin! But I concede that maybe I haven't done drugs because I was never offered any. I also know that I would like to try drugs, because they sound cool, but it's probably better that I don't, given the number of times I've clutched onto a toilet-bowl after too much alcohol. Doing anything moderately is not one of my strong points. I often proudly tell my friends that I never do anything in halves; it's all or nothing. This must be why it's easy for me to quit smoking when I want to. Shit, I've quit smoking enough times in my life to know what I'm talking about.

50

I go from sixty a day to zero with no problem because of my all or nothing theory, and thank heavens for that! Especially when having to give up smoking on falling pregnant, or when I start looking so awful from smoking that I can't bear to look at myself any longer. My eyes pop out at me from the mirror, and my skin is yellow and wrinkled, so I go and scrub in the shower to emerge as the clean non-smoker ready to face the world with sweet breath and fresh clothes. My handbag is still going to smell of tobacco for a while, but it's a good smell, because it will remind me of my great strength in going from a hundred to zero, in one fell swoop.

I wonder how I must look to Tulula now, and remember that the big thrill about giving up smoking is that I start to look fantastic again after the nicotine has stopped seeping out of my skin, and the taste of it is not so strong on my tongue. My skin starts to glow again, and I look ten years younger. But all the time I'm waiting for one of my numerous "life-wobbles" when I can turn to my dear friend Mr Ciggy, and inhale his stink through my aching lungs.

But I'm not talking to Tulula, and have only a little energy to mutter, "No. No drugs. Just cigarettes."

*And a dash of wine ...*

She looks a little happier and nods approvingly. She asks without looking at me, "Has any of your immediate family been diagnosed with mental disorders like depression, insanity or Alzheimer's?"

I hate the word "depression". I can't stand it when people are miserable and complain all the time. And Alzheimer's is also annoying because my grandfather had it and kept on forgetting who I was and greeted me all the time. An eccentric person is much more fun than a forgetful one. My father thinks that two of my great aunts were locked up in a lunatic asylum in Italy. I would rather spend time with them drinking, laughing and dancing around than sit opposite my grandfather telling him over and over that it is *me* and not his daughter he's talking to.

But I just answer, "Yes, I think there has been some Alzheimer's in the family."

She doesn't ask me for details, but scribbles again and mutters under her breath, "Have you ever had any concussions or other head injuries?" This question seems out of place. I fiddle with the hairs on the back of my neck.

*I am extremely nauseous and petrified of the big blank hole in my vision. I'm blinking, but all I can see is a shimmering circle of images with nothing in the middle. I'm vomiting the oranges I had for lunch, and I know this feeling very well, because I have felt it many times. I cannot remember my name or recognise anyone.*

*I'm waking up in a hospital room with crazy whining sounds around me and wondering what the hell I'm doing here. There's a young boy in the cot next to me who's tied to the bars and gaping at me with wide eyes, swaying from side to side, his mouth in a snarl. I'm terrified and try to recite my times tables to prove to myself that someone has made a terrible mistake by locking me up in here with the loonies.*

Tulula is tapping her pen but I won't answer until the head-bashing has stopped. My humour is back.

*My mom and I are laughing. I see her lovely teeth while we laugh about all the funny things I do when my head gets bashed in. Like the time when the school nurse discharged me early because I had fallen on my head in the corridor. I was trying to do my perfect cursive writing lesson but mixed up the letters, turning them the wrong way around, because I was confused, and couldn't see my page, or pen, or hand, and was scared because if it wasn't done perfectly, I would get detention. My mom and I are looking at the pages of my school book with the funny writing, and having a good giggle. We laugh about the time I sat on my suitcase waiting for her to collect me, and when she did, she had to come up to me and tell me she was my mother, because I just sat there like a zombie and didn't recognise her. Then the vomiting starts in the car and my head hurts like hell, and I can't see, and I ask my mom to tickle my vest. Tickling my vest takes the weirdness from the blur in my eyes, and the pain in my head, because tickling is something I'm familiar with. My mom always tickles my back. She's a good mom.*

Thank God the head-bashing stopped. I gave up horse-riding when my pony stumbled over a very big jump and stood on my face, which saw me in hospital once more. The weirdness of the head-bashing aftermath is too much to bear any longer, and I know instinctively that I must protect my dear cranium at all costs.

Tulula's pen-tapping stops and she wipes her nose. "Well, can you answer my question?"

I drift back into her room after the small realisation that my head has indeed taken some damage and say, "Yes, I've had four concussions. I was hospitalised each time."

I'm saying "hospitalised" for drama. I realise for the first time that four is definitely not an average head-banging occurrence for a standard person.

"Shame," she says, "that's not too good. Have you ever had a brain-scan?"

"No, should I have?"

She lifts her shoulders and says proficiently, "The head is a very delicate thing and there's only so much damage it can take before there are serious physical and behavioural repercussions."

That's it! My concussion repercussion is finally showing its ugly head. And I'm now even more adamant that no-one is going near it, let alone bumping it by mistake. I'm surely not going to let any shrink take a peak at my grey-matter – I'd rather eat it fried in batter with a twist of lemon. I want to go home to the shitty-couch and Pooki.

"Give me one sentence to describe your mother." It appears she's leaving the head-bashing alone.

Shit, so very hard to do in one sentence, but I give it a try anyway and simply say, "She's a good mother, and a strong person. I think she would have been more content having a career, possibly in education."

She writes in her yellow folder but seems to take quite a long time to do so. She sucks in a breath and says, "I have to tell you that your mother called me today and demanded that she be present at our consultation."

The thought of my mother being here makes the hairs on the back of my neck stand up. Nausea creeps into my stomach while the bile shoots up my throat again.

*Damn you, Babs!*

Tulula goes on, "I have to inform you that in terms of my doctor–patient protocol, I am duty-bound not to consult with any friend or family member of a patient. I explained this to your mother, but she insisted she was coming, so I had to be firm with her and tell her to back off."

*Very impressive indeed!*

It's actually quite comforting to have this privy between us. But Tulula is concentrating on her lists. "Give me one sentence to describe your father."

*God, that is so difficult!*

I fidget in my chair. "God" would actually be an accurate a word to describe him. I know I hero-worship him. Maybe a bit too much for Stef's liking?

Even though I hate it when some idiot says we should live each day like

it's our last, my father truly does. There's never been a time when he's not doing interesting things. He will spend hours into the night tying flies, making
toys for the kids, or painting a picture. The only thing I can fill my time with
is work, and shitty, difficult work like preparing feasibility studies and business plans. There's no time for play for a person like me. What the hell is the
matter with me?

But I need to answer Tulula's question. And I need to concentrate on being
benign during this question–answer session, and I speak loudly, like him,
"He's all-encompassing. Everybody is in awe of him. He's like Picasso, Einstein and Julius Caesar rolled into one."

She raises an eyebrow. I feel a tinge of marvel at the thought-process this
head-bender has made me embark upon, especially thinking about my parents. I've always concerned myself with impressing my father with my very
good university grades, and how well I perform on his "life-script" for me;
and impressing my mother with how very resolute I am … and how I manoeuvre the pull-yourself-together blanket.

Tulula is in my space again and she's checking her list. "Do you have any
brothers or sisters, and how old are they?"

"Yes, I have one younger brother."

"Tell me about him."

I really don't feel like talking about my brother because there's nothing to
talk about. There's nothing weird about him, so there's nothing to say here.
"He's a very successful financier," I say.

"Tell me about your relationship with him?"

"It's great."

*I'm looking at the doll Mommy's given me as I sit in the back of the car outside
the hospital where my brother has come out of Mommy's tummy. I hate this
bloody doll and I want to press its cheeks in until it looks weird. I've seen her
stitching the white clothing for the doll, and was very excited about getting it.
But now that she's told me I'm getting it because my baby brother is coming, I
hate the doll, as well as the new brother.*

*His stupid little face is looking up at me from the chest of the dark-skinned
nurse, as she hands him to Mommy in the front seat of the car. I want him to
disappear and get the hell out of here, because all I want is for it to be the three
of us again: Mom, Dad and me!*

I wonder why I've remembered the stupid doll-bribe so many years later. I must've been three at the time, and can't believe that I've remembered so far back in time. I remember my mother telling me that, months later, when a dark-skinned nun walked past us in the street, I grabbed my mother's arm and said, "Quick Mommy, there's his real mother, give him back!"

*But I'm getting my revenge on the silly little bugger now, because I can work the scissors and am cutting off all his hair as he giggles under the blades. I tell him to saw off an arm of an antique chair, and call my mother to witness it. He's getting into a lot of trouble and I'm satisfied, at least for a while, until my oh-so-cool-and-very-grown-up brother acts as mediator between me and my parents and they hang onto his every word.*

I don't want to talk to Tulula about my brother. I'm still my father's favourite. Or am I?

Tulula appears to be waiting to hear more about my brother, so I say, "My brother's great, just perfect. We get on like a house on f—."

We both cringe and I bite my finger. She shakes her head and whispers, "It's OK." Her whispering makes me think that she's trying to keep personal kindnesses off a secret tape-recording, which will later be used in court.

She pauses a few seconds, and then lashes me. "Have you ever had an-orexia?"

*Oh, no!*

# TULULA, SCENE 5: THE QUESTIONS THAT KILL ME

*I'm nauseous. All the food I consumed and wasted is spinning around my head. If it could fill a space, it would probably fill an oil-tanker. Or I could float in it as it reaches the ceiling of this consulting room. It bubbles and squeaks and it is sweet, chocolaty and sour at the same time. Sometimes there's a little blood floating on the top, because I know I've retched a little too hard this time, and the walls of my oesophagus have been torn by food in reverse, or my fingers have scraped the roof of my mouth.*

*I'm wearing my primary school uniform and its belt is tight, because my friend and I have just eaten an entire cake. We have read in women's magazines about girls who do this thing to lose weight. The fashion is thick tight belts around the waist, which need to make the tiniest circumference, so we need to slim down. Our bodies look weird because the puppy-fat just doesn't go away, and we certainly don't look like the girls in the magazines. We are giggling hysterically as I retch into the flower-bed while she holds my hair aside as I have done hers. The family dog comes over and eats it, and we laugh until our stomachs explode with ill-gotten air.*

I must be bemused by this bizarre memory, because my lips feel pursed and Tulula is watching my mouth. She shifts in her chair and casually says, "Take your time. I've got some stuff to complete here."

She's teasing me with that reverse-psychology shit, so I point my chin at her until she looks at her notes and I say without speaking: Yes, Tulula. It is essential to categorise food into "easy" and "difficult" vomits. Let me explain: The "easy" vomits are the things you prepare specifically for vomiting, like pancakes and cream. Or, for instance, if you're out of flour and cream, ordinary oats will do. Just cook them and douse with large amounts of sugar and milk, and Bob's-your-uncle, out it comes. These are the cheaper vomits. If you have some money to spare, "easy" vomits are also attainable by ingesting lots of confectionaries. But remember, when the baker asks you if you're having a party, appear to be enthusiastic, because there is no way in hell that one person would be able to consume all the creamy sweet junk you're buying.

She's busy writing and I'm still at her with my soundless rhetoric: Now, Tulula, let me explain all there is to know about the "difficult" vomits. These are the ones needed when the food ingested is not out of choice, like at family lunches – the ones you hate and are forced to go to by your parents. They usually happen on a Sunday with grandparents and a couple of daft cousins who go to different schools, and live on the other side of your world. If you are from Italian stock, these lunches will usually consist of venison, polenta and bitter chicory salad. These lunches feel like lead in your stomach and are very difficult to get out. But when you become an advanced projectile-operator like me, two or three helpings of fruit-salad and cream will do the trick, and help the whole lot out in a jiffy. A first good "blast" that gets the toilet-water jumping into your face is essential for an excellent emptying session.

I'm in the swing of things. Like a creamy doughnut looking for escape, I need to get all this stuff out of me, even though I won't give Tulula the pleasure. But let me tell you, Tulula, time is of the essence! One cannot wait too long to get the first projectile out, as Mr Stomach may ram his contents into the small intestine, and mental surgery and strenuous tummy pushing would urgently be required to get it back into the stomach and out up the throat. This would ensure yet another sweaty pursuit of a private toilet to get the bloody stuff out before it settles, until you're discovered by your cousin with your bum in the air, heaving your epiglottis out.

*I'm staring into the white bowl at the frothing, undigested sludge while my spit hangs from my mouth like a stream into the abyss. My sinuses are already blocked, my eyes and face are surely red, and bile pours from my nose. I need to hurry now, before I can face the world again. I have to wash my mouth with hand soap and wait for the redness to dissolve from my face and eyes.*

Tulula's still not looking at me, but I rub my face self-consciously. I know this terrible purging increased the lines around my mouth, popped the veins at my nostrils and stuffed up my teeth. I squeeze my lips together and stare at the top of Tulula's head. Oh, and, Tulula, then there's the air-freshener-availability panic. But if you're a pro like me, you've got a can of deodorant handy at all times. Excessive spraying of deodorant or air-freshener would suggest a big pooh which is what normal people do in toilets. The embarrassment from a cover-up for a pooh is far less than the embarrassment from a cover-up for tossing your cookies. Walking out of a toilet looking like you've had a fight with the devil, or leaving remnants of your battle in there, is a big no-no. Good cover-up tactics are essential, and need years of practice.

I sit slouched in my chair. Tulula is still writing in her folder, so I keep my eyes on the top of her head, and purse my lips, while I mock her again with my silent speech: Now, Tulula, one must categorise vomit venues by the functionality of their toilets. If it's a new venue, please test the cistern with a flush before eating, just to be sure. One must fill the toilet to the brim before the first flush as, God knows, Tulula, if the toilet doesn't flush a second time, you have to wait a long time before the cistern fills again. A worst-case scenario is if the toilet is blocked. When this occurs, it is necessary to scoop up the bits of floating food from the toilet-bowl and meticulously push them through the basin plug-hole, with the tap running, until people start to knock at the door to see if you're alright.

The terror of being discovered in such a predicament engulfs me.

*My grandmother is asking why I'm eating an apple after I had eaten so much for lunch, and I'm at a loss for words, but just carry on crunching into it because if I don't get some sugar into my veins after such a drastic purging, my hands won't stop shaking and I will probably pass out anyway.*

I'm angry again. Heaven's above, I've gone from mocking to mad in one split second!

*I'm sitting at dinner with my mom and dad and I wish they would stop complaining about how much I eat now because, a few years ago, I had to sit at the table to finish every last morsel of food on my plate, even the peas they discovered hidden under my knife and fork.*

*And now I feel bad for John, who works with me, because he's battling with weight. I'm enticing him to eat pastries with me during lunch hours, and we're stuffing our faces with creamy buns. He's getting fatter to the point of obesity, while I'm withering away. He's always on a diet, and says I have a constitution like an ox.*

*I've become an expert at it, after suffering red fingers for ten years, due to the gnawing of my teeth while sticking them down my throat. I no longer need to tickle my throat, but can just bend over the bowl and gently push in my stomach, as I merely will out the first projectile.*

I know now as I sit here with Tulula that the reason I don't eat sweet stuff anymore is because too much of it passed over my tongue and I'm sick of it.

It dawns on me that I vomited for an awfully long time, and stopped doing it as suddenly as I had begun, when I left South Africa at twenty-six years old and was sent on a King Air jet-plane to East Africa. I had been head-hunted by a large company for a job as project manager. And, shit, was I hot. My CV was power-packed. I was the best, obsessed, perfectionist in the business.

My pride is quickly swallowed by my shame, and a shiver runs up my vertebra.

The memory of my first and last visit to see a psychologist is with me, the one that lasted five minutes.

*My father believes I'm getting abnormally thin, and thinks I have anorexia, because it's the new teenage vogue and all over the media. I'm embarrassed, as this conversation is far too personal for my father and I to be having and I feel sorry that he has to do this, and not my mother. I reverently deny being too thin, and stress that it's because of the difficult university degree I'm taking. I even use this opportunity as a plea to him to allow me to quit my studies. But I'm physically delivered to the shrink's office by my mother, albeit kicking and screaming. This is the last time I will see a shrink, because his first question is how I get on with my father. I tell him to bugger off and lock myself in my mother's car until she agrees to take me home.*

The dreaded disease left me as promptly as it had begun, without any coercing from anyone. I fidget my bones on Tulula's chair and realise that I probably weigh less now than I did at university, because my hip bones are sticking out. But this time I'm not retching, I just don't eat. I don't eat because I have no desire for food.

Tulula hasn't encouraged an answer, and has merely sat here writing for a long time. Maybe she knows my answer, and doesn't want to scare me off by nudging me too hard. But I'm forced to answer her question. I retch my answer into her toilet-face: "Yes … but so did Princess Diana."

Tulula's quiet for a while, and I can almost feel her deciding not to pursue the anorexia thing because of the imminent time's-up. But she casually asks, "Have you ever thought of killing yourself?"

This is an easy one because I know a lot of people think about it but never really do it, just like me. I whisper, "Yes."

She's steely-eyed and stares into my pupils, asking, "Have you felt more like killing yourself lately?"

*Damn right I have!*

I'm flippant in spite of the tightening in my chest and manage, "Yes, a little, but that's probably because of shock, and I'm truly not worried about it."

Tulula gets up and shouts into nowhere, "That's it! I've heard enough! This is not anything I can help you with! You need a psychiatrist. I need to make an urgent phone call."

I'm shocked. What the hell is she saying? She's spent the last hour titivating and exposing the very depths of my mind. She has completely embarrassed me and now she's abandoning me!

She says in a loud commanding voice, "Go outside and have a cigarette. I will be with you shortly, and don't go anywhere! You need to stay here."

I feel sick. I lean into the grapevine outside her office window, and press my ear into the greenery, hoping to hear her on the phone. I almost collapse into the denseness of the leaves, and I strain to hear her, with my cigarette burning next to my face.

I can hear her speaking in hurried tones. The words are not making sense, but they flit through the window in tiny wafts: "Very unstable … denial … bad history … not helping … all the signs … urgent … hospital … fire …" And I'm surprised to hear her say, "Shame."

She emerges from nowhere, and grabs me by the arm. She marches me into her office and pushes me down into my chair. She's being very authoritative and I quite like her like this.

She sits down with a thump. Instead of doing that apex-thing with her hands, she sprawls them towards me as if trying to reach for me. "Now, you listen to me, and you listen well," she says in a staccato manner. She raises her voice, and says, "You are not the woman of the world! And you are not the mother of the year! You are going to do what I say, and if you don't, I will call in the authorities to make you do so!"

*Shit, what the hell is she talking about?*

But there's no time for me to ponder, because she yells, "You are going to hospital! You are not going to hospital tomorrow! You are not going to hospital next week! You are going to hospital now!"

I'm up like a flash and I head for the door. Looking back, I yell, "Don't be ridiculous! I have two children to look after! There's nothing wrong with me! I'm going home!"

She's up and she grabs me by the wrist. I feel the twist of her wet skin on my bruises. "I have just spoken to Stef. He knows what I am doing. So, sit down!"

I'm disgusted and disappointed with him, and I'm speechless. How can he be colluding against me?

But she's made her point. The mention of Stef's name in this room, amongst all this craziness, is like a slap in the face. Suddenly and completely out of nowhere, all of the crap we have been talking about stops smelling, and I slump back into my chair.

Tulula's stamping around her desk like she's in combat-mode, her voice on the verge of shrieking. "Your mother-in-law is flying from Paris tomorrow morning to look after the children. Stef will be taking you to see a psychiatrist. Her name is Lulu. She will be issuing you with a hospital admission directive and will prescribe something to make you feel better." She looks at her watch. "She can't see you until tomorrow, so until you are admitted, I am going to keep close tabs on you. Do you understand?"

*What the hell?*

My head spins. All I know is that if the more qualified prescription-generating shrink can't see me now, I don't have to go to hospital now. I therefore have until tomorrow to turn this all around and declare some horrible misunderstanding between me and Tulula, the head-shrinker and evil-jailer. I have never taken medication in my life, and am certainly not going to be taking any valium or sleeping pills, let alone see another bloody shrink!

Her voice quietens, but she's still resolute, "OK, now, Stef will meet you at home. The kids are staying with your friend, Clara."

*Who are these so-called husbands, friends, and family? And why are they conspiring against me with this stupid divorcee?*

She fiddles in her handbag, and takes out a small plastic tube-like container. She spills one tiny white tablet into her hand, and says with her newly gained authority, "This is not regular, but I've cleared it with Lulu. I would like you to take this before you go to sleep tonight. It will help you sleep. It's one of mine and it won't harm you."

*Ja, right!*

"Now, do you think you can drive yourself home?"

A stupid question with an obvious answer. I can fly myself to the moon right now! I'm of sound mind and faculties. "Of course I can drive. I drove here, didn't I?"

I've been driving for twenty-five years for heaven's sake! I was driving on the farm since I was thirteen! And even though there were times I did some sleep-driving, and blanking out, I have always managed. Out of nowhere, I remember the nine accidents I had in one year when I was nineteen, and the time when I drove out of the panel-beaters and straight into two policemen, and the time when I hit a man on his bicycle. I bite my thumbs, both at the same time.

# DRUG-FREE FOR THE LAST TIME

It's dark outside Tulula's rooms. I wonder how much extra time I spent with her and if she'll zap me with an overtime bill. But maybe she had some fun with me and will decide not to charge. She's peering at me through my car window, and I flinch because I thought she had gone. She mouths: "Are you OK?" and I give her a go-away look as I accelerate out of her stupid bendy driveway.

I stop at an intersection, but I don't remember seeing it on my way to Tulula. This scares me because I don't think I stopped at it. But I cast all negative thoughts from my mind as I whiz towards my glass of wine. Thoughts of booze make me happy, and I need a lot to convince Stef that I am absolutely fine, and not going anywhere.

My cellphone rings, and although it's illegal, I answer it. I like to test myself with attempting as many activities at once while driving. I put my ciggy in my left hand on the steering-wheel, and hold the phone to my ear with my right. Normally I've got Pooki on my lap because I take her everywhere with me. She would have her head out the window with a smile on her face and her ears streaming back in the wind like Speedy Gonzales.

Stef has an unusual sound to his voice, "My love, I think you should pull over at the next filling station, and I will come and collect you. Tulula has just called, and regrets letting you drive off alone, because she thinks you are a bit strained."

I should have driven over her and killed her outside her rooms! But it is an unusual request from Stef, given the high risk of getting hijacked at night. I'm a little smarted because Tulula has made my husband concerned about my mental state when the basis of our relationship is a deep respect for my intelligence and independence.

"Oh, for heaven's sake, my love, this is *me* you're talking to. I'll see you now, I'm almost there." I quickly cut him off.

My cellphone rings again, and it's Trixie. Her voice is chipper, "Hi, I spoke to Stef a while ago and he tells me he has sent you to see a psychologist."
*Shit!*

The whole world knows about my embarrassing shrink-encounter!

"I'm absolutely fine," I manage. "Really, it was just a little check-up regarding post trauma something-or-other and the doctor says I'm doing very well under the circumstances."

Trixie breathes into my ear and says, "Stef tells me that you are going to be admitted to hospital." Now I really hate her. I leave her hanging until she says, "The insurance company is prepared for contingencies like these, particularly after such disasters."

I'm still not going to talk to her, and after another pause she persists. "There is financial cover for this kind of thing and I want you to know that we have looked at your policy and there is an amount that is capped for trauma medication and hospitalisation." My interest prickles at her hinting at money because, shit, we could well do with any money right now. I muster a very croaky voice and say as casually as I can, "Look, Trixie, I'm obviously not feeling that great at the moment, but I don't think we are going to need any insurance payout for trauma."

I wait for this show of honour to sink into her head, but she says nothing, so I casually say, "Trixie, I'm fine really. Anyway, what is the sum that we signed for?"

I brace myself for the mention of money and it sounds like she's clearing her throat. Then she says, "The limit is two thousand rand." I swerve my car into the on-coming traffic. The thought of having a head-on collision and dying is exciting, but my anger quickly helps me to get back into my lane.

"Thanks, Trixie, but we certainly don't need it. Got to cut you off. I'm driving. Have a nice evening. Bye."

Any hopes of us getting any decent money out of our valued insurers are dashed, so I hang onto my steering-wheel and accelerate towards my glass of wine. I turn into a road that will take me on a detour that won't pass my burnt-down house. I shiver at the thought of the pile of blackness that was once my home, but I throttle this feeling quickly, and screech around the corner with my gate opener poised under my burning ciggy.

I'm at the townhouse and safe. My glass of wine awaits me behind the man I love, behind the front door, and behind the fridge door, where it tinkles crisply, ready to burst into my veins and fill my heart with joy. Stef is standing outside in the little garden and walks quickly towards my door to open it. I feel that he needs to get me out as fast as possible, as if I'm trapped in a car wreck. Pooki's on my lap first but I get out faster than Stef can get to me. I know I'll be better equipped to dissuade Stef from the psycho-drug-hospital-necessity with a drink in hand, so I kiss him quickly and run inside towards the kitchen without saying anything. As I'm gulping down the cool white wine, I notice that he's staring at me, as if looking at me for the first time. I don't like his look, because he always says that I'm "the tits", and he shouldn't be having any other thoughts.

I quaff two more glasses of wine and feel a little of the tension ease from my veins. Now that I can focus, I look into Stef's eyes. I've been avoiding eye-contact with him since the f—. He looks like hell. He's pale in spite of his handsomeness and his body seems to have withered. But I still sense his muscles under his shirt, and feel inadequate as his sexual partner.

And now, as if we're in a scene out of another couple's world, we are both crying. I'm shocked that he's crying because he has only cried once before, over the death of his godfather. I respect him for this show of emotion. He is so strong and I'm so weak, and I need him. He's bigger than me. Especially now, because I've fallen onto the kitchen floor and am bashing my head on his polished shoes.

It's the first time the kids are not with us since the f—. He's been strong for the kids and now he's letting go. I marvel at him and I hold onto his feet as he leans over me and squeezes his eyebrows together with his huge fingers.

I look up into his eyes and I am sure we both picture the ludicrousness of this scene at the same instant, and see mirror images of our pitiful, wet eyes and pale faces; also because we look alike. And we laugh like dragons and we can't stop, and I sprawl myself spread-eagled on the floor for more dramatic effect and say, "Gimme more wine, my baby! Shit, aren't we just the perfect pair!"

And he laughs at me like he always does, and it's comforting, and I sit up and quaff my wine, giggling madly and blowing bubbles into the glass. He's back to his usual self and sniffs his final tear-snot away and says, "I've made your favourite soup. Come and sit down and eat, my love."

I follow him and sit down in front of a steaming bowl of soup with ginger, garlic, chicken and noodles.

He's drinking beer and I'm sipping wine and I try to eat "my favourite soup", but it's difficult to swallow food, so I fake eating. We're not saying any-thing, because we both know that Stef just gets on with things. I just bloody well have to do what he says, because there is no other way forward right

65

now. His mother is on her way to look after the kids and the townhouse is small. These are good enough reasons for me to get out. He hasn't mentioned my going to hospital, because he surely knows that I will go, and I will lie there for a while, and I will be a good girl.

# CALL FROM CLARA

We sit together quietly spooning our soup as Pooki shifts under the dinner table, but our silence is broken by my cellphone ringing and we both reach towards it quickly. Maybe Stef's thinking that I can't even manage a phone call, and this makes me feel stupid again, but I've got the cellphone in my hand now, and it's Clara.

Her voice is upbeat and cheerful. I picture her graceful, fair face as she says, "Hello, honey, the kids are having a ball. How are you, honey?"

"Thanks so much for having them. Stef and I have to go out tonight and it really helps. Yes, I'm fabulous thanks. All's going so well."

Stef gives my lies an upward eyebrow over his tired eyes as Clara exclaims into my ear, "Good girl! I'm glad all is going so well! Now, I know you have a million things to sort out, but a bunch of us girls have got together and have arranged a small gathering tomorrow … in your honour."

*Oh, shit, no!*

"Oh, Clara, thanks, but it's not necessary. I'm fine and it's no big deal. I'm over it. It's been three weeks since then and I'm completely fine now, really. And besides, I have an important appointment tomorrow."

I would rather die than go to this sorry-for-you party, and I resign myself to the fact that I'm going to try to kill myself tonight with alcohol, and go straight into hospital for a bloody good reason, like a stomach pump. I will tell the nurse that I've eaten a rotten oyster and be out of hospital in a jiffy. At this time all the mind stuff will be forgotten, and Stef will feel sorry for me for having to have my stomach pumped once again. So I pour myself another glass of wine with my free hand before Stef can pour me one, like the gentleman he always is.

Clara is persistent, "Honey, I know it will be difficult for you, but we just want to see you. It won't take long and you can leave as soon as you wish. A whole bunch of mothers from the kids' school are coming too. What time is your appointment?"

I concentrate on my next lie and try to pin-point a time for my so-called hospital-admission appointment that won't coincide with the sorry-for-you party, so I chance it by saying, "At two tomorrow." I hold my thumbs.

Quite frankly, I have no clue when all these eager-beavers-who-want-me-locked-up have made my appointment with the shrink-who-has-the-power-to-do-so, but I keep my fingers crossed in the hope I've double-dated. I look at Stef and furrow my forehead in plea, but he's not reacting because he's hugging Pooki, who's sitting on his lap. I secretly thank Pooki as my loving stand-in. My head reels at the thought of tomorrow, and thoughts of my suicide-by-wine intoxicate me.

Clara has delight in her voice, "Great, honey, the gathering is at eleven tomorrow morning and it's at my house. Do you want me to collect you?"

I'm definitely not going, so I say, "No, I can't. I just can't. I'm so sorry."

She shocks me by saying, "It's alright, honey, I know how you feel, so don't force yourself to come. We will meet anyway, just to pray for you."

Clara is very religious, and I feel bad now because she is being Godly and giving and I am being un-Godly and ungrateful. She's also giving me time to think, and says after a while, "We also had a fire when we lived in Australia, and we also lost everything. I know how you feel."

*I hate myself!*

I swallow and manage to regurgitate the words, "I'll come."

She says, "Great."

I say, "Bye," and as I cut her off, I squirm, because not only am I an ungrateful bitch and an unloving wife, but I'm also an unfit mother because I've forgotten to ask after the kids, or talk to them on the phone, or kiss them goodnight.

Stef adds to my self-loathing by saying, "Why didn't you talk to the kids?" Even Pooki is looking at me strangely.

I need to vomit. I sprint up the stairs to the toilet-bowl.

Sour bile with bits of chicken and dissolving noodles squirt through my nose and eject into the toilet-water. My body is responding to an old need and my stomach doesn't require prompting. I hold onto the toilet and wrap my legs around its base. I can't cry. The only tears I have is the sour vomit that has made its way up my nasal passages and out through my eyes. I focus on the bathroom floor which is carpeted. Carpets are so disgusting in bathrooms. I can't believe that I'm wrapped around the toilet on the shitty-carpet, because I'm usually so fastidious about cleanliness. I don't touch public toilet-ware unless with a tissue, or unless I'm very drunk. But now I don't care a sod about cleanliness, or anything really. I crawl over to the bath and run the water from the rusty taps and lean over the side to watch it fill.

There's an ant struggling to climb up the slippery ceramic, so I spit on my finger so it can stick to the moisture, and flick it onto the ledge. I gently blow the spit from its legs and wait until I see it moving again. I'm content to sit here with the ant. Pooki is with me as always, like my conscience, while I wait for the water to rise.

Hopes of a successful suicide-by-wine evaporate because I would now need a pipe and funnel to get more of it down my throat, never mind a stomach-pump to get it out at the hospital. I undress and lower my bones into the too-hot water until my bum stings. My heart is in agony and submerging it in the water has made it worse. I get out without soaping. I scratch in my dirty clothes' pockets and find the tiny sleeping pill that Tulula gave me. I swallow it down with bath-water and it dawns on me that this is the first mind-altering pill I am taking in my life, besides it being a mere sleeping pill that I know everyone takes.

I pull Stef's tracksuit pants onto my wet legs, and fall into bed to await my first sleep-by-pill. But nothing happens, even though I yearn to pass out. I attempt my death-sleep. I get into my foetal position under the sheets. I bend my hands inwards and feel the stretch of my wrist muscles. I like this feeling because I'm all wound up. I'm doing my stretches inwardly and this locks me in. The only way I can fall asleep is if I fidget my feet to the tune of my lullaby, until my tendons ache. This is why I have good ankles. I've managed to sleep like this since I can remember.

# PLEA FROM JEN

My cellphone is ringing under my pillow. My heart wakes up with a painful stab and the anxiety creeps up on me like a haunted blanket. The bedroom is quiet and I feel lonely, so I reach for it under the pillow.

It's Jen. "Hope I haven't woken you, but I've spoken to Babs and she tells me you are going to see a psychiatrist today. I really don't think you should because I know you don't need one. Quite frankly, I think psychiatrists make you feel worse than you actually do. I know this most amazing woman who is a medium and she can help you. She's done so much for me, and a lot of my friends. I've never told you about her, but I've been seeing her for years. I want you to trust me and go and see her. I've called her and she can see you now. She will even wait for you. She lives close to you. Please do this for me, if it's the last thing you do for me. You won't be sorry ..."

*What the—?*

I cut her short by groaning into the phone, "Shit, Jen, just calm down. I don't know what you're talking about. I'm busy at the moment. I'll call you back." I cut her off.

*Ja, right. I'm very busy. I've just got to step out of my burning bed and enter the gates of hell on my way to the loo while the rest of the world is so bloody bored that it has to hassle a corpse like me!*

I crouch over my ribs and drool onto the carpet while I pee. I try to remember this morning. Stef must have left early for work and, not wanting to wake me, placed my cellphone under my pillow. But now I remember Tulula's little sleeping pill, and my failed attempt at suicide-by-alcohol. I am angry and I suck up my drool before it reaches the carpet. I'm not only mad at my failed attempt at getting to a hospital for a physical and not a mental reason, but I'm also mad at all these inquisitive people who are talking about my embarrassing visit to a shrink! Can't they keep their noses out of my business, and the rest of their bodies out of my life? But what to do about this weird call from Jen?

Jen, like Clara, is one of those stand-up girls, and I have the deepest respect for her. She has battled cancer and won. What shames me no end is that she now knows that I'm a weak pig who needs to see a shrink. It's surprising that she's admitted that she has seen a medium. I realise that she's probably sought non-physical help to cure her cancer. I shudder because I hear myself saying loudly at dinner parties, "Only idiots see mediums and fortune-tellers!" Jen is often sitting at the same table. I need to call her back.

Still crouching on the toilet-seat, I reach for my cellphone on the floor and drop a bit of urine on the carpet. I don't care about my splashing, and dial my friend Jen, with what feels like a ramrod in my belly.

"Hi, Jen. I want you to know that the appointment for me to see this psychiatrist today was organised by the insurance company. It's kind of a follow-up on post-trauma-blah-di-blah. I'm sure it's just a routine visit, so it's nothing weird. And also, the mothers at the kids' school have arranged a gathering for me, so I really can't make any other appointment. I really don't feel like going to this gathering either. What a ballbreaker! But I guess I need to go because they've made an effort, but still, what a pain in the arse."

I'm hoping this little lie will throw her off her mission to get me to see this funny-woman, but she says, "Yes, Clara and I have organised the do and you'd better be coming."

*I hate myself!*

"Sorry, Jen, I didn't know you were involved, I'm such a dweeb."

"It's OK, I forgive you."

*Oh, hell, she's so bloody nice!*

"I know about everything you're going through."

*Damn you, Babs!*

I know that she desperately needs me to visit this stupid woman, just like she's needed all her other friends to, and she says, "I personally don't think you need a psychiatrist because I have been to one, and they don't give a shit about you. This woman really cares and is the most amazing person in the world. She will make your whole body tingle, and you will find out a lot about yourself. All my other friends swear by her as well. She's unbelievable."

I know she will be "unbelievable" because to me she's just another con-artist. I whine into the phone. Jen's clearly not interested in anything I have to say because she says, "She's waiting for you and you have enough time to go before the party. Now that's that, my friend. You need to do this thing for me."

So I resign myself to the fact that this woman has helped cure Jen, and I need to oblige her because, dammit, I have the deepest respect for the girl.

She's also a bloody good friend. I sigh loudly. "For shit's sake, Jen, just give me the bloody address. You're a pain in the butt."

She's resolute. "You won't be sorry, I promise!"

# ENTER MAGGIE

The getting-dressed problem is with me again. Quite frankly, I could walk the streets naked with a ciggy hanging from my mouth, and a bottle of vodka in my fist, and not care a continental shit about what the rest of the world thinks of me. I'm certainly not bathing, so I wash under my arms with a facecloth, change my underwear, and pull on the same stuff I had on for Tulula. I glance at myself in the mirror. My face looks weird because my eyes seem to have got larger. Maybe my chest was so painful during slumber that my eyes popped out. I wish I had that black aerosol-can that the Replicant sprayed over her eyes in *Blade Runner*; that kind of quick make-up would be perfect for professional people like me who need a fast, vamp look without the fuss.

I'm working my top-lip wrinkles again as I blow smoke-rings against the mirror. There are a lot of cigarette butts in the basin, which is a clear signal that I am late. I know I must have blacked out, and I'm sure the stupid sleeping pill is to blame.

I wait at the security gate of the funny-woman's townhouse complex until she answers the intercom. I bite my thumb because automatic gates scare the hell out of me. I'm sweating and anxious. I don't know if I can navigate the gate opening and get through it in time, like normal drivers who actually know how they got here. I crouch forward over my steering-wheel and spin through when the gates slide open just sufficiently for my car to slip through. Visions of it closing on me make me gasp:

*My ear is pressing into my mom's belly button. We are sandwiched between a huge clinking metal lift door and its frame. My nose is squashed against the thick reveal and I smell the grease between its metal folds. I'm screaming and so is my mom, and I'm wondering why she can't push the door back. I realise that she is too weak and I am too little. Two men run over and wrench the door back. We escape just before the cage drops down. As I stare into the darkness, I know that I will never trust sliding doors again.*

I try to park as close as possible to the wall adjacent to the front door of "number fifteen". These complexes have become so dense that drivers need to be like bloody Houdini. I get too close to the wall and I hear grinding. My car is now stuck to it, but I don't care. I fall out of my open door towards the nearest bush to toss my ciggy. I suddenly realise that I probably won't be able to smoke here either. I'm getting back into my car to go home when a big woman approaches out of nowhere. She's gasping for air, probably because she's so large, and waddles over to me. She reaches for both my hands in a come-to-my-bosom gesture. She puffs into my face and says in a small voice, "I'm Maggie. I don't normally come outside to see clients, but Jen has asked me to make sure you got here safely."

She's called me a "client", and I prepare for the up-front-payment-crap. I put my hands into her outstretched ones so as not to embarrass her by pulling them away.

She's walking in step with me as she manoeuvres me down a narrow passage and into a sunny little room that smells of peppermint. I hesitate at the door but she bumps me with her big bum, and I stumble into her lair. I must be mad to allow another weirdo to frogmarch me around.

I'm shocked to see that there's a bed in the middle of the room, quite like one used in a beauty salon. I squirm at the sight and pray that I don't have to lie on it and have Maggie touch me. The thought of anyone other than Stef touching me makes me cringe – I avoid beauty salons as a rule. There is no way in hell that I'm going anywhere near the stupid bed!

On the far side of the room is a wooden cabinet, with hundreds of little brown bottles on display on its shelves. They remind me of my herbal calming remedy. Why the hell haven't I taken any this morning? Because, shit, I could surely do with a bottle of the stuff! The little bottles start wavering in my vision. I need to steady myself, so I sit on the nearest chair. I need to appear balanced and ready for her wizardry.

She hasn't witnessed my wobble. She's writing something with her back to me, which I'm convinced is my invoice. And indeed she is presenting me with it, and I am signing my cheque and passing it to her.

*What the hell am I doing here?*

She leaves me in my monkey-chair and I am happy to be here rather than lying exposed on her stupid bed.

She's still puffing and the top of her lip is wet. "Stay there in that chair. We'll spend a minute chatting first."

"Fine with me."

*God, I'm weak.*

She takes out a blue folder and slips my cheque into it. She draws a stool closer and sits opposite me. I cross my arms as she looks at me with her pig-eyes. She doesn't say anything, for what seems like an eternity. The silence between us is getting intense, so I uncross my arms and open my hands to prove that I'm not afraid of her. She seems to acknowledge this gesture because she smiles and looks prettier. I notice she's wearing a light-cotton, floral dress, like the kitchen dresses Italian mammas wear. It's loose and disguises her fatness, and the fact that she's sitting with her knees open. She takes my hands in hers once again, and rests my arms on her lap.

I leave them there for a second, but remove them to turn off my cell-phone.

"I hear your house burnt down, shame, you must feel absolutely terrible. I would be devastated if that happened to me. Are you OK? Shame … you poor girl." She shudders her heavy shoulders and adds, "I really treasure my things, and would be lost without them."

She's responded badly; selfishly. She's more concerned about it happening to her! I wonder just what her qualifications are, and what the hell Jen is doing consulting with her. It dawns on me that, because she obviously can't psycho-babble, she must do stuff to people on the white bed. I have to get out of here! My throat closes and the little bottles start to waver. I squeeze my eyes shut and open them again. The bottles settle and I pull myself together.

"Really, Maggie, material things shouldn't concern us, because there is more to life. I'm actually feeling quite good about myself because it's only the shock of the whole thing that has affected me …"

She shifts in her chair and I hope it's because she's uncomfortable. I continue. "I'm fine, really. And thanks so much for seeing me. I'm only doing this for Jen. I have to go now because I have a party to go to."

She shifts again, this time to pull her dress out of her bottom, and says, "I know you're right. We should be less materialistic but, dammit, *I* would feel like hell! And I know you are not fine." She taps my leg. "Come on, you can't fool me," she says and winks.

I jump in my chair. She appears unfazed about my showing her up. My eyes are stinging, and I feel weird. She looks at me for a while with her head tilted sideways and says, "OK, take off your shoes and let's have a nice little lie-down on the bed."

"Why?" It's all I manage because terror engulfs me.

"I work with crystals, oils and energies, and I can help you. Now take off your shoes and lie down. You really shouldn't be so antagonistic. Just relax."

I hate it when people tell me to relax! I can feel my face getting hot and I know the redness of it is giving me away. I cannot face this and I need to get out. Also, I haven't bathed and my feet are probably smelly. The whole of me is probably smelly, and the smell is probably made worse because I am sweating.

She's peering at my redness but I can't help myself, so I say, "Look, I'm really not into this. I'm very scientific."

I'm embarrassed by this stupid statement, but I need to leave with a decent excuse, so I persist, "Until yesterday, I had never been to see anyone regarding psycho or energy stuff. I was only sent to see this other psycho-woman because of an insurance requirement for post-trauma stuff. I will never be able to be hypnotised. This is not my thing. I want to go now." I quickly add, "Please don't worry about the money. I have wasted your time and I'm happy to have reimbursed you for that. I'm truly sorry. Bye now."

I stand up to go, but she gently pushes my shoulders towards the dreaded white bed, murmuring, "I am not going to hypnotise you. Now, lie down!"

# MAGGIE, SCENE 1: THE DANGLING CRYSTAL

Maggie levers me onto the bed and my head jerks backwards. I lie here like a rod, with my handbag clutched to my chest.

She reaches to take it from me, but I don't let go. We play a little tug-of-war until I feel my face reddening again, and let her take it. I look up at the rhinolite ceiling and try to focus on the plasterer's workmanship because I know all about construction. It's certainly more fitting for me to be analysing workmanship than to be having a breathless woman hovering over my reclining body. I cringe at the stupid sight I must make: clever, professional woman, flat on her back, exposed to freaky whims of herbal-witch.

Fear is with me, like the Force. But I'd rather be nuked by Darth Vadar's zapper than have this woman touch me.

*Oh, God, please don't touch me!*

She doesn't. Instead, she turns away from my rigid body. I clench my teeth. She places a very large open book on my stomach.

*What the hell?*

It's the biggest book I've ever seen, it must also be the heaviest, and it presses into my stomach. I'm delirious with fear and can't open my mouth.

She looms over me. She's got a large diamond- or crystal-thing dangling from a piano wire, and she's holding it over my feet. I manage to lift my head. "I am already sensing a lot of negative energy from you, so just lie back and let me work."

I'm so tense that I wish the bed would suck me into its folds. The brown bottles are bouncing near me. I'm terrified.

"I sense a lot of adrenalin has passed through your body in your lifetime."

*Damn right it has!*

The face of my first boss flashes before me:

*He's peering at me over his desk, squinting accusingly through his thick lenses. I'm trying to explain away yet another day late for work because of yet another car accident, burglary, traffic fine, or some other such mishap. He's smiling and calling me "Calamity Jane". I'm thinking that none of the things that happen to me is my fault. There must be some sort of evil spirit tracking me. Or I must be paying for the sins I committed in a previous life because, shit, I've done nothing to bring about my bad joss. I'm crying as I say, "Please don't fire me!"*

"You need to revisit the bad things that happened to you, in order to forgive and go forward. It would really help if you tell me about them," Maggie says calmly.

My spit is trapped at the back of my throat. I gulp. I need to throw her a decoy. Even though I'm terrified of what she's hinting at, I'm secretly impressed. Or she's merely fishing for a psycho-scoop. She's suffocating me with pity, or inquisitiveness; I can't be certain which. I consider telling a lie, but decide to give her nothing. She seems quite content to continue her diamond-dangling, and to wait me out.

I wonder if she can see my heart pounding under my shirt. I don't want to think about this, let alone talk about it. But it is here … and it opens up inside my head and pours over my tightened forehead, like pus from an untreated wound.

# MAGGIE, SCENE 2: THE CHASE

I know that my memories would blow my head off. I screw up my eyes to block them out, as well as Maggie's inquisitive face. I pretend to be in a trance. I will not give her a damn thing! But I can't elevate myself from the dusty pathway:

*My friend Lindy and me are walking towards the weir in the river at the bottom of the farm. We are tripping and giggling and being silly-buggers as usual. As we approach the weir we see them. There are four of them and they also seem to be behaving like silly-buggers, but I know that their "silly-buggers" is not brought on by youth, but rather by alcohol. I know a drunk person when I see one, even though I'm only twelve.*

*They are wearing cowboy shirts with the buttons undone and they look like The Village People. They are swaggering towards us. The thinner one shouts, "Hey! Why don't you girls come here?"*

*I'm trying to look away as they walk towards us. The hairs on my neck are prickling and I can't move. Lindy seems to be keen to talk to them. She has grown boobs and has older sisters and I have neither. And she has kissed a boy, and I could vomit just thinking about it.*

*"Lindy, let's go. Please!"*

*But she seems quite happy to stay and talk to the stupid pigs. Skinny-pig says, "You two are cute! How old are you?"*

*Now I am very scared. Black-haired-pig moves in from behind skinny-pig and walks towards us with a smile. There's a loud yell from the wooden watch-tower over the weir. I look up to see another pig leaning over the balustrading, and he's yelling, "Get them!"*

*The four of them are fast approaching. But my feet are stuck to the ground, like in my dream when I can't get away from the wolf. I have to run! Not only is fear at my throat, but I'm ashamed at having to run away like this. I'm hoping it's all a joke. Lindy must have changed her mind, because she's also backing away. They're still about ten metres from us.*

*I'm already ahead and I scream at Lindy, "Run!" She is much more athletic* than I am and soon overtakes me as we run up the hill through the khaki-bush. I hear the pounding of their feet behind us.

Watchtower-pig is shouting, "Get them!" and he's laughing. I hear the pigs in the ground-patrol panting. They're making snorting sounds and laughing.

Watchtower-pig is hooting and screeching, "Get the little chicks!"

We're nearing the bush where it thickens at the top of our koppie. I don't know where I need to go, but I'm veering off to the right, away from Lindy. I run down the other side of the koppie and into the bushes. I recognise a big prickly bush with low-lying branches because my brother and me had once found a Voortrekker pot underneath it. I know there is a hole in the ground under the branches. I dive straight through the thorns and press my shoulder against the trunk, while I kneel in the hole at its base. I thank the little jackal that made the hole, because it's big enough for me to hide in.

I blink away the sweat that's running into my eyes. My panting could give me away, so I hold my nose and let only small puffs of air into my cupped hand.

I hear watchtower-pig yell, "The other one has gone to the right into the bush. Get her!"

One of them is yelling, "Kitty, Kitty, Kitty. Come here, little pussy."

I wonder if Lindy is already dead. I hear the swishing of legs through bushes nearby, and a voice cursing at the thorns. I push my body against the trunk and close my eyes.

It's getting dark but I can stay here forever if I have to. I know they are still searching. I think about cutting my leg open so that when they find me, they might feel sorry for me and leave me alone.

I pick up a long acacia thorn and begin to drive it into my leg, when I hear, "Fuck it! The little bitch is gone!"

It's dark. I'm now certain that I'm safe because it feels like an eternity has passed and I can't hear voices anymore. All I hear are the squawks of guinea fowl as they prepare for the night in the poplar trees nearby. I can breathe normally again. My body is stiff and sore as I crawl out from under the bush. I sit on an anthill next to my bush and I pray to God and thank him for saving my life. I ask him to protect Lindy on earth, or in heaven, wherever she is now.

There's a rustle near me and it's Lindy with wide eyes and we hold onto one another for a long time. I look over her shoulder at the distant lights of our little farmhouse in the valley; the house where my parents are.

As we press our bodies together, I know we will never talk about this again. We *hang onto each other and stumble towards home with our bleeding scratches.*

*But the bush-pigs are always here. They are forever skulking in the khaki-bush on the farm where we have moved to permanently now, because the family business has crashed and we have escaped to the little cottage with little more than candles and insects ... and long trips in the stinky school bus up the hill.*

"I don't feel like talking about it at the moment!" I hear my voice out loud.

*Where the hell am I?*

But I come to. The large lady is hovering over me, and she says, "Maggie's here ... just close your eyes ... go back to sleep ... I'm with you."

I want to get off this stupid bed, but I'm so very tired ... I force open my eyes and stare at the rhinolite. I will just lie here, keep quiet, and wait her out. But I can't get away from her, or the pigs, or the farm. And I can't get off the stinky school bus:

*I stare at Lindy's big boobs as they bounce next to me on the bus. I compare them to my pin-pricks and wonder about their small size, because my entire female family has big boobs so why shouldn't I? I realise that mine haven't grown because of my shame. And I will them away under my baggy T-shirts, even though the boys at school call me "the titless wonder". My suspicions are now confirmed, because it's better having small boobs and not big ones that the three little pigs want to get a hold of.*

Why the hell am I thinking about boobs? I quickly cover my still-ungrown ones with my hands as Maggie pats me on my chest above them. I feel the weight of her big book on my stomach, and she says in a whisper, "It's OK. Whatever people inflict on you, you must forgive them. You must face them in your heart and understand them. You must exonerate them before you can go forward in life."

*"Exterminate" is the better choice!*

I sit bolt upright and the big book slides off my stomach. My anger pushes my sore heart aside, like an alien within me. My fury climaxes and spit shoots from my mouth. "Oh, really, Maggie, nothing happened to me in that sense, really nothing! But I can't bear that crap about forgiveness anyway. Get real! Forgive? Never! The stupid forgiveness-thing is a load of bullshit!"

*Slice off their balls and feed them to the lions!*

Maggie catches the book before it falls, and cradles it like a baby. She doesn't respond but merely peers at me over the binding.

# MAGGIE, SCENE 3: LUCKY ESCAPE!

I'm prostrate again. The anger still punches at my chest, so I open my eyes. Maggie closes the big book with a thud and takes it away. "Sorry ... I think I overreacted," I whisper.

I caught a glimpse of the words in the book as she closed it. The letters are tiny, and the book is huge, so it must take a hundred years to read the bloody thing, never mind understand it, and what a crock of hocus-pocus crap anyway!

I seethe. I'm disappointed in myself because I've been duped into being here. I think I was secretly hoping for Maggie to do a lobotomy, or merely rip my heart out, or something as deadly as that. I know I would be feeling a whole lot better if she had rather chopped off my head as I walked in. But all she's done is waft around with her silly dangling crystal and fake book, and made me feel tense.

*What the hell is she doing?*

Before I can react, she's taken my shoes off! "No!" I shriek. "Please don't do that! I told you that I wasn't going to take off my shoes!"

Maggie isn't budging, so I whip my head back onto the pillow and bury my fists in my eyes. She begins wiping my feet with something hot and scratchy, and appears to be oblivious to my embarrassment. She's humming quietly as she massages my left foot. Her hands are slippery and I smell peppermint. My toes seem to unravel as she whirls them around with the palm of her hand on the ends of my toenails. She rocks her big body in harmony with her rubbing and seems to be enjoying herself. I wish I could get my thumbs up to my teeth because they could do with a bit of abuse, so I bite my top lip instead.

Maggie's voice is practised. "The state of the feet is linked to the state of the body. By feeling the feet, I can pick up problems, particularly in the organs and glands."

I've heard about reflexology and am quite at ease with it. Links and messages from one part of the body to others are quite understandable.

She stops whirling my toes around and begins pressing the arch of my foot. The pain is excruciating and I gnaw my top lip. She twitters on like a canary: "Determining and healing any physical problems can often help with mental problems."

*I have no mental problems, you stupid woman.*

I'm insulted, but she continues. "Often physical problems can affect one's moods. For instance, low levels of iron can make you wake up in a bad mood."

I resolve to pump huge amounts of iron supplements into my body as fast as possible. She's on to my other foot now. Time is dragging on because the pain is killing me. But she suddenly stops massaging my foot and wipes both my feet with the scratchy cloth again.

I open my eyes. She's sitting next to me and proffering a tray, full of brown bottles, like an offering. I spit into her face, "Just a minute. Give me a second to get decent." I quickly pull my shoes on … and my dignity.

I escape to the wooden chair closest to the door and sit upright with my handbag clutched between my legs. She's got the tray of little brown soldiers in my face again. She carefully drags three bottles from their regiment and makes them stand to attention in front of my nose. "Now," she commands me, "you have problems with your kidneys, liver, and possibly your thyroid, so you need to take these three herbs. The dosage is fifteen drops under the tongue twice daily."

She passes them to me. Well, what the hell? I've already paid, and she must be satisfied that she's provided some sort of service. Soon I'll be out of here and done with her, and her ilk.

As I pop them into my handbag she whips out an invoice and says, "My products are charged separately. Thanks."

*What the hell?*

The invoice is already written out and on my lap. I whip out my cheque book for the second time, write it out to Cash, rip off the sleeve, and offer it to her.

I see my stupid self: clever, sophisticated, professional woman who has once again been hoodwinked into paying for hocus-pocus-psycho-crap she neither believes in, nor needs.

Maggie takes my cheque and tucks it into a pocket, saying, "You're still very antagonistic."

*Damn right I am!*

I have no dignity, and I have no words. I nod, and heave myself off the bed. I turn to her as I'm leaving to go, and manage, "Thank you for your time. Have a nice day." I notice the sweat on the tiny hairs above her lip.

# THE SORRY-FOR-YOU PARTY

Not only has Maggie embarrassed me and ripped me off, but she's also made me extremely late for the sorry-for-you party. She has conned me into buying some homeopathic drops for organs and glands in my body that I don't give a shit about, so I've tossed them into the trash-bin at her townhouse security gate. The only drug I care about is one that will help my heart, and it's clearly not available. So I take a few more swigs of my herb-drug while holding the steering-wheel. I've still got a lot of bottles of the stuff clinking around in my handbag, and the noise is comforting.

I'm just about to arrive at Clara's house when I'm forced to stop at an intersection by a waving traffic officer. There appears to have been an accident. There's a lot of commotion under a fallen traffic-light, and cars have slowed to a standstill.

I notice a crumpled car and wince, because it's identical to mine in colour and model. This makes me take a double look and I screech to a stop. I usually make a point of not ogling accident scenes, and pride myself in looking straight ahead while the rabble slows to gaze at the drama. But I have this peculiar feeling that I would like someone, other than me, to have some shit happen to them for a change, so I open my window and peer at the carnage. The scene that unfolds before me makes my neck-hairs tingle.

Not only is the wrecked car identical to mine, but the driver being guided to the ambulance is someone I know! She's one of the mothers from the children's school. She's friendly with Clara and would definitely have been invited to the sorry-for-you party. The party that's been arranged for me. Guests invited to the party must have passed the accident scene! Little links are sparking through my mind:

- Guests will know my car, because I collect our kids from school and mothers notice what you drive.
- Guests will know what happened to me, otherwise they wouldn't be coming to the sorry-for-you party.
- Guests will see the accident, because it's on the way.
- Guests will think that I'm the victim.

84

I stop my car and get out. I stumble towards the ambulance where the poor woman is being fitted with a neck brace. I yell at the medics, "I know this woman! Is she OK?"

One of the medics says, "Yes, she's fine. She has injured her neck but we'll take her to hospital to have it X-rayed."

I put my arms around her. She looks courageous above her neck brace. We stare at each other for a while, because I'm sure we both sense the ludicrousness of this situation. She says through her tears, "I'm sorry I won't be able to join the tea-party, but I have a gift for you. Please ask someone to take it out of my car before they tow it."

*What the hell?*

"Thank you for the present; you shouldn't have. I'm so sorry," is all I can manage.

The medic leads her away, and I stand alone on the street. My constant life-drama is playing up as usual and I'm once again at the epicentre of major chaos. Firemen are bustling about with hoses and it seems that any fire that might have been is already extinguished. I recognise one particular fireman. The alert eyes under the helmet are the ones that looked away when I cried under my burning palm tree.

And like a weird scene from *The Twilight Zone*, a traffic officer appears and hands me a large and beautifully wrapped present.

I drive very slowly to Clara's house. Even though I'm numb, I'm nervous. Nervous energy seems to spin uncontrollably around the steering-wheel, which makes me acknowledge the negative force that's enveloping me. The world is weird and black. Bad things are latching on to me. I wish Tulula was with me in my car when I pulled over at the accident.

The ornate steel gate opens before me like magic. There are a hundred cars parked in front of Clara's house.

*God help me!*

Clara's Alsatian bitch is at the window. Normally I'm terrified of her and wait until Clara locks her away before I get out of the car. But now I wish she would eat me alive. I open my door. Being mauled to death by the big dog would be better than facing the drivers of all of these cars.

The dog can probably sense the dark force that is with me, and has decided that escape is wise. I peek at my face in the rear-view mirror. Well, at least I look the part. So I stumble up the veranda steps into the reception hall of Clara's house.

A large table is adorned with snacks and cakes, and is surrounded by a myriad of lovely made-up faces. But the brows over the kind eyes are furrowed. The force of their concern washes over me like a wave, and I cry. Clara comes to the rescue and cradles me in her arms.

I'm humiliated because I have never given these women the time of day at school. All I have managed was a mere, "Hello," before hurrying to the exit gate with my kids.

I see my stupid, selfish, and pitiful self through their lovely, caring eyes and I hate myself.

Now they're driving the nails in deeper, because they are surrounding me and each one is taking turns to touch me, hold me, and ask me how I feel. I'm blubbering, so I cup my hands over my eyes and mouth. I can't hear them, nor see their faces, and I hope they don't sense my tears. I wonder how I can experience embarrassment, shame, and sadness all at once. I pull myself together and attach myself to the end of a cigarette.

An envelope is pressed into my hand, but I can't get my fingers around it because it's too thick. "We all know that you have lost everything," I hear Clara say, "and I have told the girls that things are difficult for you …"

*Oh, my God … there's money in the envelope!*

Most of the women turn away from me and pretend to be enjoying the snacks.

Clara takes my hand and whispers, "Come with me." She leads me to her lounge. Here, piled almost to the ceiling, are a million boxes, some plain cardboard and some wrapped in beautiful paper and ribbons. "The girls have put some things together for you. Some of the stuff is new, some second-hand."

*Oh, my God!*

Instead of joy, these offerings fill me with dread. I hate *things*. I picture my future in a white room with a single bed and nothing else.

I'm standing in the driveway like a dumb freak as women stuff boxes into the boots of Clara's and my car. Climbing Mount Everest would be easier than lugging all this stuff to the shitty-townhouse, let alone opening the boxes and looking at the things inside of them.

I feel floppy and drained and embarrassed and empty. I need a drink.

# ENTER DR SHAKER

I lower the back of the passenger seat in Stef's car until it's in full recline. Stef is driving and talking about business-stuff on his cellphone. I suppose he's discussing his next contract, his next invoice, our livelihood, our survival. I lie here like a diva blowing smoke at the car ceiling and thinking about dying without hurting my family.

I have no idea how I got myself dressed and into this car. What I do know is that I must have had a lot to drink last night, because I've got that sandy-eyed, tight-headed feeling. I want to puke but my throat hurts. I can't remember last night. All I remember is being buried alive under piles and piles of boxes. I must have passed out.

I stare at his beautiful profile and his sexy eye as it peers over the edge of his phone. He is washed and dressed in Clara's husband's tweed suit. He smells of soap and strength. He is my knight in borrowed armour. He always says he's my knight and I'm his princess. I flinch at the sight I must now present, slouching next to him and flicking ash out of the window.

It's a small consolation that I know he doesn't see me now. He doesn't know me. He's just getting on with things. He's doing what the doctors have told him to do. He's doing it during work hours like a scheduled meeting. He's doing what he has to do, like a man, without thinking about it and without asking questions. He is not dwelling in self-pity. But it's OK. I respect him still. I always will. I pinch my thigh until it hurts.

We're on our way to Lulu, the drug-prescriber, so that she can admit me to hospital. My fate is out of Tulula's psychologist-hands, and into the psychiatrist's. I'm sure we were meant to go yesterday but I was obviously in no condition to be moved after the sorry-for-you party. I don't want to go. I don't need to go. I'm fine. The rest of the world has gone berserk.

It's a small comfort to know that I'm letting this happen to me, because I don't have the energy to do anything about it. Everyone should be allowed to feel like this once in a while. But it's certainly no reason to be admitted to a bloody hospital.

The thought of a hospital with a lot of old codgers waltzing about, with their bums sticking out of flimsy gowns, makes me feel sick. I feel a little faint. What's really scaring the hell out of me is that I can't smoke in hospital.

I don't know where we are because I've been looking at the car ceiling on the way here. Stef is dragging me up a flight of stairs. I whine, "Oh, please, my love, please let's not do this."

He's intent, striding stair by stair. He gives my arm a tug and just mutters, "Shhh."

There's no-one in the waiting room other than a woman who appears to be the receptionist. She comes over, shakes Stef's hand, and says in a dull mono-tone, "Lulu has left for vacation, I'm Dr Shaker, and she has filled me in."

So, this Dr Shaker has been filled in by Lulu, who has been filled in by Tulula, who has been filled in by Babs, who has unwittingly been filled in by me. And for all I know, I'm here only because Tulula's made some far-fetched diagnosis by filling in an internet questionnaire called "First Twenty Questions for Prospective Client" that directs: "If questions five, six and seven are answered in the positive, patient can be referred to as a 'loony' and will generate a good cash-flow for your practice."

Dr Shaker doesn't shake my hand so I take hers and shake it like the true professional that I am. I put my chin up and say haughtily, "Yes, I am the patient, pleased to meet you."

She looks like a hippie. She's wearing a khaki kaftan-type top over ugly brown pants and seems unkempt, but then, so do I, and who cares anyway? I'm a little disappointed. She's meant to be a Bachelor of Science professional like I am, but hasn't presented herself very well. But then again, she's a stand-in for Lulu and has been found and filled in at the last moment.

She keeps her eyes on Stef. "I've come in especially to see you because I un-derstand that this is an emergency," she says abruptly. "Today I do my rounds at hospital and do not usually take private consultations."

*So, when I'm in hospital, will I become "public"?*

I'm miffed. But she seems to want to deal with me now, because she ges-tures to Stef to take a seat, and says to me, "Come with me." She's at least practising the "patient-privy" thing.

I don't want to be alone with her and hang on to Stef to indicate that it would be OK if he comes with me. Again he just mutters, "Shhh," and Dr Shaker pulls me away from him.

Her office is devoid of anything other than a little desk and two rickety chairs. We don't sit, but stand opposite one another on either side of the desk. I'm happy to stand because I won't take long. "Look, this is all a mistake." I've repeated this speech far too many times and I'm getting pissed off.

I purse my lips. "Before we go any further, Dr Shaker, I must tell you that the appointment I had with Tulula went terribly wrong and I didn't answer some of her questions truthfully. It's quite obvious that a person who has just experienced a disaster would be upset and confused. My visit to her was purely an insurance requirement for post-trauma stuff. I'm absolutely fine. I do, however, feel sorry for my husband because he's probably overreacted to Tulula's diagnosis and has had to humour her. I'm fine. I'm going home now."

I clutch onto the door handle to steady myself. She's steely-eyed and peers at me under her short, ugly haircut. "Do not open that door!"

She leans forward with her knuckles on the desk. "A doctor's diagnosis, whether she is a psychologist or a psychiatrist, is final, especially if we have the agreement of your husband. Now, just relax, we are doing this for your benefit. I have prepared a script for some medication and have a hospital admission form for you …"

I need to cut her short. I feel far superior to these bohemians and divorcees I've been subjected to, so I laugh sarcastically and say, "But you haven't diagnosed me! And neither has the doctor whom I was supposed to see. What makes me sick to my stomach is that my poor husband, who has a lot on his plate at the moment, is relying on one little consultation with Tulula that went terribly wrong, as I've explained. Now where does that leave me?" This is a very long speech for me and I'm exhausted. The clamp tightens over my forehead and the evening-wine-and-morning-coffee bile creeps into my throat.

Her voice sounds sarcastic as she says, "You don't know what you're talking about! We have discussed your consultation and have made this diagnosis on excellent information we are professionally obliged to rely upon. Very often a psychologist's consultation is followed by a psychiatrist's, if medication or hospitalisation is necessary."

She says this slowly, as if I were a child. This makes me more tired. I'm about to pass out. Little do these bloody shrinks know how professional I am and how very used I am to sophisticated dialogue. But my wit escapes me and I can't talk anymore. I am a tired child and their soon-to-be-hospitalised head-case. I slide down the door and sit on the floor like the proper loony she wants me to be.

"I need to ask you a few questions before I submit the documentation." She doesn't seem to care where I'm sitting.

*Here we go again!*

"Have you ever taken any medication for depression or epilepsy?"

*I've never even taken a bloody aspirin!*

I'm dead inside and manage, "No."

"Have you taken anything to calm you down since the fire?"

"Yes, someone gave me some herbal calming remedy, and Tulula gave me a sleeping pill. And I saw this herbal-oils-kind-of-medium woman yesterday, who has given me a couple of plant oils which I've dropped onto my tongue and, I must tell you, I feel a lot better." This is a lie but I need to get the hell out of here and back to Pooki and the shitty-couch.

She rolls her eyes and says with an audible huff, "This is what we come across all the time … and I'm so tired of it! Herbal medicine is dangerous. Being able to buy it over the counter is worse. How can you determine how many droplets fall onto your tongue? Psychiatric medication needs to be mixed in a laboratory. Are you with me?"

*Yes, I am with you, you bohemian brain-mechanic.*

She's made good sense. All I can do now is get this over with, so I mumble, "OK, I won't take any more."

"Good. Now, have you ever seen a psychiatrist before?"

"No."

"Have you ever been admitted to a psychiatric institution?"

"No."

"OK, here is a script and your hospital admittance letter. I want you to get this medication now and start taking it immediately."

"OK." Still on the floor, I slide over to her feet and take the papers from her.

I want to crawl after her like a baby as she walks out of her office, but I manage to pull myself up. I fall against Stef outside the door. He doesn't flinch. He helps me up and takes my hand and I lean against him like a child.

Dr Shaker's voice sounds practised. "She's very unstable. I want you to keep an eye on her until she's admitted. I've given her a script and admission form. You need to get the medication as soon as possible and make sure she takes it. Sorry, I'm a little rushed. I have to go."

She's gone. Stef's eyes are on me and full of sympathy. I must look like hell. I take a few swigs of my herb-drug as he tugs me out of the office.

# HOSPITAL ADMISSION

A round-faced nurse hovers above a sliding-table at the foot of my bed. She's writing notes and looks very important. I lie here, so very unimportant. The emptiness I feel is filled with shame: shame and embarrassment at the pitiful scene this must be.

There's nothing wrong with me. I am well and healthy and in a comfortable bed with a view. This is a very unusual time for me to be in bed and I wonder about it. I have never lain down to be indulgent. Even though at times I've been a mom at home, I can't rest. Relaxing on my back to read a book or watch TV is impossible. There has never been an in-between time for me. I'm either changing the world, or passed out from alcohol and too much dancing on the table. Sitting on the shitty-couch for so long, staring at nothing, was extreme behaviour. I truly hate myself even more by lying here like a stuck pig.

I peer at the hardworking nurse over my nice cotton sheets, and whisper, "I'm so sorry, there's nothing wrong with me and I shouldn't be here." I wish I was here for some critical car accident with my guts hanging out and my head bashed in.

She doesn't seem interested. I lie here as she gets on with her job. She takes my blood pressure, draws blood from my unfeeling arm, and takes my temperature. I keep my eyes closed to avoid looking at her.

She taps me on the head and offers me a tray with lots of tiny pills sprawled around a cup of water.

"Please take your medication now," she says kindly.

I draw out the dispensary sheet from under the tablets and mumble, "Please can I see what I have to take? Is this my script?" She nods.

I'm unconvinced that I should be taking any medication at all. I squint at the complicated list of medications through my haze. I try to recognise some keywords in each blurry specification:

- A word that reads like "epilepsy". Shit, I hope this is not what I think it's for, because I've never suffered from epilepsy, so it must be a homophone.
- A word that reads like "serotonin". I know that this is the stuff that the

brain manufactures because I remember reading about it in a women's magazine in an article on coping with crime in South Africa.

- A word that reads like "lamenting" or "lethargy". What the hell this is for, I don't know. But there's a hint at the word "depression" in the fuzzy small print which makes me wince.
- What seems to be some form of sleeping pill, because the small print reads "To be taken for sleep".
- An unpronounceable word that must describe a stupid antidepressant, because the small print reads "Indicated for depression". I quickly forget the label because the only thing that strikes me is that it's not Prozac, which is the only antidepressant I've heard of. I'm pleased I'm not being prescribed the same thing as housewives and Hollywood actors. This is a slight relief and eases my shame for a second.

Five abnormal things I need to force into my virgin veins! "Two fried aspirins and a quick cough!" I hear myself saying. This is all one would need for breakfast, after a night of too much drinking and smoking.

The nurse fidgets. I'm sure she needs to finish quickly with me and get busy with other patients. But I turn my head away from her and sink my cheek into the pillow. I gaze out of the window and manage as politely as I can, "Darling, I can't take this stuff. I don't know what it is. So if I don't know, I'm not taking it. My husband will collect me now. May I please use the phone?"

She giggles and shakes her head, "Come on, my dear, you are here for a reason. Let the doctors decide what you need. They know what they're doing. If you aren't going to take these medicines, I'm going to have to restrain you. And that's not necessary, my sweetheart. Now just sit up and do as I say."

I do as she says.

# WAKING IN HELL

*Where the hell am I?*

There's a smell of disinfectant and I hear the muted sound of traffic. I'm on a hard, narrow bed. There's a window to my left but I can't make out the view. I can't see very well.

My head hurts. I'm sure I'm concussed. I squeeze it all over to see if there's a bump on it. It *feels* fine, but the inside worries me: a thunderstorm is going on behind my eye-sockets. I hear a loud buzzing sound made worse by vivid flashes of colour and light behind my eyes. I don't know if I can actually see the colours, but my mind surely can. I don't understand this sensation. I'm scared.

Even though I feel detached from my body, I can feel my mouth working. But I have no saliva. My mouth is dry and I'm extremely thirsty.

I shut my eyes tightly, but the kaleidoscope of images is too frightening, so I try to keep my eyes open. I notice that there are other beds in line with mine. They seem empty but the more I focus, the more I'm able to see bumps in the sheets, which means I am not alone.

I don't care who the hell is sharing this nightmare with me. All I care about is getting out of here. I ease myself off the bed, but the ward spins, and I quickly lie down again. Where is the buzzer to call for help?

A nurse I recognise appears with a smile. "Good morning, dear, how are you feeling today?"

*I feel like dying.*

She bustles about doing nurse things and says, "It's time for your medication again. Sit up, dear, and let's get this over with."

I mumble over the sheets, "What are these for?"

"We are not going through this again and again! I have explained what the medication is for, many a time, and you keep on asking! Now sit up and do as I say!"

I pinch my brows together. Vivid images of trays and pills and nurses appear within the flashes of colour behind my eyeballs. I'm in a dark dungeon and smoking. I need a cigarette. I could eat one right now.

"Where are my cigarettes?"

"You can go down to the basement and smoke, when we are finished."

"What basement? Where am I? How long have I been here?"

She tut-tuts under her breath. "You are in hospital and very well taken care of. The medication should be starting to work, so you should be feeling a little better by now. But you've only been here for a few days, and by the looks of things, you will be here longer."

*What the hell?*

I'm marching along with my cigarettes and they're as big as I am. We're doing the frogmarch together, in step, to the imaginary basement. I don't give a damn if my cigarettes are walking next to me because I'm in a nightmare anyway, and I'm sure to wake up soon.

I'm thirsty. I swallow the little pills that have been pushed between my lips. "Where are my cigarettes? Where is the basement?"

I shuffle along with my nurse-friend. I think my bum is peeping out of the flimsy thing I'm wearing, but who cares. I'm having difficulty walking and seeing. I have never been unable to walk and see, and the sensation is frightening. But I've got the chubby arm of the nurse under my sweaty armpit and this helps. I can inch towards my cigarette in the basement.

We sit together on a hard bench in what seems like a cordoned-off area of an underground car park. This must be the smoking-zone. I think my little walk has done me good, and so has the second cigarette. I can feel the cold air around my bare ankles. I don't think we've said anything for quite a while, but the nurse seems to want to make conversation now, because she says, "Your husband's a darling. He's been here every night, at the same time, on the dot. Oh, and your aunty has been here a few times to see you."

I would rather die than have anyone see me here, or even know that I'm here. But I can't remember seeing anyone in this place, let alone Stef, or my aunt. I light another cigarette with trembling fingers.

Thoughts of Stef take me to my children. How could I have been lying flat on my back like an indulgent Pasha, while my kids are alone? Guilt engulfs me.

So here I am, with my cigarettes and shame, and sitting with a white-clad woman in a cold dark dungeon. It's as if I'm in a morgue, like a corpse. I wish I was a real one. I pull the nurse's arm towards me and tuck it under my armpit again. "I want to go to bed now. Thank you for staying with me."

# JUMPING OUT OF THE WINDOW

The flashes of light behind my eye-sockets are turning into shapes. I can clearly see a dragon with fiery nostrils gnashing at me in the kaleidoscope that has now become my consciousness.

I have to keep my eyes open at all costs. I try to settle within the coolness of the sheets but I can't because I'm quite aware of my fate and I'm very edgy. Furthermore, I've had the sense of someone watching me. I try to focus on the inmates. They all seem to be women and I count about five unmoving corpses lying around doing bugger-all but feeling sorry for themselves.

From the opposite side of the ward at the end of a row of beds, one corpse is glaring directly at me. It seems to be female because there's a hint of a pink collar under the pale chin. Its eyes are bulbous. I lift my arm and wave at it. No response. The face is like Michael Jackson's, but very white with pink lace at the chin. I'm in the music video *Thriller*. She is the zombie, and I am the frightened young girl.

The zombie's face is getting bigger. I try to close my eyes, but the dragon is here again, and I don't know which nightmare to choose. Either the zombie keeps coming at me until I'm devoured whole, or I get burnt by flames from the dragon's nostrils. And I've had enough flames around me to know that that would indeed be a painful death.

I blink furiously into this madness and scream out loud, "Get the fucking nurse!"

There's scurrying around me. Just as I'm about to be sucked into the kaleidoscope, I feel a tug on my arm and I open my eyes.

It's the dungeon-nurse-of-hell. "I think I'm hallucinating!" I spit. "If you don't get that fucking doctor over here right now, I'm going to jump out of the fucking window!"

I know that this death is possible because all the times I've thought about it are with me now, giving me power. I heave myself up and dart for the window. Strong arms grab me around my chest. My head whips back as I'm flung onto the bed. I feel a sting, and then nothing.

# EXILED TO THE LOONY-BIN

It's Stef's face and, my God, he is beautiful! He has come to save me. I am safe.

He rubs my arm, but it feels like he's doing it from a distance. "My love, we have a problem. The hospital has told me that they can't be responsible for a suicidal patient ..."

"What!"

"Yes. They need to discharge you. They have arranged for you to be admitted to another clinic." He pats me on the head.

*Who the hell is this man?*

He's not consoling me, or asking me questions, or having a discussion with me, but is talking to me as if I were one of his employees.

He turns to go, but I lunge forward and grab the hairs on his arm. "Listen to me, Stef! These stupid nurses have been giving me all sorts of crap to take, and not once have I seen Dr Effing Shaker! I think that they have given me stuff that I don't need ... this bullshit is getting completely out of control! The drugs are making me hallucinate, so this is not my fault!"

He winces and I let go of the hairs on his arm. He pats me on the head again, and is gone.

It's dungeon-nurse again, but she's not smiling like she usually does. Her mouth is twisted and her brows furrowed. As she takes my blood pressure, she asks in a voice softer than the one she uses to order me to swallow the hell-tablets, "How are you feeling, dear?"

"I'm feeling bloody marvellous. I haven't felt this good in a hundred years!"

This is an honest statement. I truly *do* feel good, despite the new accommodation arrangement. I don't know why I feel this good. It's as if a big hand is pushing away the clamp that usually grasps my head. I feel light and peaceful. I am altogether cognisant and ready to face my new world, however weird it has become. This beautiful new feeling lifts me above the hospital bed and into my elsewhere world.

"Good," she says kindly. "I'm glad you're feeling better. Here is your suitcase. Go and have a shower and get dressed. I will wait for you outside."

I didn't know I possessed a suitcase, or what's inside it, but I bounce off the bed to wash up and prepare myself for the sunshine.

I'm showered and in jeans and a white T-shirt that Stef must have packed for me. My face looks good in the mirror. I part my hair and braid two plaits. I've never worn plaits before but I feel quirky and the look suits me. There's no make-up in the suitcase but I don't need any because I look like a schoolgirl and mascara would spoil my bright eyes. I haven't had a drink for a while and wonder if this is why I look so good. I don't even feel like alcohol and this is certainly an unusual sensation. I'm the chipper clean "Heidi" and I skip out of the door.

As I bounce towards the ward exit doors, my knees bash into the spokes of a wheelchair. It's got dungeon-nurse attached to it, and she's looking at me sternly.

"What the hell is this for?" I ask with a laugh.

"It's policy. Now take a seat and I'll take you to Reception to meet your husband." I think I hear her mutter, "Poor fellow," but I can't be certain.

I ease into the seat and she whizzes me out of the ward. I feel special and float to the tune of the spinning wheels.

As we back out of the ward, the Michael Jackson zombie is still staring at me. She looks worried. The fear I had of her was unfounded. I'm being wheeled away from a bogeyman that didn't exist. What a fool I've been! But now it's too late to make excuses. The wheelchair is my unstoppable chariot.

# ENTER THE SLAUGHTER-HOUSE

I don't feel so chipper anymore. I'm reclining next to Stef as we drive to what is to be my new refuge because a stupid shrink shirked her responsibilities, and left me to fight off a dragon and a zombie all on my own. This is not my fault.

I stare at the car ceiling and wonder why I'm lying here like a dead person again. Maybe the trip in the wheelchair made me feel weak. My mind is foggy and I don't know where we're going. All I know is that I'm a shitty wife and a shitty mother. I sit up. My pull-yourself-together blanket is not working very well lately. All I manage is to find the automatic lever and manoeuvre the seat into its upright position.

We've been driving for a long time. Yellow wheat fields are spinning past the window in Vs. Stef hasn't said a word to me because he's been talking on his cellphone to other people about serious stuff happening in the real world. Not only has he had to run to the rescue of his stupid wife during working hours, but he's also had to act fast and pull a company together. The only person who's capable of ensuring a monthly livelihood right now is Stef.

"I'm so sorry, my love." He doesn't respond, but there's nothing to say, so we remain silent.

It feels like we've been driving for hours, but the car is slowing. We inch towards a big boom and an approaching security guard. There's electric fencing everywhere.

The security guard looks serious as Stef fills out the registration papers. As we near the buildings, I have the sharp impression that I have entered a schoolyard. The buildings are in face-brick and are set out like long single-storey classroom blocks. What's left of the grassy area is yellow. There's not a tree or flower in sight. I feel as if I'm going to school to write an exam I haven't studied for. I'm nervous and this at least makes me feel like someone again: I am the silly schoolgirl who's about to fail an exam, and will surely get detention. My childish plaits clink at my temples.

I peer into the face of a hefty woman in a blue apron. "We've been waiting for you. I'm Sister Bertha. Is this the patient?" She nods her head in my direction and paces over to shake Stef's hand. She hasn't bothered with me.

"Follow me." She looks only at Stef. "Let's check her in. Have you got her medication?"

"What bloody medication?" I ask. "I'm not taking any more of that crap, and that's that!"

Stef's voice is kind as he hands Sister Bertha a package, "My love, Dr Shaker has referred you to this clinic with the strict instruction that you continue with your current medication. I'm sorry, my love, but we have to do what these doctors are asking."

"It's the bloody medication that's made me sick in the head. I'm leaving now! It surely doesn't look like a hospital, more like an old-age home … or loony-bin."

Sister Bertha puts her hands on her hips and huffs at me. But I'm on a rampage. "I'm not going to be hanging around with effing loonies and old people all day long … when I'm probably the only sane one among us!"

I hope Stef's not thinking that I've also called him a loony, but I honestly feel that he's gone to the dark side with the rest of these nutters.

Sister Bertha's voice is quieter, "Now, now, dear." She's also calling me "dear" like dungeon-nurse, and I feel like a real stupid one caught in the headlights. I must also look like one with my silly plaits, and I curse myself for presenting myself like this. I should have twisted my hair into a chignon and worn my black gear and some mascara.

I stick out my chin at her, but she repeats, "Now, now, dear. Dr Shaker has referred you to our on-site psychiatrist, Dr Subramanium, and he will discuss things with you and check out your prescription."

"Well, where the hell is he? Can I see him now?" I need to speak to someone with sense immediately, and hopefully this Dr Sub-whatever will honour his allegiance to the sane and declare this fiasco a dreadful mistake.

"He only consults here tomorrow. You can see him then. Now, follow me, we are wasting time out here. I've got a hell-of-a-lot of other patients to deal with and haven't got the time to discuss the ins and outs of our operation here. There is a pamphlet that will explain all there is to know about what we do here at Amanzi Wellness Clinic."

Amanzi! There's no bloody water in sight! This place is not a bloody wellness clinic, but a dry, boring, old converted school! I hate it already and want to go home and make lots of pancakes and vomit them all out in time to do my homework.

Sister Bertha hooks a strong arm under my left armpit, while Stef gently holds my right hand, and they guide me under a wonky sign that reads "Reception".

It looks like I have no other option but to wait to speak to Dr Sub-whatever. Tomorrow I will consult with Dr Sub-whatever, who will be briefed by Sister Bertha, who was briefed by dungeon-nurse, who is the stand-in for Dr Shaker, who abandoned me to the dragon, who was briefed by Dr Lulu-whatever, who was on vacation, who was briefed by Tulula, who chin-wagged about me with Babs, who briefed Stef, who is too busy with real-world problems. And in the middle of all this head-shrinking, I've had to consult with Maggie-the-crystal-witch, who was briefed by Jen. And somewhere, peering down at me from atop, is Trixie, my fake-insurance-friend, who cares bugger-all about anything except "under-insurance", but has been nosy anyway.

I can't be angry with my poor husband. He's a businessman and takes advice from consultants who's job it is to make the right call. He has no other alternative but to remain distant from my trauma.

So here I am again, being frogmarched by yet another nurse to a room at the end of a long corridor, while Stef signs a lot of papers at Reception.

# FIRST NIGHT IN DEATH-CHAMBER

The nurses who've been bustling in and out of my room have introduced themselves, but I decide not to remember their names. One of them is sweeping the floor, while the other is presenting me with a little cup of water and pushing tablets down my throat. "We haven't used this room for a long time, and we didn't expect you, so you will stay here until another bed is freed up in the main section of the clinic."

"Washever." I'm slurring, but I don't care.

I remember that getting here meant passing a lot of empty rooms with their doors open, revealing small unmade beds. My little room is at the end of a long row of these bedrooms and I wonder why they've put me so far away from everything. There are blue curtains which open to a view of yellow grass and more face-brick outbuildings. I'm not interested in what's outside and don't spend time looking out of the window. These nurses haven't done nurse-like thinks to me, like taking my blood pressure, but seem content with sweeping the floor and making the bed.

I'm cursing the initiator of this horrid experience, when in she walks! Babs has got a positive look and a big smile.

"Hello, my love."

We hug each other but she quickly pulls away and busies herself with fluffing around the room, smoothing out my pillow, and opening up shopping bags. She's not looking at me like she usually does. Babs is a party animal. When we meet, it's to get drunk, dance around and laugh a lot. But now things are different. I am not the fun-loving drinking buddy, and she is not my collaborator. I'm the boring dopey patient and she the dreary matron.

"I've bought you a few things, my love."

*Oh, God, I hate "things"!*

Especially things that other people are giving me, but she's being so kind that I say, "Thanks, Babs, but I really don't need anything."

"Oh, for goodness' sake, my love, you haven't *got* anything! What are you going to wear while you're here?"

"I'm not staying long. I will sleep in my T-shirt and wear my jeans tomorrow. I don't care what I look like, especially in this hell-hole. Tomorrow I'm seeing the clinic's shrink, and after that I'm going." I glare at her to make my point.

"Don't be silly. Here are a few things for you."

She dumps a pile of clothes on the bed with the tags still attached, but the only thing I notice is a bright blue dressing gown and matching fluffy slippers.

"I'm not wearing that granny-gown!"

I can't believe I've just said such a mean thing, but it's shapeless, with no tie to make a waist, and big buttons all the way down from a dumpy neckline.

"I'm sorry, Babs. I love it. Thanks so much for everything."

I choose a grey tracksuit with a hooded top. I'll definitely wear this, because it's grey, like I feel. Babs has even brought little packs of panties and a vanity bag with all sorts of toiletries inside. I don't feel like washing my face or brushing my teeth, let alone putting on face cream.

Babs has gone with the nurses, and I'm left alone in the cold room. I'm alone with my buzzing head and my blue nightgown. I can't remember where I woke up today or how I got here. I remember that I tried to fly out of a high window, but I don't remember where it was. I know that I didn't manage flight on my own, but I do know that others have been moving me about, and I have not been in control of my own travel plans. I creep between the stiff sheets with my clothes and shoes on. But sleep doesn't come, only the dragon with its fiery teeth, so I force open my eyes and scratch at my wrists while I stare at the blue light through the thin blue curtains.

# FIRST DAY IN LOONY-BIN

"Cuckoo! Cuckoo! Wakey-wakey! Sit up now and take your medicine." There's a sharp pain in my neck as it's whipped up from my pillow by a strong arm.

I hit the hand away. "Bugger off!"

"Ha, ha, ha!" It's a nurse. She grabs my shoulders and heaves up the rest of my torso to follow my head.

"What the hell is the time?" It's still dark outside and what the hell is this nurse doing here?

"It's five o'clock. Time to wake up and take your medicine."

"Go away. And call the manager."

"I'll do that if you take your medicine."

"I'm not taking medicine because I'm not sick! Now just get the hell out of here and call me the manager."

"I'll do that if you take your medicine."

I need to lodge my complaint as soon as possible, but she's still got her arm around my shoulders and it feels powerful over my bony blades. I swallow the little pills with the tiny bit of water in the small plastic cup. I feel dehydrated. I'm sure my breath stinks because my teeth feel like they've got moss growing on them. I can't remember the last time I brushed them. I must have smoked a hundred cigarettes during the night because there's a pile of butts in an open lid on the bed. It looks like the lid of the face cream container, and I wonder when and how I turned it into an ashtray.

"Can I have some coffee at least?" I'm pleading.

"Ha, ha, ha! What do you think this is? A hotel? You can get yourself up and off to breakfast like everybody else."

She's looking at the pile of cigarette butts, and turns her nose up saying, "You're not allowed to smoke inside the clinic. I will have to take this up with Sister Bertha."

I ignore her smoking prohibition. "I shouldn't be taking medicine without something in my stomach. I need a coffee!"

"Ha, ha, ha! This stuff doesn't go to your tummy, my dear. It goes straight to your head."

"Bugger off! I'm not getting up and I'm not going to have breakfast with a bunch of people I don't know. Where is the shrink? Tell him to come here now!"

She doesn't answer. She's out the door. She's done her job. She needs to report to her elders.

I need to do something to thwart this sound in my head. But the only activity available to me is sleep. There's nothing in the room but me and a bed. But I don't want to close my eyes. I heave myself out of the hard bed. I wobble, and the blue curtains whirl. I manage to steady myself and shuffle my feet until I'm able to propel myself into the passageway towards Dr Sub-whatever.

There are two nurses sweeping the floor. They seem unaware of me shuffling along the corridor towards them. One nameless-nurse says to the other nameless-nurse in a casual voice, "Someone died in this room last night."

*What the hell?*

As I approach, one of them yells with some emotion, "Where do you think you're going?"

"Who died?" I hear my voice and it's high-pitched. I'm terrified of ghosts and remnants of dead people hanging around. I have a vague recollection of hearing wailing last night, but thought it was merely in my mind. The deep-throated screaming must have emanated from a dying person. This means there's a corpse somewhere in here. I can smell death and I am nauseous. This is a place for the dying and I am here and this is bad. I need to vomit, but there is nothing to come out, so I weave to my right and drag myself along the wall towards the open air.

The nurse who has spoken blocks my wobbly departure but seems a little edgy now. "Don't worry, dear, she was here a long time and she was very old. It was her time to go." She's looking at sweeping-nurse who keeps on sweeping with her head down.

"I'm not staying here for a minute longer! I'm not about to be left alone to die." I try to dash for the exit door but my feet and nausea won't allow it and I'm on the floor like a fallen broom.

Sweeping-nurse picks me up and the two of them drag me in the direction I was going. This is a small consolation, because I'm now getting the hell out of this deathly place, albeit like a raggedy doll.

Between my hunched-up shoulders, I notice my surroundings. I can't recall how I got here and I can't recall having seen anything around me, except for the blue granny-gown, which seems to be following me like a phantom.

We're out in the chilly air and shuffling on yellow grass between face-brick dormitories towards what looks like a sunroom. What must be the main entrance door to the left is boarded up with a sign that reads "Construction in Progress". The sunroom is dark and seems to be a dining area because there are a few tables scattered about and I can smell burnt toast. The tables have company. A few humans are hunched over cups of yogurt. As I trip up the stairs between my two nurses, a few raise their heads like they've heard something, but quickly continue scooping spoonfuls towards droopy heads.

I know I'm finally at the gateway of this hell when I stand in front of a brown counter that reads "Reception".

"She's here."

A robust nurse emerges from the darkness behind the counter accompanied by a thinner nurse with glasses on the tip of an upturned nose. I recognise the bigger one in my fuzziness as the one who was around when Stef abandoned me. The looks I'm getting from them make me feel like I'm in the headmaster's office. Their disapproving eyes make me tear my arms from my supporting nurses and stand to attention.

The haughtiness of my stance quickly fizzles because I see myself: very professional career woman with Bachelor of Science degree and respected mother and wife, standing to attention in front of irritated nurses in loony-bin with dishevelled plaits and slept-in T-shirt.

"I took one look at you yesterday when you arrived and I have welcomed enough patients to the Amanzi Wellness Clinic to know that we were in for trouble."

I try to focus on which of my jailers is addressing me, and mumble, "Sorry? Who are you? I'm not sure we've met."

I'm trying to sound professional but I'm abandoned by my power-clothes and black make-up. I'm not delivering an impressive PowerPoint presentation to important financiers. I'm not the belle of the ball, and I don't have everyone's adoring eyes on me. It is dark and dank in here and I am alone. No-one dotes on me. I'm a numbered inmate and an irritating one to boot. I'm an inmate who does not want to take her medication and smokes in her room.

"I met you yesterday with your husband. I'm Sister Bertha, and this is Sister Shabalala."

I squint at the silver badge on her breast and try to make out her name because I'm surely going to forget it. It reads "Dispensary". This helps. She is the lady I need to watch out for. She is not coming near me with her demon-pills after I've had my chat with Dr Sub-whatever.

"I need to see Dr Sub-whatever."

"You will see Dr Subramanium when Dr Subramanium is ready to see you. We are putting you in a new room now, across from Reception. The nurses will take you there now. You need to clean up and get yourself presentable."

"That's a waste of time because I'm going today."

"No, you're not."

Sweeping-nurse and death-nurse resume their hold on my arms. I'm weak and I need their support.

As I'm being wheeled around towards a door behind me, I hear Sister Bertha mumble, "We're in for a lot of shit from this one."

# NORA

I only have one nurse to assist me now. Sweeping-nurse has relinquished her hold on my arm and is gone. I'm being tugged along by death-nurse. I'm led into a bedroom that's cold and gloomy. It's also dark, like I've walked into night-time.

I get used to the darkness and blink my eyes to silence the din in my head. I make out three single beds along the right wall. To the left is a very large window with blue curtains, which are closed.

"Shit, it's miserable in here, we need some light." I'm taking charge because it's what I'm trained to do. I draw the curtains with some effort. But no light enters as I open them, only the dull reflection of a face-brick wall, which has been built directly behind the glazing. I'm disgusted at the misery of brick-work instead of a view. Any wall built parallel to a window opening is daft. Not only would this create drainage problems between the two buildings, but it would also affect roofing, access and ventilation. The architect of this awkward design should be ashamed, but then again, this is a public-school-turned-loony-bin and, under these circumstances, anything's possible.

There's no change to the luminosity of this terrible place, but the dull grey haze that filters from the face-brick allows a little more vision. Death-nurse smoothes out what must be my bed, which is to the right of the other two. She pats the bed and hands me a pamphlet, saying, "This is your bed. These are our rules. Please read them."

She's gone and I'm alone once more. I toss the rules into a nearby dustbin and make my way to a white door to the left past the window because it has a sign with a picture of a bath etched on it. I need to look myself in the face for a long time and blow smoke-rings against my reflection.

As I near the bathroom, a slight moan emanates from the last bed.

*What the hell?*

I gasp and jam myself against the bathroom door. Before I pass out from fear of yet another dead body, I hear a raspy, "Hello."

Is this a friendly ghost who has entered my consciousness, or is there a real person in that bed?

"Hello." The voice is still raspy, but timid.

Shit, I'm not completely mad! I tiptoe fearfully towards the bed.

A grey, wrinkled face peers up at me with sweet granny eyes behind a sharp nose.

"Please don't make too much noise, dear. I have terrible trouble sleeping." The elderly voice is shaky and irregular yet comforting and polite.

Someone is sharing my room, and the heartless nurses haven't had the grace to tell me about it or introduce us. Or maybe they've just forgotten her, like the other old lady in the death-chamber.

I introduce myself with the softest and most caring whisper I can muster, "And what is your name, darling?"

"Nora."

"How do you do, Nora? I am pleased to meet you."

I search for a hand to shake but it's under the covers. She smiles at me like a timid mouse above the fold in the sheet.

She lies here like a ramrod under a pale-blue blanket. There're no creases in the bedding, so she must've been still for a long time. The blanket covering her is worn through in places with tiny rub-balls all over it. I stare at her because she's closed her eyes and appears to be asleep.

"How long have you been here, Nora?"

The large, veined lids open and her hazy eyes are on me again. The voice is unsure and still shaky, "Oh, I don't really know, dear … maybe a couple of weeks."

"When was the last time you got out of this room and took a nice walk outside?"

"Oh, I don't go out, dear." Her eyes twitch from left to right and she looks a little frightened.

"Are these nurses taking good care of you?"

She doesn't answer but attempts a shrug of her tiny shoulders. She doesn't need to answer because I sense she hasn't been cared for.

"When was the last time you took a bath?"

"Oh, I don't know, dear … I can't remember."

I bite my lip until it hurts and say as softly as I can, "Would you like to take a nice long hot bath now?"

Her face lights up and she looks a little younger. She must have been a striking woman in her youth.

She seems unable to answer me, but her sunken cheeks redden so I pursue the bathing thing, "It's very chilly in here and a nice bath will make you feel comfortable and warm. I will help you. I'm quite capable."

"Oh, would you, dear? That would be lovely."

I trot off in the direction of the bathroom. "I'm going to fill the bath and will be out to help you in a jiffy. Can you sit up for me?"

"Not really, dear, I need to call the nurse for that."

I've turned on the taps and am back with her. I look for a buzzer but there is nothing but a little wooden bedside table with a tiny cup on it, filled with water. God only knows how long it's been here. And God only knows how she gets to drink it, because she can't sit up without help. And God only knows how she would ever be able to call for help without a buzzer, because her voice is soft and barely audible.

"Well, you just lie here and relax, and I will be back soon to give you a hand."

I trip into the bathroom to check the bath-water. I'ts just the right temperature, because I have felt it with my elbow like I did when bathing my babies. I wish I had some bath salts for her but there's none of that kind of stuff to be found, just a tiny piece of soap that looks like a well-used hotel amenity.

At Nora's bedside I peel back the blankets and horror fills me. Stick-like arms flank a flimsy nightdress of indistinguishable colour. The nightdress is crumpled around the midriff and exposes stick-like legs no thicker than her arms. I can't take my eyes off her skin. I pretend to straighten out the blankets around her in preparation for an easy lifting. Her skin is like nothing I have ever seen and I know I have to be brave now because I have a task to do. I stroke her arm. The skin is smooth, like plastic. It's so pale that it exudes no colour, just light, like the translucent white marble of a Crucifixion statue. It's the most beautiful skin I have ever seen or touched. I can trace enormous bright-blue veins across her legs, like tributaries of a river. There are so few that I'm sure I could count them. Nora is only bone, and veins and skin.

I continue to stroke her arm and my eyes sting. I secretly hope she's a little blind, because I would hate her to feel humiliated by my pity. I must put on a brave face for her, and for me.

I shake off my shock and gently cradle her torso while supporting her neck like a newborn's. Her arms creep up to my neck too, and she holds me. I wonder what to do now, because I planned on her being able to walk. I clench my back muscles and prepare to heave her up. I place my arm under the bones of her knees while supporting her shoulders … and lift. But she's like a feather and I've got her against my breasts.

I feel her breath on my neck as she says, "Thank you, dear."

I place her body, like a facecloth, on the edge of the bath. She can manage this without my holding her, which is comforting. I'm not a nurse and not used to seeing other people's naked bodies, let alone a frail one like this that feels as if it could snap any minute. I need to be brave now. I decide to spare her dignity in front of me and say, "Would you like me to help you undress and get in?"

"Oh, I don't know, dear."

I compromise for both our sakes, "Don't worry, Nora. Let's try to do this together. I will lift you into the bath. You can keep your underpants on and take them off in the water when you are sitting. I'll unbutton your nightdress and lift it up so it doesn't get wet when I lower you in. When you are in the water you can hold a facecloth around your front while I pull your night-dress over your head." Her body is so narrow that I'm sure the facecloth will cover most of her. "Then I'll leave you to bathe. I'll keep the door open, so you can just call me if you need me and I will help you. Do you think you can manage all of that?"

Her eyes dart around again. She takes her time to answer because I'm sure my plan is quite confusing for an old ducky like her. So I sit beside her on the edge of the bath while she ponders.

"ok, dear, I think I can manage."

She smiles bravely at me and I smile back. We are both ladies, and prud-ish ones at that, but we will get through this together.

I move behind her and gently unbutton her nightdress and pull it up to under her shoulder blades. They protrude from her luminous skin, as do the knobs of her spine and the ridges of her ribs. Now I see where all her skin is hiding. It hangs like pastry and ends in folds above her large panties.

She turns her head over her shoulder and says to me, as I stand behind her, "I hope I don't smell, dear."

"Of course you don't, love."

I hook her nightdress under my right arm so that it doesn't lift up any further. I cradle the underside of her knees to begin our descent into the water.

There's a bang and a shrieking voice, "Hau! What are you doing?" It's an-other nameless-nurse and her eyes blaze at me and Nora.

110

I replace Nora on the edge of the bath and quickly pull down her night-dress to cover her nakedness while she clings to me like a baby.

I meet our intruder's eyes with fire in my own. "I'm bathing Nora. I'm doing what you should be doing every day! She tells me she can't remember when she last took a bath and that's deplorable!"

I want to use the f-word and tell her to f-off, but I won't swear in front of Nora.

Her bum presses into me as she reaches for Nora. "Suka, wena!" I've worked on enough construction sites to know that she's telling me to bugger off, in Xhosa.

She huffs. "You are not allowed to do this job. This lady is my patient to look after. I will make the washing."

She grabs Nora by the shoulders and pulls her upright, exposing her folds, and her veins, and her nakedness. I want to tug Nora's bones back to my chest and hide her away, but I stop myself short, because a tug-of-war would rip poor Nora in two.

I let go, and Nora manages to stand on shaky legs. She gazes at me like a wet puppy. "It's OK, dear."

The nurse nudges me out of the door and slams it with a thud. I seethe … and I'm so terribly sad.

# FIRST QUEUE FOR CLINIC-SHRINK

With a cigarette dangling from my lip, I drag myself along the wall of the reception area in pursuit of an escort. There's no-one around to show me the way to the doctor, so I will find him myself. I stumble into the dull sunroom. There's no-one here and, judging by the dishevelled tablecloths with crumbs on them, breakfast must be over. Come to think of it, I can't remember the last time I ate, but I'm not hungry. Weirdly, I also don't need a drink. I feel slightly out of body and there is still a buzzing noise behind my eyes.

I avoid turning left towards the death-chamber and shudder. I leave what must be the main block, and cross the yellow lawn towards what seems like another section of the clinic. I stumble around to find my bearings and make my way towards the grey steps of a school-like corridor. Flanking the corridor to my right is what looks exactly like rows of classrooms.

A woman rushes at me from the first classroom and yells, "Where do you think you are going with that cigarette? You are not allowed to smoke in undesignated areas!"

I don't like to be spoken to like this. I am not a mere number, nor am I a raving lunatic, and I deserve respect.

I drag on my ciggy and support it daintily in the air with upturned fingers, saying as politely as I can, "Sorry? I don't think we've met. Who, may I ask, are you?"

She appears to want nothing of my courteous chatter and attempts to lunge at me, so I toss my ciggy into a bush. She pushes out her chest and says, "I am in charge of the Activity Centre. Now, where do you think you are going?"

She hasn't provided her name, but what the hell is an activity centre doing here? I feign disinterest and grasp for a lie. "I have been sent to see Dr Sub— the psychiatrist. I have important matters to discuss with him."

I'm trying to sound professional in the hope she'll think I'm a drug rep. She giggles into my face. I'm self-conscious. I'm in scruffy jeans and a wet, crumpled T-shirt. Not only am I wet, but I must have kicked off my shoes to bathe Nora, and my plaits are probably looking rather tatty by now.

She takes my hand like a child's and leads me up another few steps towards a row of people who are pasted along the face-brick wall of the corridor.

"These are Dr Subramanium's rooms," she says with a little laugh. "Wait here in the queue for your turn to see him." She trots off with a twinkle in her eye.

I'm terrified. The figures slouching against the wall are probably loonies with serious mental conditions. I have never been in the presence of anyone truly sick in the head. I feel the chill of a breeze against my wet T-shirt and my feet are cold against the grey concrete. I skulk towards the back of the queue, keeping my head well down. I'm facing the backs of what I sense are about four men. They are leaning against the wall like gangsters and haven't turned around to look at me, nor are they talking. I do as they do and lean nonchalantly against the brickwork and light a cigarette. I have three boxes tucked tightly into my jeans' pocket so I have enough to wait out my time. As the smoke bellows through the cold air, all of them turn on me.

*Don't look at me! Don't come near me!*

They form a circle around me and are close approaching. I keep my head down. I will not make eye-contact.

"Hey, chicky, lend me a fag."

"Score me a smoke, man!"

"Me too, hey!"

One chap inches much closer to me than the other three and says in a whiney child's voice, "Aw, please may I have a cigarette as well? I promise I'll pay you back." He's very close to me now and I feel claustrophobic. But he has a tremendous smile and a placid presence, like a gentle giant.

*Whew!*

All they want is a cigarette. All they give a shit about is that I've got a stash. This is good. Without looking up I quickly hand four cigarettes to the giant with trembling fingers. He swiftly pockets them all and the other three are on him. They jostle him around and try to grab at his jeans' pocket. He giggles madly and seems to be enjoying the little game.

They've got their cigarettes. Their heads are together while they light up. Their backs are turned again and they puff away.

But Gentle Giant is with me still and says, "Please can I have a light? I promise I'll pay you back. My name is Samuel, Samuel Krishna." He has thick black curly hair and a bad shave. Little bits of tissue are stuck all over his jaw with spots of blood on them. He is handsome, but not in a sexy way. His childlike eyes and gaping mouth disguise his handsomeness. He looks like a young boy with the potential to be a supermodel. He puts the cigarette awkwardly between his lips and bends towards my lighter, and I say, "Pleased to meet you. May I call you Sam?" He nods energetically.

He hasn't asked my name, and I'm glad. My name is not my name now. It's a nice name which smacks of a normal me in a normal world. Standing here with my stupid plaits, awaiting another head-bending, puts me far away from the real world. I decide that if anyone in this awful place asks my name, I shall call myself "Lamby". This is what my father calls me, so it's not far from the truth.

Sam scampers to the front of the queue screeching, "Hey! Come on, you guys, that's my place in the queue and you've stolen it again!" One of them grips him around the neck and pulls him towards the concrete floor while another mock-punches him in the stomach. All three of them are laughing as they jostle him around.

"Hey! Leave him alone!" I shout. They shove him towards me and he trips into my chest.

He holds onto me momentarily and pulls himself upwards towards my face. "They are so horrible to me. They never let me keep my place."

He whimpers like a puppy and I pat him on the arm. "Don't worry, Sam. Stand here with me. I've got lots of cigarettes."

"Oh, goody!" I hand him my lit cigarette because he seems to have dropped his own in the scuffle, and he's full of smiles.

A woman calls from the door in front of the queue, "Samuel! You can come in. Dr Subramanium will see you now."

"Oh, goody!" He skips past the queue. One of the bullies goes into a kung-fu position and kicks him on the bum.

I don't want to be left alone with these thugs and I miss Sam. But their backs remain turned and they seem content to lean against the wall and stare into space.

# ENTER CRANIUM

I don't know how much time has passed while I've stood here outside the doctor's waiting room, but Sam and the three oafs have all gone in and come out again, one by one. Each one of them has galloped out hooting savagely, except Sam, who stopped for a quick smile and another cigarette, and skipped merrily down the corridor chanting, "I promise I'll pay you back. I promise I'll pay you back."

I wonder what made the inmates hoot on their exit from the rooms, but then again, this is a loony-bin and, having had some experience with Tulula, a good head-tickling can indeed be funny.

I must have smoked a hundred cigarettes and have been content to stand here and stare into space, contemplating death before my appointment with God, who will give me wings for a swift flight out of here. I realise I'm about to have a very professional meeting with a very professional doctor who is about to discharge me for very professional reasons, but I can't remember his name! Let alone *pronounce* it. I know it begins with "Sub", and I think it ends with "ium", but I can't be sure. I can't call him "Sir", because he'll definitely keep me here if I do. I decide to call him Cranium. After all, he *is* a bloody skull-doctor!

I'm led by a woman, whose face I don't look at, into a little brown room with an enormous brown desk that seems to take up all the brown space. Perched at the end of the desk with his back against a window is my ticket out of here. I feel bedraggled and dizzy but not self-conscious anymore. I will rely on my professional tongue. I'm a qualified and clever woman of the real world and this is a meeting between graduates which will be held with decorum and elicit excellent results. I picture myself on the telephone telling Stef that all's OK, and could he please come and fetch me.

I plonk myself in what must be the patient's chair and face the man I've been waiting for. I'm a little unsteady and my vision is fuzzy, but I'm finally able to focus on him.

He has creamy coffee-coloured skin and an Asian look. He has dark, black hair but his sideburns are white. His face is elongated, with a long nose. He has a very long neck, atop a very long upper torso. Everything about him is stretched, even his ears. His eyes are beautiful and very round, seeming to defy his overall longness. I imagine him with glasses, but he's not wearing any, so he's probably younger than he looks. All in all, his appearance is placid, and he seems harmless enough.

He doesn't say anything but merely sits looking at me, as if he's waiting for me to speak, like a headmaster awaiting yet another excuse for tardiness.

I decide to wait him out. This is a far cry from my consult with Tulula, who lashed me the moment I sat down. But maybe this is just another psycho-tactic recommended in their psycho-degree, called "Options for Setting the Scene on First Consult". I try to sit up straight, albeit with difficulty, because I'm still feeling wonky, but a good posture speaks volumes.

I notice a yellow folder in front of him. I lean slightly forward and squint at it to see if I can read anything on the cover page, but all I see is my name in very large print. I have become a yellow folder; I'm reduced to hurried sentences on paper.

We sit like this for a while until he tilts his head down over my folder and begins to flip through the pages in slow motion. Without lifting his head he says, "Why do you think you are here?"

*What the hell?*

One of his eyes is still looking at me! I'm dumbstruck, but I manage to close my mouth with a gulp. He hasn't flinched but keeps on paging through my folder while the eye remains focused on me. The bloody thing is not moving in his bloody skull! I'm terrified! I need to think quick! I need to pull myself together! I mustn't panic! So I gather some quick rationale from somewhere inside my now very fuzzy head. He has a glass eye. So what! We all have imperfections, so what the bloody hell! He has white side-burns, which means he must have been practising for a long time. He must have seen a million patients who have reacted just like I have. If he or they thought his glass eye was an impediment, he would not be a psychiatrist, and I would not be sitting here with him. He must be all the more fantastic as a psychiatrist to have overcome this awkwardness. I must *not* react. My determination helps, so I put my shock aside and lower my unaffected self into his unaffected presence.

I haven't flinched, and I'm proud of myself. I sigh and slump into my chair. But I can't remember his question, so I sit up and ask, "Sorry? What was your question again?"

Both eyes are back on me. He is completely calm and says, "So, Miss, why do you think you're here at Amanzi?"

His face is expressionless, but I can't take my eyes off the eye. I'm fascinated. He shifts in his chair and I realise that my mouth is open.

I shut it and suck in my drool. "Sorry? What was your question again?"

"Why do you think you are here?"

I get my professionalism well behind me and sit up straight. I suck in as much air as I can, and say, "I'm glad you ask me this, doctor, because one of my friends arranged an appointment with a psychologist, which was quite unnecessary, and went terribly wrong, which landed me in hospital, where they forced me to take a lot of drugs, which, may I add, I have never taken in my life, not even an aspirin, which caused me to hallucinate and resulted in me play-acting that I would jump out of the window, something I would never contemplate doing because I'm a very well-balanced woman who would never be so selfish as to do a thing like that to my dearly beloved family."

I've been exhaling while talking and I'm sure my voice sounds weird. I suck in some more air and try to finish. "All in all, it's a terrible mistake that I've been admitted here, there is nothing wrong with me and I'm absolutely fine, and I respectfully implore you to professionally acknowledge this unfortunate turn of events, and discharge me without further ado."

I'm very tired after this and feel confused. I slump back into my chair.

"Tell me about yourself."

*Shit! He hasn't heard a word I've said!*

I need to splash my face. This is my last and only opportunity to prove that I'm not meant to be here and to get the hell out.

"May I please use the restroom?" I don't wait for an answer and escape the confines of his room in search of water.

I'm in front of a mirror in a small bathroom next to his rooms. The bathroom smells of disinfectant and urine. This smell is real – I'm not waking from my recurring dream with acid up my nose, but living a nightmare with loony-urine splashed on the floor.

I take out my plaits and twist my hair into a tiny bun at the nape of my neck. I can't really see my face because the anxiety that's clamping my brows together makes it impossible. It's as if there is a big hole in my vision, like when I had my concussions. But I know what needs to be done here, so I splash water on my face and slap my cheeks until they sting. Hanging over

117

the basin, I remember that I haven't brushed my teeth. Blowing stinky cigarette-breath over Cranium is certainly not going to get him onto my side. So I foam up the basin soap into cupped hands with some water, and gargle with it. I do this a few times until I'm sure I smell better, and go back to my chair.

He's on the phone. He doesn't say anything into it but merely goes, "Hmmm. Hmmm. Hmmm." And then, "Bye, dear."

He's back on me with his perfect eye in his elongated face and says, "Tell me about *you*."

*Oh, God.*

I'm tired of talking about myself. Tulula has completely exhausted this indulgence. But then again, it's probably another chance to display my confident self and pursue my discharge.

I'm still very tired, despite the new hairdo and slapped cheeks, but I gather all that's left of my professional abilities and draw on my interview experience. I prepare to regurgitate my curriculum vitae.

"I was born in 1963. I'm a qualified Bachelor of Science graduate and Project Manager. I have used my qualification well and have achieved great success in the construction and finance industries. I have worked abroad and gained international experience. I have owned my own multi-million-rand companies and gained tremendous respect from my peers."

This is boring me to death and I'm so very tired. I try to picture myself in a professional environment where what I have to say counts. But I am so very, very tired. Both his eyes are unmoving. I push on with difficulty.

"So, I have always been a very active businesswoman and quite a workaholic. Because of my great success in business, I never wanted marriage or children, but when I was twenty-seven, I met a man in an aeroplane who immediately asked me to marry him. I instinctively said yes. We got married, we had two children, we bought a house, and it burnt down."

*What the hell am I on about now?*

I'm suddenly angry and shout out, "It burnt down! So what? Other than this little hiccup, you can clearly see that I'm a highly professional business executive and fantastic mother and wife! I'm a very balanced woman with her head screwed onto her shoulders, and I surely don't need any psycho-mumbo-jumbo from you! I think I've had enough of that in the last few days to last me a lifetime! All in all, I'm a very well-adjusted and sane person and I am not meant to be here!"

I catch my breath and lower my voice, "So can I go home now?"

He still hasn't budged. In fact, I can't remember him moving at all. He clearly hasn't heard a word I've said, because he glibly says, "Tell me about your fire."

*No! No! Not that! I don't want to talk about that!*

"I don't want to talk about it, because it has nothing to do with why I'm here! That happens to a lot of people and it's not the end of the world! People get over that kind of stuff and so will I. Everyone I have spoken to since it happened has had the decency not to talk about it. Even my friend, Clara, who's had the same thing happen to her." I'm hoping this will make him feel bad, but it clearly doesn't, because he remains stolid.

I realise that I haven't actually talked about it other than briefly with Maggie, who seemed more concerned about it happening to her. My tears begin to pour like tap-water. Crying is a small consolation, because ever since taking the bloody drugs, my tears have completely dried up.

"You need to go to your room and rest. I will see you again in two days."

I sniff back my tear-snot and manage a choking squeal, "I can't sleep for shit's sake! Have you not heard a word I've said? All these stupid drugs are making me hallucinate, for God's sake! I can't sleep! Do you understand? I can't sleep!" This is a half-truth, because I haven't managed to sleep properly since the f—, with or without drugs.

He scribbles something on a piece of paper and seems impervious to my outburst. "I will give this to Sister Shabalala. I have prescribed something to make you sleep."

I glance at him through my teary haze and I manage to look at both his eyes at the same time. But more tears are here. I don't want any more medicine that will affect my head and take away my tears. I need my bloody tears!

I sense I've lost my battle and feel desperately alone. I manage to raise my voice, even though I'm limp. "I don't want any more medicine that stuffs up my head! I want something to help my heart! Is that so bloody difficult, for God's sake!"

# SPACESHIP

I stumble into Nora's chamber with my heart in my mouth and dried salt-tears on my cheeks. I've pulled myself together, but I'm too tired to think about my lost battle with Cranium. I'm here to stay for another day, so I'll think about it tomorrow. I always have tomorrow. For now I need to concentrate on how to pass out in the face of the looming dragon behind my tired eyes.

The room smells of instant soup. Xhosa-nurse is at Nora's bedside. "Sit up, Granny, and eat your food!" She proffers a tray with covered plates. It must be lunchtime.

Even though I'm weak and have little energy to offer the real world, I need to involve myself in Nora's fate.

I manoeuvre the tray from under Xhosa-nurse's peeved-off face and place it on the bedside table. "Excuse me! I have something to discuss with Nora. Just wait a minute on the side." I nudge her away from the bed and step closer to Nora.

She clicks her tongue at my intrusion, but she obliges with a shake of her head and a huff.

"Hello, Nora. How are you feeling after your bath?"

"Hello, dear. Much better. I've managed to sleep well. How are you, dear?"

"I'm super, thanks."

I'm hoping she can't see my dried tear-stains. I know I look awful and I'm sure I must smell, because I haven't washed since I got here. Xhosa-nurse is hovering near me, but I don't care what she thinks of my appearance. I secretly hope I smell bad.

I focus on Nora, who's eyeing the food-tray, and she says, "I need to eat my lunch now, dear. So please won't you excuse me for a while?"

Xhosa-nurse shoves me and I push her away, still keeping my eyes on Nora. "Now, listen to me, Nora! You cannot eat in bed! Eating in bed is sad, because it makes you depressed. Even happy people who eat in bed get depressed. You need to get up at mealtimes and eat in the dining room. You need to walk and talk and eat away from your bed, because you will feel a lot better if you do. So, let's get you up, and I will take you to the dining room."

Nora is clearly reluctant to face the outside world, and her eyes shift. "I always eat here, dear. I prefer it that way. Maybe we can have lunch together in the dining room another time. Thank you for your concern, dear."

I concede. Nora is hungry and her food is getting cold.

Xhosa-nurse is in my face again and shouts, "Hau! Suka, wena!" She nudges me aside with her bum and hauls Nora up over the little tray. I collapse back into my emptiness and my heart aches. The buzzing noise behind my ears is debilitating. I need my death-sleep.

It's Xhosa-nurse again and she points at my face and says sternly, "Lunch is served in the dining room. Go eat!"

I walk towards my bed and say to the pillow, "I'm not hungry and I'm tired. I want to sleep. So I'm not going."

I collapse onto my bed and pull the edge of the blanket over my feet. I need to wriggle my ankles until they are sore.

The door slams and I lie here and stare at the bricked-up window in front of my bed. I need my death-sleep. I get into my foetal position under the sheets. I bend my hands inwards and feel the stretch of my wrist muscles. I like this feeling because I'm all wound up. I'm doing my stretches inwardly and this locks me in. The only way I can fall asleep is if I fidget my feet to the tune of my lullaby, until my tendons ache. This is why I have good ankles. I have managed to sleep like this since I can remember.

Bang!

The bloody door's open again! It's Xhosa-nurse with a little tray under my nose. "The doctor says you must take this. He says you must eat before you take your medicine."

"Oh, bugger off!"

I curl further into my foetal position and put my fists into my eyes until sparks flash behind my eye-sockets. I'm not eating! I'm not taking any more drugs! I moan into my pillow and decide that I will act out a loony-fit. I'm here anyway and that's what's expected.

My loony-shoulders are yanked up and I peer into the face of a nurse who seems to know what she's looking at: a raving head-case in need of a fix! Her actions are automated. She clasps me behind my ears and shoves the hard little things between my lips until my neck arches backwards. "Drink!" The plastic mouse-cup is here.

If I weren't a lamb to the slaughter with Tulula and Maggie and Dr Shaker and dungeon-nurse and death-nurse, I'm surely one now. I'm on the altar with my neck bent back and my eyes bulging from their sockets. I gulp down the pills.

This is amazing! I'm sitting in the cockpit of a spaceship. I am the co-pilot and I'm pulling levers and pressing icons on the touch-screen of a vast illuminated instrument panel in front of me. I know what I'm doing. The pilot sits close to me on my left under the domed glazed fuselage. I know my pilot well, and he is gentle. He is in charge and very capable of flying this thing. His body is much bigger than my human form. He has a green, elongated head that ends in a cone. He has no mouth. His eyes are large and kind and he nods at me like we are partners. He likes me; we are a team. He is not talking to me but I can hear his instructions. We are flying this thing together in the starry skies. The view enchants me.

This is not a dream, because I am awake and I know it. I can *feel* the touch-screen of the instrument panel and the soft chair under me. All my physical senses are alive. We are on a mission together. We are content, and we fly in silence through the magical universe.

But I'm having two experiences simultaneously. I'm taking mind-instruction from my fine-looking pilot and I'm in my bed in Nora's chamber. I know where I am and why and how I got here. I peer over to my right and there is Nora. She is sleeping soundly. A little snore emanates from her sheets.

I have just been in a spaceship. I was not dreaming, because dreaming is different. I *was* in the spaceship, I *was* the co-pilot, and I could *feel* and *smell* everything around me. I am fascinated, fearful and confused at the same time, but my travel in space has left me lifted and I feel relaxed because my pilot and I achieved a successful flight. But now I am here with Nora and the bricked-up window, even though I've just stepped out of the cockpit.

I am adamant that all my previous drug cocktails were to blame for my dragon hallucinations. The drugs must have messed with my head and my virgin brain-cells must have been bombarded with strange messages and reacted badly. They must have been warning me to stop the abuse. Yet my experience in my spaceship was different. It could not have been a hallucination.

I'm analysing the difference between my two experiences when Cranium walks in. He sits on my bed in the darkness while Nora snores away. He doesn't say anything, but just sits on my bed and stares at me.

"What time is it? How long have I been sleeping?"

"That's why I have paid you a personal visit. I was concerned about you. You have been sleeping for twenty-four hours."

"Shit! You've got to be joking!" The last thing I remember was Nora eating in her bed, so that makes it lunchtime on my third day here. I try to lift my head, but it's heavy on the pillow and won't move.

He puts his hand on my arm and says, "Let's try to get you up, shall we?"

I don't want him touching me. The thought of him so close is unnerving, so I gather myself and hop out of bed with my spinning head in tow. I brace my knee against the edge of the bed and stand to attention.

He's obviously pleased with my effort and says, "That's good." But he must have also noticed my wobble, because he says, "You are a little dizzy because you haven't eaten. Lunch is served and I want you to get out of bed and go."

I remember my spaceship. "I've just experienced the weirdest thing. I have told you that the cause of my getting kicked out of the hospital was my drug-induced hallucinations. But I've just had a very interesting and very real experience in a spaceship. All my senses were active and it was completely unlike my normal hallucinations, which were quite bizarre and confusing. What do you make of this?"

As I speak I start to feel more like me and not some tired bitch with an attitude and a buzzing head. The long sleep did me good. I wait for a professional answer to my interesting question.

He doesn't answer, but takes out a pen and small block of paper from his shirt pocket. I was hoping he was offering me a cigarette.

"I am going to prescribe something that will help." He scribbles on the block, and is gone.

*What the hell?*

I'm left alone with Nora's snoring. I'm left alone with a science problem to solve without my professor. I'm left alone with the prospect of taking more drugs along with the five medications that were passed on to Cranium by Dr Shaker. I'm all alone against the head-benders and their white scripts. I don't need my pull-yourself-together blanket anymore. I will add sleeping pills and spaceship nukes to my cocktail, and enjoy the effing ride. But now it's lunchtime, and I have a mission.

# BERNARD

"Nora ... Nora ..."

I pat her arm until her lids open to reveal darting grey eyes. "It's me, Nora. Are you OK?"

She's a good riser, unlike me, and flashes me with her still-lovely and very intact teeth. "Yes, dear, I'm fine. It's so good to see you again. And how are you? You have been sleeping a long time, but don't worry. The nurses have been in and out to give you your medication."

"I'm sure they did, Nora. But now it's lunchtime and you promised me a lunch date."

Her smile broadens between her sunken cheeks. "That will be lovely, dear, but I look so awful in my nightdress and have nothing to wear."

"Don't worry, Nora. No-one here will look at you. They're just a bunch of loonies who only care about themselves. If it makes you feel any better, I haven't bathed and I must look a mess. You and I will look a right pair."

She giggles at this and I have the blue nightgown ready. It's the granny-gown that Babs gave me, and I can't wait to give it to Nora. "This is a present. See, it still has the tags on it. Now let's put it on and go and have a party."

She giggles, "That's so lovely, dear. But I would like to put on some make-up."

"Sure you can, Nora. Where is it? I would be happy to make up your face. I'm a professional make-up artist." She winks at me and we both giggle.

In a grubby little make-up bag in the drawer next to her I find some old sticks and tins of make-up that look as though they were bought in the fifties. I find some beige base and massage it into her soft skin. I find a tin of blue eye-shadow and dust a little bit onto her wobbly lids as carefully as I can. It's electric-blue and I don't want her to look overdone. I leave out the mascara because she has no eyelashes and finish off with a light pink lipstick on her thin, lined lips.

"There we go. All finished. You look beautiful."

I help her up, and proffer a small vanity mirror. She smiles at her reflection and seems pleased. With a grimy comb I smooth the few strands of her hair over her scalp and down the nape of her neck. Her little slippers are worn and her nightdress is threadbare, but I soon have the blue granny-gown buttoned and we are ready to go.

I quickly scratch the sleep from the inner corners of my eyes, slick back my hair and re-elastic the greasy mess into my usual bun at the nape of my neck.

"See, Nora, look how revolting I look. We are Beauty and the Beast. You're the princess and I'm the dirty scoundrel."

She pinches my arm and giggles again, "You are lovely, dear. Don't be a silly-billy."

I hook my arm under hers and escort her as if we are a lady and gentleman on our way to a fancy dinner-hall. We're out of our dingy room with its bricked-up window and she shuffles along next to me. I'm impatient and excited to get her out, but she's walking so slowly that I yank her along to keep her in pace with me.

*What the hell?*

I'm startled by Bang! Bang! Bang! The banging is accentuated by loud drilling. We've passed the reception area and face an enormous gaping hole in the opposite wall. Bits of steel reinforcement and electrical cabling are sticking out of its edges. There is dust everywhere and blue-uniformed builders are scuttling about bashing and crashing. I'm horrified!

I grab the arm of a passing nurse. "What the hell is going on here?"

She seems annoyed with me, but I can hardly hear her over the din. "We are doing some alterations but that's none of your business! Now, move on."

I shout into her stupid face, "Like hell it's none of my business! We are patients here and noise and builders on the loose are definitely our concern!"

But she's gone. Nora is mute and squeezes my arm. I pull her closer and we duck under a loose lintel and stumble into the makeshift dining room, or sunroom, or whatever the hell this is. The little tables are still scattered about, but they are covered in dust and debris.

Bang! Bang! Bang!

I yank a tablecloth off a nearby table and use it to clean the one I've chosen for us next to the window in the sunshine. I find table-settings and serviettes and set our table. We are alone but for a solemn-faced matron, who waltzes up to our table and glibly says, "Lunch is over."

I turn my face on hers. "Like hell it is! It's only one o'clock. Call the manager. Or bring me a menu, if you know what's good for you!"

She laughs. "Do you think you're in a hotel or something?"

I feel sorry for Nora, because I'm being the disgruntled patron, and she the embarrassed date. But I don't need to discomfit her any longer because the matron says, "You will eat what you're served. I'll see what's left over."

Nora's clutching her serviette and still seems distressed. I need to cheer her up, so I scamper outside onto the yellow grass in search of a flower for our table. I find a weed with tiny purple flowers, and stick it in a glass between us. I sit back in my chair and say, "There we are. Isn't this romantic?"

"Thank you, dear." She seems to be cheering up.

The matron is back and dumps two trays with covered plates on the table. We face some slop and rice, accompanied by custard and jelly. Nora seems delighted with these offerings and chirps, "This looks lovely, doesn't it? I'm quite hungry."

She eats in silence while I wobble my jelly.

I force a little custard down my throat and wait for Nora to finish before I ask, "May I have a cigarette, Nora?"

"Certainly, dear, I don't mind at all. My husband used to smoke."

I keep my ciggy away from her face and ask with some difficulty, "Where is your husband?"

"He died a couple of weeks ago. His name is Bernard."

*Oh, no!*

I shouldn't have asked. I shouldn't have asked, because now she is crying under her electric-blue eye-shadow. I shouldn't have asked because I've probably reopened a hole in her fragile chest. I hand her a stiff paper serviette and ask as gently as I can, "Nora, would you like to talk about it?"

She's composed herself and mutters into the distance, "We were married for sixty-three years. We never spent a minute apart. And now he's dead."

My heart jolts and I say a silent prayer that I will die before Stef does. I wonder why she's here, because she is completely sane, like I am. "Why did you come here so soon after his death?"

She winces. "Bernard did everything for me, dear. He did the shopping. He paid our accounts. He changed the light bulbs. He was a kind and giving man and treated me like a queen. I did nothing but care for my roses. I knew nothing about the day-to-day running of our home. I didn't even know how to turn on the TV. When he died I was lost."

We sit silently as she stares out of the window. Her pain smothers my own, and somehow I feel a little better because hers outstrips my stupid, selfish

126

heartache by a mile. I fiddle with my serviette and want to cry with her, but I don't have any bloody tears. Tears are necessary now; they are highly important.

She settles and seems quite peaceful again. She must have been a loving wife. She must have been patient and interested in her husband. She must have doted on him and made him feel like he was the only person in the universe. And they must have been the best of friends. I know that counts a stack, because Stef and I are best friends and our marriage is good. I marvel at the solid nature of men. Men are so delightfully simple: all they need is love. They behave perfectly well given this antidote. And they need to be satisfied.

I redden at my thoughts of Nora having sex, because I'm sure she would snap. I pinch my knee under the table and wish for a marriage of sixty-three years like Nora and Bernard.

But why the hell did she land up in this Godforsaken place after such a long and normal married life?

Nora sits nibbling her food. But I need to ask her one last question. "Why are you here, Nora?"

I can't hear her answer because she's mumbling into her chest. I catch some words like daughter … burden … afford … and she finishes off with, "This was the only place that agreed to take me in."

If I were left alone after sixty-three years, I would surely go nuts and kill myself. It dawns on me that it must be very difficult for old people to kill themselves, because it requires much physical exertion and lots of bravado. I undertake to kill myself before I'm too weak to do so.

I picture Nora slowly dying in her bed in the darkness without Bernard and the TV, while her roses die in the garden. I picture her stupid bloody daughter finding her like this because she probably hasn't had the decency to visit her mother in an age. I curse Nora's family and I curse this bloody place and all the bloody places like it, and I curse the bloody nurses and bloody shrinks who don't give a shit about anyone.

Bang! Bang! Bang!

"Fuck this!" I yell at the gaping hole in the wall.

Nora's head lifts and then drops again, and I stutter into her face, "Shit, I mean damn, I-I am so sorry, Nora."

"Don't worry, dear, Bernard used to swear like a trooper. I think 'fuck' is the perfect word to use right now."

We giggle like mad and slop-nurse is here. I see us through her eyes and I'm pleased she sees two hysterical nutcases, because that is what we need to be in a nutty place like this.

I don't look at slop-nurse, and say, with my nose turned up to the ceiling, "Dear gracious Nora, would you like to take a stroll with your perfect gentleman?"

"I would truly love that, dear sir. Let's get the fuck out of here."

# AMANZI SCHEDULE

Nora must be exhausted from our walk. Snores escape her gaping mouth in the far bed. I listen to every snore, because this means she's breathing. The rasping has stopped a number of times and I've tiptoed to her bedside to put my finger under her nose. She seems to manage getting through the snoring pauses but I've been jumping back and forth between our beds all afternoon.

I can't sleep anyway and this at least is keeping me busy. I lie here day-dreaming about my kids and feeling guilty. Pooki's little face is here with her eyes like a seal's and she's desperate for me. Even if she hates it when I fiddle with her ears, she wants me to fiddle with them now, because she misses me. But I try to get all the little needy faces out of my mind before I'm forced go to the bathroom and vomit up the custard I had for lunch. I try to focus on my walk with Nora.

I'm so glad for her because she was happy to be in the sunshine and was stopping to look at insects while I picked weeds with flowers to bring back to our dreary room. She shuffled along so slowly that I had to stop myself from yanking her forward and telling her to hurry up. All around us was yellow grass and face-brick. I don't remember anything else but the dreary surround-ings, and a bunch of people having a braai on the sunroom terrace.

There must have been about six of them and, by the looks of them, they had no place being here. They were not behaving like loonies. They were jolly and chatted to one another, while a few of the men turned meat over the coals. Like a typical Sunday lunch around the braai. They didn't seem fazed about Nora and me waddling by like two old codgers, but one of the men did give us a loud catcall. I told them to fuck off and yanked Nora in the opposite direction.

The bed between us remains empty and I'm glad. I wouldn't want a real loony polluting our company. Evil lunacy is sure to get into Nora's open mouth and stop her breathing forever.

I'm not anxious like I normally am, but I'm bored. My anxiousness has been replaced by boredom, and it's easier to deal with. I've never been bored because I'm always too anxious. Either I try to sleep using my wriggling-ankle-death-sleep tactic or I'm overexcited and thinking about entering politics. I loathe the word "bored" and forbid my children to use it in front of me. There's no place for boredom in a world filled with a million things to do.

I get up and waft around our beds. I find a laminated paper on Nora's bedside table that reads "Amanzi Schedule".

| 5.00 am | Rise and shine | *Like hell!* |
|---------|----------------|--------------|
| 5.15 am | Medication | *Bugger off!* |
| 6.00 am – 7.00 am | Breakfast in Dining Room (Main Block) | *Never have I eaten breakfast so not going.* |
| 7.00 am – 8.00 am | Free Time | *Always.* |
| 8.00 am – 10.00 am | Activities in Activity Centre (Top Block) | *Not on your life!* |
| 10.00 am – 10.30 am | Morning Tea in Tea Room (Main Block) | *Irrelevant.* |
| 10.30 am – 12.00 pm | Psychiatrist Consultation in Headmaster's Office – Days of consulting to be advised (Top Block) | *Definitely.* |
| 12.00 pm – 1.00 pm | Lunch in Main Block | *Nora's special time, so we will be there.* |
| 1.00 pm – 2.00 pm | Free Time | *Nora's walkies.* |
| 2.00 pm – 4.00 pm | Afternoon nap | *Can't sleep anyway, so a nap's out.* |
| 4.00 pm – 4.15 pm | Afternoon Tea in Tea Room (Main Block) | *Irrelevant.* |
| 4.15 pm – 6.00 pm | Group Session in Gym Room (Top Block) | *Never! Unless I'm bored and want to laugh at the loonies.* |
| 6.00 pm – 7.00 pm | Free Time | *Always.* |
| 7.00 pm – 8.00 pm | Dinner in Canteen (Top Block) | *Only if Nora goes! Otherwise I'll eat in bed with her and we can entertain one another so we don't get depressed by eating in bed.* |
| 8.15 pm | Medication | *Bugger off!* |
| 9.00 pm | Lights out! | *Says it all.* |

I remember that I chucked my copy into the bin but I'm so bored that anything to read is welcome. I throw myself onto the middle bed so that I can hear Nora's snoring more clearly, and take time to reread it.

At the bottom of the sheet there's some more writing: "Please note that times and venues are subject to change without notice and visiting times are only allowed in patient's free time."

I don't bother to read the other small print because I haven't been doing anything on the programme and neither will I. In any case, none of it is actually achievable in all the dust and noise of the construction work, so what the hell do they expect?

There's no time allotted to ablutions – this reminds me that I haven't washed in days. Stef has to be coming to see me at some point. I hope it's tonight. So I drag myself to the bathroom to make myself presentable, albeit putting on the dumpy grey tracksuit Babs gave me. I wonder what Stef will think of me looking like a bored housewife. He'll probably think I want to look this unappealing because sex would be like death, given my recent track record.

There's a shower-head over the bath and I'm sitting under the soft spray with my knees tucked under me. The water is cool, so I must have been sitting here like this for a hell-of-a-long time. I wonder how I got here, because I can't remember undressing. I also must have left Nora so long that she might have stopped breathing for good.

I gather myself and spin through my usual bathing routine as fast as possible, careful not to slip on the wet floor. There's no clean bra in my suitcase and I need one because my nipples stick out like pin-pricks. But the tracksuit is big and dumpy and hopefully the thick fleece and pocket-bumps will hide my boobies away.

Nora's still alive but she's also still fast asleep. I nudge her shoulder gently and her eyelids open. "It's nearly seven o'clock and it's dinner time. Let's get going. I'll help you up."

I notice dry drool on the sides of her mouth. "I'm far too tired, dear," she whispers. "I think the fresh air made me sleepy. I'll take my dinner in bed, if you don't mind."

I don't push it because, given the amount of time she's lain here in her bed, her first outing has probably exhausted her. So I will leave her alone to Xhosa-nurse and the covered plates that smell of instant soup.

# STEF VISITS WITH ROSE AND LAPTOP

I can't find the canteen in the Top Block because all the lights up the corridor are off. There's no activity, so I presume dinner is off. I'm not hungry anyway, so I can go back to Nora and watch her breathe while I wait for Stef's visit.

I notice that the sunroom is lit and I can see occupied tables through the cottage-pane windows. The dinner venue has been changed without notice. I find an empty table which fronts a poster of Winston Churchill on the wall. I squint at the writing underneath his portrait: "Even this man had it! Would you employ him?"

What the hell this means, I don't know, but slop-nurse is here and a tray with covered plates is plunked in front of me. I open the lids and it's the same as the lunch-slop. I stare at my offerings because I don't want to look at the diners.

I don't remember ever eating alone before.

*We are dining at a fancy candle-lit table. The waiter is placing a linen serviette on my lap and asking, "What would the madam like for an aperitif?"*

*"Double vodka and orange, please. No wait, some champagne. No, I've changed my mind, just bring a bottle of good Sauvignon Blanc, and I'll start on it right away."*

*Stef confirms my last request to the now very confused waiter, who's skulking away in a huff. Stef has also just gone through a number of table changes, because I've tried to find the table furthest away from everyone, or the table with the best view, or a bigger one. He has done this with grace and follows me around with an apologetic smile to the waiter in tow.*

There's a nudge on my shoulder and a voice behind me: "Hello. Would you like to meet my parents?"

*No thanks! Go away!*

It's Sam with the unshaven stubble and the child's mentality. "Hello. How are you this evening, Mr Krishna?" I'm glad it's him because he's fun. I like him.

"Can I have a cigarette? I promise I'll pay you back."

"We'll have a cigarette after dinner, because we're not allowed to smoke here, but I would love to meet your parents."

"Oh, goody, that would be fun. My parents are over there."

I look in the direction he's pointing and see an elderly couple hunched over their food, just like all the other loonies are. While staring at the patrons, I notice that all the other tables are occupied by groups of three or four. In the far corner, a lone blonde chap sits at a table, hunched over his tray like I am. He looks up at me as if he senses my eyes on him. He has a nice look about him, but we both look down at out plates at the same time.

Master Krishna seems to have forgotten about introducing me to his parents and sits opposite me with a big smile. "Can I get my food and eat with you?"

He probably doesn't want to lose his chance at a cigarette, but I capitulate and say to his stubble, "Sure you can. But won't your parents be upset?"

"Oh, no!" He giggles. "They visit me every day."

I can't be bothered with their family issues, and we sit opposite one another like old friends. Sam has made me feel like I've known him for years. He seems relaxed in my company and is full of warmth and smiles, like a child. I prefer the company of children and animals over adults.

He gulps down his food while I wobble my jelly. He swallows a mouthful and looks up at me with gravy running into his stubble. "They've stolen drugs again and Sister Bertha is very angry. She keeps on asking me if I have stolen them, but I don't even know how to get in there. She says that if she catches the robbers, she'll call the police."

He looks scared and his bottom lip pops out at me with remnants of gravy on it. I reach over and put my hand on his arm. "I'm sure you're not a robber, Sam, but do people really steal drugs here?" I can't imagine anyone wanting to take any more drugs than have been shoved down their throats.

"It's only the other patients," he whimpers. "I've seen them do it. But they are nasty and they hurt me and kick me all the time."

My heart flutters as an immense presence fills the dining room. It's Stef. He's with Sister Bertha and she's full of pomp and ceremony as she bustles in next to him.

"Your husband's here to visit you," she says with authority, as if I don't know him. I scowl at her until she goes away with a smile at Stef, and a curtsy.

He's in a black suit with the crisp white collar sticking out above the lapel. I'm pleased he's found the black suit amongst the old clothes we were given at the sorry-for-you party. This is more his style. He's not wearing a tie and his top button is open. He's got his casual and sexy power-look. He's so handsome that I could faint, and I look around at all the loonies in the hope that they see how lucky I am. No-one raises a head at him except Blondie, who quickly resumes his eating. Stef's got a black briefcase in his hand which makes him all the more appealing. He's my modern-day knight in shining armour wielding a briefcase instead of a sword, but his message is still, "I'm here, I'm yours, and I've come to save you."

I stare into his beautiful green eyes like a dumb lamb, but now that he's close, I see that he's unshaven and he looks tired. I fiddle with my bun and pull a strand of hair out of it so that it hangs over my eye.

I give Sam a go-away look, but he's unresponsive and stares up at Stef's tall form with his mouth open. He doesn't get the message, so I say, "Stef, meet Mr Krishna. Mr Krishna, this is my husband, Stef."

"Oooh, he's so handsome." Stef doesn't shake his hand.

"Can you leave us alone, please?" His eyes are kind but stern, and Krishna ducks away to the safety of his parents.

"Hello, my love."

"Hello, my love."

"Can we step outside to talk?" He says this with urgency. I'm sure he needs to escape this nutty eating-hole forthwith.

We face each other in the cold night air outside the reception area. He draws one red rose from the inside of his jacket and hands it to me.

I sniff the sweet rose-smell of the outside world. "Thank you, my love, it's beautiful."

Words are unnecessary, especially now. We talk through our eyes with an enormous amount of electrically transmitted chemistry. Our love and friendship still holds us tightly together, and I am relieved. He is with me still.

I open my mouth to speak, but he puts his hand up towards my face, and says quietly, "Listen to me, my love. I cannot go down with you right now."

I don't say anything to him. I don't whine and scream and perform. I don't tell him about the drugs that have been forced down my throat, or the staff, or Nora, or my bricked-up window. I want him to go now. He wants to go now. I want him to get the hell out of here before I become "the arse" and not "the tits".

He hands me the briefcase. "I've brought you a laptop so that you can play Tetris, and I've brought you your cellphone, and a carton of cigarettes."

"Thanks, my love."

He knows me well. When I need to focus, I don't read books but lock my-self away and play Tetris until I'm better. I can play for hours with my ciggy hanging from my mouth and burning my eyes. This is the only thing that re-laxes me. This is the only thing that stops my bloody brain from over-revving. I'm grateful for the Tetris and I'm grateful for the cigarettes, but I don't need my cellphone. I cannot use it in here, because I'm not *me* here, and I wouldn't know what to say to my friends or family who live in the real world. I don't want to talk to anyone. I just want to play Tetris, and smoke, and listen to Nora's snoring until I die by "death by Tetris" or lung cancer, or something as excusable as that.

He kisses me lightly on the mouth, and is gone. I'm sure I hear him sniff.

# CALVIN KLEIN

I hate waking up. I push my face into the hard, smelly pillow that stinks of loony-scalp. My head still feels unusual, but better. My thoughts are still fuzzy but the head-clamp has gone. I haven't been visited by my dragon, or my spaceman. I miss the latter and our starry expedition. All in all, my head feels a damn sight better, which doesn't really help, because it's my heart that needs attention, not my head, which has always been so very well screwed onto my strong, professional shoulders.

I squirm into my foetal position as Xhosa-nurse nudges my face. "Wake up! It is five o'clock. Time to take the breakfast. Time to take the medicine."

I let her do her stupid nurse-stuff because I feel numb. I let her grip my jowls and stick the pills behind my lips because my head-clamp is not here and my neck feels floppy. This is easier to handle than it was yesterday.

I haul myself up. I need to check on Nora. She's snoring through her skeleton jaws and I'm comforted. I'm still wearing my depressed-housewife tracksuit, and reach for my deodorant. This will have to suffice for a wash-up because I don't have the energy to go through a bathroom ritual, let alone take a pee. I don't remember drinking anything besides the water in the mouse-cup for tablet-taking. I have to get away from the bricked-up window.

I'm shuffling in Babs's too-big blue slippers along the passage to the right of the reception area and away from the exit doors. I feel like I'm in a slow-motion video. I have never moved like this. My actions are always quick and solidly in the direction I'm heading. Now I have to think about every step and it's quite a nice sensation. Focusing on the mechanical functionality of my body helps my head to focus too, albeit only on my body's movements.

There's a door to my left that's closed but has a sign on it that reads "Tea Room". I open it and enter a large, dimly lit sitting room with brown walls and brown carpets. Everything in this place is brown or face-brick. There are brown couches along the walls to my left, which remind me of a teachers' tea room. Teacups and saucers are ready on a table, but there's no tea in sight because it's not teatime yet. I could do with a cup of coffee, but I will not go to breakfast to get it. I will stay here until the loonies have gone to the Activity Centre.

I make my way through the Tea Room and out through open doors onto a small terrace with two rickety steel chairs facing more yellow grass. I plonk myself down on one of the chairs, careful not to topple over. I tuck my knees under my chin and light my first morning ciggy. I'm enjoying my slow-motion actions with trembling fingers and I'm secretly acting out loony-antics, like the ones you see crazy people do in the movies. I exaggerate the trembling fingers on purpose while I light my second cigarette.

I'm doing the same thing I was doing on the shitty-couch in the shitty-townhouse. I'm on a shitty steel chair in the shitty loony-bin, and smoking. I can sit here like this forever, as long as no-one bothers me, and as long as I have my cigarettes. I don't give a damn about my health, or what I look like, or anything, really. I know that I shouldn't kill myself, because that would be selfish. I want to kill myself. I recognise this feeling because I have felt like killing myself since I can remember.

The pins and needles in my calves are becoming extreme because I've crunched up my legs under my bum. My veins must have stopped working because my legs are dead, and completely unfoldable.

Even though I'm on a medication-cocktail that supposedly helps my mind, the killing-myself thing is still with me. I think it always will be. It's become a part of me, like one of my genes. I've accepted the danger of it as much as I've accepted that I'll never go through with it. Thinking about doing it with the knowledge that I'll never do it is my own shameful yet private and perpetual network. No-one will ever know about this stupidity, and I scratch my arm to confirm it.

I light another ciggy and, as I blow the smoke into the cool air, I realise that my death-network is slightly different now. The anxiety that triggers the process is not as severe. Usually by now the clamp that grips my forehead would have moved down my thorax, pushing the life out of my heart with such intensity that my mind has to tell it to stop beating. Whatever I'm taking must have something to do with this. Maybe the sluggishness I'm feeling is slowing down the process, giving my mind enough time to redirect the clamp before it grips my heart.

As I marvel at the trembling of my hands, I realise that my thumbs aren't looking so raw and have actually started healing. So maybe the will to damage them has also been impaired by the medication. I force myself to chew them.

I have no clue what drugs I'm taking. I do know that I'm getting a lot, because there are a lot of different colours, shapes and sizes sprawled around the water cup. I can probably blame my hallucinations on the fact that I have lain here, and in hospital, for so long that my mind is playing tricks. My mind has probably become so bored that it has got up to childish pranks. I have always filled it with actions to perform on my mission to be the perfect wife, mother and professional. And if I find myself lacking in spunk, I drink, so that I can get my body onto the table and excite my friends.

I try to recall the medication-cocktail that was first prescribed by Dr Shaker and picture the hazy script I saw when I was still so alive and feisty in hospital. But the only words that flash through my mind are epilepsy, serotonin, lamenting or lethargy, sleeping pill, and the unpronounceable anti-depression stuff that thankfully isn't Prozac. Cranium said he was going to give me more, or stronger, sleeping tablets, and I wonder if he gave me something else to take my spaceman away. Shit! This probably makes it about six or seven bloody pills that I'm having shoved down my throat each day.

A door bangs somewhere behind me and I almost fall off the rickety chair and burn myself. I quickly scoop up the enormous pile of cigarette butts at my feet and shove them into my empty cigarette box.

"Uurgh! Fuck! Fuck this!" The swearing shocks me.

*Who the hell is that?*

My drug-analysis is interrupted by a large muscular man who walks past me and stands with his back to me as he faces the yellow grass. He's wearing well-cut designer jeans that are slightly too big and expose the thick top band of Calvin Klein underpants. He must be wearing a designer T-shirt as well, because it's so well fitted that his abs are sticking out nicely, revealing muscular arms exposed at the right kink above the bicep. His hair is ruffled and has that on-purpose bed-head look which adds to his masculinity, but maybe he has just woken up, like me. He looks sexy anyway. I see all this from behind because he hasn't bothered with me. I'm sure he doesn't even know I'm here.

He sticks his hand into the back of his underpants to have a good bum scratch, I'm sure. I cough. He slowly looks around at me, but keeps scratching his bum. This patient also doesn't give a shit about anyone, least of all me. I probably look like an old dried-up bat to him, and why would he bother having manners in front of a loony anyway? I've never felt so unattractive in my life. In the past, at this stage of the girl–guy thing, I would be shunning his flirtatiousness and batting my eyelashes.

"The fucking nurses must have taken blood again last night! Look at my fucking arm." He looks my way but doesn't make eye-contact and proffers his nice bicep for me to ogle. There's a bloodied piece of cotton wool with a plaster stuck over it underneath the bulge.

"They've taken blood again without asking me and this time I'm going to sue the bastards. My father's an attorney and he's going to sue their fucking arses, just you wait and see. I don't want to be in this fucking place again! I'm clean for fuck's sake!" Although he's using the f-word a lot, he has an excellent English accent which hints at private schooling and money.

He must have taken drugs because he had a blood test last night and he's still here. It dawns on me that this young boy, presenting himself to me on this little patio in this loony-bin, is a drug-addict. This place is not only a loony-bin but a bloody rehab clinic! I'm incredulous and horrified at the same time. Not only are there loonies here, but druggies as well, neither of whom I have ever had the misfortune to meet.

I stare at the plastered cotton wool on his beautiful bicep, and mumble through the smoke of my trembling cigarette, "That's an unfortunate situation, and highly dubious, to say the least."

I don't want anything to do with this fool and, as if on cue, he waltzes off saying, "Highly fucking unfortunate and highly fucking dubious, to say the least!"

I'm glad he's gone because I want to be alone. I want to sit here and focus on the yellow grass peeping through the sand, and think of nothing.

# FORMAL MEETING WITH CRANIUM

I've forgotten about Nora while I've been blanked out on the Tea Room terrace. But she's still here snoring through her open mouth. I bend over her and kiss her cheek, but she doesn't stir. She's not kicking, but she's alive, and that's what counts for an old ducky like her. I speed my way through a wash routine, put on the same grey tracksuit, and get my arse moving to be first in the queue for Cranium.

I pass the Activity Centre on the way up the concrete school steps to his office. I peer through the classroom window and notice a few loonies wearing baby-aprons and throwing paint at one another. There appears to be no supervision and this is probably why they are behaving like naughty kids. A red blob smacks the panes in front of my face. I duck and escape to my queue.

No-one is here and this is good. I bang on the door that reads "Headmaster's Office" and it's quickly opened by the no-name woman, who must be Cranium's secretary. I push past her and ask, "It's consulting time on your schedule. Where is the doctor?"

She turns her back on me and opens the first door to the left as a gesture to go in. Cranium is on the phone, and without looking up at me, says into it, "Hmmm. Hmmm. Hmmm. Bye, dear." He hangs up.

I'm certainly not going through the silent-time with him again, but I don't want to hear him speak. I am the one who's got lots to say today, and he needs to listen.

He doesn't speak. His round eye peers at me from his elongated head and I'm in familiar territory. I don't sit down. "I'm here to see you today because I need to lodge a formal complaint."

I give him enough time to let this sink in. I am not expecting a reaction, so I push on, "The lady who shares my room is not taken care of. When I moved in, she hadn't been bathed. I find this unacceptable. She has not been taken out into the fresh air and she is made to eat in bed. And *you* should know that anyone who stays in bed to eat will surely develop depression. I'm very unhappy about this and if there was an SPCA for humans, I would surely report it."

He's his usual mum self, so I continue, "And although it's none of my business, I don't know why she's here. She shouldn't be here. There is nothing wrong with her, because I've spent a lot of time with her and she's completely sane. Not only is she sane, but she's an impeccable lady."

He starts to tap his fingers on the brown desk, and I see his good eye widen for a second to align with his elongated head. I know that he can't comment on another person's state of mind, but I'm glad I'm making my point.

I haven't finished. "I would like to lodge my second complaint. The construction work that is being undertaken here is disturbing the patients." I don't know this for sure, but the constant banging is sure to conflict with the banging in the loonies' heads, or if there wasn't any head-banging in the first place, like in Nora's case, it would surely cause it.

I lean on his desk and glare down at him. "How in heaven's name do you think you can fix patients, or create a peaceful atmosphere for healing, with this racket going on? I can even hear the bloody noise from here, and it's already making it difficult to concentrate. The work is also not being done professionally. No-one is cleaning up the mess at night and there is dust and filth everywhere."

I secretly hope that the noise and filth of construction work rids us of the loonies, and the sexy druggie to boot. But it's affecting Nora and Krishna, and I worry about them.

Cranium speaks, "You haven't been attending meals and you haven't been attending the morning and afternoon activities."

*You haven't heard a bloody word I've said!*

He's turned me from concerned patron to indignant brat! I can't stand anymore and slide downwards into my chair.

"I will never attend the stupid activity sessions! I am certainly not going to be doing any finger-painting with insane people. I am a professional woman. I am not going and that's that!" I stick my chin out at him. I feel like a schoolgirl.

He raps his fingers on the table. "If you don't go, I can't assess your progress, and I can't sanction your discharge."

"But I can't do anything physical because the stupid drugs are making me lethargic! What the hell do you expect me to do?"

He stops rapping his fingers on the table. "Time's-up. I've got other patients to see."

# MANTRA MAN

I stumble out of Cranium's office like "the fallen". He has not acknowledged my complaints. Domestic issues like care for the aged, excessive noise, and filth are probably not within his control. Or he just can't be bothered, because he's probably as sick of this place as the nurses seem to be. I need a bloody drink but my mind won't accept the message. Maybe I've been given a drug that stops my usual craving. This is the only thing that makes sense, because I know for sure that this is the longest time in my life that I haven't had a glass of wine, or any booze for that matter. I go through the list of my favourite drinks and none of them is appealing. Shit! How strange is this?

I *do* know that my body will crave a supplement for its usual alcohol intake. Maybe that's why I'm smoking so much. I think about the druggie and resolve not to mix with him. I can't let him influence me, because my body might be telling my brain to get its feelers out for other mind-altering stuff.

I try to rekindle the delight of a sip of crisp white wine while I watch my feet leaving footprints in the dust as I make my way past the sunroom.

"Hellooo, dear."

It's Nora, and she's sitting at our table. There's a glass on the table with a weed in it. It looks fresh and my heart skips a beat because she's probably gone to the trouble of picking it herself. Her lovely teeth glint at me over the little purple flowers. I'm so glad that she's made this effort to dine with me. I think I love her.

"It's so nice to see you here, Nora. Sorry to have kept you waiting. Has the maître d' taken your drinks order? Shall we treat ourselves and have a bottle of champagne? How about some oysters?"

I take her veined hand and kiss it like a gentleman. She giggles as slop-nurse dumps the lunch trays with covered plates onto the table.

I try to look serious. "Thank you, waiter," I say to slop-nurse. "If you play your cards right, a very large tip is reserved for you. Bring me your finest champagne." Nora giggles again and so does someone behind us.

It's Blondie, and he nods at me with a smile.

I nod too and smile. "Hello."

"Hi." He quickly puts his head down again towards his plate.

The rest of the dining-team are sitting in groups of two or three and are chatting away like normal people bantering in a normal restaurant.

The sounds of clinking cutlery and chatter are interrupted by some lunatic singing:

Hare Krishna Hare Krishna
Krishna Krishna Hare Hare
Hare Rama Hare Rama
Rama Rama Hare Hare …

The singing gets louder and the noise is now on top of us. Oh, for heaven's sake! It's the Krishna man! Samuel Krishna fancies himself a Buddha disciple. I wonder what his real surname is.

He's repeating the song and dancing around our table with his arms in the air until one of the other patrons nearby yells, "Shut up, you idiot!" and trips him.

He stumbles into our table and finishes his song in a whisper. Nora looks terrified. "Don't worry, Nora," I say. "This is Samuel, please don't be scared. I've met him before."

I try to sound like a parent. "Sam! Stop your nonsense! You're upsetting Nora. Calm down and go and sit outside. I'll meet you there and I'll give you a cigarette after we've finished our lunch." He only looks at Nora and seems a little frightened of her.

"I'll wait for you outside. Promise you'll come?" he whispers.

I picture him sitting outside, kicking his feet back and forth to the tune of his mantra for a hundred years, until I finally show up. "Of course I'll be there, Sam. Now, run along!"

He skips out of the sunroom, making a big detour past the table next to us. Nora hasn't said a word, and we finish lunch in silence.

Nora crosses her knife and fork and says, "Poor chap."

I nod. "Yes, it's a shame, because he's handsome and kind. But then again, ignorance is bliss."

She nods at me over our weed. "I'm quite tired, dear. Do you mind if we skip our walk today?"

"That's fine, dear. I'll walk you to our room."

I've helped Nora get under her blanket, and I've sat beside her and waited for her snoring. I'm sitting on the little patio outside the sunroom waiting for Sam while I smoke a ciggy. Unexpectedly, he wasn't waiting for me, but I see him sitting at a patio-table with his parents. I probably should go over there and introduce myself.

I move across to their table. "Hello, I'm Lamby. Pleased to meet you both." The old man gets to his feet and shakes my hand while Sam's mother greets me with a reserved nod. She probably thinks I'm a loony and is expecting me to start singing or something. Now I regret my pseudonym because it surely smacks of lunatic.

"What did you say your name was?" It's the father.

I can't think quickly enough, so I say, "I understand you are Samuel's parents. He's lucky that you visit him often and that's nice." I don't know what else to talk to them about. They probably don't want to talk to me either. I turn my attention to my friend. "Would you like that cigarette now, Sam?"

"Ooooh, no! I don't smoke." He says this looking at his mother.

I'm quick to his aid and blabber, "Oh, yes, how silly of me. I already offered you one and you said no. Please forgive me, Sam."

He looks relieved and keeps his eyes on his mother, but she addresses me in a stern voice: "Samuel is forbidden to smoke, so please don't offer him cigarettes. He's not well and doesn't know what he's doing. So it's up to you not to be a bad influence. You need to hide your cigarettes away, because he will find them and smoke the lot. He's a very naughty boy!"

She says this as if Sam wasn't here and I feel sorry for him. But he seems accepting of her insults because he stands near her with his hands behind his back, swaying from side to side with a mischievous grin on his man-child face. "Mom, tell her about my rock band. Tell her I'm a writer. Tell her about my poems."

Mother seems irritated and says, "Shush, Samuel, now sit down and stop your nonsense!"

I don't believe Sam can actually play an instrument, or even hold a pen, but he surely can sing, and I want to know more. "That's nice, Sam, what's the name of your band?"

"The Grooving Krishnas!"

He starts singing the mantra again, but his father stands up and pulls him onto his chair. "Shut up, Samuel. We've spoken about this before. You're not to embarrass your mother!" Sam's highly agitated. He's shaking his head and jumping up and down on his chair.

I'm secretly enjoying this and want to add a bit more fuel. "Calm down, Sam, I'm really interested to hear about your band, and your writing. Tell me about them." His parents slump back into their chairs.

Sam seems to have calmed down and looks at me with his big, beautiful eyes above his stubble. He puts on a serious face. "My band is excellent. We've even been the opening band for UB40 in Botswana. We're excellent! We're brilliant! I want to play for you. I want you to come and see us. When I go home again, you can come to our big house and I'll get the guys together and we can party. You'll love it. I'm so excited to show you what we can do. Our house is huge. It's awesome. You'll love my room, I painted it all by myself and I've got awesome rock-band posters everywhere. Promise you'll come when I get home."

His parents are unmoving and glare at their plates, but I don't care about them and say with enthusiasm, "I would be honoured, Sam. And tell me about your writing."

He becomes excitable again, jumps up, puts his arms into the air, and starts singing the mantra. His father gives an audible huff and yanks him back towards the chair. "Samuel! Do you want me to call Sister Bertha?" Sam sits quietly and seems to have excused himself from our presence, like a passing breeze.

I glare at his father but he says with a patient sigh, "Samuel is a very talented boy when he's well. He's published books and poems and we are very proud of him. But please leave us alone now. You see what you've done to him. Now please, go!"

*Well, stuff you too!*

I pat Sam on his shoulder as I leave, and he whispers, "Thank you, Lamby. Promise you won't go forever."

# BEN

I have left Sam in the firm grip of his parents' tough love and I have left Nora snoring towards her death. The sadness I feel for them eases my own. I need to get as far away from the sunroom patio as possible. I need to find myself a nice little hole to blow smoke out of.

Activity-nurse is in my face. "Where do you think you're going with that cigarette? It's four o'clock and time for our group session in the Gym Room."

*Like hell it is!*

"Come along! All of you! And that includes you." She grabs my cigarette, and it burns my fingers as she whips it through them. "Visiting time is over. It's time to get going."

She chucks my ciggy onto the yellow grass and claps her hands at the patio crowd as if they were nursery-school children. A few of her children are reluctantly leaving their visitors at their chairs, and dragging their feet towards the Top Block. All their heads are stooped and there's a lot of moaning going on, except for Sam, who's chanting, "I'm the teacher's favourite. I'm the teacher's favourite."

He clasps activity-nurse's hand and tugs her up the stairs with the rest of the loonies behind them. He has unwittingly created a diversion.

*Thank you, Mr Krishna!*

As the visitors file out, I feel I'm finally left alone and slump my track-suited bones onto the nearest chair while I light another cigarette between the blisters on my fingers.

"Hi." I'm looking into the green eyes of Blondie.

"Hi." I really don't feel like talking to anyone else. I've got my hands full with Nora and Sam, and drug-addicts who complain about the illegal extraction of blood.

I sense him edging closer. "I've found an ashtray," he says. "We can share it. Do you mind if I sit here next to you?"

"Yes. Whatever." Ashing on the floor won't make any difference to the dust around here anyway, but maybe I'm just being a bitch, so I change my tune and say, "Yes. Thanks."

He sits next to me on a rickety steel chair like mine and lights a cigarette with fingers trembling, like mine. His hands are scrawny and his knuckles are raw. He doesn't say anything. I don't want to look him in the face. I can smell leather, and it squeaks as he lifts his cigarette to his mouth. Out of the corner of my eye I try to size him up. His jeans are pale and worn and his knees are popping out through the denim.

He has a nice clean face but it's also scrawny, like his hands. "Looks like we've escaped the finger-painting," I say.

"Fuckin-aye!" He laughs and I join him until we both cough through the smoke. Now that I've heard him swear in this manner, I presume he's a lot younger than he appears.

"My name's Ben." I can't give him my stupid pseudonym, because it was clearly misdirected at Sam's folks and I've learnt my lesson, so I give him my real one.

He leans down towards the ashtray on the floor to extinguish his cigarette, and winces. "Ow! Shit!"

"What's the matter? Are you OK?"

"I think I've just ripped my stitches open!"

"Eeew, I just hate when that happens." I'm making a joke because he's probably up to some loony-tricks.

He must sense my disbelief and says with some difficulty, "No, I mean it. I've just had an operation." He zips open his leather jacket and pulls up his T-shirt. There's a big white bandage that's stuck down by a see-through bandage to the hairs of his lower belly. Bright red blood is seeping through the gauze.

*Oh, yuck!*

Why the hell is he here and not in a hospital? I look away from the oozing blood. "What the hell happened to you?"

"I had my appendix out a cupla days ago. Ow," he winces as he pulls his T-shirt over the bloody bandage and zips up his jacket.

"Shall I get you some help? That looks bad!"

"Naah, it'll be alright. I'm OK now. Can I offer you a cigarette?" He's being brave, like Stef, and I'm starting to warm to him.

"No thanks, I can't smoke those. I think my lungs would fall out if I tried." I light up my own and we sit together in silence, my inquisitiveness prickling. I can't resist anymore so I ask, "But what are you doing here?"

"I went completely ape-shit when I woke up from my anaesthetic. I fucked out badly so they sedated me and brought me here."

"Oh," is all I can manage.

"Ja, they buggered up my head so badly with all the drugs they've given me that I react like this after anaesthetics. I was off the drugs this time, and coping, but some of the drugs must have been left in me, because I reacted the same way as before."

"Before what?" I ask.

"Ja, I had to have an emergency operation. I tried to kill myself again. The first time I tried to hang myself in my folks' bathroom, but I fucked up because the rope was too short and I couldn't kick the chair away. All I did was twist my neck. But my folks found me gripping the rope at my neck and I was put onto drugs."

My mouth's dry, so I close it and try to make some spit so I can talk, but all I can manage again is, "Oh."

"Ja, the last time I slit my wrists, but my mom found me before I could bleed to death. Check this out." He pulls his jacket sleeves up to reveal purple stripes on his wrists. "I'm a bit fucked up, hey?"

"Oh."

"But that was two years ago and I was cool for all that time. The fucking operation fucked me up again, and now I'm here because they think I'm going to try to commit suicide again."

"Oh."

"But I'm still cool now. It's just the appendix operation that made me go wacko. I attacked the doctor when I woke up after the op, and punched his lights out." I look at his raw knuckles. The top of his hands are full of scabby scratches.

I pull myself together and peer at this man who's actually had the courage to try to kill himself. But I still can't manage speech and he's talking to me again. "Shit! I had just got my life back together again and started a new business. I've got a big order for air-conditioning units and the buyer is probably wondering what happened to me. Being locked up here is a real fuck-up."

I want to talk about the air-conditioners and not about him, and finally manage a sentence. "Oh, so you're in the air-conditioning business?"

"Ja, I'm an engineer."

"Shame, man!"

But now I am confusing myself in my attempt to think about his air-conditioning units and not his failed suicides. I whisper, "Do you mind if I ask you why you tried to commit suicide?" A risky question, so I quickly add, "Sorry, I didn't mean to ask you that."

148

"That's OK. I haven't talked about it to anyone in two years." I curse the bloody shrink who put him on medication without chatting about this first. And I brace myself for his answer.

"I tried to commit suicide because I killed my girlfriend."

"Oh."

"Ja, she was on the back of my motorbike and I had an accident and she died … and I didn't."

It's a small relief that he didn't murder her, but I feel so sorry for him. I sense his terrible sadness as it flits through the smoky energies between us.

He sniffs. "I find it difficult to talk about since it happened two years ago."

"All I can say is that what happened to you …" I'm about to say, "was not your fault," but hear myself saying, "was such a fuck-up!"

*What the hell?*

It was a stupid thing to say, but he seems to like my answer, because he nods his head with a laugh and says, "Fuckin-aye!"

I try to think of something sensible to say. "Shit! It wasn't your fault, it was your destiny." That sounds phony and I regret saying it.

"It *was* my fault. I killed her. Her parents never want to see me again. We were engaged."

"Shit, that's even more of a fuck-up."

I hear a door bang and laughter coming from the direction of the Activity Centre. "Let's hide, Ben. I don't want them to find us and make us do the things on the stupid schedule."

"Fuckin-aye. Let's split."

We find a tree behind the death-chamber. I'm not scared of it anymore because Ben's story has overshadowed my fear. I sit down and lean against the tree-trunk and he stretches out on the yellow grass in front of me with a wince. We stay like this in silence, smoking our cigarettes and impressing each other with how well we can blow smoke-rings.

It's getting dark. My mind has been so absorbed with getting into Ben's brain that I've forgotten about Nora. I reach over and hug him. "I've got to go, Ben. I'm looking after the old ducky who's sharing my room because no-one gives a shit about her in here."

"Ja, I've seen the two of you around. That's cool. I'll see you at dinner."

I head off towards my Nora, and as I trot away I hear him shout, "You're a cool chick!"

His comment makes me feel a lot better about myself than I have in ages.

# SISTER BERTHA

Our room is dark as I enter. My ears prickle for the sound of Nora's snore. But the dank air is deathly quiet. Panic fills me, and before I get to her bedside, I screech, "Nora, are you here?"

No response.

I find the light-switch at her bedside table. The blankets appear to be flat but I can't be certain. I haven't got used to the dim light from the inadequate little lamp, and I pat the blankets feeling for the bump of her tiny body. She's not here!

My heart pounds under the zip of my tracksuit top. I'm paralysed. I am startled by a bang at the door. "Nora! Is that you?"

"For goodness' sake! Why are you yelling?" I make out the angry features of Sister Bertha as she fast approaches me in the darkness.

"Nora's not here!" I scream. "Where is she?" I'm out of control. She grips my shoulders and shakes them until my head wobbles. "Is she dead? For God's sake, answer me, woman!"

"Now, calm down! Nora's fine. Her daughter has come to visit her and they're having supper together."

I collapse onto Nora's bed with my head in my hands. I want to cry but there are no tears. I will wait like this while my heartbeat slows and until Sister Bertha gets the hell out of here, and leaves me alone. The mattress dips beside me. I don't look up but an arm is around my shoulders. "When I first laid eyes on you, I thought you were going to give us shit."

I wait for my scolding, but it doesn't come. Sister Bertha is speaking softly as she sits by my side. "You have been good to Nora, my darling."

But I'm angry, and without lifting my face from my hands I whimper, "I've had to help because the staff around here doesn't give a damn about her."

I can feel the moisture of her breath on my ear as she whispers slowly, "You have to understand that the nurses deal with a hell-of-a-lot of shit and don't make a hell-of-a-lot of money. After long shifts, they have to stand in hell-of-a-long queues for a taxi, which will take them to a township, while the patient whose bum they've just washed is asleep in clean sheets. You have to understand why most of them have become like this."

I lift my face and see her eyes for the first time. They are kind, but I see the fatigue in them. "Thank you," is all I can say, because of my immense relief that Nora isn't dead.

"Would you like to go to dinner and eat something? You will feel a hell-of-a-lot better if you do."

I couldn't think of anything worse. My heart and head have been overwhelmed by the events of today. My shoulders slump and their muscles drag from my neck as I say, "I've had a big lunch today and I can't eat any more."

"That's OK. I understand. Let's get you up and into your bed. I'll bring you a cup of tea."

Sister Bertha bustles out and I sit in my bed against the cushions she's placed behind my back. I kick off my track-shoes and try to relax. But the things I have experienced today are sitting on my chest and I stare at the bricked-up window. She returns with a smile and a tea tray.

She sits next to me on the edge of my bed as I sip my tea. She seems content to stay with me. I imagine that the only time she has off is when the loonies are at dinner. It's comforting to lie here with her. I don't feel the need to talk. She pours herself a cup of tea saying, "Don't mind if I join you."

"Sure." She slurps her tea. "How long have you worked here?"

"About five years now."

"Shame, you must be exhausted, what with dealing with all the loonies."

She laughs and says, "Darling, I'm used to it. I've been dealing with them all my life."

"Oh?"

"Yes. My mother was a prison wardress and handled the mental state of the inmates." She uses finger parenthesis when saying "mental state" and raises her eyes to the ceiling. "Why the hell they bothered about the *feelings* of rapists and murderers, I just don't know."

She has a slight Afrikaans accent, but isn't struggling with the "th" of English.

She shifts closer to me on my bed and says, "We lived at the prison and us kids went to school there as well, so I spent most of my time with my mother, while she handled the criminals' nonsense. Trust me, I can read a person when I see one."

"So you thought I was going to give you shit, did you?"

"I surely did when I first saw you. I thought you were a spoilt brat with a bad attitude. Most of the people I've dealt with in my life have been off the streets with nothing to their names but their stuffed-up lives."

I want her to tell me more about all the stuffing up of the people, so I shift into an upright position on my pillow.

But she continues with her story. "When my mother lost her job, we found ourselves on the streets with nothing. There were six of us kids. My father had left my mother before she had my baby brother. A private safe-house took us in for a while, but there were too many of us kids for them to support, so my younger brothers and sisters were put into an orphanage."

She's a hard woman with the unhappiness of her life tucked away nicely, just like my mother's. My sadness goes to my mother. I am indeed the spoilt northern suburbs bitch; nothing like these women.

She's finished her tea and pours two fresh cups for us. "But there's not only bad news. Me and my mother found jobs in a private mental clinic in Johannesburg. Soon we had enough money to buy a flat. And we got my brothers and sisters back. We got the OK from the orphanage and we took them home, one by one. This was a hell-of-a-complicated procedure and we nearly lost the youngest to a foster home. There are time limits and all sorts of things which allow a mother to get her child back, if she can afford to and if her home is OKed."

She looks over my head. "A lot of bad things happened to some of them, going from one foster home to another, but me and my mother got them right. Today they are all happy and successful, and getting on with it."

"Shit! That's a hell-of-a-bloody story! You should write a book."

"Ja! It would be a bloody good book, hey? Maybe I will when I'm old and grey and, hopefully, if I haven't gone mad by then." She seems to be thinking about her book. "Ja, but I won't put swear-words and sex in it."

We laugh. But I need to know more about her, so I ask, "So what made you come to this place?"

She slurps her tea and says, "When my mother died, I couldn't face working without her. We were very close and the asylum started to get me down. So I applied for the position of Head Matron here and got the job. That was five years ago and, God only knows why, I'm still here." As if as an afterthought, she adds, "But this place is different from the other institutions where I've worked, because it's more for drug-abusers than the mentally disturbed."

"Oh, really? I thought this place was for loonies only."

"No, darling. You, Ben, Nora and Samuel are the only ones here that aren't substance-abusers."

Surprising indeed! This makes only four of us, out of what seems to be about twenty patients. So, I have had sixteen druggies polluting my air without my knowing it. I wonder if Tulula or Dr Shaker had put some stuff about the amount I drink into my yellow folder. But I'm not an alcoholic, really I'm not! Maybe I did drink a little too much. Come to think of it, my eyes aren't as puffy as they used to be.

"That's weird," I say, "because I've only made acquaintance with the other three, and not the druggies." I figure this means that we head-cases intuitively know one another and stay away from the druggies.

Sister Bertha shakes her head. "I will take a loony over a druggie any day." She's used my words and this amuses me. But she's also taking me into her confidence. I feel like I'm in the real world again.

I feign disinterest and stare at the window. "Why is that?" I can't wait to hear why she favours loonies over druggies.

"They arrive here and quickly establish themselves into the pecking-order. We get the girls who sleep with guys for favours. We get the rich executives who control everyone. They pretend to be clean to get a discharge, only to come back here in their flashy cars with a hidden stash for more favours from girls. We have to watch the dispensary like hawks. They'll steal any bloody drug they can get their hands on."

I remember Sam telling me about the robbers. "Yes, I've heard that this goes on here. What a bugger!"

She shakes her head over her tea cup and sighs. "We find them raving in their beds. These types of drugs are bloody dangerous if you don't take them regularly. They also stay in the system a hell-of-a-long time. I've heard that if you don't get off them slowly, you can have a bloody seizure, or heart attack, or something."

*Shit!*

I hope that my veins can expel the toxic shit from my own system as soon as possible.

Now I know that wild dogs are sniffing around us four, and the thought is a little chilling. I recall the barbeque that Nora and I witnessed. These were not normal people laughing and chatting over a normal Sunday braai, but a bunch of schemers, thieves and drug-addicts.

"Whew!" is all I have for Sister Bertha.

The door to our room opens to Nora's delightful face next to Xhosa-nurse, who guides her towards her bed. Sister Bertha greets Xhosa-nurse with a professional nod and is gone.

"I'm so glad to see you, Nora! How was your dinner and how is your daughter?"

She doesn't answer. I go to her bedside to help Xhosa-nurse get her under the sheets. But as I smooth her hair back and tuck the few strands between her head and the pillow, I see that she is crying and I'm a little embarrassed. I leave her to her tears and tiptoe back to my bed.

# CELLPHONE'S ON

I still can't sleep. No matter how hard I wriggle my ankles and twist my body into its foetal position, sleep won't come. I've downed my drug cocktail with new enthusiasm and lie here waiting for whichever one of the pills to do its job.

Stef hasn't visited. All I can do is wriggle my ankles until my bones crack ... and listen to Nora's snoring.

I think I feel claustrophobic, but there's no space in my gloom to accommodate this emotion. I'm trapped. I decide never to allow my children to keep pets in cages, because now I know how the little things must feel – cramped up and alone in a tiny cage with no food and green water because the kids have forgotten how cute they were and that they need to eat. In fact, Nora's gaping profile makes her look like a rodent and my mind starts making strange pictures. Nora the Rat and Michael Jackson are looming behind the kaleidoscope, and this spells trouble.

I shake my head in the face of my dragon and turn on the little bedside lamp. I throw the tea-tray serviette over it to dim the light and seek out the briefcase that Stef brought me.

The sight of my cellphone in the briefcase makes me gasp. It's an unusual connection to my usual world. I take it out and study it in the light. My new fingers are over my old fingerprints on the phone, and the last month's events swirl around my head. I have forgotten about every other soul in my previous life, other than my children and Pooki, who have turned into phantoms and tug at my guilt-strings. I have pushed the outside world from my mind because I'm ashamed of being here. Stef has briefly stepped into this world, and this intrusion is all I can cope with.

Gingerly, I turn it on and punch in my pin. The screen flickers and the beeping starts. It continues for so long that I stick it under my pillow to muffle the noise lest it wakes Nora.

The beeping finally stops and I sit upright. The digital voice is in my ear. "You have twenty-six new messages. First message:

155

"You are not answering your phone! Babs tells me that you are on your way to see that psychologist. I thought we had discussed that and you weren't going. I want to know what's going on. Please call me as soon as you can."

Beep.

"You are not answering your phone! I have spoken to this psychologist-woman and demanded to know what's going on with you. She didn't want anything to do with me. Please call me."

Beep.

"You are not answering your phone! For God's sake! What's going on? I'm worried about the children. Please call me!"

Beep.

"You are not answering your phone! I'm very upset about this. Please call me!"

Beep.

'You are not answering your phone! I've been to the townhouse to find out what's going on. Stef's mother was there with the children. I didn't even know she was here. I felt like a fool, because I'm your mother and I should know these things. I'm very upset that you haven't called me. Stef's mother doesn't know what's going on either. I don't know why you're in a hospital. Please call me as soon as you get this message!"

Beep.

"Your name has been selected from our lucky draw. Please come to our launch party to see what you've won. Lot's of time-share opportunities for you to choose—"

Beep.

"Stef tells me you've been moved to another hospital. He couldn't tell me anything and said he was in a meeting. Why have you not called me to tell me what's going on with you? I'm quite annoyed! And I'm terribly worried about the kids."

Beep.

"Hi. It's Trixie, just wanted to—"

Beep.

"For God's sake, what's going on? Can someone please call me! I can't read hieroglyphics!"

Beep.

"It's you father. You mother's worried. Call her."

That's the last straw! I turn off the phone. Both my thumbs are bleeding and drool is dripping from my mouth. My head-clamp is back and the acid is creeping up into my throat.

I keep chewing my skin through the salty blood on my thumbs. My heart aches. It aches for my home, it aches for Stef and my children and Pooki, and it aches for my mom. She is a good mother. She is a worried mother. She is worried about her daughter, who's been loafing around and talking to mad people without a care in the world other than her bloody cigarettes. I hate myself and want my heart to bleed empty.

I tuck my phone into the side pocket of the briefcase and yank out the laptop. I cross my legs and open it on my lap. It's on and I'm gripping the mouse as it slides over the wobbly tea tray next to me.

Start ... Programs ... Games ... There's no Tetris! I rip off some more skin from the side of my thumbnail.

FreeCell ... click. Don't know what this is but let's try it. I need to focus.

# FREECELL FRENZY

Good; aces at the bottom. Click. Where are all the spades? Click. Don't collate too many spades unless I can do the same with the red hearts or diamonds. Click. The king, queen and jack are at the top so that's lucky. Click.

I love this game! I love it when a suite's complete and the cards flutter up. This game is organised. Thanks heavens the cards are ordered and stacked and aren't all over the place like in *Alice in Wonderland*! That would surely freak me out and suck me down into this bed and into the dark dungeons of this hell-hole!

"Congratulations! You win! Do you want to play again?"

*Sure, you fool ... let's go!*

Shit, this one's impossible! I love the impossible ones. Restart game ... Solved it! I'm getting good at this: red, black, red, black, nine, eight, seven, six. Click-snore, click-snore, and flutter. Nora's still alive. Click, click, click.

"Goooood morning, ladies! Rise and shine!"

*What the hell?*

All I can see is red and black and kings and queens, and the little man who has become my digital companion at the top of the screen looking left and right at my cursor. I am numb. This is excellent!

But the elation doesn't last long, because I now know I'm in Amanzi and I sure know the strong arm of Xhosa-nurse as she whips my head up to give me my potion.

Sister Bertha is next to me as well. "What are you doing on your computer?"

"Just playing games ..."

"Did you manage to get some sleep?"

"I can't sleep."

"That's surprising. Let me see if I can get Doctor to prescribe you something a little stronger."

"OK."

I would love to take something a little stronger. I've never been unable to sleep because my death-sleep tactics have always worked. I'm now craving being comatose.

She's back at my side with the plastic cup and I gulp down two tiny blue pills. Xhosa-nurse is singing a lullaby and busying herself with washing and dressing Nora. It seems like the vibes in the room have got better since Sister Bertha and I became friends, and I wonder if it's because I now know more about these two sisters' lives, or if it's because I'm not being so hostile.

Sister Bertha pats my head as Xhosa-nurse stands next to her, beaming down at me with her big white teeth. "You must sleep, mama. We wake you at ten tomorrow so you can be ready in time for mister doctor."

# MOTORBIKE RIDE WITH BEN

I'm exhilarated! I'm singing! I can't remember the exact words of this song, but I'm singing it as the wind whips my hair into my mouth:

It's the weekend and I know that you're free,
To put on your jeans and come on out with me,
I need to have you near me; I need to feel you close to me,
Kshhh, Kshhh,
I need to have you near me; I need to feel you close to me,
Doo, Doo, Doo,
You and me will go motorbike riding in the sun
and the wind and the rain,
I've got money in my pocket; tiger in my tank,
And I'm king of the road again,
Yes, I'll meet you in the usual place,
I don't need to think; it's just your pretty face,
I need to have you near me; I need to feel you close to me,
Kshhh, Kshhh,
I need to have you near me; I need to feel you close to me.

"Yahoo! Faster! Faster!"

Ben's got me on the back of his motorbike. I'm hanging onto his leather jacket like a monkey. I look down at his strong hands as he grips the handlebars and there's blood pouring from his knuckles like red paint blown onto paper through a straw. I peer over his shoulder at the long road ahead disappearing into a spearhead as it oscillates over the distant hills of the Karoo. I feel like flying. I want to take Ben and his motorbike with me. But I'm attached to his back so I'll have to grip him between my knees to get us both up.

We whiz through a swarm of insects and they prick me in the face and sting my eyes. "Ben, be careful! Don't go so fast!"

Now I'm scared. I can't look at the road ahead anymore and focus on the smudgy tar spinning past my knees. I have a bad feeling about this. I hope

I don't feel pain before I die on the tarmac. I try to let go so that I can flap my arms to get us airborne. I want to fly but the ground moves too fast. I'm scared of being whipped from the back of the motorbike by the wind before I can get enough flaps going to get us up.

I'm not meant to be here on this motorbike with Ben. He's got the wrong girl on the back. This is a terrible mistake, so I open my thighs to loosen the grip I have around his waist.

"Sorry, Ben, I have to let you go!"

The wind blows my voice back and away from his ears, and he doesn't respond. He's concentrating on keeping his motorbike steady while avoiding the insects.

Someone's got my arm and is pulling me off the motorbike. It swerves.

"Hello, hello, are you awake yet?"

I land with a thud and blink away my confusion until I can see. I'm in a bed and I peer into Sister Bertha's face.

My jaws are sore and, as I unclench my teeth, relief rushes through my veins like champagne. Shit! Sister Bertha was here a second ago when she gave me the little blue tablets. I wonder why she's back so early. She was to wake me for my appointment with Cranium, so I sit up quickly to prove that I'm not a dozy-head and am ready to face the world.

"We were worried about you. How are you feeling?"

"Better thanks. My batteries have been charged. I'm ready for the doctor. Just give me a minute to shower."

"Darling, you've been sleeping for twenty-four hours." She doesn't elaborate. This is the second time that I've passed out for so long.

"Shit!" is all I manage.

"It's Saturday and the doctor doesn't consult on weekends, so you're off the hook. Stef called early this morning and said he was bringing lunch. He's bringing your children to visit you."

. *What!*

The thought of my two innocent children here amidst this craziness is overwhelming. I don't want them here. I don't want them to be confused by Sam's stupid singing or frightened by Nora's veins or Ben's bruised fists. I'm angry. How could Stef allow them to see their mother in this hell-hole!

But they are probably confused and need to see their mother. Knowing Stef, he would not have told them the whole story, so that's OK. I need to get

161

a grip on myself! I need to wash up, and present myself like an indulgent lady resting at a health hydro. But anxiety is still choking me. What about the loonies!

"I don't want my children to see me like this. I don't want them to see all the patients."

"Children have the most amazing capacity for acceptance. A hell-of-a-lot more than adults do, my darling. You need to console them, but they need to know the truth."

I can't do this. "I can't tell them the truth now. They've gone through enough. I will tell them when they're older. I don't want them to be upset."

"There's an old grandstand at the far end of the clinic. No-one goes there and it's a nice place to have a picnic. I will take them there when they arrive."

Sister Bertha is flipping brilliant! I hug her. "Thank you, you're a saint."

But now I worry about my drugs. I've been sleeping for a whole day, which means I've missed two doses. Thoughts of my collapsing and going into cold turkey in front of my children send shivers down my spine. "What about my drugs? Shall I take a double dose quickly?"

She laughs, "No ways! You'll be a walking zombie. I've told you before that if you don't take your drugs on time and every day, you're in trouble." She used the word "seizure" when telling me about what happens to the druggies who steal head-drugs, and I'm sure she's trying to be subtle. She adds flippantly, "We'll top up your drug levels later."

*Shit! This is scary stuff!*

The toxins that have been driven into my mind-networks need to be topped-up, so that I won't die, or have a seizure, or become a zombie! This inherently makes me an addict and the thought paralyses me. I'm confused and terrified and anger pumps at my temples. I hate to have to do things that are necessary, at necessary times, because I live my life doing whatever I want, and drinking whatever I want, whenever I damn-well feel like it!

"Shit, Sister Bertha! All this stuff is terrifying me. I feel like I'm playing a doped-out freak in someone else's movie! I'm also bloody angry. This whole bloody experience has been like a comedy of errors, but I don't think it's very funny!" I realise she probably doesn't get the "comedy of errors" thing, so I say, "All in all, I feel like a floppy-doll who's been fed mud from a spoon by a little child." I also feel abandoned, but I don't say that. I push my palms into my eye-sockets and try to force my head into the pillow. I need to press my eyeballs into my skull so that my sleeping tears will leak out.

The mattress dips beside me but I don't uncover my eyes. Arms slip under my head and I'm pulled up into soft breasts and the sweet smell of washing-powder. "I understand that what's happened to you isn't your fault. But Sister Bertha's here, OK, girlie" She rocks me against her breasts.

"Shit! I need to hurry! Sorry Sister. I've gotta get ready for my kids." I pull myself away from her.

# BLESSED ARE THE CHILDREN

White mist and cigarette smoke envelop me, and I can't see anything. I adjust the temperature of the shower spray and sit in the bath with my knees tucked under me. My children are to visit me today, and my heart throbs. I feel weird and slightly out of control. I know that I should have taken the stupid drugs at the right time during the past twenty-four hours instead of snoozing away like an indulgent housewife. Or maybe I'm just being a mental hypochondriac, because Sister Bertha has scared the hell out of me by explaining the dire consequences of missing medication. I need to be myself when I see my children today, because their impressions of me in this weird place need to be sound. But all I want to do is crawl into my bed without drying myself and play FreeCell until I disappear into the aces, queens and jacks.

*I can't make out the pink roses on my wallpaper because it's too gloomy in here.*

*I must be invisible. I mustn't make a sound, so I cover my head with the blankets and pinch my nose so I can't breathe. Not even Mitcho is here to hold onto. He's stopped purring and has gone before I could grab hold of him and grip him to my chest under the sheets. He knows what's coming as well as I do and has scampered out my room just in time. He's a very naughty cat!*

*I can't hold my nose forever and try to let a little bit of air in to keep me alive. Acid is mixing with blood in my nose and terror grips my forehead. I have to plan my escape just right because I know the ghost will take his time here before drifting down the passage to terrify my brother. I know he visits my brother too because we usually crawl into my parents' bed at the same time. I'm always a little ahead, so I know he visits me first.*

*I know he's gone when the air in my room lifts, and allows the smell of jasmine, which grows through my window, to filter into my nose and take the acid away. I've got to be quick because I know he'll spend some time in my brother's bedroom, which will give me just enough time to make my escape. So I cup my hands on either side of my eyes to allow enough vision to make my way to the safety of my parents' bed. The dash down the hallway is like running through the horrible pictures of hell that the Bible-studies teacher shows us. As if she knows, my mother is expecting me. She holds the blanket open at her side of the bed and I crawl in beside her to wait for the pumping at my temples to stop. Then my brother is here, and we are all safe between the sheets.*

*We don't talk about these nights. I'm eavesdropping at the study door and listening to my mom as she talks on the telephone. "I've never in my entire life felt such evil! I woke up last night to a presence in my room. I opened my eyes and saw a man standing in the doorway. I could see him perfectly. He was dressed in a suit and wore a hat. He stood there for a long time and then disappeared. Then Lamby came into our room, as she usually does, and there was a child standing next to her. The little girl was smaller than she is and was wearing a long white nightgown. She was standing close to Lamby and seemed to want to clutch onto her. Then Lamby said in a very adult voice that was not her own, 'I'm very irritable!' So I told her to go into my bathroom and have a drink of water. As she walked into the bathroom, the little child followed her in, and was gone."*

*As I press my ear to the study door key-hole, I am strangely comforted. I will never tell my mother that I heard this conversation. But now I know she knows, and will be expecting me like she does, with the sheets open just enough so that I can slip in beside her and feel her breath on my neck as I close my eyes.*

The plastic shower curtain is sticking to my back. The water is cold as it drizzles onto my head and past my ears. I don't know why I'm brooding over these ghostly memories because I have forced myself never to think about them.

*I'm eavesdropping on my mother again. She's chatting to her friend. "We were having drinks in the lounge after dinner, and Dawn suddenly froze ... she started talking in a strange voice ... the curtains lifted on their own." And I hear my father's stern voice as he says to my mother, "I never want that stupid bitch in our house again." Dawn is quite nice, but her kind, pretty face turns into an ugly witch's one.*

God only knows why I remember Dawn. Maybe the dragon opened a hole in my mind to allow the memory in. I'm not scared anymore. I am here in this cold white bathroom in this cold black asylum. There is no evil here. There are no ghosts, or ghost hostesses, just loonies and druggies. But today

I need to be a good mother. Today I need to expel any scary thoughts from my children's minds. I have to comfort them and tell them everything is OK. I am their mom.

I smudge the mirror with a piece of toilet paper and try to make out the condition of my face. But I can't see my eyes. All I see is my mother's face.

*It's still dark and I can't see the tiny pink roses. I'm listening to "The Finger of Fate" on the radio that I have just got for my birthday. I need to keep it on the whole night, because I don't think the ghost will come if he hears the voices coming from the small black box. But my mother switches it off and tells me to get some sleep because I have a test tomorrow. She and my father are going out again, and we will be left alone with Annie, who will probably fall asleep in the kitchen. Annie's told us that the man with the hat walks up and down the garden boundary wall all night and she thinks that's very funny, but my brother and I don't. She's painted strange red crosses with loops on the top all over her bedroom floor, so she thinks she's safe. But I know we're going to hand out some terror of our own tonight, because it's when my parents go out that my brother and I start the fighting. We will chase each other around the house with kitchen knives, until one of us manages to lock himself in the bathroom. By this time, Annie will be awake and hysterical and threatening to tell our parents.*

*I hate it when my parents go out. I hate it when my mother comes into my bedroom to kiss me goodnight because I don't want her to go. But her beauty overwhelms me. Her eyes are thickly painted and she has glued eyelashes onto them. She has pinned that fake ponytail that I like to play with onto her own hair and has twisted the lot into a beehive. She kisses me on the head and wafts out of my room leaving the smell of jasmine behind.*

I see my mother's face as I stare at myself in the reflection. She's a beautiful mom, and she's a good mom. She's protected me. She's given me the pull-yourself-together blanket and now I need to draw on her strength and prove my worthiness to my children.

They are visiting me today and I need to get my act together. I clean the mirror with toilet paper until my image clears. I twist my wet hair into a chignon with some old rusty hair-clips. I've got Nora's make-up case, and make my face up, careful not to look like some crazed freak. The image of my face is important, especially to my children. I've lined my eyes with a pencil and applied a touch of rouge. I don't look as beautiful as my mother.

# MOTHER AND CHILD AT GRANDSTAND

It's cold and icy. My boobs shiver under my grey tracksuit top and I squeeze them together as my ciggy smoulders under my face. I'm sitting on the bottom seat of the grandstand as I wait for Stef and my children, who will be shepherded here by Sister Bertha.

I haven't noticed the grandstand because it's at the far boundary of this schoolyard prison. It's alone and derelict, without its usual audience, just like me. The seat is cold and I worry that I might develop piles. Maybe if I sit here long enough I will get the dreaded bum disorder and have to go to hospital for a real reason.

I'm full of guilt, and heartache, and worry about my new mind-drug addiction. I'm at the epicentre of all that has happened until now, and the events of the past few weeks unfold before me, like a sports match:

- I have escaped the burning palm tree and the clutches of Trixie.
- I have put on a brave face for all to see, and behaved like nothing happened.
- I have tucked the horror of the flames away, because I have tomorrow to think about it.
- I have faced my duties as a mother and prepared the lunch-boxes.
- I have bought an expensive bed for Stef and me to sleep in.
- I have obliged my friends and consulted with Tulula and Maggie and Dr Shaker.
- I have gone to the sorry-for-you party.
- I have lain prostrate in hospital and allowed myself to be wheeled out like an invalid by dungeon-nurse.
- I have checked into Amanzi like a good girl.
- I have swallowed the medication-cocktails.
- I have accepted the stupid blue granny-gown.
- I have tried not to look at Cranium's glass eye.
- I have visited hell, the dragon, and the spaceman.
- I have seen blood from Calvin Klein's arm, and from Ben's stomach.
- I have watched Nora snore, touched her silky veins and bathed her.

- I have cried without tears for Nora and her beloved Bernard, for Sam and his music, and for Ben and his manslaughter.
- And I have kept to myself and haven't harmed anybody.

The experiences I have endured spin around me like chariots. I shiver in the icy wind. The dismal situation that I'm in has also rendered me a shitty person because:

- I have abandoned my children and Pooki.
- I have been unable to touch Stef or have him touch me.
- I've told a few doctors and nurses to bugger off.
- I have abandoned my cellphone and its connection to the outside world.
- I have abandoned my mother and made her worry.
- And, worst of all, I have pretended to commit suicide, and this foolishness has landed me here!

And all through this torment I have not gained a thing! Nothing has changed in the way that I feel. Nothing has changed my personality. Nothing has happened to my brain other than its fuzziness and its experience of a couple of hallucinations and the way it has slowed my walking. I'm a bloody fool! But I am still so very sad.

The only positive thing I can think of is that I haven't had a drink in ages. Maybe I should be grateful. Who knows? I secretly wonder if Stef has packed a bottle of wine.

Hanging over my head like an umbrella over my madness is one stark fact: my house has burnt down and my children are alone. The ladybird with the black-spotted red carapace is me.

"Mommy! Mommy!"

I pull myself together and run towards my children. They are coated and wearing woolly balaclavas. Their ears are covered against the breeze and they are warm and cared for. A little heat creeps into my bursting heart. Their eyes get bigger as they approach me and they visibly falter before I can grab them to my chest. It is like a moment locked in a vacuum.

"Come here, you little fools! Mommy's fine!"

They don't seem convinced, and stand in front of me with a little distance between us. They peer at me with eyes I've never seen before. It's as if they've grown up while I wasn't looking, or maybe I've grown down and become a stranger to them. Tears I no longer have burn behind my eyes. I'm grateful for the bloody drugs because I can't cry now. I need to prove that I'm fine, that I'm their mom. That I'll never change.

But they stand here like children having to greet a stranger and are scared and shy. I choke and leap towards them with the biggest smile I can muster. "Hey, you little idiots. What's up? How are you doing?"

They look at each other for encouragement, but don't budge.

This is not working and I look over their heads to find Stef, but he's standing on the top seat of the grandstand, looking down on us, with his arms folded like a Greek god. He's not going to help. He's leaving this to me. I understand.

I approach my little chickens slowly and put my arms around their shoulders. "OK, you guys, let's sit down and Mommy will tell you everything. You are big now." I can't bloody remember how old they are or when their birthdays are. I close my eyes and rattle the fuzziness in my mind and quickly work out that Mackie is four and Mouse is seven. They are so little, they have come out of my stomach, yet they now tower over me. I'm little and they are big. They are big adults facing the flames on their own.

*Blessed are the children.*

I put my arms around their shoulders and they feel stiff, but they tuck themselves under my armpits instinctively. I draw them down on either side of me and we sit on the bottom seat of the grandstand, staring at nothing.

I feel Stef hovering somewhere above our heads. He probably hasn't told them anything. The Mars–Venus thing comes to mind. Securing his family's financial survival would supersede any necessity to chit-chat with the kids about the mental condition of their mother. I'm OK with this, but my babies are here and they are obviously worried. They haven't seen their mother for days on end … I can't work out how many.

But the two of them are here, their little bodies are attached to their mother's and they need to know what the hell is going on. I squeeze their shoulders towards my breasts and shake them. "Listen to me, guys, Mommy is staying at this hotel because Mommy needs to rest. Mommy is very sad." They both look up at me at the same time and I feel their shoulders soften. "Mommy is very sad because of the f-f-ire."

I've got to stop calling myself "Mommy", because I'm sounding like a fool, so I continue more seriously, "I have lost my home and all the things in it. All the things in our home were things I had been collecting since I was small like you. I have lost my photographs and my diaries. And I know that you have lost your things too and I'm sure you miss them, but all your toys were old and buggered and were a lot of crap anyway and we can buy you tons more." I like to swear occasionally when I talk to them, because it relaxes them. I have told them that only when they are old can they swear, but they love it when I do and it works this time because they both giggle.

I know I'm not giving them the true reason why I'm here, because picturing their mother trying to jump out of a hospital window would truly stuff up their minds and have them crawling around on a psychologist's carpet when they're adults.

I extinguish the burning flames from my mind and whisper into their up-turned faces, "Anyway, do you understand why I'm sad, and do you understand that I need to sleep a bit just to feel a little better? And it's only because you are safe that I can do this. I want to thank you so much for letting me be sad and have a nice sleep. I'm coming home soon and then everything will be the same again."

They both stand up at the same time and kiss me hard on the mouth and hug me until I choke. Mackie pushes Mouse away from my neck and Mouse pushes him, both trying to get a better grip. My heart is beating so hard below my tearless face that I can't breathe. I can only clutch onto them and bury my face in their balaclavas until we are all three lifted into the clouds, far away from this God-awful place.

I manage to lift my head from the fabric of their jackets. "So, guys, are you cool with all of this?"

They both nod energetically and say in unison, "I love you, Mommy!"

"Thank you, guys. I love you more than you love me."

Mackie and I are good at this game and he says, "No, I love you more. I love you more than the world and the stars and the sun."

Mouse hugs me as I say, "No, I love you more than the universe!"

They put their heads together and yell, "We love you more than eternity!"

The game is over now, because how can you beat loving someone more than eternity? So Mackie says, "Can we go and play now?"

I smack them both on the bums and say, "Push off, the two of you silly-buggers!" They're off up the steps of the grandstand, laughing and trying to push each other over.

Stef sits next to me, kisses me lightly on the mouth and quickly busies himself with unpacking a picnic basket. I can sense his annoyance, but I understand. He must be wondering what the hell he's doing on a bloody grandstand in the freezing cold on a Saturday afternoon with a loony-wife in an unappealing tracksuit.

I put my arm around him lightly enough not to appear needy. I hate to appear needy. I know men hate it, most of all Stef. We are both from families that don't show physical emotion. We are two independent people of the world. This is the basis of our respect for one another, and our friendship.

I look into his ear and say, "I'm sorry about this, my love. It's not my fault and I still don't know why the bloody hell I'm here. This place is like hell itself. Please get me out of here."

He doesn't turn his eyes to me and says, "What did you tell the kids?"

"I told them that I was sad and needed to sleep." Shit! I sound like an indulgent pig.

"That's cool. I haven't told them anything, just that you're fine."

"Oh? But I'm not fine. I can't bloody sleep and when I do, I pass out. The bloody drugs are killing me ..."

He puts his big hand up towards the sky. His ruby graduation ring glints, like a warning. I shut up. We sit together and stare into the distance, saying nothing.

We're eating bread with chicken drumsticks and salad from Tupperware. The kids are jumping up and down the steps around us, sipping cooldrink from cans and playing silly-buggers. Stef hasn't brought any wine and the absence of alcohol between us over a meal is a strange experience. It's actually quite boring.

I sense a finality in his voice as he says, "I don't want to stay too long because it's cold out here for the kids and I've promised I will take them to a movie."

This meeting is over. Stef has to move on. "That's nice. Thank you for bringing them. I think they both feel a lot better."

Mouse yells into my ear, "Papa's brought Pooki to see you. She's in the car. Come and say hello to her."

Things wouldn't be right if I didn't have the chance to explain my stupid predicament to my other child.

As we say our goodbyes in the confines of Stef's car, Pooki jumps all over me and bashes my teeth with her head and pees on my lap in excitement. I fiddle with her cool ears and hug her tightly as she wriggles under my grip. All she wants is to kiss me to death through her gnashing teeth and never let me go. I am her shadow and she is lost without it.

They have kissed me and hugged me and I have told the kids that I'm now going for a nice massage and to have my nails done. They seem happy. I stand here in my bedraggled tracksuit and wave goodbye to Pooki's sad seal eyes as she wags her head on the back-rest while the car edges away.

I think I've stood here in front of the security gate gazing after my departed, packaged family for a long time, because Sister Bertha is walking towards me with the security guard and a huff. "We couldn't find you at the grandstand. Are you alright? And how are the kids?"

"They're fine." I'm not, but I don't say it.

"That's good," she says with a happy face that looks like its homely cheeks are trying to cheer me up. "What did you tell them?"

"I told them that I am sad and resting. I also told them that I'm about to have a nice massage and have my nails done. Any chance of some pampering?" I think of Xhosa-nurse roughing me up and filing my nails. My sense of humour is back at least. My humour is my friend, as much as my ciggies are.

She laughs and the security guard is gone. "Come on, let's get you back inside. Samuel is quite worried about you and has been wondering around asking everybody if his parents chased you away."

"Sam wants a cigarette."

I want to take lots of my medication. I want to get into bed without washing or brushing my teeth or taking my clothes off, because Pooki has peed on me and I want her smell with me. And then I want to play FreeCell all night to the beat of Nora's snoring until the screen gobbles me up.

It's been a bleak and shitty day.

# POOR ADVICE FOR BEN

I wake thinking about Ben and I'm strangely of lighter mind, as if his trauma has filled some of my own bleakness. I have told him that I would think about his ordeal and try to find out how I could help him. But I still don't know what the bloody hell to tell him, because if I had killed someone and then tried to kill myself, I wouldn't want to hear any sympathetic crap from anyone, because nothing can turn things like that around. Especially because the cause of the deaths he has to deal with have not only been involuntary but voluntary as well, both caused by him, and that's a huge lot of shit to swallow.

But I miss him and his quiet and tormented demeanour and will go to breakfast to find him. I will also try to avoid talking about the serious stuff. Nora's snoring is loud and clear, which signals at least another day of life, and this gives me some time-out for Ben.

Xhosa-nurse hasn't appeared today to stuff shit down my throat, but has left the mouse-cup on the bedside table with the myriad of tiny tablets for me to swallow by my own volition. This is unusual and she must be aware, like me, that I actually require the stuff now and don't need coercing.

I at least try to look a little more decent and take a little longer in the bathroom. I don my jeans and T-shirt. Today is too grey for the grey tracksuit and besides, it's starting to smell too much of deodorant mixed with old sweat.

I'm waiting at the dusty little breakfast table for Ben. I'm also waiting for my mind to react to my medication and concentrate on trying to feel a difference. But I'm still me. The only thing I know is that I need to take my medication diligently because I don't want to have a seizure.

I hate Sundays. Sunday tells me that tomorrow's school, or that I need to wake early and get my lethargic arse to the office and change the world with my latest feasibility-study presentation. The yellow grass outside spells winter, but it's grey and raining outside – strange for a Johannesburg winter. Coupled with the face-brick of my surroundings, this Sunday is a very miserable one indeed.

Ben walks in as expected. He's a man and I am certain he will be present at breakfast. Men eat at defined times and are not like women, who don't eat all day and then stuff themselves with unhealthy junk food when they get home from work. Or maybe it's just me who does this, but anyway, I have this firm belief that men do the right things at the right times, no matter how screwed-up they feel.

I wave at him and he meanders through the druggies towards my table. "Hey! How's it going?" Again I feel the difference between our sexes, because he is chipper and I'm the morning zombie.

"Pretty crap. I hate Sundays."

"Shit, so do I. What's to eat?"

There's no yogurt or dry cereals on presentation today, but there are covered plates on the table. This must be "special Sunday breakfast", like in a boarding school. I remove the tin lid from my plate. The food looks like aeroplane food. But I've always liked aeroplane food and Ben and I sit together and swallow the stuff without talking. I'm eating a substantial meal in this place for the first time. I don't taste anything, but I am eating, so that's probably good.

Ben looks up from his scrambled eggs. "Have you thought about what I told you?"

*Shit!*

I know my brain thought about it in a dream and this is all I've got for him. I'm certainly not a person who analyses dreams and tries to find meaning in their messages. Relying on a weird message in a dream is sure to create actions-by-suggestion. My fear of mind-power envelopes me, so I push away the dreadful images of me trying to lift Ben off his motorbike between my knees, and find myself blabbering through the plastic eggs, "Shit! I've given it a lot of thought, but this is a tough one."

"Fuckin-aye!" He's wearing his leather jacket again and I can smell its odour as it squeaks under his armpits.

"Again, as I said to you before, what happened to you is a total bloody eff-up." I can't believe what's coming out of my mouth, but he keeps on eating as though it's OK.

I don't know what to say to him, but what I do know is that I can't give him any of the bullshit that you read in sorry-for-you cards.

"Listen, Ben, I think you have to try to get your head right all by yourself. I don't think anyone else can help. I'm sure there are no anti-sadness drugs for such a thing."

174

He looks at me intently, but I know I'm not saying the right things. I always speak without thinking and blame it on some stupid star-sign prediction I once read in an even more stupid women's magazine that said: "Sagittarians always say the wrong thing at the wrong time." So I always put my foot into things because the stupid prediction told me I would, which further proves my mind-power theory.

But Ben's not getting up to go, and is still looking at me intently over his toast. So I continue putting my big foot where it's not meant to be. "A plus would be if you found a girlfriend you could love again, and who you could talk to about this. Maybe she'll feel so desperately sorry for you that she'll love you even more, in spite of herself, and you will stay together forever. And just maybe, in the distant future, you'll accept what happened to you and look at it like God gave you no arms or something, and it becomes part of you. Quite frankly, I think the only thing you've got going for you is time … that's if you don't try to kill yourself in the meantime."

*Shit!*

What a crappy thing to say! But he hasn't flinched, and he's still here, so I try to improve on my nonsensical talk by adding, "Killing yourself would be such a waste of a really decent guy who's got a lot to give this screwed-up world. I think someone else is waiting for you out there and, if you do yourself in, you will be robbing her of a cool life-experience with a cool guy."

This is such bullshit advice, but it's the only answer I can give him because I've tried to find something good in the bad. If someone gave this advice to me right now, I would tell him he's a bloody fool.

Ben looks sad. "I don't think I could ever replace her. I'll always be looking for someone who doesn't look like her, or looks like her. I dunno which? Shit! Fuck!" My advice has definitely not helped and we're both mute for a long time.

But it seems he wants more of my bullshit, because he's still looking at me intently, so I say glibly, "I just don't know what advice to give you, Ben, because the thing that happened to you is unfair to say the least. And the only thing I can compare it to, is being born without arms or something. All you have left to do is cope with the thing or die."

Now I've made another stuff-up, because he *has* tried to cope and he *has* tried to die, so I say, "Shit, that doesn't help does it? Because you *have* tried to cope with killing your girlfriend and you *have* tried to die."

He smiles. "It's cool to talk to you. I think I feel a bit better."

I'm glad he's said this, because I find myself saying, "You see! All you need is a girl like me to talk to about this over and over again so you don't feel alone, and maybe one day you'll feel like you've talked about it enough and can just get on with living your life. I really think that talking to someone helps and maybe that's why people see shrinks. Crying in front of a stranger you've paid, is by far easier than crying in front of someone you know, for free."

"Ja."

"And I just want to add that I feel so sad for you that I could die."

"Thanks."

And that's that. I don't have any more to give him now and I hope the conversation is over, because it's killing me.

I suddenly realise that Ben hasn't asked me why I'm here and I hope he never does.

# TEDDY BEARS' PICNIC

Ben and I finish our breakfast in silence. We munch dry toast while staring into nothing. I've successfully managed flight by a lot of arm-flapping, lifted myself off the back of his motorbike and left him alone on his journey through the Karoo.

It's still drizzling, so we search out a covered place, free of the druggies, and are puffing away on the little terrace in front of the Tea Room. Ben shifts up the plastic wrapper of his cigarette box and taps out tiny smoke-rings from smoke he has blown through the hole burnt in the wrapper with his cigarette. I follow suit and blow even smaller rings by lightly tapping my cheeks. Ben uses one hand to crack open his Zippo. He squeezes the lid and the base of the Zippo with his first three fingers and it pops open, like magic. He flicks the Zippo against his leg and it's alight. As I suck in the gas from my lighter to light it in my mouth and do my dragon trick, Sister Bertha walks in.

"What the hell are you two you doing?" She's got a big smile on her face, but I feel like a child who's been caught smoking in the schoolyard.

I blow the gas from my mouth and choke, "Nothing! I am just having a smoke."

"You've got a visitor."

*Oh! Shit no!*

"Oh?"

"Clara is here to have lunch with you. She's waiting at Reception."

"Oh?"

It feels like I've just had breakfast, and the thought of entertaining Clara is daunting. She is so bloody nice and so full of the joys of life. Her enthusiasm will surely kill me. I'm also in no state to receive normal people from my normal life in this abnormal place.

Ben gets up and his jacket squeaks. "I'm going. Have fun. See you later."

He and Sister Bertha are gone and I'm left alone to contemplate how to react to Clara. The pull-yourself-together blanket is not what's needed here, but rather a rocket up my bum. Clara's joy and energy will surely demand a good reaction from me.

I've slapped my cheeks and am practising smiling when in walks the beautiful Clara with picnic basket, and Sam, in tow.

*Shit!*

This is a double whammy! Not only do I have to be the normal me in the normal world, but I have to deal with Sam as well! But I focus on Clara. "Oh, my God, Clara! What are you doing in this God-awful place?"

We hug and I squirm because Clara is very religious and I feel like I'm going to be zapped by God's staff and sent directly to hell. Clara turns her other cheek and presses it against my own and our embrace lasts a long time. She's squeezing me so hard that I can't move or breathe and I wonder where she's found such strength in her small body. I manage to pull myself from her grip and look into her beautiful face. It feels like she is the hen and I am the little chicken, and I realise that I probably look like one because my eyes have started to pop out at me from my reflection in the bathroom mirror.

"God, hon, you look awful!" She always calls me "hon", and I'm comforted even though she's saying I look like shit. She's crying.

"Clara! Don't cry. There's certainly no reason to cry!"

"Sorry, hon, I just can't bear to see you here."

"I'm fine, love. Really I am! I'm just resting here and there's nothing weird going on, I promise you."

But Sam is here and buggering up my illusion, because he's also hugging Clara and he whines into her ear, "Don't cry! I'll look after her!"

*Oh, shit!*

Clara is startled. "Hey! Steady young man! Who are you?"

The twisted grin is on his man-child face and a bit of drool drips over his stubble. "I'm Samuel, Samuel Krishna!" He puts his hands into the air and starts dancing around. "Hare Krishna Hare Krishna Krishna Krishna Hare Hare Hare Rama—"

"Shut up, Sam! Stop it! You're scaring Clara and disturbing us! You are a very naughty boy!"

Clara's eyes are big and for a second it seems as if she's a misfit like one of us. Or maybe she really is a loony, because she's always so bloody happy and maybe that's a mental disease in itself. The buzzing in my head has started again.

Sam stops singing but still dances around us with his hands in the air. He looks particularly crazy today because he's wearing striped pyjamas and his hair is standing up as though he's just woken up.

I grab Sam's hands from the air and pull them down to his sides. He obliges and whimpers, "Please can I have a cigarette? I promise I'll pay you back."

Clara's usual joy and confidence seems to have been flattened by this scene. I give Sam a cigarette and light it for him. "Shit! Don't worry, Clara. Sam's a lovely man. I keep his cigarettes for him so he's just come to get one."

Sam starts dancing again. "Oh, goody! I've got lots of cigarettes! I've got lots of cigarettes!"

Clara manages a little giggle. I don't want to scold Sam again, so I leave him dancing around us and he says over my head, "Hello, Nora! Do you want to go for a walk with me?"

Nora is here too! She ignores Sam and says to me, "I feel so energetic today, dear. I've had a nice long sleep. But don't be cross with me because I had my breakfast and my lunch in bed and I didn't get depressed like you said I would. Today I would certainly love to go out with you. I'm wearing my macintosh."

Although Nora is completely sane, hearing her words through Clara's ears makes her sound as daft as Sam does. She's also piled on lots of make-up. She's used the electric-blue eye-shadow but has applied it right up to the underside of her eyebrows, and she's wearing bright pink lipstick that has been applied as though a clown did it. She looks completely out of her cotton-picking mind!

"Good morning to you, Nora," I say. "You look lovely. This is a very good friend of mine, Clara. Clara, this is Nora, who's also a good friend of mine and is completely sane like the two of us."

I've said a stupid thing again and I wonder if Clara now thinks that I've also lost my marbles like these two dolts standing here. She shakes Nora's hand.

I take Nora's other hand and say, "Dear, I think you've put on a little too much make-up. The mirror in our bathroom is not very clear. Let me fix it for you."

"Oh, I'll do that," says Clara, who's still giggling. "I would love to fix your make-up."

She spits on her finger and lightly smoothes the blue eye-shadow over Nora's floppy eyelids.

"Oh, thank you, dear. I feel like a princess," Nora says.

Clara uses a serviette and wipes away the lipstick to follow the contours of Nora's mouth. "There you go, hon, you look much better."

"Thank you, dear. I will leave you two to catch up. Oh, I've brought your cellphone, dear. It's been ringing all morning." I'm sure I didn't turn it on.

I don't want my cellphone, but I take it from her. I know my mother is desperately trying to get hold of me, but I've successfully tucked her away. I know I will need to let her out and face a very personal conversation with her about where the hell I am. But I will think about this tomorrow, so I put my arm under Nora's armpit and help her down the steps of the patio and onto the muddy yellow grass.

She hops off like a spring chicken. I wave at the back of her macintosh and she's gone.

Sam is no longer in our space but I see him giggling at the window of a red Porsche parked very close to the Tea Room patio. Its wheels seem to be stuck in the mud and the streamlined bonnet is raised above a small ditch. The windows are misty, but my senses tell me that they're not misty from driving in the rain. Maybe I'm imagining it, but I see the Porsche rocking slightly.

Sam seems very excited and is rubbing the side windows and cupping his hands over his eyes against the glass. "Oooh, they are doing naughty things in here!"

What's going on hits me like a freight-train, and I run over to Sam and grab him by his elbow. I drag him back to the patio and sternly say at his drooping head, "Come with me, Sam. That's not a nice thing to see for a young man like you."

Clara takes Sam's hand. I'm embarrassed for Sam as well as for Clara, but I'm also extremely angry, so I yell at Clara as if my explanation will mitigate this bizarre situation. "These bloody over-sexed druggies! I thought this prick had left this place but the stupid addict is back again and scoring a bonk from some dumb, rehabilitating schoolgirl!"

I'm back at the Porsche. I bash the window with a closed fist. "Hey! You in there! What's going on? Are you in trouble or something?"

Clara and Sam giggle behind me. I continue to bang on the window but the mist is coming from the inside and I can't see anything.

There's a firm hand on my shoulder and it tears me away from the window. "I will deal with this! Get going!" It's Sister Bertha and I allow her to frogmarch me back to Nora and Sam, who each take a shoulder to finish the man-handling, and walk me into the Tea Room. Now I really feel like a bloody loony and I flop against the happy lady and the man-child.

Clara is full of authority, but her joy-factor hasn't left her. "Don't worry, hon, the nurse is right. You don't want to get involved in that."

Sam hangs onto her, but she seems happy with his clinging and cradles his shoulders. "Thanks for helping out, Clara, but I'm not a lunatic like all of these people, at least not yet."

"Don't be so serious, hon! This is so bloody funny I could die! Have a laugh!"

Sam is quick on the uptake and chants, "Have a laugh! Have a laugh!"

I'm the schoolgirl who's not allowed to disturb the class but just can't help herself. My guts explode. I fall to my knees on the brown carpet and laugh and laugh and laugh. I don't give a shit if I'm sent out of the classroom again or if I get expelled from school for good. I know I'm out of control, but where the hell are my laughter tears? I dig my fists into my eyes in the hope that by pressing my eyeballs into their sockets, some liquid will escape. I don't care if it's blood that comes out. I don't care about anything. I just want to laugh with laughter tears until I'm expelled by the headmaster.

I think a long time has passed because all is quiet and I'm no longer laughing. I see black sparks behind my eyes so I remove my fists from them and try to make out my company through the haze. Clara and Sam are standing above me like two statues. I find it comical that they are at a loss for words and I'm slightly disappointed that Sam hasn't joined me on the floor.

My voice is high-pitched and not my own. "Don't be so serious, the two of you! This is so bloody funny I could die! Have a laugh!"

But all I get are two pairs of big eyes on me: one pair blue and saintly and the other brown and terrified. Clara's arms reach for me. "Up you get, hon. Let's have some lunch, shall we?"

"Oooh, can I have lunch with you? I'm hungry." Sam has recovered and this is reassuring.

My cellphone in my jeans' pocket presses against my bum. I hope it cracks in half. I wipe my face and heave myself off the floor and into Clara's arms. She seems back to her happy self again and says with an enormous smile, "Of course you can, Sam. I'm so glad you're hungry, because I've made lots of sandwiches."

I would rather stay on the carpet with my fists in my eye-sockets and my phone stuck up my bum than face putting something into my stomach. My FreeCell is calling me. I've become familiar with Clara's big rectangular Tupperware and I anticipate the smell of egg mayonnaise sandwiches with chopped lettuce sprinkled over the tiny triangles. The ones she offered me while I sat stupefied on the shitty-couch.

She busies herself with preparing our picnic. Even though we're in the brown-clad Tea Room, she throws a blanket onto the floor, and positions small cups, plates and serviettes on it like a bloody teddy bears' picnic. The smell of egg fills the air and I sit next to Sam on the carpet while we smoke cigarettes. I couldn't care less if we're not meant to smoke in here, because I'm slightly out of body and, if we're caught at it, I'm sure to lift myself out of here mentally or start laughing again like a loony. I surely deserve a little loony-leeway and couldn't give a shit anymore.

Sam is in teddy-bear heaven and devours sandwiches like he hasn't eaten in ages. Clara is smiling and pouring juice into wobbly plastic cups. I make a good attempt at swallowing doughy lumps of bread and egg.

This joyous little scene is interrupted by the harsh screech of my cellphone ringing. I answer it automatically and say, while spitting egg onto the phone, "Pronto?"

"It's your brother. Where the fuck are you and what's going on? Mommy's been calling you and you're not answering your phone. She wants to call the police."

I cough up egg and laugh into his ear. I'm feeling very naughty. I want to shock the socks off my brother's steadfast feet, so I say through my laughter, "Oh! Didn't you know? I've been admitted to a lunatic asylum."

"Fuck! What the hell? I thought you were in hospital?"

"Oh, I was for a while, but then I tried to commit suicide by jumping out of the window, so they kicked me out and sent me here. Isn't that a laugh?" I'm not going to say that I *didn't* jump out of the window. I wink at Sam and Clara, who also laugh because the three of us are too far gone to be serious now.

"Fuck! Are you alright? Shit! This is serious!"

"Ja, you're telling me! Now you know why your sister has been behaving strangely all your life. I'm just another loony, and now I'm here where I be-long."

Sam and Clara are now laughing very loudly and my brother is in my ear, "Fuck! Who the hell is there with you?"

"Oh, it's just Sam, here, speak to him." I shove the cellphone into Sam's eager hand and expect his best performance.

It is surely forthcoming, because Sam's using his high-pitched voice as he speaks into the cellphone, "Hello, Lamby's brother! I'm Samuel, Samuel Krishna!"

*This is delightful!*

My brother is a big business man, like Stef, and I picture him at his desk perusing a multi-million-rand contract.

"I have a rock band," Sam says. "It's called the Grooving Krishnas. Do you want to hear me sing?"

I think I hear my brother say, "Sure," but I can't be certain. There's no stopping Sam now, because he's singing his mantra into the phone.

I leave him singing into my brother's ear for a long time, but grab him when he starts to dance out of the Tea Room with my phone. I say loudly close to the phone, "That's enough now, Samuel. Thank you very much! You can sit down now and finish your picnic like a good teddy bear."

I eagerly press the phone against my ear, "Hello?" I doubt my brother is still on the phone.

"Fuck! Call Mommy!"

# MOM VISITS IN THE RAIN

My medication has been doled out an hour earlier this afternoon and I wonder if it's because the clinic is short-staffed on a Sunday, or whether Sister Bertha is afraid I lost my marbles at the Porsche window and needs to give me my drugs earlier. I've taken my normal dose, and the top-up, to get me up to my benchmark drug level. I try to convince myself that the stuff will start to work soon and make me feel better, because that's what it's meant to do. I have noticed however that my skin is smoother. Maybe I'm not frowning as much as I normally do.

I'm contemplating the power of head-medication as I lie on my bed engrossed in FreeCell. My cellphone rings, and the laptop mouse slides off the tea tray. I quickly grab the phone so as not to disturb Nora, who's been out walking most of the afternoon and is fast asleep. Her snores are softer and I'm pleased.

"Hello."

"Finally! I'm on my way to see you." It's my mom.

"OK."

The phone's gone dead and, in a funny way, I'm glad she's coming. Even though I will be obliged to tell her all the terrible stuff that's happened to me, she's still my mommy and I need her.

A hundred games of FreeCell have helped me to focus. In spite of the recent fanatical events of analysing Ben's manslaughter, Clara's teddy bears' picnic, Nora's blue eye-shadow, Sam's singing to my brother on the phone, and the bonking-druggies, I have my pull-yourself-together blanket securely around my shoulders, with my head balanced very nicely on top of them. I'm ready for my mother.

It's started raining again. There's a fine sheet of drizzle in front of the face-brick behind the bedroom window. I can hardly see it because no light can make its way into the narrow crevice between the buildings, and all I can think of is the poor design of the thing and whether the rain is getting into the substructure. I'm thinking about the principles of my engineering degree on water-proofing, when in walks Xhosa-nurse.

"Your mama is here. She is waiting in the car. She wants you to go to her. She does not have the umbrella and she says she will stay only for a short time."

*Shit!*

I've been playing FreeCell at the same time as pondering the fate of the building. I must be getting good at it because I can now play it without thinking. But my mother is waiting for me in her truck and I need to go to her quickly.

I must look like hell, but there's no time even for a pee. I dash out of Reception and into the pouring rain towards the parking lot and my mother's truck.

She's had her little 1.4 litre truck since I can remember, even though my father drives a smart 4×4. I hear her saying as she always does, "I love my bakkie. It still goes like hell and I'll never get rid of it." I used to ask her to park far away when she collected me from school because I would have been mortified if any of my friends had seen us drive off in such a wreck. She would park out of sight without a word of complaint. I think of my "Pilly". For the first time I'm not embarrassed by her rusty little truck.

I crank open the door and the sight of her overwhelms me. She's sitting with her ciggy in hand and she looks sad. Her normally tanned face is white and there are pockets under her eyes. She doesn't appear happy to see me and gives me a scolding look. I feel guilty because she must be mad at me and I know she's been worried, but she's allowing me to explain myself by coming here in the pouring rain on a shitty Sunday afternoon.

I edge in beside her on the bench seat and slam the door twice until it closes. I light a cigarette and we both sit here smoking and saying nothing as the windows fog up. We have this ciggy-camaraderie between us. I remember her saying, when I started smoking, "Great, now we can smoke together!"

I'm pleased she hasn't told me to pull myself together or scolded me about abandoning my kids. I'm pleased for the silence, and her presence.

She extinguishes her cigarette in the truck's ashtray and, as she blows the last smoke from her lungs, says in an authoritative voice, "I'm not at all happy about all of this! I am very upset that I've been left out of the picture. I've been calling Stef, but he hasn't returned my calls. I am your mother and you should have called me. I am worried about the children. For goodness' sake, you could have called me!"

I start to talk in my whiny dealing-with-Mom voice. "I know, Mom. I'm a big shit. But I feel so bloody crap that I just don't want to talk. I don't need to be criticised right now and ... I'm sick to death of hearing you telling me to pull myself together."

I have *never* talked to my mother like this, but I can't stop myself, because I'm stuck here inside with her in the pouring rain outside a lunatic asylum.

"I just can't talk to you now, Mom."

I watch her intently as she lights another cigarette. No-one can light a cigarette like my Mom. She puts her head up and smokes like one of those Victorian ladies. "Oh, for goodness' sake, you know you can always talk to me," she says as she delicately puffs through poised fingers.

"But, Mom!" I'm whining again and I hate my voice when I talk to her, but I can't help myself. "I can't talk to you because I'm a stupid, weak cow and I think that I always have been. I will never be as strong as you and that's that."

She has always told me that I'm different because I'm strong, and that I should hold my head up high at school and university, because holding my head up would put me above the rest of the rabble. And I surely have held my head up. I've been called an aloof snob too many times.

I wait for her lecture, but she doesn't give it. All she says is, "I'm not that strong, you know."

"Oh?" is all I can manage, because she *is* strong and I need her to be.

"No, I'm not that strong at all. I've had to be strong because my life was up to shit and if I hadn't been strong, I wouldn't have survived."

I remember a wrinkled black-and-white photograph of her as a little schoolgirl with her two little plaits looped under, like Heidi's. Memories of stories about her youth make me shudder through the smoke.

My four-year-old mom looks at me from the black-and-white photograph. She has been chucked into a convent boarding school because her parents are getting divorced. Her father doesn't care about her and is probably pleased to see the last of her, so that he can have his life back again and chase women at will. Her mother will become an alcoholic and will continue drinking and mourning her husband until the alcohol finally kills her.

The little girl's mother is a Sagittarian like I am. But my mom, who's a Leo, proves her strength when she finally leaves the convent at eighteen to drag her mother off the streets of Johannesburg when the police call to tell her that her mother is lying drunk on the pavement once again.

I picture her sitting on her little bed in a row of many on her first night at the convent. She visits her grandmother on weekends, but her granny is soon to die, leaving her to spend her weekends and holidays stuck in the convent.

I'm sad for my mom's sad life, but I can't help myself blurting out, "Mom, I know you've had a shitty life, but that doesn't really help me, because all your shitty life did was make you unable to nurture properly."

*I can't believe I've just said this!*

I'm sounding like a stupid shrink in the movies and I hate my voice as it regurgitates this stupid psycho-babble.

"I don't like what you're saying! I have been a very good mother to you."

I don't want to talk about this anymore, because we will get ourselves into a terrible catch-22 situation where we will be saying the same things over and over again until I fall out of her truck and we're not on speaking terms.

So I try to end the circle by saying, "You have been a good mother, but we're not much of a physical family and never hug one another."

This is a mistake. "But your father's family wasn't either," she says. "I didn't have a family to speak about ..."

This has got to stop, so I put my head into my hands and whine, "OK, OK, OK. I don't want to talk about this anymore. I feel so crap I could die anyway, so why bother!"

She's resolute in spite of my childish antics. "Don't say such a silly thing! What's the matter with you anyway? I can't read hieroglyphics!"

I keep my face buried in my hands because I don't want to look her in the face, and I say into my palms, "I dunno what the matter is. I just want to die."

"Well, you've had a terrible shock because of the fire—"

"No, it's not that!" I look through the misty window.

"Then what *is* it, for God's sake?"

"I don't know!"

We both light cigarettes again. We both don't care that the cab is filled with smoke and that we can hardly breathe. But I've been asked a question and it's spinning around my fuzzy head. "I dunno. I dunno, because I've been thinking a lot about *me* for the first time in my life, and I think that I've wanted to die since I was a child."

My mother doesn't scold me, so I continue. "I think that I wanted to die because I used to think about ways of killing myself when I lay in my bed counting the pink roses on my wallpaper. All I remember about my past is feeling sad. As I'm saying this to you, I really *am* thinking about it for the first time."

"Well, what could I do? You used to lock yourself in your bedroom all the time and you never wanted to see anyone."

I forgot about locking my door. "But, Mom, doesn't that tell you something?"

"You were a moody child and that was that. Anyway, it was the sixties, and there was none of all this modern rubbish about psychology and stuff."

"But, Mom, isn't it a bit strange for a little girl to have behaved like that?"

"I couldn't do anything about it. You were a strong-willed little girl and we couldn't get near you because you always locked yourself in your room."

"But, Mom, you were the adult and I was the child."

"I don't know what you're trying to say."

I repeat the sentence very slowly. "You were the *adult* and I was the *child*."

"I was a very good mother to you."

We're getting into an even bigger never-ending story. I want to lie on her lap and have her tickle my back, like she used to. She *is* a good mom. Maybe I'm being a brat and making excuses for my stupid self. All I know is that I have been so bloody anxious and sad all my life. When I have tried to think of the reason for this, I can't come up with anything. Nothing bad has happened to me!

I always tell people that I've led a charmed life and I'm indeed a lucky girl. But terror grips me because, more than the ghost and failure, I fear happiness. Just when my life began to be beautiful again, disaster struck, like it always does when happiness is coming. I was the happy housewife who had just refurbished her kitchen and re-thatched the roof. I was the happy housewife who had the best husband and children and was the envy of her friends. My life was a bloody symphony. But then the anti-happiness devil struck again and this time he burnt my house down.

I shake off the soot and I'm back with my mom. "I know you were a good mom. But I think I was born with a problem, because nothing bad happened to me when I was small and I have no excuses."

I can't talk anymore so I lean towards her over the creaking seat and hold onto her. We don't cry, each for our own reasons.

"I think you need to try and let the doctors help you, and I think you probably need to take something to make you feel better," she says into my wet hair.

188

I'm still holding onto her. I start to feel uncomfortable, and a little embarrassed. I think she does too, because we pull away from each other at the same time. I pull my tracksuit jacket closed and zip it up until the teeth pinch my throat. She sits upright and poises a ciggy between her Victorian fingers.

"OK, Mom. I'll try. Shit! I think you need to write a book about your life. It would be a bloody good story. Maybe I'll write it for you one day."

"I think so too."

We both manage a laugh as I wrench open the rusty door and stumble out of the smoke and into the dark drizzle.

# LOSS OF A DAUGHTER

I wake up playing FreeCell. I'm amazed because I think I've been playing entire games from start to finish in my sleep. I see the cards and remember the order of them with my eyes closed. This is a little frightening but it's a damn sight better waking up in the middle of a card game than waking up on a guillotine.

But the dream-game is over and the cards scatter over my pillow. I'm left alone with a head without cards and too much time to think. I concentrate on the timing between Nora's snores as I stare at the wall above her bed.

Something is niggling at me. I know I wanted to tell my mother something very important as we sat in her truck last night. I hate forgetting things. I always forget the most important thing, because it's probably the most serious. I chew my finger in the hope that the nibbling will help me remember.

I turn my cellphone on and dial my mom. I need to talk quickly because I don't want to touch on yesterday's conversation. I need to say what I have to say fast and efficiently.

My mom clearly doesn't want to go there either because she says in her sleepy voice, "I'm still in bed." I picture her in her bed with all her little dachshunds sleeping around her and under the blankets. I can hear her lighting her first cigarette as she says, "It was nice to see you … finally."

I'm quick to the chase. "Listen, Mom, I forgot to tell you something important yesterday."

"Hmmm?"

"I don't want you to tell Dad anything about me right now. I don't want you to tell him I'm in a loony-bin." The thought of my father visiting me here makes me nauseous.

"Oh? But I've already told him."

*Oh, God. No!*

"Shit, Mom! Why did you do that? What the hell did you tell him?"

"I told him that you were under strain and in a hospital and that I thought he should come and see you."

*Over my dead body!*

"Listen to me, Mom! I don't want Daddy to see me here! Do you under-stand?"

"I don't know what you're on about. He's your father, for heaven's sake!"

"I'm not denying that, Mom, but can't you understand why I don't want him to see me here?"

She clearly doesn't, because she says, "OK, I'll tell him you don't want to see him."

*Dammit!*

"No! That's not what I mean, Mom. Don't tell him that! What I'm trying to say is …" I feel like shaking my mother through the phone line, or kick-ing one of her dachshunds off the bed! "… that I don't want *him* to see *me* here, and not that *I* don't want to see *him*! It's the other way around! Don't you get it?"

The acid begins to creep into my chest because I know I'm nearing one of those mother–daughter fights and this time I don't think I have the capacity to call her back to apologise. She's heading for that fight, because she sternly says, "I think you're being a silly girl! I'll tell him not to come. But I still think you're being a silly girl!"

She's definitely going to tell him that I don't want to see him, because I've probably confused her, but I've done my best and now I need to concentrate on a very difficult game of FreeCell, so I say, "Thanks. They're calling me to breakfast. Love you. Bye."

I'm left to the difficult game and the even more difficult image of my father being here and seeing me so weak. So I edge up the difficulty level and throw myself at a very juicy game of FreeCell.


There's activity in the air affecting my concentration. Doors are banging and I can hear the mutterings of disgruntled nurses from behind our bedroom door. I know very well by now that activities in the Activity Centre take place between eight and ten in the morning. I have refused to throw paint around with the druggies.

As far as the rest of the schedule is concerned, I might have breakfast if Nora wants to join me, and I will most definitely attend my session with Cra-nium at ten-thirty. I have a lot more complaining to do about the noise and dust of the construction work and I have a new complaint I wish to air about the bonking-druggies.

I'm startled by Xhosa-nurse, who's in my face with the mouse-cup and the muti. "The doctor says you must go to the painting in the Activity, please."

I swallow my poison with a determined quaff. "Mama," I respond in her accent, "I am not a nana. I am not the baby. I am not going to play like a child! *You* can go to play with the children!"

She explodes with laughter. "Eish!"

I love her for her sense of humour and add, "You can tell the masipa sangoma that I'm very tired and I have to take care of the magogo, Nora!"

Her eyes widen at the word "sangoma". I'm sure she thinks Cranium is one. She leaves with her tray and her laughter and I get to the business of getting Nora up and washed and ready for walkies, so that I have an excuse not to finger-paint.

Nora is in excellent spirits. We've slurped our yogurts in the dining room like normal people and are waddling along on the yellow grass picking weeds. I feel like I'm the same age as she, because my body is still moving slowly. One of the tiny tablets is to blame for sure, but I'm comforted by my resolve that, as soon as I'm out of here, I will wean myself off the crap and get back my lively step. But for now, the two of us are walking along step by step like two old codgers, and this suits me fine.

As we approach the end of the death-chamber, I notice a woman at a parked car struggling to lift a wheelchair from the boot.

*Shit! I know this woman!*

I leave Nora's side and walk over to help her. I feel I'm in some bizarre dream where the faces of people from your past are willed into your vision for no reason. You haven't seen them in a hundred years and if someone mentions their name, you don't remember them, but the dream brings them back. Or maybe I've still got the electricity thing around me and events, like the coincidental car crash, are willing themselves into my energised space.

"Sarah? Is that you?" She lifts her eyes from a spinning wheel of the wheelchair, but they're not the eyes I remember. Sarah was a friend from school and was always so cheery under her blonde bob. She still has the bob, but her usual bright eyes are empty pools.

"Oh, hello," she says without emotion.

I'm not about to chit-chat in the face of her cold demeanour, so I get busy helping her contort the chair from the tiny boot. I leave her to shut the boot as I wheel the chair down the concrete slope towards the wing at the end of the death-chamber.

192

I stop at the sliding doors to wait for her, but I can't stop my tongue from wagging. "It's been so long since I've seen you. What are you doing here?"

She doesn't look at me as she takes the handles from me. "My daughter is here. She was involved in a car accident. Her head was damaged. She can't remember her name."

She's doing the as-if-a-recording thing that people do when they have to tell other people about something bad that happened to them, and my heart breaks for her but, as usual, all I can manage is, "What a stuff-up."

I've said it very quietly and with a lot of emotion, but she seems peeved by my comment because she nods her head at the sliding doors and is gone without further ado.

I stand here dumbstruck. Nora is with me and she takes my arm as though I'm the older ducky. She must have overheard the conversation because she says, "There's nothing in the world like a mother's suffering over the injury or loss of a child. Come on, dear, let's get back to base."

As we leave, I gently grip Nora's frail arm on one side and pinch my thigh as hard as I can on the other.

# BAD SESSION WITH CRANIUM

I'm still pinching my thigh in the hope of a big bruise as a physical reminder of how lucky I am that I'm not Sarah. As Nora and I pass the top section of the clinic, I see Cranium's queue. I need to be there.

I know the answer before I ask, "Are you coming to see the doctor, Nora?"

"Goodness gracious! I'm old enough to be his mother." That says it all.

I giggle and nudge her arm for more of her chatter while we edge our way towards our parting at the queue.

She is giving me more because she says, "He tried to analyse me when I got here, but I told him that I was far too old, and if he found anything wrong with my mind, it would be far too difficult to remedy because it's so old that it's probably set in stone like a fossil. I told him that he would probably need a geologist's pick to get at it and I was certainly in no mood to have him try, especially because I had just lost Bernard."

I grip her a little more tightly against my breast. "Shame, dear."

I feel her shake her bony shoulders as she says, "I did actually tell him that I was old enough to be his mother."

She hasn't mentioned his eye and I respect that. She's a gracious lady. "Good on you, Nora! You could probably teach some of these shrinks a thing or two."

She giggles, and I continue, "In fact, maybe patients should get a prospective shrink to answer a questionnaire with questions like: 'How many crappy things have happened to you in your life? And, if so, please specify.' And, 'What have you gleaned from these experiences and how do you think they help in helping others?'"

We're having such a good laugh that I've forgotten about my queue. "Oops, I'm going to be late! I'll see you later." I kiss her on her velvet cheek.

As I jog up the stairs to secure my place in the queue, I think of Tulula. Maybe Babs was right when she said she relied on her as a psychologist because she'd gone through the hell of divorce. I would only ask a shrink one question before I allowed her to dissect my head, and that is: "Do you shop a lot?" Her answer would lead me to a myriad of other questions like: "Do you need the stuff you buy?", "Do you think you're materialistic?" etcetera, and I'll have her wrapped up in no time. I quickly dispel the urge to ask Cranium these questions because I'm sure he won't think it amusing and will probably keep me here forever.

I find Ben and Sam standing together near the front of the queue. Because I couldn't give a shit about the druggies, I push in front of a few of them and edge towards my friends. I take Ben's hand and say, "Ben was keeping my place."

Calvin Klein is the one who has to let me in and he says, "Give me a cigarette and I'll let you in!"

"I beg your pardon, young man? Who the hell do you think you are?" I'm talking to him like Nora would, but he's probably around my age, so I feel stupid as I say it.

"Fuck off, bitch!"

*Huh!*

I'm scared because now he's got his face in mine and I can smell his aftershave. I edge closer to Ben. "Oooh! Be careful Lamby! He'll hit you like he always hits me," Sam says.

But even though man-child has tried to help, Ben's my real man, and he grabs Calvin Klein by the balls. I can't believe what I'm witnessing, but I'm secretly thrilled. I pretend I'm an actress in a movie and that this is happening on screen. I back off and clutch onto Sam as Ben keeps his grip on Calvin Klein's crotch.

I'm waiting for a strong reaction from him, but there is none. He's just sinking lower and lower towards the concrete floor with his face in a baby-scowl.

Ben's voice is strong, "You don't talk to her like that! Now, apologise to her and get to the back of the queue!"

"OK, OK, OK. Lay off. Sorry, OK?" He scuttles to the back of the queue cradling his crotch and I'm sure I hear him say, "Bitch," over Sam's hysterical giggling.

"Thanks, Ben."

I'm not going to tell Ben that he was being far too aggressive. Nothing like this has ever happened to me other than the time Stef gripped the neck of a biker-boy because he burped sitting next to us at the movies.

Things have happened very fast, and Ben, Sam and I lean against the wall breathing heavily through our newly lit cigarettes. I feel close to them because we are the *true* head-cases.

The queue in front of us is getting shorter by the number of times faceless-nurse is calling out, "Next!" and Sam starts to fidget again.

"What's the matter, Sam?" I say.

"I dunno. Every time I go in there, I don't know what to say to the doctor. Oh, Lamby, tell me what to do."

"I'm sure you know what to say to the doctor by now."

"It's always the same. He always asks the same thing and I always say the same thing. Please help me. I love you, Lamby. Please come in there with me."

I don't want to ask Sam what they talk about, because I truly don't want to know what's wrong with him. But he's said he loves me and I think I love him too, so I say, "OK, I can't come in with you because I'm not allowed to, but I'll try to help you."

"Oh, goody!"

Ben is standing in our little circle, but he doesn't help me out this time. Suddenly I get that devil-may-care attitude again. "OK, Sam. I think that because you've said everything you need to say to the doctor and because he's said everything he needs to say to you …" Sam looks confused, so I stop elaborating and say, "I think that you should sing him your Krishna song."

He's delighted, because he's jumping around chanting, "I'm going to sing for the doctor! I'm going to sing for the doctor!"

I hear someone at the back of the queue saying, "Shut up, you fool!" but I don't care, because Sam has his task set, and he's no longer anxious about seeing Cranium.

"I think you should also do your dance while you sing. What do you think, Ben?"

"Fuckin-aye, Sam-the-Man. If you do that, I'll give you a packet of cigarettes."

"Oh, goody!"

"Samuel, will you come in now." It's faceless-nurse and Sam is gone as the door slams in front of us. Ben and I put our heads together and press our ears under the sign that reads "Headmaster's Office".

Sam's singing is like music to my ears. But Ben and I can't keep our ears pressed to the door any longer because we're buckling down and laughing. We hang onto each other and try to laugh silently, but I feel I could explode and I sense Ben could too.

We haven't got time to explode, because the door is wrenched open and faceless-nurse is above us holding Sam by his elbow. He buckles down to our level and Ben grips him in a bear-hug. Sam isn't laughing, but is content to be with us on the floor.

I hear a loud and clear voice above our madness, "You can come in now!"

Ben trips forward, still holding onto his stomach because I'm sure his stitches have split open. He's in front of me and it's his turn to go in, but a strong arm reaches from behind him and grabs my shoulder. "The doctor wants to see *you* now!"

*Oh, shit! I'm done for!*

Both of Cranium's eyes are steely in his long head. I'm still hopeful that Sam hasn't told him who made him sing and dance in his session, but my hopes are dashed when he says, "It's a very serious offence to tamper with patients' sessions, especially Samuel's, because he has a very serious condition and we are in the middle of very serious therapy. You are jeopardising the length of time I have to keep him here."

But he's made me feel sorry. I feel like the schoolgirl who's made a teacher cry and when you look at it from her side, you actually feel pretty crappy for what you've done. I would rather die than lengthen Sam's time here.

"And because you've jeopardised Samuel, I am going to be extra vigilant when it comes to your assessment."

*Shit!*

"I'm sorry."

He grunts. "I hear you've not attended any sessions in the Activity Centre. We take it very seriously when a patient refuses to attend. As soon as you start cooperating, things will be different for you."

I picture myself ducking paint as the druggies flick it around the Activity Centre. "Look, I'm sorry about Sam, but I don't need any help. I'm fine. I don't need any bloody help from anyone, especially if it's helping me to hold a paintbrush like a child."

"I will see you the day after tomorrow, and I trust you will have attended the sessions by then."

I get up to go because there's nothing more to say. Faceless-nurse drags me to the exit door with a, "Next please!" Ben trips past me and there's blood on his white T-shirt under the open zip of his jacket. "Are you OK, Ben? Your stomach's bleeding again!" It must've been from laughing.

He grimaces as the nurse pushes him past me towards the door. "I'm OK, I'll live. Are you OK?"

"No! I've just got my head chopped off because Sam told him who set him up. Plus I have to go and finger-paint this afternoon. Promise you'll come?" I'm whining like Sam but I don't care.

He turns his head back at me as he's marched through the door and says, "Of course I'll come with you. I dig art!"

# PSYCHO ART

There's a sign-in book on a school desk of the Gym Room that is the dreaded makeshift Activity Centre. Ben is in front of me and eagerly ticks the block next to his name on a spreadsheet headed "Activity Attendance". He gives me the pen and I notice that my own name is listed in the column perpendicular to date headers with a lot of red crosses against it. I wonder how Sam is able to fill in this Excel spreadsheet, because it's not very clear, so I spend some time bending over the book and mentally fixing the format.

I love spreadsheets. I've written so many programs that I want to sit here and redo the clumsy thing. This would be far more stimulating than painting stick-men on poor-quality paper that bubbles when the paint dries. I'm proud of being a mathematician, not a hippy artist. I groove on any stuff that has to do with maths.

In spite of my misgivings about the ability of loonies and druggies in the arts, I notice a lot of good paintings on the walls. I can't take my eyes off the paintings.

*I'm under the tree outside the Engineering faculty at university. I'm eating an apple and smoking alone as usual as I swot the summary notes I've made for the pending exam on Metallurgy.*

*I'm annoyed by my construction family because it's their fault that I was goaded into this tiresome degree. The course is so bloody difficult and the lectures last till nightfall. But I have to finish my degree and get a job.*

*I sigh through my nervousness over the pending exam and force myself to find some joy in the thing I love most about my studies. So I envelop myself in my tutorial on a Fortran problem and mentally type out the MS Dos language in green font on the dull screen: "Go to", and "If cell X is greater than or equal to cell Y, write:" and "Generate random number".*

*I think I've determined the volume of soil to be moved and re-used in levelling a building-site using the theory of vectors when a bunch of Fine Arts students in cool hippie clothes meander past me laughing and chatting. They are surely going to have a lovely afternoon engrossed in a delicious art project on the "Marvels of the Modern Picasso", while I will be stuck here doing science laboratory work until it's dark. I remember the career counsellor saying he'd analysed my profile and that I'm a difficult case indeed because I'm leaning towards the arts, but the mathematical side of my brain is strong. "Good luck in your career decision," he said. "Thanks a lot, you fool. Now, what the hell do I do?" But I don't have a choice in the matter. I fulfil my father's life-script for me and enter the Sciences.*

*I feel like a complete nerd and wonder what the Arts kids must think of me, because my only stature at the university grounds is stuck to a ticker-tape machine in the science laboratory, or stuck to the scope of a theodolite on the rugby-field. I also stick out like a sore thumb because I'm one of few girls studying Quantity Surveying. But I block out all desire to be one of the Arts students, and concentrate on getting the best marks for Metallurgy.*

Someone squeezes my bum and says over my shoulder, "Hey! Sign the stupid thing! Let's get a table together before they're all filled."

It's Ben. I've been standing with pen poised over the stupid sign-in form and thinking about my compulsory aversion to the arts. Maybe my unwillingness to attend these "arty" sessions has something to do with it? I don't know. But fooling around with paint with a bunch of idiots is definitely not my thing, regardless.

There's newspaper on the desks which are arranged in rows, like in a classroom. Ben, Sam and I rush around like school kids and find three desks next to each other. There's a lot of scrambling going on as the druggies push each other around trying to find desks next to preferred friends, like we have done. Sam is giggling and activity-nurse is slapping his hands as he tries to open the little bottles of paint that have been placed on our desks.

In front of us are rectangular pieces of glass, which I'm certain are secondhand windowpanes. I feel that I'm about to start an exam because activity-nurse says, "Right! You have your paints, you have your brushes, and you have your media to work on. Get to it!"

*Now what?*

I must be the only one who hasn't swotted for the exam, because there's silence as everyone gets busy with opening bottles and testing paintbrushes. Sam's got his tongue stuck out and he's concentrating on pouring different colours into a lid and mixing them together. Ben's leather jacket is squeaking and he's bending over his desk intently.

I open the bottle of black paint and select the thinnest paintbrush.

200

Time has slipped by without me because I'm sitting next to Sam and Ben on the edge of the concrete walkway with our finished works on the grass in front of us. We have managed to sneak them out of the Activity Centre, despite the strict instruction from activity-nurse that they are to remain the property of the clinic until discharge. God only knows what they want to do with them. Maybe Cranium is going to analyse them and decide on our state of mind by how much black paint we have used, and if we've suggested lunacy in our compositions.

Nora waddles up to us and stands behind us on the concrete. I'm pleased to see she's out and about. Ben fetches her a chair and places it next to me. The four of us are together in the sunshine as the paint dries on the glass.

"These are lovely, dears," says Nora. "Maybe I'll join you next time. I used to be quite good, you know. Bernard had my paintings framed. It's a pity I don't have them anymore. My daughter had the Red Cross collect everything from my home when she sent me here."

I hate her daughter even more, and I place my hand over Nora's.

I pick up Sam's glass-painting and hold it up to the sun. He's smudged the glass with greasy fingers already, but what he's produced is amazing. He's managed to blend the three primary colours of paint we were given into a psychedelic image of an electric guitar. He's produced the exact shape of the thing. Secondary colours shade outwards from the primary shape of the guitar so that it appears to be raised from the surface of the glass. I wonder what there is to analyse in this creation, because there's nothing abnormal about it.

"That's awesome, Sam! You're a good artist." I must have pleased him, because he's panting.

Ben's picture disturbs me. He's covered the glass with black paint and pressed his face onto it. He's stuck a piece of string in the wet paint which has now dried, and secured it in place like a noose around the base of his face shape.

It's Nora who scrutinises Ben's picture for the longest and says, "Oh, my goodness, this is a little sad, dear."

Ben laughs. "Tell me about it! But I think it looks quite cool."

I nudge Ben with my elbow as if to say, "Don't tell Nora that it's you on the glass." But he doesn't and I'm relieved. I wonder if Cranium will work it out, because Ben doesn't need any more time here than I do. He needs to get back to his big order for air-conditioning units, and find a nice girl he can talk to.

"Your picture is quite nice, dear." Nora's looking at mine now and I'm unconvinced by her criticism. I'm embarrassed because it's crap.

"Oh, it's really boring compared to the others."

I've painted a lake scene in black with a row of trees at the bank reflected in the water. I've made sure that each tree-shape is directly mirrored in its reflection in the water. It makes me even sadder to look at than Ben's, and I hate it so much that I want to smash the stupid piece of glass on the concrete floor. I think that the others feel the same, because no-one else has made any comment, other than Nora, who's being polite.

Ben holds his piece of glass up to the sun. "Why the hell do we have to leave these pictures here?"

I gaze at the impression of him hanging by the neck. "Maybe it's because the doctor wants to analyse them so he can decide how sick in the head we are and how long he needs to keep us here?"

A funny memory comes to mind and I say, "Stef went to a convent boarding school and got up to all sorts of nonsense because he hated the school and the nuns and the beatings, so he was sent to see the school psychologist. It's funny that they had a psychologist in a convent, because we never had one in our public school and just had to take the smacks on the knuckles, while the boys got cuts – hidings on bare bums, with a whip."

I feel stupid explaining this. But I remember my red knuckles and wanting more of the beatings to have something tangible to hate my teachers more.

I return to my story. "Stef's school was in Europe and maybe they were a little more advanced in psychology-crap than schools in South Africa." The three of them are looking at me intently. "Anyway, he was sent to this school psychologist-woman who made him draw some pictures on a piece of paper. So he thought, 'Bugger this!' and drew a nun with an axe in her head."

I'm treading on dangerous ground, but what the hell. We are in a loony-bin and there's no denying it, and anyway, I can't keep myself from my usual attempts at shock value.

But it's Nora who says, "And then what happened to him, dear?"

"He got expelled. All because he was full of shit and knew that a drawing like that would not be tolerated. Anyway, he was eyeing a school closer to his friends in Paris, which was one of the few that would accept him." I'm sure I've been talking too fast for Sam, because he's staring at Ben's picture and rocking backwards and forwards.

Ben laughs and says, "Sounds like my kind of man!"

"Me too!" Sam seems to have left the mystery of the hanging man and is back in the conversation. "I also paint things that make my mom cross."

We all look at him. "Ja, I once painted a guitar high up on the front of my parents' house when they weren't home. I nearly fell off the ladder, but then I had to hang onto the window until my parents called the fire engine to come and get me. But I had already finished my painting, so I didn't mind waiting for them to get me down. And also it was too difficult for my mom to climb up and give me a hiding. But the fireman told me it was the biggest guitar he had ever seen and then the newspaper man came and he took a photograph of my painting. But then my dad called a policeman to stop him putting it in his newspaper ..."

This is the longest conversation I've heard from Sam without him breaking into song and getting agitated. But Ben cuts him short. "Oh, crap, Sam! That's a big lie! Stop fibbing!"

"I'm not fibbing! I promise you! It was the biggest, coolest guitar in the world. My Mom had the wall painted over the next day. You believe me, don't you, Lamby?"

"Sure I do, Sam. I believe anything you say."

"Thank you, Lamby. I love you more than Krishna."

I'm trying to work out if he means he or Krishna loves me more when Ben huffs. Nora turns to him and says, "Believing my husband's stories was what made our marriage so good."

Sweet, simple advice. I'll remember it forever.

"I am going to paint another big picture when I get home," Sam says, "and then I'm going to invite the doctor to come and have a look at it. He'll know that I'm much better and won't make me come back here again."

"Like hell, you idiot, he'll have you shot!" It's Calvin Klein. Ben leaps up after him, but he's tripped down the stairs and is out of sight.

# OLD FRIEND

Dinner has been served in the top canteen without notice, but we've sent Sam on a sniffer-trail and he's found it. He, Ben, Nora and I are sitting at a table eating battered fish and chips from a buffet. The place feels like a hotel breakfast room and I feel like I'm dining in a normal environment and not in a makeshift sunroom at a shitty little table with dust in my teeth.

But my table guests are from a different world from mine, and I'm still surrounded by a lot of bombastic druggies who are making too much noise and seem to be sniggering at us. The four of us chat like old friends, but it's quite difficult to hold a decent conversation with them. I have to say "Oh, absolutely, dear" to Nora, and "Fuckin-aye" to Ben and "Stop eating with your mouth open" to Sam – all in different voices. Expressing my trapped artistic desires today in the Activity Centre has also exhausted me.

I gaze at my jelly and switch off from my friends, who seem content to babble over their battered fish. I miss Stef. He made an appearance at seven o'clock with a rose and a kiss on the head and left without acknowledging my loony-friends or the druggies. His night-time visits are like a dream, wherein the knight arrives on his horse to save you, but you're tied in chains. So he leaves you to the fiery nostrils of the dragon, while you watch the quarters of his steed gallop away. But then you wake up and you know you don't need anyone, because you are not a princess. You live in the real world, and you can only rely on yourself.

So here I am with my loonies in my own reality, staring at my jelly. Although my heart and head are not, the rest of me is fine. I am here and there's nothing I can do about it but move along in the general forward direction, and get on with it, as I usually do. There's always tomorrow to think about it.

"I love you guys! You are my bestest friends in the whole wide world! Please can you be my mother, Nora?" Sam is on his feet and is hugging Nora from behind her chair.

"Like hell she'll have you, you moron!"

This comes from one of the druggies sitting at the table next to us.

Sam winces like he's going to get a slap on the head, but Nora places her veined hand on his shoulder. Ben turns on the intruder like a viper. "Keep your cow-nose out of our business!"

She *has* a cow's nose because she's wearing a nose-ring, and there are more rings in her eyebrows. It's a girl-druggie and she's got the devil-may-care look down pat, just like the ones in the movies. Her hair is short and she's tied tufts of it into little bunches all over her head exposing her scalp in criss-crosses. She's not wearing make-up, but she's somehow managed to maintain the greyness under her eyes to tell the world that she's one cool and sassy drug-addict with complicated psychological issues.

People like this scare the hell out of me because the look suggests volatility. I will definitely keep out of this, so I peer down at my jelly and shift myself out of view behind Ben's leather jacket.

Girl-druggie proffers the typical intelligent retort, "Fuck you!"

I don't sense anyone else joining in the furore, because her own table guests seem quiet and unmoving, but Ben's not letting go. "Listen to me, chick," he says, "he has done nothing to you. His was born like this and there's nothing he can do about it, unlike you bastards who fuck up your own lives and those of the people around you. You all should be shot, which would save people like us a lot of time and money!"

Shit, this is a little harsh!

I worry what Sam must make of Ben's appraisal of his condition, but he's covering his ears and Nora is holding him. I feel sorry for the girl.

She's on her feet and shouts into Ben's face, "What the fuck do you know about me? What the fuck do you know about my fucking life?"

She bursts into tears and runs from the dining room shouting, "Fuck you! Fuck you all … and the horses you rode in on!"

It's quite an eloquent statement for a supposedly down-and-out druggie and now I find her interesting and want to hear more. But it's Sam who stands up and tries to get her back by shouting, "Sorry, lady! Sorry, lady!" Ben grabs him by the shoulder and pushes him back into his chair.

Nora closes the scene by saying, "Poor girl."

We don't say anything for a long time. I think we are all pondering the things that make people do what they do, and the things that push them over the edge and into a place like this. Even Sam is quiet. We sit silently around the scattered crockery. I know we don't sleep anyway, and the longer we remain in this dining room together, the longer we don't have to face the night alone.

Ben, Sam and I are quietly smoking our very necessary after-dinner cigarettes when our weird space is invaded by the very familiar presence of a man I haven't seen in years.

I'm shocked. He's an old friend whom I had completely forgotten. Even though I'm in a strange place and his presence is completely inopportune, his familiarity is welcome and delights me. We haven't seen one another in a long time because we had a difference of opinion. His wife was the reason for our fall-out. He divorced her. She is dead. I blamed him for the sadness that consumed her before she died and I hated him for it. She was my soulmate and I hers, and her passing nearly killed me.

It is as if she has guided him to me. Maybe this bloody place has brought something positive into my life. I suddenly feel at peace with him. I want to hug him and cry.

Thank heavens I can't cry, but I manage a good laugh over my false bravado. "What the hell are you doing here?" I couldn't care less how he's traced me here. He's here and that's all that counts. I expect a clever, witty answer from him because he's highly intelligent. He's also funny and I have missed how he made me laugh.

His answer is like honey. "Shit, kid, I heard you were in a hospital, but this takes the cake."

He's looking at my dinner guests and manages a laugh that doesn't sound like his own. But the casual manner that I knew is still with him, because he stands to attention, clicking his heels, bows, and takes Nora's hand to kiss it. "It's very good to meet you, madam. I hope you're single, because you could be a delectable date." I love the way he speaks, like Richard Burton in *The War of the Worlds*.

Nora's delighted. She surely knows how to handle a man, because she winks at him and says, "I'm far too old for you, young man. When you're a bit older, make sure you give me a ring."

She's being witty, but he's quick to the uptake and says, "Diamonds before sex, that's what I say." She giggles.

He's still standing to attention and says to Ben and Sam, "How do you do, dear fellows?"

They both stand up and shake his hand. It's as if he pulls us all together as he sits down, as if one of our party. Ben and Sam are behaving like normal men being introduced to a normal man in a normal environment.

I can't take the smile off my face. I want to hug him to death. But I settle down in my seat and gaze at him like a dumbstruck schoolgirl. I hear myself blabbering, "I know it might be strange for you to see me in a place like this, but you know my house burnt down …"

*Oh, no!*

"I heard so. Sorry about that, kid." I don't want him to say any more.

I wince at the paltriness of my reason for being here compared to Nora, Ben and Sam's reasons. I address my table quests, "Listen! That's not the reason I'm here, guys! Some stupid shrink who tried to analyse me for some post-trauma psychology-shit admitted me to hospital and I tried to fake suicide by jumping out the window and then they sent me here so it was all a big bugger-up. And now they won't let me out!"

"Shame, Lamby! Sam says excitedly. "You and me are the same! We shouldn't be here!"

But my old, reliable friend comes to the rescue. "Well, that's a conundrum in itself. What can I do for you, kid?"

This is the first person that I truly believe wants to help me, but the shame of my predicament makes me want to justify my being here, so I say, "Well, I'm here because of a stupid mistake, but Nora, Sam and Ben are here for a bloody good reason."

I can't stop my stupid self! "Nora here lost it when her husband died after sixty-three years of marriage and was abandoned by her stupid uncaring bitch-of-a-daughter. Samuel here thinks he's Hare Krishna. And Ben here killed his girlfriend and tried to kill himself – twice!" No-one says anything.

I feel dizzy and completely out of control. For the first time since I've known him, my old friend is at a loss for words. He takes a cigarette from my packet and lights up. He's never smoked.

# MEDITATION

I'm lying on a stinky mattress on the floor in a small office next to the Activity Centre. What the hell I'm doing here, I just don't know. My days seem to be blending into one another. Time is irrelevant to me. My only clock is the Amanzi Daily Schedule. I don't know how long I've been here looking after my loony-friends, or how long I lay in the hospital with the inviting window, or how long I sat on the shitty-couch like a zombie. All I know is that it's been a hell-of-a-long time that my kids and Pooki have been abandoned by their mother. I need to vomit.

Coupled with my now very laboured physical movements, I've been blanking out, only to find myself blowing smoke-rings with Ben, or walking with Nora picking weeds, or playing FreeCell while she snores, or finger-painting with the druggies, or chatting to Cranium. Cranium seems to be tolerating me, and my respect for him is growing. Ben, Nora and Sam haven't mentioned my insensitive outburst the other evening. My love for them is also growing.

This is the first time I'm not absorbed in something ... other than my current shame at being prostrate. I can't remember what I look like, but I must look like shit. Or maybe I secretly want to look like shit, like girl-druggie. But I keep my eyes closed in the hope that no-one can see how pitiful I am. I wonder what my mom would think if she saw me lying here. I would surely disintegrate if my father did. He hasn't visited me and I'm glad he hasn't witnessed my humiliation. Mom has visited every day since our session in her bakkie. She's allowed me to stare into space and say nothing, and must realise that my pull-yourself-together blanket was burnt in the flames. Clara and Babs have visited a few times and have been gentle company as well. They've allowed me to behave like a doped-out chain-smoker with nothing to say. They've been sworn to secrecy and, as far as I know, no-one else knows I'm here. I've enjoyed listening to the Richard Burton voice of my dear old friend. He's visited often. He's brought back my laughter and it feels good. He's also removed some of the absurdity of my being here and has helped me to see Amanzi as some weird stage-show. Our leading actor is Sam, who never fails to excite. I know he's not humiliated and I'm happy to make him happy, and that's all that counts for the boy.

The embarrassment of lying here is becoming extreme. Laughter creeps up my chest like butterflies looking for an escape. I start to laugh. I try to stop and squeeze my nose. I feel like I'm in school again. Ben is lying next to me, but he's not laughing. All he's got to offer this terrible predicament we find ourselves in is, "Fuck! What a ballbreaker!"

I laugh even more. I'm on my back once again like I was with Maggie-the-crystal-witch and, once again, I'm powerless and out of control.

"Quieten down, the two of you!" It's activity-nurse and she's sitting poised on a little stool to my right. There's a window behind her and the curtains are drawn but light still fills the room.

I open my eyes to plead with her over my toes. "Please, nurse, I really don't want to be here. This is ridiculous!"

"This is part of our Amanzi programme. Now settle down. I'm still waiting for another patient."

Sam is here too and it seems he has fallen asleep. So it's just Sam, Ben and I who have been forced to attend this whatever-activity. I'm glad that Nora hasn't been made to lie here with us. I manage to stop giggling and start to do my feet-fidgeting thing as we lie here waiting for the other patient, but quickly stop it because I don't want activity-nurse to think I'm agitated.

"You've kept us waiting. Lie down over there next to Sam. You know the drill."

A big sigh. "Whatever!" It's girl-druggie, and she quickly lies down without looking at Ben. I wonder why she's been chosen to join us loonies for this session.

Activity-nurse says in a low, practised voice, different from her usual high-pitched one, "I want all of you to relax now. I want you all to close your eyes and listen."

I hear Ben mumble next to me, "Oh, fuck."

I hear a loud click and then another followed by an ear-piercing screech. "Oh, sorry, just a minute, I need to rewind." She's got a bloody tape-recorder!

A woman's beautiful voice speaks over soft background music. "Today, as we lie here together, we are going to try to unload our minds of all outside thoughts and try to focus more on our spirituality ..."

*Oh, no!*

Now that I'm concentrating on the voice in the crackling tape-recording, it sounds a lot like activity-nurse's, but I can't be sure. If it *is* her in the recording, she's making a very good effort at sounding like a spaced-out guru, and I have a sneaky suspicion that we loonies are in for some half-baked version of someone else's hocus-pocus. Given my strict rule of avoiding the power of suggestion, I'm now not only embarrassed and compromised by lying on the floor like a fool, but I'm also terrified of being possessed by some unprofessional voodoo crap.

Ben grunts next to me as I stifle a nervous giggle. I must say, however, that I wouldn't mind "unloading" my mind. I have always wished it were empty, even just for a second.

Since childhood, and whenever asked to make a wish, I have silently whispered, "Give me peace of mind." I realise this is a bloody serious wish for a little mind. But I still wish for peace of mind every time I put my toes into the sea.

Crackle, crackle ... "We are deeply rooted in the earth, yet open to the higher powers of the cosmos. Independent, yet inextricably connected to all of life. In order to prepare ourselves for this journey ..."

*Oh, no!*

It bugs me when people say they are on any kind of journey other than going on holiday. I can't hear what the tape-recorded voice has said about her bloody spiritual journey, but now she's on about some sort of preparation crap.

"In order to prepare for this session, I want you to relax. I want you to think of nothing but your body ..."

I hate it when people tell me to relax. It must be the most annoying thing someone can say to another person.

"I want you to imagine your body as a link between heaven and earth, and to try to connect your physical embodied existence with the sacred and spiritual dimension of being. Aligning the spine and opening the channels that run through the centre of the body encourages an unimpeded circulation of energy, which, in turn, contributes to wakefulness on all levels: physical, mental, and spiritual ..."

*This is far too complicated for loonies. What the hell is she on about?*

"To help you achieve this, I want you to close your eyes gently in order to be aware of what is occurring in your inner consciousness rather than suffer the distractions of the world outside ..."

My eyes *are* closed! I would rather keep them closed than face this pitiful scenario.

"Relaxation drains stress from your body. It cleanses your body from head to feet, with the dirty energies being drained into the floor ..."

This draining thing is more apt for the druggies, who are indeed in need of a good purging.

"To help you achieve this, I want you to imagine your body getting heavy and sinking into the mattress. Concentrate on all the parts of your body and imagine them getting heavier and heavier until you feel as if you are sinking deeper and deeper into the mattress. Start with your shoulders and arms and work your way down to your legs. Feel your body relaxing and sinking deeper and deeper. Now feel your hands and your fingers sinking deeper and deeper ..."

I don't know if I'm lying down properly or where my arms need to be, or if my palms should be facing upwards or downwards. Come to think of it; I'm sure one needs to be in the lotus position or some such contortion to be able to meditate. A vision of Buddha comes to mind and I think of Sam. Being an avid Krishna follower, I'm sure he does this all the time. I'm quite sure that lying down is not the best way to achieve this kind of crap and this is why he's fallen asleep.

"Concentrate on relaxing all the parts of the body and breathe in and out, in and out ..."

*OK, breathing is easy.*

"Breathing exercises focus the mind on the physical act of breathing. Become aware of the way your chest rises and falls each time you breathe, bringing your consciousness close to the here and now and away from the problems of yesterday and worries of tomorrow ..."

*Now, why go and bring the word "worry" into this?*

Now I have to start the relaxing thing all over again.

"Focus on your breathing while relaxing your body. On the inward breath, feel the body expand as you bring fresh energy into it. On the outward breath, release all the tension that is being held in your body. Bring the breath deep down into the abdomen by releasing the abdominal muscles and letting the abdomen expand. Now move the breath up into the rib cage and feel the broadening around your ribs. Now raise the breath a little higher and feel your upper chest expanding. On the outward breath, relax your upper chest followed by your middle chest and then release the air from your abdomen by drawing your abdominal muscles in and up. Try to feel your breath flowing like a wave, your inward breath connecting with your outward breath in a nice rhythm ..."

I've stopped breathing because now I'm totally confused. I don't know where my breath comes from anymore or how to let it out. So I will just do some heavy breathing and see if it works.

Crackle, crackle ... "Feel your inward breath rejuvenating your body, feel your outward breath relaxing your body, releasing tension from your body. Feel your shoulders relax and feel them dropping as you breathe out, releasing the tension in your shoulders. Feel the release spreading down through your arms and into your hands. Feel your entire body letting go with each outward breath ..."

I'm quite impressed with my efforts in trying to relax and breathe, and it's actually quite a nice feeling to just let go for a while. No-one's looking anyway, and I could merely be seen to be sleeping. So, what the hell, I'll just keep breathing and letting my body sink into the mattress.

The voice seems far away now but I hear it still. "You are totally relaxed. You are at one with the universe ... Now, imagine you are floating up a hill towards a big beautiful tree on the horizon ..."

*Yes, here I am!*

I imagine the tree. I float towards it like in a dream. I float up a hill covered with soft yellow grass, gently flattening and rising to the rhythm of the passing breeze. The tree is enormous and aged and sacred and green. It is a scene I have seen in many movies. All that's missing is a little girl on a swing under its branches, or someone standing at a grave, or a cowboy riding off into the distance behind it.

"Or if you wish, imagine being in a place you truly love and are at peace with. Picture the scene and go there ..."

My arm is extending from my body. It actually is! I lean forward and reach for the soft rippling sea water. I touch the water and feel its coolness. I can see my hand as it ruffles the water and makes ripples which are smaller around my finger tips and then get bigger as the circle of tiny waves moves outwards. I can smell the sea and sense the overcast weather. It is cold. A light drizzle speckles the water. The waves are small and lap around my feet. There is no colour. My arm and my toes and the water and the sand are in black and white. I know this beach. It is the beach at Hout Bay in Cape Town. The one I love. The one I walk on when it's raining and overcast. I am here.

*What the hell is going on now?*

I see wrinkles around an eye. The eye is closed and unfamiliar. But I see the eyebrow. I know its shape. It's my eyebrow. This is my forehead. This is my eye. I am a mirror held closely to the side of my temple on the right side of my face. I see myself and marvel at how I look with my eyes closed. I have never seen myself with my eyes closed.

My skin is not its usual colour but like a black-and-white image in a film. It's like I'm seeing myself through the lens of a video camera as it moves around the contours of my face. I scrutinise my laughter wrinkles and the shape of my nose. I look funny with my eyes closed. My lids are heavier than I imagined. My face looks peaceful.

Terror grips me. But I can't stop myself from looking at my face. I'm fascinated. I'm moving upwards. I can see my whole body now. I can see my upturned palms and my grey tracksuit with my thin body in it as it lies on the mattress. I must have turned my palms upwards and didn't know it. I can see everything in this room. I see Ben and Sam and girl-druggie and activity-nurse. Ben and girl-druggie have their eyes closed and are lying haphazardly around the room on their mattresses, just like I am. Sam has his eyes open and seems to be looking at me. I see the nurse as she holds her finger on the small rectangular button of the tape-recorder on her lap. The tape-recorder is about to slide off her knees, but she catches it in time and replaces it on her lap, still keeping her finger poised over the button. She's looking down and doesn't notice me above her head. I'm like an unseen balloon.

*What the hell is going on now?*

I'm moving out of the little room and down the passage towards the light. I'm out of the door at the end of the passage and there's a big tree in front of me. I don't recognise it because it wasn't here when I came into this place. I turn left in front of the tree and move silently down the stairs of the corridor. I'm no longer high up but am lower down near the concrete steps. There are many people passing me, but their shapes are grey and fuzzy. Everything is still in black and white. Some are walking up the steps and some are walking down. I can't make out their faces. Most are looking down at their feet as they manoeuvre the steps. Others are just sailing by like phantoms. They scare the hell out of me.

A sharp nudge. "Wake up! Let's go and have tea and biscuits. I'm starved."

I'm awake! I have not just woken up; I have just landed! I'm relieved and frightened and fascinated. I struggle to my knees and hang onto Ben's jacket.

"Come on," he says, "get that body up!" He lifts me and I feel like a doll, but I'm comfortable with his arms around me. We are friends and he's here to lift me up.

As we make our way down the long passage towards the door to the outside corridor, I resign myself to the fact that what just happened to me is merely a drug-induced hallucination. The stupid little experience is tucked nicely away under my pull-yourself-together blanket. We exit the doors and step into the corridor. I stop dead in my tracks. The tree that I thought I'd imagined and that helped me to expel any thoughts of going down this passage a few minutes before, *is* here! I'm shivering and I hang on to Ben's jacket again.

I blabber into the leather, "I thought that we were in the room next to the Activity Centre, the one that *doesn't* have a tree in front of it. And now I realise we were in the room at the top-end of the corridor, the one that *does* have a tree in front of it."

"Wakey-wakey! Get with the programme. The room next to the Activity Centre is for group discussions and head-shrinking. The room we've just come out of is the lotus-hocus-pocus room. And what's all this crap about which tree is where?" He puts his hands into the air and makes claws with his fingers while howling into the distance with his mouth shaped like a wolf's.

His little show of bravado doesn't make me laugh.

# SIGNIFYING NOTHING

*Obi-Wan Kenobi: These aren't the droids you're looking for.*
*Storm-trooper: These aren't the droids we're looking for.*
*Obi-Wan Kenobi: He can go about his business.*
*Storm-trooper: You can go about your business.*
*Obi-Wan Kenobi: Move along.*
*Storm-trooper: Move along ... move along.*

*My heart is beating and I'm floating. I've finally had the courage to rip off the wallpaper with the little pink roses. I gaze lovingly at my poster of Luke Sky-walker. The force is definitely with me as well.*

I chew my finger. I can't work out the difference between the power of the mind, or moving with your mind. Even if I try to force it out of my mind, the terror of my experience in the lotus-hocus-pocus room envelops me. It is here and it won't let me go.

Ben, Nora, Sam and I are having breakfast together. It feels like they are normal people in the normal world, having breakfast and talking about normal things, and I am the freak consumed by freaky things, like a true mental patient. They should go home. I should be here. I should be here long enough for Cranium's head-bending to wrench this stuff from my mind!

"You look bad, Lamby!" It's Sam.

*I couldn't give a shit what I look like!*

"I'm just tired, Sam. I think this place is killing me."

"Shame," he says. "Can I have a cigarette? I promise I'll pay you back."

Ben and Nora have chosen not to comment, and I'm glad Sam has changed the subject of my appearance. I give him a cigarette and light it for him. My head feels even more screwed-up than it ever has, and my heart is still sore. But it's my head that's worrying me the most. At least it takes precedence over my bleeding heart for once. So I concentrate on forcing the slippery yogurt down my throat, but the slime is moving down my oesophagus, just in front of my brain.

I don't want anything near my brain, let alone food. I don't want it disturbed. I want it to keep quiet and still inside my cranium.

I can't stop myself from analysing the events of last night. My stupid professionalism is surely to blame, because I've been taught to analyse things. I always analyse things – far too much for my, or anybody else's, liking. I just want peace of mind, and I'm sliding my feet into the sand under the receding white foam of the sea and wishing that my head would turn off.

But thoughts of the weird phenomenon won't leave me. Now that I'm sitting here in the sunroom with the smell of breakfast in the air, I cannot believe that I tested this out-of-body thing while lying in the bath last night. Although it pains me, I try to recall how and why I did the stupid thing!

*I've wedged a chair under the bathroom door handle. I'm secure in the vacuum created by the safe enclosure of the bathroom. The warm water laps over my belly and the hot steam covers the rest of my body that's exposed above water level, like a blanket. All I feel is the hard porcelain behind my neck and the cool on my arms as the steam evaporates from them.*

*I can't feel the coolness on my arms anymore and even my neck has become numb. Terror grips my throat. My body feels nothing but my mind is filled with dread. Dread over what I'm about to put myself through. Dread of drowning. This is not a good place to be trying it. This is not a good place to be trying it at all. But I can't stop myself from trying. I want to prove that what happened to me in the meditation room was nothing but a mind-induced hallucination. I'm forcing myself to keep my head above water. I don't want my body to be left alone to drown! I don't want anything weird to happen!*

*I'm watching the black-and-white movie again. I see the side of my eye again. I see my laugh wrinkles, and my profile, and my closed eyelids that appear too heavy. I see my outstretched arms and my burning cigarette in the soap-tray. And I see my breasts as they peek like little pyramids above the water. I see myself above myself and I'm terrified. I open my eyes to stop it … and it stops. I'm back. But the terror is still here.*

I scoop up the rest of the yogurt and force it down my throat. I knew then as I know now that I will never try it again, like art. I will not allow myself to do it. I am a professional woman of the real world and there is no space in my normality for such a mind-blowing phenomenon. I will drink myself to death to forget it if I have to. But now I'm certain that I can do the mind-travel thing whenever I want to. But I don't want to. I don't want my mind to leave my body. Ever!

"Ever!"

*Shit, I'm talking aloud instead of thinking!*

Ben and Nora's eyes are on me as Sam shouts, "Never, ever, ever!"

"Dear, you don't seem very well this morning." It's Nora.

"Fuckin-aye, chicky! What's up? You look like shit, and you're talking to yourself." It's Ben.

"I'm just tired. I can't sleep in this place. I miss my family. I want to go home."

Nora puts her hand over mine and I realise I've got sticky yogurt on my fingers. "I think you should go and see the doctor, dear. I think you should try to convince him that you need to go home." I want Nora to hold me like a mother holds her baby. I want her to cradle me and stroke my hair and tickle my back and rock me to sleep, even if I've messed yogurt all over myself.

"OK. I'll try."

"Please get me out of here too, Lamby. I want to come home with you."

Nora pats Sam's hand. "Now, now, Samuel, finish your breakfast and then you can take me for a walk."

"Oh, goody!"

It's only Ben's eyes that remain on me. "Do you want to talk about stuff?"

"No thanks, Ben, there's nothing to say really. I'm fine. Really I am. I'm just a little tired."

"OK, but I'm here if you need me."

As the three of them get up to go, Ben says, "Come, on guys. Let's go to the Activity Centre. Today we're making statues or some shit."

They've all had the decency not to say any more and, as they leave, they go silently, like they're leaving someone in mourning. I light another cigarette and put my head into my hands with the hot end poised above my eyebrow. I don't care if it burns me. That, at least, would feel good.

The thing that I always say is with me:

*I'm repeating it over and over in my mind as I stand over the cauldron on the school stage. Even though it isn't my line, I can't stop myself from repeating it. I'm supposed to be saying, "Fillet of a fenny snake; In the cauldron boil and bake; Eye of newt and toe of frog ..." while the three of us witches toss plastic frogs and snakes into the black casserole dish that is the cauldron. But the stupid*

nerd of an acne-face has been chosen to act as Macbeth, and say the thing that
I want to say over and over again. He's been chosen to say one of the most poi-
gnant things I've ever heard in my young life.

I repeat, sotto voce, lest the druggies think I'm daft and treat me like they do
Sam, the marvellous thing that Shakespeare wrote. I repeat the marvellous
thing that I've memorised so well and that I shout over people's heads at dinner parties when everyone, including me, has talked such a load of crap that
I feel ill and want to vomit.

> She should have died hereafter;
> There would have been a time for such a word—
> To-morrow, and to-morrow, and to-morrow,
> Creeps in this petty pace from day to day,
> To the last syllable of recorded time;
> And all our yesterdays have lighted fools
> The way to dusty death. Out, out, brief candle!
> Life's but a walking shadow; a poor player,
> That struts and frets his hour upon the stage,
> And then is heard no more: it is a tale
> Told by an idiot, full of sound and fury,
> Signifying nothing.

And if I'm very drunk and can't remember the exact words that I knew so
well at school, I summarise the thing with a slur.

> We strut and fret upon the stage of life,
> Saying much,
> But signifying nothing.

Why the hell I've always been impressed with Macbeth's take on life, I just
don't know. Maybe it's with me again, as I stare into the depths of my empty
yogurt cup, because it begins with: "She should have died hereafter ..."

# GOODBYE CRANIUM

I fart into the plastic stool but I don't care because I'm alone at the table in the sunroom of Amanzi Wellness Clinic and now that Ben, Nora and Sam have gone to do their activities, there're only druggies around me.

I only have Shakespeare at the bottom of my yogurt cup and he would probably laugh about my farting and write a sonnet about it like Miller did in *The Crucible,* wherein some poor man is trying to prove his wife's innocence and her accuser declares "a fart on Thomas Putman".

I'm whispering: "We strut and fret upon the stage of life; signifying nothing," as Macbeth smiles upon me. Shakespeare won't leave me alone. He's setting up a play with the sunroom as our stage. Ben, Nora and Sam are hanging about like village idiots and hovering in the wings are the witches: Tulula, Maggie, Dr Shaker and dungeon-nurse. Sweeping-nurse is cleaning the stage floor because there's a lot of dust left about in setting up the stage. Cranium is happy with his disguise and very important role as Lady Macbeth. Death-nurse and Xhosa-nurse are booing the bourgeoisie while Sister Shabalala is shooing away Calvin Klein and girl-druggie, who're drinking from the cauldron and eating frogs' legs.

And centre stage, lying on an altar, is Lamby. She's extremely anxious because she's forgotten her lines and keeps repeating: "Much ado about nothing." Sister Bertha is with her and places a gentle hand over her bleeding heart.

"What the hell are you still doing here, girlie?"

"I forgot my lines ..."

*Shit!*

The last person in the world I need to be talking crazy to is Sister Bertha. I'm lying over my arms while drooling into my yogurt cup and talking to myself like a true loony.

At least the sunroom is empty. But Sister Bertha looks concerned and says in a soothing voice, "The doctor wants to see you now. He's consulting in the reception area because the construction work has moved to the Top Block."

I bury my face in my hands and, under the darkness between my fingers, I take out a ciggy and light it under my nose. Sister Bertha doesn't tell me not to smoke in here and I'm glad because I would smoke anyway and we'd probably end up in an unnecessary argument, which would take away the pity in how she's found me here. I need my cigarette, and her pity.

I have to lift my face from my hands because the smoke is asphyxiating me, so I clutch the top of her hand and say without looking at her, "Sit down with me for a minute, love. I need to talk to you. It's important."

She drags out a plastic chair and sits opposite me and her eyes touch mine in their mistiness. I must smell because I can't remember washing today. Events of yesterday have left me immobile and unable to wash or brush my teeth. I determine the poor state of my face by the odd look in her eyes. She turns her palm upwards under mine, and holds my hand.

I whine like a child into her adult face, "I really shouldn't be in this place. I'm like the ladybird who's left her children alone."

She raises an eyebrow because I'm probably sounding crazy again, so I say, "I've been thinking about the rhyme because it's got the fire-thing in it. I know I'm full of nonsense, but I promise you, I'm actually a very nice and normal person."

*That sounded dumb. But, shit … I just said "fire" out loud!*

She closes her eyes and nods, and my voice loses a bit of its whine. "I've had a little trauma and that hurts, but it happens to a lot of people. And I haven't told you this yet, but I made a big mistake when I was in hospital because I faked a suicide attempt. I know this sounds crazy, but I'd been given so many drugs that I was hallucinating. I felt abandoned by the psychiatrist who was meant to be taking care of me, and I wanted someone to see how desperate my situation was …" She doesn't say anything but keeps nodding with her eyes closed.

"I need to go home now because, as much as the doctor thinks I should stay, I'm causing my children pain. I need to go home to them. Do you understand what I'm saying?"

"I do, my darling. Now, come on, it's not for me to analyse you. Let's go and see the doctor."

Even though she hasn't waved a wand and got me out of here in a cloud of smoke, her simple words, "I do," are enough for me. She understands. Maybe she always has.

I wriggle the numbness from my bum as she lifts me from my plastic stool. "Come with me, girlie, the doctor is waiting for you."

I've been led into so many consultations, like a circus monkey. This time I don't feel like the monkey, but rather like a little child whose mother is taking her to the dentist and telling her it won't be sore. She doesn't come with me into the small ante-room behind the reception area, but leaves me outside the door to make my own entrance. She squeezes my hand, and lets me go.

In contrast to the brown Headmaster's Office with its brown walls and brown carpets, this little room has a large window which allows in a lot of sunshine. The desk takes up most of the space, so it feels like the only things in here are Cranium, me, the desk and the sunshine. His face looks fresh in the sunlight and I notice its maturity by the expression-lines above his eyebrows. The light illuminates my yellow folder and he doesn't look at it like he usually does, but looks at me. The intensity of his stare feels like a laser zapping into the depths of my head. The scribbled words on the loose sheets from Tulula and Dr Shaker and whoever else at the hospital are no longer important, because he's focused on me. I feel that he's inside my head for the first time.

He smiles for the first time. "I hear you've been a good girl."

I don't know if this is a question or a statement, but I keep quiet. I make sure not to return his smile because I need him to know that I'm serious.

He keeps on smiling and says, "The people at this institution are knowledge-able and there is continuous dialogue between us. We monitor our patients."

I'm not sure what there is to monitor about me, because most of my time has been spent hiding away with Ben, Nora and Sam, or playing FreeCell in the dark. But I still don't say anything.

He continues with a kind face and outstretched hands. "I want you to know that the fire will always be with you. You must accept this. There will be times that you will see something that reminds you of it and you will feel a little pain, but this will go away and leave you in peace one day."

He's walking me through the burning embers of my home but, God help me, I never want to remember the things I had or the walls of my house.

I bring my thumb to my mouth and quickly withdraw it.

But he seems to be preoccupied and hasn't noticed my attempt at thumb mauling. "Records of your first consultations with doctors are with me here in this folder."

Again I'm reduced to a nameless character in a yellow folder, but he continues his dialogue over my cynicism, "I think there are underlying issues that you need to revisit. I've made an appointment for you with the psychiatrist you were meant to see before you were admitted to hospital. She's back. I want you to see her when you go home."

I shout into his face, "Does this mean you're letting me go?"

"Yes."

"When?"

"Your husband is collecting you tomorrow. The psychiatrist I'm sending you to will keep me informed of your progress." I don't care about the psychiatrist. My overwhelming sense of escape is like a fresh breeze on my face.

I slump down in my chair. I wish I had tried to remember Cranium's name, and could say it properly. He's been gracious and kind. He's sat opposite me with his glass eye while I've behaved like the spoilt brat that Sister Bertha thought I was. He's analysed me like he was supposed to. I was sent here, and he did his job. He's a good doctor. I want to hug him tight, but his eye may pop out, so I restrain myself.

"Thanks for all you've done for me. I'm sorry I was such a bitch," is all I manage.

His smile broadens. "It's OK. I'm pleased with your progress. You're going to get through this. Now, off you go. I've got other patients to see."

# GOODBYE NORA

I can't play any more FreeCell. I can't play because it's a waste of time. As much as I've pleaded for my release, the thought of leaving fills me with dread. I'm not going home like a woman cured, as if I've just been to a spa. I'm not going home with my nails freshly painted and peppermint oils in my nostrils. I'm going home like the girl who came in here, with a head full of dread and a heart full of ashes.

Worst of all is that I can't face saying goodbye to Ben or Nora or Sam. I'm not sad to leave Sister Bertha and Xhosa-nurse, because they've said so many goodbyes to so many patients.

I've chosen not to have dinner with my mates, because I don't want to face them. This is not a movie in which the farewells to my loony-friends are expected and tearful as we kiss and hug goodbye at the asylum porte cochère. I can disappear without a trace and without sad goodbyes.

I'm fully dressed with my shoes on, and tucked securely between the sheets. The door is wrenched open and Sister Bertha eases in beside me.

She doesn't meet my eyes but seems to be looking at the face-brick behind my window. She says in a voice that's trying to carry sympathy, "Nora's gone."

I look at Nora's bed and an arrow of guilt pierces my heart. There are no blankets or pillow on it, just a grubby mattress with a dent in the middle. I've been so consumed by my going home that I've completely forgotten about Nora!

I hate myself and I'm speechless, until I manage, "Has she died?" Tears are stinging behind my eyes.

"No, darling, of course not. Her daughter collected her this afternoon to take her to an old-age home. It was quite a surprise."

I hate Nora's stupid daughter just like my kids must hate me. I imagine poor Nora lying alone in an old-age home with no-one to take care of her. But Sister Bertha is helping. "Here, take these, they'll help you sleep."

The tablets ease down my throat. My bedroom door is closed silently. My dungeon is empty. Nora has gone. I don't need my death-sleep tactics tonight. All I need to do is push my fists into my eye-sockets until my brain leaks out my ears and I pass out.

# EXIT THE LOONY-BIN

Stef has signed me out and I've told him to wait for me in the car. I'm standing in my room for the last time and can't take my eyes off the bricked-up window. I feel a nudge. It's Xhosa-nurse. "Gijima! Your husband is waiting."

I turn on her and pull her big bulk to my chest. She puts her arms around me and I feel her enormous boobs pressing into my ribcage. I say over her shoulder, "Hau, mama, I will miss you. I have left my suitcase and my clothes here because I don't want them. So you can give them away if you want."

"Thank you, mammie, I will give them to the pikinins."

I leave her quickly and rush out to find Ben. He's eating scrambled eggs in the sunroom. I try to sound flippant. "I'm going, Ben. Give me your number."

He smiles up at me and says as he swallows his egg, "Cool for you."

I've got my cellphone poised and he gives me his number. I punch it in. "Thanks, I'll keep in touch. Let me know about the air-conditioning order."

"Will do. Cheers. Catch you later."

I should hug him but I can't. He stares at his plate. I remember that this was what he was doing when I first clapped eyes on him.

I fall out of the sunroom and rush to the parking lot. I hope I don't bump into Sam. I don't want him to see me go. I secretly hope he's sick enough in the head to forget me and my cigarettes.

I sit next to Stef in his warm car and it feels like I've just arrived at Amanzi. The absence of time between my coming and going has obliterated my stay. The only thing that remains with me is Ben's cellphone number.

My thoughts go to Ben and Sam and Sister Bertha. I try to convince myself that this is not a movie where an emotional ending is expected full of promises for the future. Maybe the drugs have something to do with my inability to feel. I squeeze my cellphone between my legs on the car seat. It's safe, with Ben's number saved as "Ben Loony-bin".

I stare out of the window. I recognise the wheat fields in flashing Vs as they spin past the window in reverse. Stef and I haven't said anything to each other, as usual, but the dependability of the good company we share is still here.

I break the silence and say, "Where are we? And where in the hell was I? I don't have a clue. Isn't that funny?"

His stern profile above the steering-wheel tells me it's not so funny, and he says, "About sixty kilometres east of Johannesburg."

I don't ask for more details. "Shame, my love. It was a hell-of-a-way to drive to visit me. I know you're busy and it's a far drive and far away from the kids."

"My mother was with them. Of course I had to visit you."

I don't know if he visited me because he had to or wanted to, but I don't push for an answer. I've completely forgotten about his mother being at the townhouse. I cross my fingers and ask as casually as I can, "Is she still here?"

"No, she left this morning."

*Thank God!*

"I've booked for us to go to France and visit my father. He's paying for the flights."

*Oh, God! No thanks!*

The thought of getting this body to pack a suitcase, get on an aeroplane and chitter-chatter with French people is nauseating. The thought of having to conjure up passion for the vineyards and olive groves and French country-side is unbearable. I want to stay in the shitty-townhouse. I want to stare out the window and sit on the shitty-couch with Pooki, until a frosty Friday when I wake up well in the head and able to face the world.

I'm desperate. I raise the pitch of my voice and wail, "But your mother's forbidden us to see your father with his new girlfriend. She said she'll never speak to us again. She said she'll disinherit you! We can't go, my love!"

"I don't give a shit. The kids need a holiday! We're going and that's that!"

It's a very unfair thing for a mother to tell a son not to see his father, even though his parents are going through a divorce. For almost ten years he's been up to his ears in court cases and verbal abuse from his mother about his father. I know neither of us wants to discuss his parents' divorce.

"But we haven't got our passports. They're burnt."

"Oh, my love, our passports were the first thing I sorted out. You and the kids had your ID photos taken. Don't you remember?"

I can't remember.

He reaches under my seat and takes four passports from his black pouch and puts them on my lap. "Have a look yourself."

225

I'm only interested in mine because I'm sure I didn't have my photo taken. But here I am on the little photograph. I look like a foetus. My eyes are popping out and my face is pale. It looks as though I'm forcing a smile, but maybe it's a snarl or I'm clenching my teeth to hold back the vomit. It's a sharp smack on my present face to see my old one looking so bad.

Stef must read the horror of my self-discovery. "Shame, my love. It was the day after. You were probably still in shock."

I notice that he hasn't used the f-word. I hold my breath and mutter, "The day after *what*, my love?"

"Since then."

"Since *when*, my love?"

"Since the house burnt down. Since the fire." He says this without flinching.

So bloody easy! And there I was! Like a brat from hell! Slouching around like a spoilt Pasha in a rehab clinic, just so that I could be taught to say one bloody word out loud! What a waste of time and money! I don't say anything.

I stare out of the window at the looming skyline of Johannesburg and pinch my thigh. I know I *have* to go to bloody France, put on a smile, and face the world. I *have* to go and be with his family and drink rosé and laugh and chat and be me. I've just learnt how to say the word "fire", and now I have to go to bloody France!

"When are we going?"

"In two days. Oh, and the doctor has arranged a follow-up consultation with a psychiatrist tomorrow afternoon."

*What?*

The puke shoves its way up my throat. I've got anxiety-acid and vomit coming up my oesophagus, so I open the window and stick my head out into the spinning air.

"Close the window! Are you mad?"

I close it and slump back into my seat.

# HOME TO MY BABIES

Pooki pees on my lap and knocks my teeth before I can get out of the car. She shakes with joy and I squeeze her to my chest until she whimpers.

The kids are at school. This will give me time to doll up and look fabulous when they come home and see me.

"The kids are so excited to see you."

"Shame, my poor little babies. I feel so bad."

What awaits me as I walk through the front door is the hugest flower arrangement I've ever seen in my life. The sight of the colour in this dreary townhouse hurts.

"Thank you, my love; you shouldn't have. I'm not worth it."

"The kids wanted to. They chose it themselves."

I know this is a lie because Stef did the choosing, and it was his idea, but I don't say so. I notice that his eyes are watery and this hurts too.

"This is from me." He hands me a brown paper bag.

I don't want a bloody present. I don't want things! I try to smile and say, "I don't want anything, my love. I'm not worth it."

"Open it, you'll laugh."

I open it. Inside the bag is a yellow T-shirt. The only thing that crosses my mind is that yellow doesn't suit me, but I say, "Thanks, my love, I'll put it on."

I unfold the T-shirt. It's got black writing on the front that reads:

PSYCHIATRIC WARD
OUT-PATIENT: 33854/44923-345

*What the hell?*

"Cool, hey!" He giggles.

It's *not* cool and it's *not* funny! I hate the stupid T-shirt even more now, but I gulp, and say, "Ja, it's cool, my love, thanks." I could rip the bad-joke-yellow-thing in two. I crumple it up and put it back into the bag.

I seek out my shitty-couch. It looks like it's missed me. I've missed it too, and I still want to sit on it all day, drooling over my bleeding thumbs, fiddling with Pooki's cool ears, and smoking. I want to tie myself to it so that no-one can get me to see another shrink … or go to France.

I light a cigarette and say, "Shall we have a glass of wine?"

"The doctor gave me strict instructions that you can't drink while you're on your medication. He said it's highly dangerous and will affect your progress."

*What bloody progress?*

I've progressed, I'm fine, and where the hell do these bloody doctors want me to progress to? I plan to drink a lot, then puke, then take the tablets, but, "Oh," is all I manage.

"I have to go back to the office. I've got meetings all day. Are you alright to be alone, my love?"

*I want to be alone.*

I say it to myself like Greta Garbo. I want to say the words out loud and imitate her husky voice, but then we would both laugh and that would hurt.

Stef kisses me, but without passion, which I'm pleased about, because I still feel like a corpse. Any love-making with me would be necrophilia.

He's gone and the silence of the townhouse pulsates in my ears. After the banging and crashing at the loony-bin, and my own head-banging while talking to Cranium, Sister Bertha, Ben, Sam and Nora, the din of the silence hurts my head.

I pour a glass of wine as Pooki lifts her paw at the fridge door and looks at me accusingly. I'm going to have a long, hot bath and get into bed. I'll wake up to find this has all been a dream. I will dress up, put on make-up and be ready for the arms of my children.

# ENTER LULU

Sister Bertha's wise words about the acceptance and maturity of children ring in my ears as I sit in the waiting room of Lulu, who is to be my new loony-head-bender.

*Blessed are the children.*

Mackie and Mouse welcomed me with open arms yesterday afternoon. They asked if I'd had a nice rest and were ecstatic that I was home. There was no blame or confusion, just their delightful acceptance.

I had pulled myself together, albeit with a lot of wine, and made a fantastic dinner like only a good Italian woman can. Quaffing the wine was easy, like riding a bicycle. Stef didn't reprimand me for drinking, I'm sure because he was hoping the wine would bring me back to my old self. We ate dinner like we normally do, chatting about the kids' school day and how they hated their teachers and the food at the canteen, and we had all laughed, even Stef.

Mackie told us that he was scared of burning alive and asked if we were safe in the townhouse. We discussed safety issues against fire in the home. We promised to put a ladder in their room, so that they had an easy escape from the second floor of the townhouse if there were a fire. Mackie thought it would be cool to escape a fire and couldn't wait for the ladder to arrive to practise his escape.

We talked about how cool it was to be on the news, and how the helicopters had circled our burning house. And how cool it was that we lived in the townhouse now, because it was small and their bedroom was closer to ours than in the old house.

Stef reprimanded Mackie for lighting matches and burning things outside. He told him about "The Dreadful Story of Harriet and the Matches" from *Struwwelpeter*. We promised to get Mackie the book.

Later, I took Mackie and Mouse under the sheets, and into the warm feathers of my breast. No death-sleep tactics were necessary. The quiet beating of their little hearts elevated me above my own bleeding heart, and sleep was easy.

There's a women's magazine on my lap. I turn the pages gingerly because magazines in waiting rooms are full of bacteria from sick people who don't wash their hands after making a wee. There are other patients sharing my space and thumbing through magazines. The waiting area serves a number of psychiatrists. People have been called to see doctors other than Lulu. I dread my own call-up.

I've driven my car here all by myself. I've followed the directions given me by the receptionist. All my faculties are with me. The people sitting here with me are all probably batty, or bored, or in need of conversation. Out of the corner of my eye I analyse the group around me. I can't stop myself from analysing things.

There's a man whose head is bent towards his lap, but he's not looking at his magazine. He seems sheepish and unwilling to lift his head. There's a very thin young girl with a tattoo on her wrist, who seems irritated by her mother and keeps pulling her hand away from her grasp. There's a man working on a laptop, who seems to be preparing a report.

I feel the sorriest for the girl. I want to edge up beside her and discuss vomit-techniques. I also want to tell her it's dangerous, in the hope she'll stop, but I know this will be pointless, because it will stop on its own when her environment changes.

A good-looking woman in stilettos is paying her bill at the reception desk. What her mental illness might be eludes me, because her appearance radiates confidence. As I'm trying to make out the reason for her seeing a shrink, my name is called and I drag myself out of my seat for yet another unnecessary head-shrinking by yet another unnecessary psychiatrist, other than Cranium, whom I actually miss.

# LULU, SCENE 1: INTRODUCTIONS

*God, she's beautiful!*
Her lovely blue eyes quickly lift from yet another yellow folder and alight on mine as I enter her office. She's got purple hair, cut short and gelled into spikes, which makes her look like a pixie. The colour of her eye-shadow matches her hair and emphasises her sparkling eyes. She's funky, and this appeals to me.

"Howzit?"

"Howzit?"

The atmosphere is relaxed and I am comfortable in spite of my heavy heart.

Lulu leans back and wedges her knees against the edge of the desk so that her chair tilts backwards. I notice she's wearing a lot of layered clothing: a slinky wrap over a long-sleeved top over a vest, in charcoal and blues. All in all she looks very stylish.

"You look great," she says. "Where did you get that jacket? It's awesome."

I'm in my usual vamp, professional, black garb. I'm pleased with the general way she's chatting to me.

"Someone gave it to me, so I can't tell you where it's from, but thanks anyway. Can I smoke in here?"

"Sure, doll." She's called me "doll" and I want her to hold me up like one. "I also smoke."

*Cool bananas!*

She takes out a nicotine-stained tea saucer from her desk drawer and places it between us and I say, "Have one of mine."

"I smoke the same brand."

*Even better!*

We light up like we're in a bar having a glass of wine together. I'm damn sure that the chemicals between us are working. And here is another inquiry to add to my "shrink-questionnaire": "Do you have a good vibe with your shrink? If so, you're sure to connect. This will make her job easier in dissecting your head – and yours even easier to tell her how to do it."

She pages through the yellow folder again. I know now that personal yellow folders are privy between doctors, and wonder how the hell they get the information to one another so fast.

"Shit," she says, "they put you on a lot of drugs!"

*Tell me about it!*

I like the fact that she's getting down to the drug-stuff right away. Still studying the notes in my folder she asks, "Why the hell have they put you on stuff for epilepsy? Have you ever had a fit, or fainted?"

"No." I've definitely blanked out a lot, but I choose not to say it.

She nods her head over the long list of drugs. "Have you been feeling lethargic lately?"

*Shit! Have I?*

"Yes."

"The stuff they've given you may be overkill. If you're the kind of girl who's usually full of energy, this stuff will make you feel like a zombie!"

I'm glad she's as concerned about the shit I'm taking as I am, and is cutting to the chase as quickly as possible. I like people who don't dilly-dally. It's a sign of higher intelligence.

She flips over the pages and writes the date on top of a brand-new sheet. She throws her pen down and leans back in her chair, tipping even further back than before. "We'll deal with your prescriptions later," she says with a mischievous smile.

I resign myself to wait for the only important discussion I need to have with her. The drugs must go! So the wait will be worth it.

She tears out another piece of paper from a pre-printed block and, without looking at it, ticks a number of items and puts the sheet in front of me. "I first want you to go and have a few blood and urine tests. We need to check out your thyroid gland and sugar levels. Irregularities in your body can often be the cause of shit happening in your brain. Even an excessive nasal-drip can affect your moods. We should also check out the effects of dairy products on you, etc."

*Now, this makes bloody sense!*

I secretly hope that I have some blood or mucus disorder, so I only have to pop pills that fix my body and not pills that mess with my mind.

She tears another pre-printed sheet from yet another block and scribbles something on it. "I'd also like to send you for an EEG. We need to check out any overactive brain activity, etc."

*What the …?*

"What's an EEG?" I've heard about in it passing. "Do I have to lie in a wind tunnel and have my head dissected in little layers? I really don't think that's necessary." But maybe it would be interesting to see the damage done by my many concussions.

"No, an EEG is not the kind of brain-scan you're thinking of. That's a Magnetoencephalography, or an MRI. What I want to do as a first step is an Electroencephalogram. Unlike a CAT, PET or MEG scan, an EEG picks up natural electrical signals the brain produces and uses little pens to translate them onto graph paper."

My head spins to keep up with these complicated words, but all I can say is, "OK. Cool." I'm sure I've got a dumb look on my face so I furrow my brow and nod in the hope she thinks I'm clever.

"But let's deal with that later. How are you feeling?"

*Excellent question!*

"Pretty crap."

"Looking at the shit you've been through and the stuff you're taking, I'm not surprised. Are you still feeling like killing yourself?"

*Excellent question!*

I remember that this was the last question Tulula had asked me, and my answer tipped the scales. "The killing-myself thing is a lot of bullshit because I would never do it."

"OK, doll. I know that you had a fire. That's pretty tough and you may want to talk to a psychologist about it, but I'm not here for that. I want to talk to you about other things."

*Wonderful!*

# LULU, SCENE 2: MOOD DIAGRAM

Lulu tears a piece of paper from an exam pad and shoves it in front of me with a pen poised above it. She draws one horizontal line in the middle of it and says, "OK, this line represents the state of mind of most of the world's population. I'm talking about the ones who seem to glide through life without a worry in the world."

I understand exactly what she means. I've always envied these kinds of people so I say excitedly, "Like my brother. No shit ever happens to him. Unlike me …"

She cuts me short like she's got no time to waste, and says, "Yes, like your brother," as if she knows him. She writes, NORMAL, upside down on the line, and draws another line far above it. I'm impressed with her upside-down writing.

"Now, this top line represents the state of mind of people who are eccentric, or geniuses, or creative. People like Einstein, or Churchill, or Mozart. Are you with me?"

"Sure!"

Without labelling the top line, she draws another line way below the middle line. "Now, this bottom line represents the minds of people who are constantly sad or depressed."

"Got it!"

I'm a little apprehensive now. I would rather not associate with depressed people. She hasn't labelled the bottom line either, but it doesn't matter because I understand the diagram. We both drag on our cigarettes. She lets her ash fall onto the paper and brushes it off as if she couldn't care less. I like her even more.

She passes me the pen. "OK, where do you fit into this little picture?"

*Shit!*

I take it reluctantly because I honestly don't know where the hell I fit in. I wiggle the pen in circular movements above her drawing for a long time and then a laugh escapes me. She laughs too, takes the pen from my hand and draws a line from the normal line to the top line and then through the normal line again down to the bottom one. I take the pen from her and continue the line repetitively up and down and up and down until I nearly start drawing on her desk. We both giggle. It's the first time I've laughed in a while, but her company is easy and I feel that she's carrying me, like she carried my pen.

She takes back the pen. "OK, jokes aside!"

She draws another line way below the bottom line and she looks me sternly in the face. "This is the one that's not so funny."

In big upside-down capitals she writes a label on it: SUICIDE.

"Some people get so depressed that they go here. And this is what shrinks look out for. This is why I always keep my phone on."

I'm impressed that she calls herself a "shrink". I'm also impressed that she keeps her phone on. I'm sure she's a pro at getting her patients to reconsider death, or life, or whatever.

I put my finger just above the suicide line and, careful not to touch it, say, "I've never gone here."

She nods, but she's still got her eyes on the paper, and has labelled the line just above the suicide line: DEPRESSION.

*Shit!*

I pull myself together and try to save my grace. "But I go up to the top line a lot. I love to be full of energy, and inventive, and creative. It's a complete high for me!"

She labels the top line: MANIC. I like the term because I'm happiest when I'm manic and usually consider entering politics at this time.

"Are you a little scared when you're up here?"

I think about this and I know that I am because I know that shortly I'll be at the bottom line again, feeling empty and crap. I think that maybe this is why I fear happiness. "Yes, I'm shit-scared when I'm up here, because I know that what goes up must come down."

She grins. "That's a good way of putting it."

Funnily enough, I'm not so worried about this up-and-down stuff because I know that what's down also has to come up, and this is definitely something to look forward to. Not that I think I could ever be happy again when I'm so low.

The thought of any of my friends or family knowing that I hit the depression line now and again sends a shiver up my spine. No-one should know about this little discussion. It's my own private movie.

"You seemed to shiver. Are you OK?"

"Yes, I'm fine. This is all a little embarrassing though. I thought I was one of the normal ones."

"Don't worry, doll, there are lots of people who are like this. These are the people whose moods shoot so far up from the bottom or middle line that their brains over-rev and they invent something, like Da Vinci, or write music, like Mozart."

"Shit! I feel privileged. Were Da Vinci or Mozart or Einstein manic-what-evers?"

She laughs and says, "There has been some research that shows that some of our geniuses were, but then again they didn't consult with me, so I can't be certain." She winks. "Consider Van Gogh, who cut off his ear in a state of depression, and Churchill, who called his bad moods his 'black dog.'"

Now I know why there was a poster of him at the loony-bin. "Fascinating stuff."

Lulu puts a frown on her pixie-face and says, "Although you can ascribe creativity to this kind of behaviour, the repercussions are serious." She taps on SUICIDE and looks me straight in the eyes.

I frown as well. "Got it!"

"Some creative people at the top line only go down to the 'Normal' line, and that's fine. It's when they go down to the 'Depression' or 'Suicide' line that things become serious. This kind of behaviour needs to be monitored, and often patients need constant medication to keep them in safe bounds."

I fake a haughty face and say, "Well, *I* wouldn't want medication because I live my life in constant anticipation of my 'highs'. I would rather die than not have them. This is what makes my personality. It's part of me. I'll suffer the crap moods down here on the bottom line, just to have my highs!"

"Don't stress. There *is* medication that keeps you normal and allows you to be *you*, and enjoy your highs. All you want is not to suffer the massive downs and deep depression. The kind of depression that comes out of nowhere, like a disease. That's why medication is so important."

I don't say anything because Lulu's torn off another sheet and is drawing again. As if an afterthought, she puts it aside and takes out the one with the four mood lines again. I admire her indecisiveness because this makes her human. I'm in good company with people who swap between ideas and decisions in a random way. She waves her pen over the horizontal lines like a wand.

"I'm just thinking about one of my patients now, and I want to give you a little example of the seriousness of these mood changes. He's highly intelligent and heads up a large financial company. He also suffers manic episodes." I'm comforted. "He comes in here when he's worried about a big decision he needs to make or is on the verge of concluding a contract. I can pick up where he's sitting on his mood-chart. If he's wavering off the 'Normal' line, I tell him not to make decisions or sign contracts. He's on medication, but I still keep tabs on him."

I remember the chap with the laptop in the waiting room and say, "Very interesting."

"Yes it is. So you see how important it is to recognise where you're sitting on this chart? Where you are mentally can affect all aspects of your life, your business, your relationship with your kids, their happiness, etc."

The hairs on my neck prickle at her mentioning my kids. I really try hard to appear normal so that they aren't privy to my lows, but realise that they can probably sense them. They must know that the smile on my face is false. I hope they turn out normal, because if *my* influence is anything to go by, they could land up here.

"Do you think this explains why I've had such bad joss in my life? I was called 'Calamity Jane' at the office."

"Yes, because abnormal mood swings can cause poor decision-making. You also stop listening to your instincts. You shouldn't try to ignore them, or try to bargain them away. You need to listen to them, doll. Try to work on this."

I'm impressed! How the hell she's managed to hit the right buttons, I just don't know.

# LULU, SCENE 3: NAUGHTY LITTLE NEURONS

I'm fascinated by how Lulu speaks. It's as if she spends time structuring her sentences before saying them. Unlike me who blurts out any bloody thing without thinking. I'm able to follow her because she talks like she's reading from a textbook and allows me enough time between sentences to absorb what she's just said. As much as this has turned out to be a lecture on the functionality of the brain, I love every minute of it.

She tosses the mood-chart aside and resumes her drawing on the second sheet. "OK, now these little circles represent the neurons in your brain." She draws a lot of circles haphazardly on the sheet. "Each one of these little cells is charged with electricity, which reacts to nearby cells, like messages through a magnet. There is enough electrical energy in each neuron to cause a lightning bolt."

*I love this stuff!*

It appeals to the scientist in me, brought about by an exacting degree in Physics. The concept of electrical energy flowing through the brain is fascinating. Now I'm sure humans will be moving things with brain-power in the future. My own reliance on the negative energies around me is reinforced. Popping a light bulb, mentally, surely needs a lightning bolt.

"I love this stuff! I did Physics at university, but this is the kind of science that I should've been studying!"

Lulu continues her science-in-the-head lecture, and I'm all ears. "Neurons react to one another and create networks of behaviour. For example, one neuron gets a message which triggers another message in another, etc., until the brain has created its own little circle of behaviour, which is the same, time and again. For example, you walk into the street and a bus is tearing towards you; what do you do?"

I won't answer the obvious and she knows it, because she continues, "You jump back onto the pavement to avoid being crushed. This network exists in your brain where one cell tells another what to do, which tells another, which tells another, until the network closes like an electrical circuit, and you jump to safety. In other words, little networks spinning through our brains at all times dictate our behaviour."

She can probably read the fascination in my eyes, and she continues, "For instance, a woman comes home and her husband says something that makes her angry, like he usually does, and she hits him over the head with a frying pan, and he throws his newspaper at her, and on and on and on …"

"Like history repeating itself!"

"Exactly! Both their neuron-networks are triggered by his first statement to her, and their behaviour is repetitive, and will probably cause a divorce if they don't get mental help. This is what psychologists or marriage counsellors do: they help people break the networks that dictate certain behaviour."

*So bloody simple!*

"Cool, this is all very clear to me. I'm glad you haven't asked me irrelevant things about my first memory, or how I get on with my parents. A clear understanding of the science of the brain is all you need to fix yourself."

"That's my job. It's the psychologists who do the psychoanalytical stuff. They assist us in recognising the triggers of our actions and help to break the networks that land us in trouble. They have a very important role to play."

She flips through my file and says without looking at me, "As much as I believe you have an aversion to this kind of therapy, I do think you may have a couple of things to revisit. Maybe you should think about it."

My so-called-psychotic-partner-issue is the only thing that comes to mind, but there's no way in hell I want to talk about him. He can burn in hell for all I care. I want to dig an acacia thorn into my leg, but I squeeze the cheeks of my bum together and say, "I'm fine and none of that analysis-crap is for me. I certainly don't have any issues to deal with, and if there were any, I can sort them out on my own with all these scientific explanations." I wave my hand over her drawings like I'm swatting a fly.

She doesn't answer. But I want to get back to analysing the naughty little neurons, so I say, "I also think that a confused head brought about by dodgy neurons can cause bad energies that mess with external forces as well."

She nods. "So do I."

It seems she likes my enthusiasm and I'm sure that the electrical energies between us are positive. She's surely a woman with sense, and I give her the biggest smile I can, in spite of the acid in my chest.

# LULU, SCENE 4: WHAT MAKES US TICK?

Lulu whips out yet another piece of blank paper, and draws a cross section of a brain, putting the ear and the nose in the right places. Her drawing skills are abysmal, but I like the crudity.

She draws a circle behind the ear and says, "This is the emotional lobe of the brain. You know of course that the brain consists of a number of sections, which are responsible for different thoughts and senses and stuff?" I nod energetically with my eyes fixed on her drawing.

"The emotional part of the brain is actually within the temporal lobe, which is also responsible for language, hearing, vision, and memory. But let's just call this the 'emotional lobe.'"

I eagerly lean forward over my elbows to spur her on. "Cool."

"What causes depression is as follows: Say one little cell is not quite right, like it's a bit deformed or sick ... say it's like a pimple." She draws a little circle in the middle of the emotional lobe and starts scribbling over it. "What happens is that all the other little cells crowd around it to try and fix it, like they're worried about it or something." She draws other little circles around the one she's scribbled over, with lots of arrows pointing at it. "They're so busy being little doctors and trying to fix it that they forget about their real job, like properly responding to your environment and making you feel the things you should be feeling, emotionally. Got it?" I nod quickly.

She leans back and says, "So that's why people feel empty and numb. They can't cry or laugh and just feel up to shit. This is the kind of depression that's not brought on by something tangible like a death or divorce. It's not anyone's fault. Got it?"

*So bloody simple!*

"Shit! That's so bloody simple!" I certainly understand what she's talking about, because as much as I search for reasons for feeling so low, I just can't find any. I can't get out of bed, so I lie there like a zombie. The only thing I feel, like an instinct, is terribly embarrassed because I'm lying there like a lazy cow with no excuses. And Stef doesn't know what to do either, so he brings me a cup of tea and says, "Just sleep, my love."

I think my enthusiasm for all this science stuff exhilarates Lulu, because she's animated as she eagerly works on her head diagram again. She draws another circle behind the ear and says quickly, "OK, I want to show you just how important the sparks between your neurons are. This is the memory section of the temporal lobe." She draws a horizontal line through it and numbers the two sections 1 and 2.

"We have 'Memory Level One' and 'Memory Level Two'. Number One is the stuff we see or hear that's not really important to us. Like, if I said, 'Five six seven one two three', you wouldn't give a hoot because it means nothing to you."

I've already forgotten the numbers, but she doesn't need to explain so I quickly say, "Ja, got it."

"OK. Now, Memory Level Two is the stuff that you remember because it's important to you, like your mother's face, or memories of your childhood. Like, say you played the lottery on that number I've just rattled off, and won a million. You'll never forget the number and would be telling your grandchildren about it when you're old and grey. That number would sit in your Memory Level Two forever."

"Got it."

"Now let me tell you about déjà vu, like when people say they have an increased sense of familiarity with something they're experiencing."

*This is sure to be good!*

Everybody knows about déjà vu, and I continue to humour her with my eyes. She says, "What happens with déjà vu is that ..." She draws a kind of lightning bolt between the two memory sections, "... a neuron in Level One makes a mistake, for whatever reason, and sparks a reaction in Level Two, like a misdirected thunderbolt. What happens is that your Memory Level Two thinks it's getting old memories, and is tricked into believing that this Level One memory belongs to it, and that it's reminding you of an old memory, and not a new one. Of course, all this happens so quickly that the time it takes for the miscommunication between the two levels is almost immeasurable. So you feel that the stuff that's happening around you is happening exactly as you've experienced it before, even though you've never had this experience before."

I wait a bit until I've worked it out. "That's bloody brilliant!"

She smiles like sunshine and says, "Cool, hey!"

She definitely likes my enthusiasm. I also think we've developed a mutual respect: she knows I can measure the tensile strength of a steel beam in a soccer stadium; I know she can measure the tensile strength of the neurons in a psycho's head.

This wonderful vibe between us is making me delirious. It's like a union between two mad scientists, with lots of stuff to debate through the night over a bottle of vodka.

# LULU, SCENE 5: THE FUNNY-SMELL THING

Lulu's cellphone rings and I hate the interruption. But my inquisitiveness prickles in the hope I'm going to hear her talk someone out of killing herself. So I lean back in my chair and light two ciggies and pass her one so she understands that I don't mind that we're being interrupted. I can hear a hysterical voice on the other side, and she says into the phone, "You neurosurgeons are all the same! Just calm down. I'm sure he's into you …" She winks at me. This is obviously not a suicide case, and I stop concentrating on the voice.

The long pauses between dialogues with her neurosurgeon-friend allow me time to mull over what we've been talking about.

Something niggles at me. The drawing of the nose on the cross section of the brain reminds me of something Tulula said in our 20-Questions session.

Lulu puts the phone down and stretches her arms out while leaning back into her chair and says, with her ciggy hanging from her mouth, "Sorry about that."

"No problem. While you were talking, I remembered something Tulula asked me. What's all this about the funny-smell thing?"

She licks her finger and says, "This is very interesting."

From under the pile of papers, which are now strewn all over her desk, she hauls out the picture of the brain with the ear and the nose on it, and slides it towards me. She stretches over the drawing, and draws a line from the nose, past the memory and emotional circles and down, what I presume, is the throat.

I lean forward over the drawing, and she says, "This is the nasal cavity. Now check out how close it is to the memory levels."

I try to work out where she's going with this, but she's explaining it before I can think. "A lot of the things we do and think have been carried through our genes since we were cavemen."

She leaves my ancestral monkey hanging in the air as she offers me one of her ciggies and lights up for both of us. We're certainly chain-smoking during our exhilarating discussion.

We blow smoke at each other and I say through the haze between us, "That makes sense."

"OK, now the four basic smells that we experienced while living in our caves were ..." She pauses for drama, "... rotting meat, urine, fire and musk."

I'm excited. "Shit! Of course! What was the musk?"

"The musk must have been from the plants we would crush to—"

I quickly finish the sentence for her as the beauty of its rationale dawns on me: "... to do our cave-paintings."

She nods. "Exactly!"

I can't stop myself from adding to this stuff, and I think I'm babbling in my excitement. "The smell of urine must've been strong because we must have pissed in our caves like animals. And of course, we had no refrigerators, so meat would rot. And of course, the smell of fire was always prevalent, especially in winter. So basically, these four smells were all we really recognised, over millions of years! Shit! This is fascinating!"

I'm glad the f-word is smouldering in my ancestors' cave and not mine. She doesn't need to explain the link between the olfactory senses and the memory levels, because I've got it, and she knows it.

"You've got it. So, the brain remembers these basic smells, and again some little sparks interfere with our olfactory senses and tell us we can actually smell them, even though the source of the smell isn't present. It's only these four smells that we shrinks look out for. I see this poor guy who constantly smells smoke, like burning matches, and it's freaking him out. But now he understands where it's coming from, and we're dealing with it ..."

I'm not sure how one would expel a smell that's already lodged in one's subconscious, but what I do know is that I don't smell the musk anymore, only the acidic smell of urine at the end of my repeating nightmare.

As if an afterthought she says, "I used to consult this old lady when I did some pro bono work in the squatter camps. She was beside herself because she continually smelt something rotten. She was constantly cleaning her shack and washing her private parts."

"Shame, man. Is she OK now?"

"Yes, all fixed up."

She reads something in my yellow folder. "You seem to have experienced a lot of the things we've talked about, which may suggest a twitchy temporal lobe. I want to take a peek at your activity levels. That's why I suggested an EEG."

"Does this mean I'm a clever chick?"

She doesn't answer. Maybe she thinks I'm weird. As much as I've tucked the mind-travel thing safely away under my pull-yourself-together blanket, memories of my strange experience at the loony-bin are with me still. Maybe electrical energy was responsible for the mind-travel. Who knows?

But I don't want to talk about this stuff because I think she's got enough information on me to suggest that I've got a high dose of electrical energy sparking between my neurons.

What I *do* want to talk about is my bad joss when I'm going up and down between feeling low and being manic, so I say, "I'm sure negative electrical energy has been responsible for a lot of my bad luck. And I mean a lot! I've had so much shit happen to me, but thank heavens I can always put it aside to think about tomorrow … like Vivien Leigh says in *Gone with the Wind*."

"Ja," she says, "I remember that. It also struck me as some kind of avoidance. We all say we have tomorrow, but tomorrow never comes, and we never seem to sort out anything, hey? I do the same thing, so don't feel alone." I could kiss her.

# LULU, SCENE 6: THE GLORIOUS CHEMICALS

It's dark outside and I look at my watch. Our consultation was only meant to be half an hour. "Shit, Lulu, we've been here for almost two hours!"

I could sit here and chat about all this stuff through the night. All that's missing is a bottle of cold white wine and two crystal glasses. I hope she's not going to give me the time's-up thing.

"No sweat, you're my last patient of the day and it's been great to chat to you. Don't worry, I'll still only charge you for half an hour."

*Shit, she surely is one of the good ones!*

"Shit, doll," I say, "you're one hell-of-a-person! It would be cool to crack open a bottle now and have a little toot together. It's drinkie-time."

She doesn't reply to this but I catch her writing in cursive on top of the page: "A?" I know the A stands for "Alcoholic". The question mark next to it tells me she's obviously not sure whether I'm one or not. I point at the A. "Ah-ha! I've caught you out! I know what the A stands for! That's funny. But I truly am not one. My grandmother was, and knowing what my poor mother went through with her, I'm nothing like her."

Surprisingly she also laughs, but not sarcastically like I've just done, but out loud with a twinkle in her eye. She says, "People who seek alcohol are looking for a tranquiliser," as if this explains it all.

I don't want to discuss this any longer, and apparently neither does she, because she's back on her brain-diagram again and drawing a lot of spindly lines all over it.

She says without looking at me, "OK. Now, with all these electrical impulses going on in your brain, you also have the chemical stuff that's released, which causes or stops different emotions. You know, of course, about serotonin." I've heard about it and I nod.

She says with animation, "This is the most glorious stuff, and if we didn't have it, we would all surely die."

"Oh?"

"Yip!"

"Shit!"

She's into her lecture again. "Serotonin has a lot of functions. It's located in the stomach, where it's used to regulate intestinal movements. You also get it in your neurons and central nervous system, where it regulates mood, appetite, sleep, muscle contraction, and some things like memory and learning."

She continues drawing wavy lines over the brain and says while she's doodling, "It's also found in plants, fruits, vegetables, fungi and animals. It does the same kind of thing to them as it does to us."

"Wow! And I thought it was just a head-chemical."

"It also has the most amazing capability of switching off our consciousness. That's why you hear of people who don't feel anything after a serious accident. The serotonin pumps through the brain and allows them some time to recover. It's like an anti-shock drug."

"Shit! Bring on the serotonin!"

She raises a finger. "But be careful here. It's a hell-of-a-thing to monitor because an incorrect dose can cause physical problems. It can also mask or enhance other character traits. Incorrect administration of the stuff can increase the risk of suicide in some patients, for example."

*I don't need serotonin!*

"But going back to the natural way it helps the brain: a lot of my patients who've been abused or raped—" I close my eyes and put my hands up towards her face to tell her I don't want to talk about this kind of stuff, but she's finishing her verdict, "A lot of my patients who suffer abuse tell me that they seem to elevate themselves from the situation, and that they actually feel nothing. They say that it's as if they're looking down on themselves as the abuse is happening."

I cup my hands over my face, and all I can see is the light of her desk lamp, shining through my fingers. I hate talking about this kind of stuff and I certainly don't want to think about it. But Lulu is at it again, as though she wants me to be strong or something. "So you see how amazing serotonin is? In fact, if we didn't have it, we would probably die of the pain and suffering that life imposes on us."

"Amazing! Now, can we talk about something else, like Uri Geller."

It's dark outside, and memories of working late at night alone in my office are with me like dread. She looks at her watch and says, "OK, doll, we both need to get home to our domestic duties. We'll leave together."

She wipes out the saucer that was our ashtray with a tissue, and opens the windows of her office.

"I want to give you some papers to read." She gets up and passes my chair.

I stretch my arms as if I'm waking up, and get up to follow her. She's shuffling about in a small storeroom off her office, where shelves are piled with yellow folders, files, papers and other junk. "I've got to tidy up this place one day," she says. "I can never find anything." She passes me a pile of photocopies, the pages of which are stapled together in sections. I glance at the big heading on top of the pile: "Bipolar Disorder – January 2002."

I've heard about this Bipolar-thing in passing, and it seems to be the new vogue sickness that everyone's talking about, especially Hollywood actors, whom I've read about in stupid tabloids. Whenever some actor has been caught taking drugs or drunk-driving, there's always some bloody reference to her having Bipolar-whatever. What a load of crap!

I follow Lulu out of her office and towards the elevator. This stupid reading matter on something that has absolutely nothing to do with me is definitely not for me. I'm certainly *not* going to read it and will seek out the first dustbin to toss this pile of rubbish.

I'm stuck close to Lulu in the elevator as we head our way to the ground floor. I find myself saying, "Do you believe in spiritualism? I mean, it's a far cry from psychology, but what are your thoughts on it?"

"Yes, I do," she says. "I think it plays a big role in who we are as human beings."

"I don't know why I asked you. The question popped out of nowhere."

We're in the car park and a security guard ambles over to see us to our cars. I need to say goodbye to Lulu, but don't know whether to shake her hand or hug her. I choose the latter, and she hugs me back with oomph.

As I walk away I wonder if I'll ever see her again. "Shit!" I yell across the increasing distance between us, "I forgot to tell you, I'm going to the South of France in two days … on a bloody holiday! I would rather stick hot pins in my eyes than go!"

She shouts into the darkness, "Wow! That's so cool. Just enjoy it, doll. You're a lucky girl. You need to go and have your blood tests chop-chop. We can do the EEG when you get back. I'll fax the script to you as soon as I get your results."

I'm relieved my brain-probing has been put on hold, because there's no way any machine is going to pick up anything, given the amount of mind-altering drugs I'm on. The only thing it will sense is my heart rate, and that will be as slow and dull as the pulsing of my debilitated neurons. And like hell am I taking any new drugs with me to France!

# THE FRENCH PRACTITIONER

Shh, shh, shh …

I lean my elbows on the terrace table, cup my hands over my eyes, and peep at my audience between my fingers.

Shh, shh, shh …

I don't want them to look at me because I'm so bloody embarrassed I could die.

Shh, shh, shh …

I don't want them to be here.

Shh, shh, shh …

I only want Stef here.

Shh, shh, shh …

I don't want his uncle, or his grandmother, or his father, or his father's girlfriend to be here. I don't want them to witness what I have to go through now. I want Uncle Gerhard, Oma, Manfred and Jacqui to push off and leave me to deal with this alone.

Shh, shh, shh …

No-one is saying anything, but I feel their disapproving eyes upon me like an unspoken scolding.

Shh, shh, shh …

The only thing I want to hear is the song of the cicadas. Their perpetual song, like water-jets from an irrigation system, is strangely consoling. Their pulsating shh-shhs seem to mask the throbbing in my head and help me to focus on keeping calm – and avoiding a seizure.

Like an irrigation system being turned off, their song is interrupted by the sound of a car chugging up the long driveway. Their pause is brief, and they quickly return to vibrating their tummy muscles to produce their mesmer-ising clicking sound. My audience gets up to meet the car; only Oma stays because she's old and can't get up without assistance. I hear hushed greetings on the driveway behind me.

I straighten myself in my chair and prepare for this horrible meeting. I think I look OK because Jacqui has given me a dress that looks like the ones worn by country girls in old French movies. It's lavender-coloured and drawn into the waist, and makes a swishing sound when I walk. It's a sexy, feminine dress and completely lost on me because I feel like a hermaphrodite. I've tied my hair loosely behind my neck, and, all in all, I must *physically* present a happy French maiden.

I feel like the doomed maiden in Pagnol's *Manon of the Springs*, or perhaps I feel as lost as she did. Stef has told me that Pagnol's *My Father's Glory* and *My Mother's Castle* are set in this exact region. To normal people this must be a marked experience; it's lost on me, and I feel guilty for being blasé.

I don't want to think about endearing things like the little Pagnol skipping over Mount St. Victoire, which is behind me. I don't want to think about the adoring relationship between father and son as they hunted the *Gallinetes Cendrées*, which probably ran for its life like a ghost, right here under my feet. So I stick my thumb into my mouth and look at the vineyards of Aix-en-Provence while I await the French practitioner.

It's so beautiful here it makes me want to vomit. The glory of the place is eluding me, and the memory of the passion I used to have for this kind of splendour is hurting. Anyone would give their eyeteeth to be sitting here on this terrace, in front of a French villa, overlooking endless vineyards and olive trees, which look like the glossy pictures everyone aspires to in homemaker's magazines. Anyone would sell their mother to be sitting here amidst all this beauty, in a sexy French dress, with blonde hair tied loosely at the neck, while the cicadas sing to the mistral. It's so beautiful that anyone would be inspired to write a poem or a book about it, full of descriptive words and wine and wonderings.

I feel Oma's eyes on me, so I whip my thumb from my mouth. She's working her mouth and a little grunt escapes its vertical wrinkles. She's Austrian and doesn't speak English or French, so she only talks to me in grunts. She's probably saying, "What the hell's the matter with you? I've gone through a World War and raised four children with nothing to my name but an old rooster and an orange for Christmas. You are not injured or malnourished, so why in God's name are you having a bloody house-call from a doctor?"

I don't give a shit what she thinks. She's so old that she probably can't see very well, so I put my finger back into my mouth and chew off the bit of dried skin that's been tempting me.

"Bonjour!"

*Oh, my God!*

A scrawny, tanned little man, with thinning hair and a casual checked shirt appears at my side with my audience circled around him. He extends his hand to shake mine. I don't get up, but I put a big smile on my French-maiden mug, and give his wet palm a squeeze.

I concentrate on my French accent, "Bonjour, monsieur."

He carries a black doctor's bag. It's creased and worn, so he must be experienced. Manfred has told me that he's the only available doctor he's managed to find at short notice and that he's had to drive two hours to get here. I'm extremely embarrassed that he had to drive so far to make a house-call for a waste-case like me.

I hope he speaks a bit of English, so I say as well as I can, "Excusez moi, monsieur docteur; je parle Anglais; mais je parle Français un petit peu. C'est difficile pour moi mais j'essaye." I've learnt these sentences like a parrot. They're the ones I throw at all French people I meet, and I've even practised the accent. But the frowns I usually get tell me they still smack of "merde Anglais".

I'm hoping he'll burst forth in perfect English, but he doesn't look at me and keeps his eyes on Stef, which probably means he doesn't understand a word I'm saying. He must already despise me because he thinks I'm just another "Anglaise" invading the South of France like Peter Mayle.

"Je ne suis pas Anglaise," I stutter, "je suis Sud Africaine." He nods, so he must be pleased I'm from Africa and not an English enemy from across the channel, and he's probably made an effort to comprehend my shitty French. But it's clear that he's not capable of speaking to me in English, and it's clear that my French isn't good enough, which means we'll have to communicate via Stef. This will make this meeting even more horrific than its subject matter.

He sits down opposite me as does my audience. I'm sitting at the head of the terrace table, which makes me feel like I'm chairing a meeting. My haughtiness is quickly squashed by the fact that they are chairing me, and want me to admit my craziness like an employee about to be fired.

He accepts a glass of rosé from Stef, and when my glass is also filled, I notice that he doesn't raise an eyebrow at my drinking, but merely raises his glass and says, "Santé!" I finish my glass with a gulp and so does he.

He says something to Stef with a smile full of sunshine, "… problem?" He puts a funny "ya" at the end of his words, typical of Provencal lingo.

I abandon trying to understand what the hell Stef's saying, and switch off. It's actually quite pleasant to leave the details of my sorry predicament to someone else to explain.

Stef talks for a long time and, as he speaks, the doctor's eyes widen. Given that Stef says what he means without elaboration, I'm sure he's got to the point and explained my dilemma without adding too much pathetic detail.

I pick up the words "bagage" and "aéroport" and "médicament" which tells me that Stef has explained that I was on medication, and that I had stupidly packed the stash in my suitcase, and that my suitcases hadn't arrived at the airport, and that my medication was lost, and that the airport company had declared it missing and couldn't promise its return, and that I had finished the little I had taken in my handbag on the flight two days ago, and that I needed more. As I put all of this together, I know that the negative energy is still around me, like the fire-demon, because it was only *my* suitcase that was lost, and not Stef's or the kids'.

Stef has probably explained that we've had the script faxed here by Lulu, but that none of the medication I'm on is available in the local pharmacies. And that basically, I'm in the shit. I've finally explained to Stef that I probably need to stay on the stuff because, if I don't, I will probably have a seizure or a heart attack or something as delightful as that.

I really hope he hasn't explained all the nitty-gritty details. "Did you tell him what the medication is for?" I ask.

"Yes, my love, I've basically told him everything."

*What the hell?*

This means that he probably knows that some other shrink thinks it's necessary, because I'm a bloody loony in need of a head-fix. I grab the bottle of wine and fill my glass, as well as the doctor's.

He sips it gingerly without looking at me and says to Stef (what little I can pick up), "situation ... très sérieuse. Impossible ..."

The wrinkle between Stef's eyes deepens as he nods at the doctor. He turns to me and the crevice between his eyes smoothens. "My love, there's a little problem. He says he can't prescribe medication unless he's made his own diagnosis, and if he's satisfied that you actually need it, he will try to prescribe similar medication."

*What the hell?*

I can't believe what I'm hearing! I've just had my medication changed by Lulu, who supposedly has given me stuff that's different from the rubbish I was taking in the hospital, which had been changed twice by Cranium in the loony-bin. And now I'm going to have to take some other crap that's supposedly similar to the stuff that replaced the crap I was taking ... only if

I act out some loony-antics that this French bloody practitioner can believe, and therefore medicate for!

I feel like the circus monkey again. I whisper into Stef's face, "If I'm going to have to have a fucking private consultation, I want it to be fucking private!" I tilt my head and eyes at my audience.

Stef says something to his father in Austrian, and they all get up to leave. As Oma is helped up from her chair and onto her walking sticks, she scowls at me and grunts. She surely understands what Stef has just said.

I smile at her. "Danke, Oma. Ich bin müde."

I'm not sure what I've just said in German and neither is she, because she merely works her mouth in and out over her gums and is gone with the others into the kitchen.

Now it's just me, Stef, and the French practitioner circling the bottle of wine. Stef pours the doctor another, avoiding my glass. The doctor quickly quaffs his and, holding up the glass to the sunshine like a true connoisseur looking at the last swirls at the bottom of it, says, "Magnifique!"

Stef fills it again like a man au fait with the French spirit of generous hospitality, and talks at the doctor's now reddening face. I'm not sure what he's saying, but I assume he's giving his own reasons why I'm on head-medication. I wish I could hear his take on my predicament. It would surely give me a clear insight about where I rate on his scale of respect, and whether he still thinks I'm the "tits".

"What did you tell him?" I ask.

"I told him you were stark raving mad and that I had committed you to an asylum because you were threatening suicide and becoming a danger to yourself and those around you."

*Typical Stef-style!*

I don't expect anything less from Stef. He always cuts to the chase. Moreover, I know he wants to get rid of the doctor because wine flowing like this would surely see him at our dinner table, and passed out on the couch.

The doctor doesn't utter a peep, but his black eyes and red cheeks say it all. I know what's needed now. I've got the empty plastic containers and silver pill sachets in my pocket. Like a magician hiding a coin, I gingerly take them out and hand them to the doctor, careful not to expose how many there are to the chirping cicadas. He lowers his glasses from his forehead and peers at the labels for what seems like an age. I'm sure he's thinking that I must indeed have some English blood in me, because French people, especially the ones from the South, would never need such crap. Any mental illness is quickly sorted out by a good day's grape-picking in the scorching heat. My shame burns at my temples as he scribbles a number of line-items into a doctor's script book, and chucks the page at Stef.

Stef folds the script and puts it into the back-pocket of his shorts as he gets up to shake the doctor's hand saying, "Merci beaucoup, Docteur. À bientôt."

I understand what he's said and again, in typical Stef-style, he's telling the doctor to be on his way. He gives the doctor a solid handshake and patronising smile.

The doctor's gone, and Stef and I sit together on the terrace saying nothing, as usual. The only thing I'm able to muster is, "Shit! Was that a ballbreaker or what?" He doesn't respond.

Shh, shh, shh …

The cicadas are making me tired. I can't believe I'm so tired. I haven't moved my bum off the property since we arrived here two days ago. I've worn my happy-mommy mask and desperately tried to be a fun-loving, doting mother to my kids. Maybe this is why I'm feeling so exhausted. Furthermore, I've insisted on doing all the washing, and spent hours hanging the large sheets, towels and clothes on the washing line at the back of the villa, like a crazed freak in the wind.

Stef gets up. "I'll go into Aix and get the stuff. The kids can stay here and swim."

I hear the kids' screams over the noise of the cicadas, from the pool on the hill behind us. They seem to be having a ball with the neighbour's kids. They're so engrossed in "regard moi" and diving and splashing in the pool that I feel I can safely leave them here with the family.

So I say to Stef in Greta Garbo's husky voice, "I'm going for a walk. I want to be alone."

# MY LEGIONNAIRE

I haven't taken in where I am, because my emptiness hasn't allowed it. But my footsteps down the sandy driveway boost my energy, and I become a little more aware of my surroundings. I've got Lucky in tow, and she keeps me focused. This helps too. I'm comfortable in the presence of dogs, more so than humans, and miss my Pooki. She's probably lying in a little cage at the kennels, pining for me as if I've died. But Lucky's not privileged like Pooki. She's a pavement special. She was rescued by Manfred and Jacqui in Ghana, and she's lucky to have been found, and even luckier to be living here with them in the countryside. But she's old and blind, and I need to make sure she sticks with me as we trundle down the driveway. She seems to know where she's going, so I follow her.

I keep my eyes on her bobbing bottom, which is much higher than the rest of her. The front legs are half the length of the back ones, and the poor dog seems to be a hybrid of different-sized dogs whose genes are unevenly spread, causing an awkward lopsidedness. Even though she's a mongrel, I feel close to her. We're both Africans in France, like fish out of water. She's happy to be out and walking with me, and I'm slightly comforted by the fact that I can give some pleasure to somebody, albeit a lopsided rescue dog.

I haven't told anyone, but I've kept the last dose of my medication from my hand-luggage, and carefully cut the tiny pills up, so as to keep taking little bits and not shock my brain. I don't want it to think that it's been totally deprived of its mind-altering influence. I remember Sister Bertha's advice on the dangers of quitting suddenly, but maybe I'm looking forward to a seizure, like suicide.

What I do know is that I'm feeling strange. I'm feeling slightly out of body and light-headed. Although there's still no change to my sadness-level, the wooziness is quite nice. Maybe my veins and head enjoy the relief of the drugs being drained, like expelling a long-held pee. I don't want to think about my head any longer, so I lift my eyes off Lucky's bottom and into the sunlight.

Stef explained where we were on our arrival, but I took no notice. As Lucky and I near the end of the driveway, I recall his words. The estate is situd at the end of a small village called Puyloubier in the foothills of Mount St. Victoire. The village is special because it's the last village adjacent to the mountain. The estate is even more special because it's the last privately owned property at the end of the village.

As much as I was in a haze as we drove through the village on our arrival, I could sense its aura. It's quaint and has all the ingredients of a typical French village, like the ones only film producers find. The bowling area is park-like and situated in front of the town hall. The men playing pétanque are like permanent fixtures, like actors in a perpetual play. They're even dressed appropriately in black pants and open-neck shirts and herald bottles of water-like liquid, which they quaff between boules and curses. There's one bakery, which has a monopoly and has been owned by one family for hundreds of years, one primary school, and one of everything else. There are also a few bars, restaurants and art galleries.

As we passed through the village, the density of houses lessened until we reached what was the end of the public road and the beginning of the estate. It was huge in comparison to the rest of the properties which, Stef explained, had once been part of one estate, but had been broken up by family squabbles. Although this is a typical ingredient of urbanisation, the village remains small and the buildings retain their original state and colouring. So yes, it's pukka, like in the movies, and I'm lucky to be here walking on set, with Lucky tripping happily in front of me.

We near the end of the driveway, which divides the olive groves from the vineyards, and I expect Lucky to hit a right and head towards the village centre. But she's off to the left and passes an enormous stone pillar which reads "Legio Patria Nostra – Capitaine Danjou". I read Latin at school, so I know that means "Legion of our Nation", but I have no idea who Captain Danjou is. Stef has told me that the property adjacent to the estate, at the end of the public road, belongs to the French government, and is the retirement village for invalids of the French Foreign Legion. I shouldn't be here, so I whistle at Lucky to stop. But she quickens her pace and disappears around the bend.

"Bonjour, mon petit chien-chien!"

*Who the hell is that?*

The voice is male and gruff. I jog around the bend and come face to face with a big man in a vest. He's leaning over his large belly and roughing-up Lucky, who's pouncing around his feet with her tongue hanging out and a big smile on her face. His eyes are on mine as he swirls her around. There's a naughty twinkle in them, which makes me a little nervous. I'm from Africa, and I certainly know that walking alone is not recommended, so I mumble, "Bonjour." Keeping my eyes on Lucky, I find myself shrieking a little too hysterically, "Lucky! Come here, you naughty dog!"

I'm not sure if I should've tried my French, but he would have worked out I was English anyway and still had his way with the "merde Anglaise salope!"

Lucky's become overexcited, and he pushes her down, still keeping his naughty eyes on me. She obeys his command as he lunges at me with an extended meaty hand. I can't take my eyes off the bottom of his belly, which is exposed under a too-short vest. The creases underneath his belly-bulge disappear into the top of his pants and I notice that his fly is open. As much as I've tried to appear unperturbed by him and to act with decorum, fear engulfs me, and I find myself backing away. But his lunge towards me is unyielding, and the meaty hand clasps mine in a hearty handshake.

"Bonjour, madam, Salute, Buenos días, Guten Tag, Nee hao, Nostrovia. And a very good day to you, pretty lady!"

This multilingual greeting catches me off-guard, but the open fly still worries me and I can't take my eyes off it. He must notice the direction of my stare and jumps back and turns around saying, "Excuse me, dear lady. I do apologise!"

At least his snake is in its cage, and I manage, stupidly, as I feel my face burning, "Excuse *me*."

I can't put a nationality to his face because it looks universal, but it's nice enough, and now that he's grinning, the twinkle in his eye, which I thought was full of sexual advances, is merely a twinkle full of jolliness.

He beams at me and growls, "You are English?"

The mistral must have blown over him and into my nostrils, because I smell sweat and ethylated spirits. This must be the remnants of some cheap alcohol, and fear wells up inside me again. But I say as politely as possible over another potential menace, "No, no, not at all. I'm from South Africa, but my father is Italian and my mother half-German and half-Russian." I feel stupid saying it; us South Africans don't know where the hell we're from.

"Ah-ha! This explains your beauty. Mixed blood, especially the blood of our Allies, is a good recipe for good genes and exquisite beauty."

I'm not sure what he means by "blood of our Allies", because I don't know who he swears allegiance to, or which war he's referring to. And I'm certainly not sure of his opinion of my beauty, because I've been feeling like an ugly toad. But I like the compliment.

His head and face are shaven and, although he sports a large belly, he walks erect and has a military air about him. He must be a legionnaire.

"I'm sorry," I say, "I know I'm not allowed to be here. I'll go now." I grab Lucky by the scruff of her neck and begin dragging her away from the soldier.

"Of course you can walk here! We have many tourists coming to visit the barracks. And anyway, you are walking with the famous Gustav!"

I didn't know I was walking with the famous Gustav, but he hooks his arm under mine and we're walking together along the road. He teeters a little, I'm sure because of the alcohol, and I hold him up. But he's in good company: maybe he's being so familiar with me because he can smell wine on my own breath.

A military-type van tears towards us and I grab hold of Lucky's neck and hold her still while Gustav retains his grip on my arm. A man wearing a beret in the passenger seat shakes a finger at Gustav, as if in a warning, but he gives the middle finger to the back of the van as it speeds away from us. I like his oomph.

We've passed two small bends in the narrow tarred road and seem to be ascending a small hillock. I keep my eyes on Lucky's bottom and she seems content with my new-found company, and trots ahead of us. Gustav is slightly out of breath and I'm not surprised, given his size.

I feel rivulets of his sweat on my arm and I'm slightly nauseated by the hairs under his arms, like bushels growing from his vest. I'm sure his armpits are rancid. I swallow hard and, trying to squash my squeamishness, I say, "You speak very good English. Where are you from?"

"I'm a Belgian," he says with pride. I know the Belgians hate the French and vice versa, but not as much as the French hate the English. Gustav is not a typical Belgian name. I'm sure he's made it up.

I don't want to smell his sweat, so I block my nose without touching it, and speak from my mouth, "So you must also speak Flemish, and of course you speak French."

"I speak Flemish, French, Spanish, Italian, and German. I also speak some Russian, and a bit of Mandarin, Korean and Arabic. And of course you know that I also speak perfect English."

I like his lack of modesty and agree, saying, "You speak superb English!"

I've heard that the palates of people who speak many languages from an early age don't shape to suit one particular language, making good pronunciation in all languages easy. But he has a very strange accent. In fact, I've never heard English spoken quite like this. It lacks the typical accent of any particular language and I can't put my finger on the lingo. If I had to choose, I would say it's more like English spoken by a German who's had the highest education in an English school. The lingo lacks the usual German lilt, but sounds more like Latin spoken without an accent.

I'm impressed by his multilingualism, and admit, "The only other language I can speak is Afrikaans, which is quite useless internationally. I'm hopeless with languages. My brain can't grasp them." I think my brain is so full of maths that it keeps trying to solve a problem when posed with a grammar issue, and crashes like a computer. I'm actually quite ashamed of my inability to speak another language. My father speaks Italian and Bergamasco, a northern Italian dialect, my mother used to speak German, my husband speaks French and Austrian, and my kids are fluent in French. They certainly haven't inherited my deficient language gene.

He laughs and says into my ear, like he's telling me a secret, "I had to learn these languages because I had missions all over the continent, and I've fou  t alongside many different nationals."

I picture Gustav full of grit and gumption, hiding out in the mount with Telly Savalas in *Kelly's Heroes*. I nudge him and say, "You must be brave and very clever!"

He stops us short by tugging on my arm, and says to the sky, "I' best!"

We laugh together and say nothing for a while as we reach the top of the hillock. The view is breathtaking. I'm walking with my brave legionnaire in God's country. Huge olive trees creep up the slopes of St. Victoire to the left, and to the right, as far as the eye can see, are rows upon rows of vineyards. I notice a number of grey-haired men working the fields, and assume they're retirees of the Legion. They certainly don't look like invalids, and I'm a little miffed at the unfortunate term used for these men.

The picture of a working vineyard is like an impressionist painting. I find myself tearing away from Gustav's grip and opening my arms to the sky, shouting at the top of my voice, "My God, this is beautiful!"

"Ah-ha! She has passion!" And he lowers his voice to a whisper as he retakes my arm. "Even though there's a little sadness in her eyes ..."

# THE KILLING FIELDS

I don't want to be reminded of my sadness, and I don't want to talk to Gustav about it, because the special moment we're having together has made me feel normal again. He doesn't know I'm a freak who's just been discharged from a loony-bin. Any mention of that crap in this beautiful setting will suck him down to hell with me and I'm afraid I'll lose him like in *Alice in Wonderland.* So I change the subject. "Does this entire wonderland belong to the Legion?"

I don't look at him, because his face is too close to mine as we walk arm in arm, but he says with pride and laughter in his voice, "As far as the eye can see! This all belongs to me, because I'm the most famous legionnaire of all."

I don't believe him, of course, but I'm enjoying his bravado. I say, "That's fantastic! Why are you the most famous?" trying not to sound cynical.

"Because I've killed the most men!"

*Shit!*

I don't answer because I can't find the words to respond, but I secretly want him to tell me all the grisly details about the killings. I want to introduce Stef to this man. I know he's Stef's kind of man. Stef was in the French army and has all the qualities of a soldier. I just hope Gustav didn't kill any Italians, or Germans, or Russians, because this would be too close to home.

"Did you kill any Italians or Germans or Russians?"

"Mostly Koreans, Algerians, and Iraqis, but I've also killed about five or six Italians. I didn't kill them in their own country. They were just in the wrong place at the wrong time."

"Oh."

I'm sure he didn't kill them in South Africa. And luckily my family immigrated to South Africa a hundred years ago, so the slaughter of my relatives is too distant from my blood-line for me to feel offended. But what I *am* left with is the macabre significance of keeping company with a professional murderer, even though his reason for killing was the "Patria Nostra".

He's huffing and puffing and the smell of alcohol on his breath intensifies with each exhalation. The sweat that's pouring from his hairy armpits is staining my pretty French dress, and it's starting to stick to me. I need to let go of him, so I say, "Let's sit down for a while."

There's an enormous tree to the right of the road, and it seems to be the only shady spot to escape to in this scorching heat. The road in front of it ascends again and he's surely going to need the rest before I walk him to his barracks, wherever the hell they are. The heat is quite unexpected. It's much hotter here than in South Africa.

I unfasten his arm from mine and say, "Let's sit under this tree."

He trips into the bush and scratches around in the undergrowth, and I get a glimpse of the crack of his bottom as he bends down. He emerges with a large rock which he dumps on the roadside, gesturing for me to sit. I feel like Falabella in the *Asterix* books, and he my obliging Obelix. I wrap my dress around my legs and bum, and find the most comfortable spot on the rock to sit on. He collapses on the sand next to me and sighs as he stretches out.

He's relaxed, because any civility would be lost on a man who's experienced so much horror. I'm relaxed with him, and not at all compromised by his devil-may-care manner. In fact, I find his joie de vivre attractive. Lucky's also relaxed and lies next to him in the sand. She must like him, and this is more proof that he's a good man. He's closed his eyes and seems to be sleeping.

I tuck my arms under my knees and rest my chin on them as I crouch on the rock beside him. I need to take in where I am and try to feel the magic of it. I've become so used to the sound of the cicadas that I have to concentrate to hear them. The terrain here is typical of the South African Highveld and reminds me of home. The sand is pale and rocky and the grass is yellow and wispy, like on the farm where I grew up. Only the vineyards are out of place.

He yawns loudly and, without sitting up, offers me a small silver flask. "Drink the blood of our land, my dear lady!"

*Sure thing, my soldier-man!*

I push the thought of his gob on it aside, and swig the liquid. It's not at all a cheap taste and reminds me of Aquavit. It goes down well and I say through a cough, only to make him think that I'm a delicate lady, "That's very strong! Would you like a cigarette?" I'm sure he smokes too. The stress of war would surely warrant it. He takes one, still lying on his back.

I can't resist it, so I say, holding my thumbs beneath my dress, "Tell me about your missions." I want to say "killings".

He sits up with some effort and turns his grizzly face on me. "Why is a young lady like you interested in such horrible things? I don't want to taint your innocence."

"I'm not so innocent, you know. I'm not a little Parisian princess. I'm a strong farm girl from Africa and I can handle it."

"Ha! She has gumption! Maybe we can meet at the bar later and if you get me drunk enough, I might tell you."

"Then my husband will be very jealous and will challenge you to a duel, and you will surely be killed because he is a strong Austrian mountain goat, and you will be too drunk to defend yourself."

His eyes twinkle. "I'm terrified! The Austrians are exceptional war men and very brave. I would like to meet him. Maybe he can drink with us to-night?"

"If it's a drink challenge you want, he'll drink you under the table. He can drink enough to kill a horse!"

"Yes, the Austrians are good drinkers! I like him already!" He passes me the flask again and I take a long swig.

This conversation is getting stupid and I'm sure he's keeping me talking because he doesn't want to talk about his missions. So I put a little puppy wail into my voice and regret doing it as I say it, "Pleeeze … just tell me one weenie little thing."

He winces as if I'm pulling a knife from his stomach and groans, "You know a little about the Legionnaires, no?"

I've heard the story many times from Stef. "Stef's grandfather was a legion-naire."

I peer into his face to seek his approval, but he doesn't say anything. He merely purses his mouth and nods, as if appreciating a good wine. So I finish the story I know so well, "Stef's father was Austrian and fought for the German Army until 1945 under the ordinance of the Anschluss. He was probably a little crazy after the War, and joined the Legion, which he served until 1955 in Corsica and Algeria. He returned to Austria in '55 and saw his son, who was already sixteen, for the first time."

I'm surprised I can remember the dates, but I was good at history at school and learnt my lessons like a parrot. He's still nodding and pursing his lips, this time in appreciation of the stuff in the flask, but he seems interested enough and asks, "What happened to him?"

"He was diagnosed with lung cancer but refused to stop smoking and died in '58. Would you like another cigarette?"

He laughs and takes one, and I finish my little story, adding, "He received a Christmas card from the Legionnaire General who praised him for his honour. We named our son Maximillian, after Stef's grandfather."

"That's an honour."

I tempt a small conflict with my soldier, and say into the sky and not into his face, "I've heard that in order for legionnaires to be accepted, they have to be a special breed, or completely crazy, or troublemakers, or criminals, or something like that."

I can't believe that I've referred to Gustav, or Stef's grandfather, as potential criminals, and immediately blame the hardtack we've been drinking, but he laughs out loud. "You certainly got the crazy-thing right, but they stopped enlisting jailbirds a long time ago."

I wonder if Gustav was a rescued jailbird, because he falls in the "long time ago". I wonder if they still accept crazy guys or troublemakers into the Legion. I provoke him by looking into his eyes and asking, "What made *you* join?"

His eyes are misty. As he takes a swig from the flask, he says, "I joined in 1949. I was just a boy of eighteen. My father was a legionnaire and was killed in the War. My mother committed suicide after his death, so a friend of my father got me in."

I don't say anything and neither does he. A bus screams past us and hoots as it swerves and tries to avoid Gustav's legs, which are stretched onto the roadway. He doesn't move them, as though he wants the bus to run over them. "That's the bus that takes the legionnaires to and from Aix every day," he says casually as he looks at his feet on the tar road.

I'm ashamed for thinking he was a jailbird. My heart aches for his mother, who took her life due to sadness. My heart pains for Gustav, who was left motherless. Stef left home at sixteen and has all the ingredients of a man like Gustav.

I don't say anything until Gustav says, over his feet, "My father's friend paid for my passage over the Straits of Gibraltar to Algeria and gave me a letter of recommendation to enlist there. He was sent to fight in the Indochina War. I never heard from him again, but word has it that he was killed landing by parachute in Dien Bien Phu."

I wonder how he remembers all this. I'm sure the killings and the alcohol must have affected his memory, but he continues, as though he's talking to himself. "Initiation was tough in those days. We were buried in the desert sand up to our necks, and left there for two days in the sun of the day and the frost of the night. They returned to get us out and would piss on our heads until the weakest of us pleaded for water, or mercy. Only the resilient ones were accepted into the Legion."

*Shit! This is tough stuff!*

I don't want to hear any more, so I bury my face in my hands on my knees, and say into my pretty French dress, "Shit, I want to cry." More accurately, I *need* to cry, but my tears still evade me.

He gives me no sympathy as he takes the conversation in the direction I wanted and, like a well-deserved punch in my face, says, "That was only the beginning for us. The insults and abuse continued until they felt we were fearless enough to slit a man's throat like slicing an apple ..."

I take another swig and say under my hand on my forehead, "I don't want to hear any more about that stuff."

He puts his Obelix-arm around my shoulders and says very close to my ear, "You've got me drunk, and I'm telling too many secrets."

But I can't abandon my soldier, who's opened up to me. So I pull myself together and say, "Tell me about your missions."

"I might have fought alongside your husband's grandfather, because I also did Algeria. I then did Korea, and the Suez Crisis. I did my last mission in Zaire." He's saying he "did" these missions like someone saying they "did" a crossword.

He says with a lot of regret in his voice, "It was in Zaire that I was wounded and condemned to leave and live out my life here like a drunken good-for-nothing."

I wonder what it was that made him an invalid, but I've heard enough about the action and don't want to talk about it anymore. And it seems he doesn't either. He heaves his big body up and says, "Let's get going." He takes my hand and pulls me off my rock.

My head spins and he teeters, and we hang onto one another. We must look like two hobos with their gutter-dog after a drunken night on the street, but I don't care. I feel privileged to be in his company.

We don't walk arm in arm again. Maybe we both feel that we need to prove to the other that we can handle our alcohol. As we're nearing the summit of the hillock, I remember the pillar at the entrance to the Legion and ask, "Who's Captain Danjou? Did you know him?"

He laughs over his breathlessness. "He was one of the first legionnaires, and lived long before my time. He was killed in 1863 in Mexico. That was the war that made the Legion famous. But we lost all our men except one or two. Danjou had a wooden hand which was sliced off in battle and stolen by war-scavengers. It was later recovered, and now it's displayed in the Foreign Legion museum in Aubagne."

"That's a gruesome story. How can you remember all this stuff?"

"Don't forget, my dear lady, I'm the famous Gustav! Although they call me an invalid, my mind is as sharp as a razor-blade!"

# MARY MAGDALENE

We ascend the next hillock, and Gustav is panting like Lucky. The road levels out towards the entrance of what seems like a large Bastille.

He opens his arms towards it and says, "This is our headquarters. This is where the famous Gustav lives and sleeps. This is where the famous Gustav makes little pottery souvenirs for the tourists."

I don't say anything.

"We also make good wine here."

This is a small consolation and I hope he gets to stamp the grapes. There's a large parking lot to the right of the entrance. The Bastille is surrounded by tall fortress-like walls. The trees flanking the road to the Bastille are gigantic. This place feels historical, and I marvel at my good fortune to be staying on an estate so close to such an important piece of French history. I squint at the words on a large archway over ominous gates: "Légion Etrangère Institution des Invalides."

Gustav stops at a large pillar. Lucky also stops and peers lovingly up at him with her tongue hanging out. There's a niche on the corner of the arch with a pious-looking stone figure in it, about sixty centimetres tall, which looks like the holy figure of the Christian Mary. The niche has a mesh cover over it, which I'm sure has been put there to keep the figure safe from the marauding hands of tourists.

He stands in front of Mary and makes the sign of the Cross from his forehead to his belly and to the left and right of his hairy armpits. He says, looking up at her, "Now, this is the most interesting."

I edge closer to him and feign enthusiasm to match his. I wonder if I should make the sign of the Cross like he's done, but choose not to.

He says with his arms outstretched towards her. "This is not the Madonna. This is Mary Magdalene, the most important of Christ's disciples."

Even though I'm a Catholic, have been baptised, and had my first Communion, I still get confused between Mary Magdalene and Mary, Mother of God and the Madonna and the Virgin Mary. They always look the same in pictures and statues. It's only when a Mary-figure is carrying a Baby that I know She's the Mother of God, so She must be the Madonna, but She's often depicted without the Baby, and this is when I get confused. I'm also not sure if Mary Magdalene was a virgin, like Jesus' Mother.

I fidget my feet and nod in the hope that he's not going to quiz me on the Bible, because I'd probably fail. But he asks, "See the shell behind her?"

The shape of the shell is barely distinguishable. I make out the fan-shaped spines of what appears to be a scallop carved into the stonework behind Mary's head. I don't want to expose my ignorance about religious symbols, and keep my response simple, "Yes, I see it."

He continues talking like the famous Gustav who knows much more about everything than anyone else, and says, still keeping his eyes on Mary, "The shell is a symbol of pilgrimage." He points at the shell and says, "See the cross above the shell?"

"Yes, I see it."

"It's the sign of the Knights Templar, which is a symbol of their mission in protecting her and her vessel. It is said by some that the Knights Templar built this building as a kind of headquarters, and used it as a refuge and a pit-stop for pilgrims." I've heard of the Knights Templar, who I think are like the Freemasons, but I don't know much about them. I'm not sure what he means by Mary's "vessel", but I keep nodding beside him.

He must sense my fake understanding, but continues: "After Christ's death, Mary escaped persecution from Jerusalem and left with her vessel and her brother Lazarus, and a disciple called Maximinus. They travelled in a small boat with no rudder or mast, and landed accidentally at Saintes-Maries-de-la-Mer near Arles. It is said that she went to Marseilles and converted the whole of French Provence to Christianity."

I feel a tremendous sense of the realism of this story, and it appeals to the scientist in me. It seems highly plausible, because the people in the Bible must have been common folk like us, with common feelings, and behaved like we do in times of need or persecution. I wonder if the "vessel" Gustav referred to is a "baby", because it surely is the same shape. But I hate it when people say that Mary must have slept with Christ and had his child, because Jesus was sinless and this is highly blasphemous. But then again, he was a man and she was a woman, and women often sleep with their bosses because they look up to them, just like I did. They may have slept together after one of his sermons, when they were both feeling exhilarated by his words, and were full of respect for one another … and passion.

267

And maybe she fell pregnant because I'm sure there was no contraception two thousand years ago. I'm sure the rhythm method wasn't discovered yet. "Do you think Mary and Christ had a baby?"

He looks down at me and winks his naughty eyes. "Maybe, maybe not. Who knows for sure?"

But he seems more interested in the plight of Mary and says, turning his adoring eyes upon her again, "Mary later retired to a cave on a hill nearby here called St. Baume, where she lived for thirty years and gave herself up to a life of penance, like a nun."

My maternal instincts prickle in my bosom and I wonder: if she did have a baby, what happened to it? I do know that, as a mother myself, it wouldn't be so healthy for a baby to live in a cold, dank cave. But what does make sense is that, if the baby was taken away from her or died or something, she would have been very depressed and given up and gone to live alone and mourn. I know that if anything happened to my kids, I would not only want to crawl into bed forever, but I would definitely contemplate suicide. But Mary, like my own mother, was obviously a lot stronger than I am.

But who would know any of this for sure? I can only put myself into her shoes. She must have been wavering around the depression-line on Lulu's diagram, just like me. And then again, there have been times, fleeting moments before another boring date with another boring man, whom I yet again had to pretend was cleverer than me, when I've considered becoming a nun.

I feel a deep sense of compassion for Mary Magdalene and ask, "What finally happened to her?"

It seems Gustav likes my enthusiasm. "The French believed that, when she died, her body was taken to an oratory that was built for her by St. Maximinus in a town that is now called after him. St. Maximin is very near here." He points over the valley to the right of us. "Every year, at around this time, her skull is placed in a gold shrine for all to see."

This is now very real to me and, for the first time, I feel a deep respect for the words in the Bible. Given the realism of the stories Gustav has told me, any implausible or unfinished Bible story can be explained by imagining how we would react to things, as common folk. I like stories that are plausible. A strict education has made me desirous of plausible solutions.

And now that I think about the realism of the Bible, I think I *do* believe in miracles and healings. They must surely happen when there are enough people together, who are singing, and chanting, and thinking and wanting the same thing, because if Lulu's right, one neuron has enough energy to cause a lightning bolt. Enough of them sparking off in one room would surely create some movement or altering activity. In order for people to start to work up a common frenzy, they *must* have faith and spirituality. Maybe I'm spiritual after all, because it's when I feel out of body that I become frenzied, and create things, and make things happen. This probably happens when I'm wavering around the manic-line on Lulu's diagram.

My head spins again and I feel quite pissed. Gustav must also be feeling pissed, but given his large size compared to my small frame, I doubt the alcohol has travelled through his system as fast as it has through mine. Trying not to slur, I ask, "Shell me more about the tell."

*Shit!*

He must not have noticed my booboo, because he says, "The shell, as I've told you, is a sign that pointed the way to pilgrims. Centuries ago, pilgrims would travel to Jerusalem to help fight Christian persecution. The shell and figure of Mary Magdalene point towards Jerusalem, and show the way. Pilgrims have been travelling for centuries to visit the body of St. Jacques in Spain, at the Cathedral of Santiago de Compostela in Galicia."

"Who's St. Jacques?"

He looks quizzically at me, like I should know, and says with a little frustration in his voice, "He was the brother of John. We call him St. Jacques, but the English call him St. James. It is believed that he was the founding member of the Knights Templar."

I'm getting confused by all of this, and don't want to ask him any more questions I should know the answers to. I think he's referring to Jesus' disciples, but I don't ask, and choose to keep nodding my head.

He kneels down, holding onto Lucky for support, and says, "People still take the pilgrimage to Jerusalem and Spain today." He must be getting tired.

I step closer to the column and press my cheek against the flagstones. I also need some support, but my mind is still spinning. I didn't know all this religious travel was still happening in modern times, but there's obviously a lot I don't know. I also can't remember what the link is between Mary and the Templar guys, and St. Jacques and St. Max-whatever. But the Saints must have been Mary's buddies, because they were all disciples. And if St. Jacques was also a disciple who knew her, he must have decided to make it his business to protect her, or her baby, or her vessel ... whatever that is.

I can't remember if the shell points to Jerusalem or Spain, and try to work out where it's pointing by doing my "Never Eat Silk Worms" thing, to remember where North, East, South and West is. I try to work out the direction of Jerusalem from here, but I can't remember if the South of France is above or below Israel. My head spins and I'm woozy.

Another van like the one which passed earlier pulls up alongside us and I grab Lucky's neck. This time it stops and the man in the passenger seat, wearing a beret, opens the window and gestures at Gustav to move on with his thumb stuck out, like a hitchhiker.

Gustav does the fuck-off thing that the Italians do by punching his arm and lifting his fist at beret-man, and shouts, "Salopard! Enfoiré! Fils de Pute! Bordel à queue de pompe à merde! Va te faire voir chez les grecs!"

I've heard this kind of swearing in French a lot, and I know he's saying very bad things to the back of the van, but I try to ignore it by saying, "I must get home now. I'm sure Lucky is thirsty. Thank you so much for …"

But he's already turned his back on me and is walking away. He raises his meaty hand above his head and waves in my direction, without looking at me. He stumbles sideways but regains his step and says, "Merde!"

I have to hold onto Lucky because she's pulling me in Gustav's direction. She must love him and want to go home with him. But I hold onto her until I see him stumbling through the massive doors, and into the Institution. As I watch his bulky frame disappear, I'm hurt that he should be referred to as an invalid, because he has all his faculties and the most remarkable memory. Maybe he's dubbed an invalid because he's become a raving alcoholic due to the horror he's experienced. But I choose not to think about why any longer.

Although I feel the wrench from my legionnaire, and wonder if I'll ever have the fortune of seeing this gracious, intelligent and brave man again, I'm left with an amazing revelation: he has revealed the very depths of his soul to me. He has shared his humiliation at being pissed on the head. He has talked about his missions. He has risked dismissal from the Legion by standing in front of the statue of Mary and telling me secrets I'm sure he's not allowed to reveal. He has read the sadness in my eyes. And I'm sure that I'm the first dim-witted tourist who didn't mind his sweaty armpits and accepted his arm under mine, and drank from his gob-smeared flask. I'm honoured. He's made me feel normal again. I miss him already.

I must've been standing here looking at the big gates of the House of the Invalids for a long time, because I've forgotten about Lucky and now I can't find her. I whistle for her and begin to walk back home with my heart beating. I see her bobbing bottom on the road in the distance. She must've decided to go home a while ago. I fear leaving her alone on this road, where legionnaire vans drive too fast, and I jog to follow her. It's difficult to run with so much booze in my veins and nicotine in my lungs, and I realise that I'm also frail and unfit. I've got a headache because my brain has been filled to the brim with delightful information, and I've drunk spirits after wine. I know that this makes for a very sore head. I haven't given the time of day a thought, but it's still very light and the sun is still high in the sky.

I'm huffing and puffing and, as I run up the road away from the Legion, I feel like I'm being watched. There's a mighty presence from the vineyards to my left, and I'm scared. The adrenalin helps, and I pick up speed, keeping my eyes forward to avoid the presence.

*I'm running to my mother's room because the ghost has visited.*

I'm out of breath and I can't run anymore, so I drag my body up the sandy driveway towards the villa. I'm walking like a gorilla, but I'm too tired to care. I'm also hot, so I head towards the swimming pool to the right of the house. I need to jump into it with my clothes on, just like I usually do when I'm drunk and need to sober up, or when I need to hide in its depths. But this time I need to jump into it to wash away Gustav's sadness, and his sweat, from my pretty French dress. I also need to gargle with the chlorinated water to wash the smell of alcohol from my mouth. I jump into the water and my dress billows around my head, but I flick my tail like a dolphin, and swim underwater until my lungs ache.

I burst from the surface on the shallow side like a person baptised, ready to face my family, albeit like a drowned rat in a wine barrel.

# MARY MOTHER OF GOD

My belly is extended to the proportions of pregnancy. It aches so badly that I'm battling to walk upright. I'm walking like a gorilla again. I should have heeded Oma's advice when she, the kids, and I, sat around the large barrel on the terrace, pitting mirabelle to make jam. Oma gestured to me to stop eating them, but they were sweet and delicious, and for each one I pitted, I ate one, not heeding her advice. And she laughed through her gums as my belly blew up and the pain made me wince. And I laughed through my agony along with her, because she doesn't laugh a lot, and I was happy to entertain her.

I need to be alone to expel the fermenting gases from my belly and walk the route I took yesterday with Gustav. I now know what Oma means when she says in Austrian, "To hold back a fart is like committing suicide."

Not only is my tummy sore but the back of my neck is stiff because I've been hanging washing all morning. I've washed my French-maiden dress and am wearing it again. I've unbuttoned it at my midriff. It's late afternoon. This is when the French take their siesta, so there'll be no traffic on the road, and no-one to see me. I've also drunk a lot of rosé again.

Here I am, walking through an impressionist painting, with big belly, sore neck, new head-drugs in my veins, and rosé on my breath. I don't have Gustav to hold me up, or Lucky to show me the way, but the road to the Legion is simple enough, and the pressure in my stomach is eased by farts with each step.

I can't stop thinking about Gustav. And I can't stop thinking about the presence I felt from the vineyard at the top of the hill.

I near the top of the hill where the Legion becomes visible. I turn right and walk towards the vineyards. But the presence must have gone, because there's nothing here but rows of vines, and what seems to be a shrine, like the one that Gustav showed me of Mary Magdalene.

But this shrine is different. It stands alone and is made of stone with an arch over the top. There's a stone figurine in it that also looks like the Mary he showed me, but there's no shell behind her head and she's wearing a red dress and blue cape. Her palms are open and one arm is outstretched towards me. She's protected by a mesh grating like Mary Magdalene was, but there are fresh-cut pink roses at her feet. There's a well-trodden path in front of the shrine. The flowers must've been placed here by local people.

I feel an overwhelming sense of piety, and I don't know why. I've never felt this before. I found it ludicrous when our catechism teacher told us to pray in front of a statue of Christ or Mary.

I button up my dress. My stomach has deflated and I need to look respectful for Jesus' Mother. I close my eyes and I don't know why. I bow my head and I clasp my hands and I don't know why. This isn't the kind of thing that I would usually do. But now I'm faced with a dilemma: What in God's name should I say to Her?

I clear my throat and focus my eyes upon Her. I say out loud, "Um … Hello, Mary."

This is ridiculous. I'm talking to a statue. But I say, "I know that You're not Mary Magdalene."

I've no clue where I'm going with this, but I say, "I'm sure You are Mary Mother of God, because yesterday I visited Your daughter-in-law with Gustav. And as sure as God made little green apples, I didn't feel like this."

It feels like I've blasphemed, so I quickly say, "Sorry for saying that … um … I'm not saying that Your Son was her husband, but let's just assume it for a moment …"

I feel Her disapproving eyes upon me, like a mother's, so I say, "I know You know I'm probably a little pissed, but I've only had two glasses of rosé, and I was far more pissed yesterday, because that stuff I was drinking with Gustav had an extremely high alcohol content. So please, don't think I'm mumbling like a drunk. I'm of sound mind and have all my faculties about me, and I'm really quite serious about talking to You."

My head is clear and so is my stomach. In fact, I don't feel my body, just the vibes between us flowing over me like a crystal-clear stream.

I keep my eyes on Her and say, "I just want to tell you that I've been feeling pretty crappy lately. In fact, my heart is so sore I could rip it out. You see, my house burnt down a while ago, and I've tried to analyse why I'm feeling so sad, because I know deep inside that I'm not mourning the loss, but I'm mourning myself. I think that maybe I've been allowed to think about *me* for the first time in my life, and what I see is not a very pretty picture."

The tears are behind my eyes again, but they're not coming out. I wish I could expel the tears like blood from my eyes, like one of those stigmata things, and show Her just how sad I am, but I can't.

I press my clenched fists into my forehead and say with my eyes closed, "I think I've been feeling anxious and sad my entire life, for no reason, and I just don't know what to do about it. The stuff these doctors have given me isn't helping, because my heart feels the same as before: empty and sore."

I feel a little selfish talking about me and my sorry heart, so I say, "Listen, Mary, I don't want to sound selfish and I hope You're not mad at me."

And now, all the good things I have flood over me like champagne, so I look into her eyes and squeeze my hands together until my knuckles crack, and say, "I know I've got my prayer all mixed up because I've talked about my sorry predicament before thanking You. So I just want to say thank you for my wonderful children and my husband. And thank you for setting us up so nicely to meet on the aeroplane. Because given how shitty some husbands are, to find a man like Stef, I must definitely have deserved it by being a good girl in a previous life or something. We've made angelic children who are good and kind and gentle, so I'm sure that the match between him and me was made in heaven. I thank You so, so, so much for my privileged life."

Her eyes are still upon me and I think I've said enough for one day, so I close my eyes again and make the sign of the Cross, and say, "Thank you again, my dearest Mary. Cheers. Have a cool day. I love You. Amen."

# LETTER TO MY CHILDREN

It's early morning and I'm alone on the terrace of the villa, sipping coffee and smoking my tenth cigarette. It's so early that the cicadas haven't woken up yet to start vibrating their tummies and making a racket. I can't sleep anyway, and prefer to be awake. Sleeping pills are no longer prescribed for me. Given that I never took any prior to this messy loony-bin and drug-pumped situation, my body is probably trying to adjust and put itself to sleep without assistance. I curse all the stupid drugs!

The silence and solitude help me to focus. The days at this beautiful place are spinning by without me. I know we planned to stay a month, but I'm not sure how long we've been here. I know we lost our home at the beginning of May, and it's now somewhere in July or August because this is when my kids have their French school holidays. I'm not sure how long I spent in the hospital and loony-bin, but it must've been quite long, because I can't have spent thirty days sitting on the shitty-couch staring at nothing. I'm a sorry case, and I hate myself for being such an immobile, lazy cow. All I know for sure is that going home to a pile of ash is something I don't want to do or think about. I hope I'll be here a lot longer. I hope I'll be here forever.

I want to stay here forever because I've become emotionally involved with Mary. I've become quite attached to Her. I need to walk to the Legion twice a day to chat to Her. I gaze out over the vineyards towards Her and realise that this has become my ritual. I've become obsessive about it. I need to spend an hour with Her on my way to the Legion. I need to touch the ominous gates and turn around and walk back towards Her. I need to walk in a straight line towards Her and keep my eyes fixed on Her shrine, as it bobs in my vision. I need to keep my eyes on Her as I pass Her and wave goodbye saying, "Thanks for the chat. I'll see You later."

Now I always remember to thank Her before asking Her to help me. Sometimes I wish She could reach out through the mesh of Her shrine and tear my bleeding heart out, like in a horror movie or like those strange doctors in South America who reach into people's bodies and fix them without any incision.

There's a lot of debris on the paving under my feet, because there's construction work going on at the villa. As much as I feel the destruction of my home has wiped out any desire to build again, construction never leaves me alone. It even followed me to the loony-bin, where alterations drove the inmates battier than they already were. It's as if I've been on a building-site since I was born. It follows me like my shadow and now I hate it. I kick aside the building rubble from under my feet, and force bricks and mortar from my mind.

Shh, shh, shh …

The cicadas have woken up to the heat of a new day, to start drilling their noise into my brain again. I'm not sure if my revised medication-cocktail is working properly yet. However, I've noticed that when the anxiety wants to creep up my throat and clamp my forehead, it feels like there's an invisible hand that pushes it back down into my stomach, not allowing it to raise its ugly head and make me want to crawl away and die. This is a new but nice sensation. The medication must be working on my brain … even though it can't penetrate my heart.

I squeeze my brows together with one hand and give my chest a bloody good thump with the other. Why the bloody hell hasn't a scientist found a cure for a bleeding heart yet? Sleeping pain away is also a lot of nonsense, because the brain must store the sadness messages delivered to its neurons, and add up the pain like the cumulative expenses in a cash-flow. I'm sure that a large dose of serotonin injected into the heart would do the trick.

So yes, my heart feels exactly the same as it did before. I need to top up its happiness-level and take the edge off by drinking a lot of rosé. I'm most definitely of the opinion that I need alcohol and nicotine instead of drugs.

I light another cigarette, even though I know it will exacerbate my hangover. I peer down at the exercise book I've been writing in. As I glance over my words, I can't believe how crappy my writing is. Not only is my spelling terrible, but the sentences are too long. And now that I'm looking at what I've written, the content is pathetic. If I ever have the time to type this lot in Microsoft Word, thank heavens I'll have the assistance of "spell check" and "Fragment (consider revising)".

My writing reads like one of those books I pick up in a bookstore that starts with, "I was walking through the forest with the birds singing and the wind in my hair and the crunch of pine-needles under my feet …" or "I lived in a small house with no money and I had a very sad life …". I don't bother to read on, and scratch around for another book with a catching cover that I hopefully won't be able to put down. I spend hours picking up books and reading first sentences and end up buying the first one I looked at, but will never read it, and probably give it away. A lot of people buy those self-help books, which I can't be bothered with. It's probably because I've never read them, and not learnt how to help myself, that I find the choices of books so difficult. I need to start helping myself!

All in all, my writing is feeble, but I try to reread my stupid words. I want to make sure they're at least comprehensible. I want to leave something for my kids. I miss my diaries. My kids would have kept them and hopefully read them when I was dead, or when they were bored.

I force myself to reread my writing. There are a lot of inserts between words, and stars with circles around them and arrows pointing everywhere. I've squashed small writing between the lines and into the margins. I wonder how writers of the past, who wrote by hand or used typewriters, managed to produce books that were so eloquently written. Given the poor state of my inserts, editing, afterthoughts, and writing in the margins, this would have taken a person like me a hundred years to produce, let alone produce something readable. I've headed my script:

*My Dearest Beloved Children: The Hole in my Life-line*

I open my left palm and gaze at the small hole in the life-line crease. It's a distinct hole, like a pock-mark. I've always wondered why it was there. But I'm feeling the worst I ever have, and I'll probably die early, so the hole is in the right place – slap-bang in the middle of my life-line. I cast these macabre thoughts aside, and continue reading my notes to my children. As I try to read the scribbled words I've been writing over the past few days, I hate my sorry self:

*The need to write to you began during my time spent at an institution …*

It's a pretty crappy way to start. Jumping the kids straight into the loony-bin thing is enough to cause their own shock and trauma. I need to change the beginning. It mustn't be dreary. It must captivate. I skip the first paragraph and skim over my words.

*I begin my script to you with no idea how it will turn out or what it will become. It is born out of the need I have mentioned, which I must explain before I begin …*

This is definitely reading like one of those books I wouldn't buy. I light another cigarette and push on.

*I sit here in the early morning with pen in hand and the back of an old notepad after another sleepless night, traumatised by haunting and disturbing dreams of our beautiful home which, due to my great distance from it now, has become a ghost, its image never to leave my subconscious and always to be at my mind's side …*

There's a big arrow inserted at the end of this sentence. I squint at the tiny words written between the lines. They seem full of pity and over-expression, but I try to make out the poorly written sentences.

*A rather perverse need brought me to its scene again before we left for France. I needed to indulge my deep sorrow of it. I walked through the blackened and perilous walls, the thick debris of thatch and remnants underfoot. The charred remains of our things more recognisable than if unscalded …*

I remember that Babs came with me to visit the ruins, and had taken a photograph of me as I scratched around in the ash of my bedroom, hoping to discover something intact and unscathed by the flames. Now that I think of it, this was a rather bizarre thing for her to do. But as I try to visualise my stupid self, scratching around in the aftermath like a war-scavenger, I can also smell it. It's as if the sickly sweet smell of wet burnt plastic will be stuck to my nosehairs forever. I pinch my nose and read on.

*The thick carpet of ash weighted by the burnt remnants of our furniture and melted glass was all that was left of our past. The most tremendous wrench was seeing what was left of your little bedroom, the sad remains of your teddy bears, an arm of a doll, the eyes of a panda staring at me from the blackened mass. What wasn't burnt was stolen the next day when we were gone, the most dreadful theft being a hundred goldfish from the fishpond in the garden. Who in heaven's name would steal inedible little fish from a burnt and abandoned home? Even that which was under water didn't escape the flames …*

278

Blah, blah, blah … This is unbearable! I wonder why I wanted to tell the kids how miserable I felt about losing our home. The dreary words are insufferable. I skip a lot of the ash stuff and get back to what I recognise is my description of where we are now, to draw a picture for the kids. I need them to see me at this time in our lives. These chapters read more like my chipper self. I must've written them at a different time, either very pissed, or in a better mood.

*Uncle Gerhard is a painter and is staying in a hired caravan behind the villa to help with construction work. He's dolling up the place and painting the shutters green with white frames around the windows to give it a typical Provencal look. I've learnt that one can't just build on willy-nilly in France like we do in South Africa, but have to keep strictly in accordance with the existing structure of the building and maintain its original colour and village-feel …*

I picture myself in my beautiful kitchen, the one that is no more … It dawns on me that I refurbished the kitchen when I re-thatched the house, just a few months before the fire. I smashed down the existing kitchen and built a smaller one. I did this because the hoteliers I worked with pointed out that the bar-area of a hotel was always designed as small as possible, as people are drawn towards confined areas where they can brush up against one another and have a drink. This was a strange concept for me, but the more I analysed human nature and our desire to be together, albeit unwittingly, it made sense. So I used the existing large kitchen as a pantry and extended off it a small oblong area which made for a 1.5-metre-wide working area, between stove and preparation worktops. I ensured that portions of the worktops had no under-counter cupboards, and placed a few bar-stools along them with leg-room. Guests would squash their bodies into this tiny space while I cooked. The atmosphere was delightful. Memories of my kitchen and cooking with friends around me hurt. I push them out of my mind and lean over my exercise book. I need to concentrate on the here and now.

*The villa is still looking pretty shabby because Jacqui bought it in a poor state of repair. Fixing up these old buildings is a costly exercise which is often overlooked by eager purchasers who think they're getting a bargain by buying a bit of French history. The vineyards and olive groves were also left unattended too long and need tons of work …*

I look down at my lily-white hands and realise that people on estates here work the vineyards like dogs. Jacqui's hands are not like a woman's but rather like the cracked old hands of a poorly paid labourer. I also notice the callous on my index finger, caused by my pen from eighteen years of writing diaries. I yearn for my diaries, so I try to chew off the calloused skin as I read on.

*As you know, Mommy is a builder. Having estimated many a construction project, I always add on a huge contingency because experience has taught me that the anomaly of building can catch an owner off-guard and break the bank …*

… or his marriage! The bloody wife is always involved in domestic building projects and this is a recipe for disaster, because men need to stick to the budget while women like to add and change, without regard for finance. Here's the Venus–Mars theory proven again, but in this instance, I'm the man.

I've written a lot about the building industry and have no clue why. My writing reads like I'm doing another feasibility study where the figures need a lot of tweaking. I skip all the technical stuff and read the last sentence in my chapter about the construction work going on at the villa.

*But Jacqui seems to have her hand on the finance and will hopefully get her money back, because she's planning on turning the villa into a guest house …*

The thought of arbitrary people being here makes me a little jealous. I'm becoming much attached to it and want to keep its splendour, and Mary, all to myself. My notes continue in a less technical manner.

*The atmosphere here is energetic because everyone is involved in repair in one way or another. Even you kids have been helping and have been standing precariously on ladders while Uncle Gerhard holds you up, keeping his hands over yours on the paint brushes. However, I have stayed away from the building work because I keep seeing what should be done. If I got involved, it would consume me to the point of madness. I have found solace here by separating the whites from the colours and hanging a lot of washing. I've also thrown myself into my other passion – cooking. It's a fight to make the meals here because French people live to eat and love to cook. But I seem to get my way and have been making the Italian food I normally cook for you at home, like rabbit with red wine and rosemary, which you pick for me from the hillside, artichokes in white wine and parsley, and aubergines in garlic and parsley and Jacqui's homemade olive oil...*

Instead of being the party-person and entertaining everyone like a demented freak as I usually do, I realise that my quiet focus on domestic practicalities is how I've created my worth here. I must remember to write a cook book for the kids, including all our family dishes from the north of Italy.

I'm bored with reviewing my notes. I've written a lot of pages about our time here: the guests coming and going, our mission to make Oma laugh, Uncle Gerhard's life in Austria, and what my kids are saying and doing. I'm so used to writing my diaries that day-to-day simple living is what I love to describe, even though it makes for boring reading. The loss of my diaries hurts, so I put the thought of them aside. I realise that I've forgotten to write why Mommy spent a long time away from her children when they were sad and confused. So I tear out all the pages I've written, crumple them up, and chuck them onto the pile of rubble under my feet. I turn a new leaf, and write:

*Why Mommy Was Such a Wimp*

*Dearest Mouse and Mackie, I'm not sure how old you'll be when you read this. Right now you are seven and four years old; it's 2002. We are spending your French school summer holidays with Opa in Puyloubier, the South of France. I've spent some time writing to you about the time we're spending here. I hope you enjoy reading it, because it's nice to read about the cool things you did when you were children.*

I pick up the crumpled pages I threw away from under my feet, and smooth them out. I'm such an irrational idiot sometimes! I've got to learn how to stop myself from flying off the hook! I light another ciggy and poise my pen above the page. I'm a schoolgirl:

*I spent my years at school laughing my head off because I was shy. Most of my school years were spent outside the classroom I'd just been kicked out of. I never did anything bad at school, just laughed and laughed and laughed. This made it impossible for my teachers to teach me. I did, however, do well at school in spite of my many detentions. But I never came first in anything, or got any prizes at school, other than "hundred per cent attendance certificates".*

I'm hoping this will help my kids feel that they don't have to live up to me or walk in my shadow. It's only their mom who's the fool; certainly not Stef. So here we are with a good balance between parents. But I need to give them some faith in their mother, so I write:

*Now that I'm big and had a tough university education and lots of work experience, I feel a lot more confident. I know this sounds a bit swollen-headed, but I think that, coupled with lots of work experience, I've had enough disasters happen to me that I hope I can give you some pointers. What's really cool too is that, because I've had a lot of shitty things happen in my life, I can help you with anything shitty that happens to you. Even if nothing shitty happens and you still feel sad, talk to me, or someone else who knows about this. Feeling sad for no reason is not your fault. It's caused by a pimple in your brain which makes you feel lousy. Sometimes people call this "Depression".*

There you are, girl! Not only can you say "fire" out loud, but you can also say "depression"! I print in capitals:

*NO MATTER WHAT, I'LL ALWAYS BE HERE FOR YOU. I'M HERE TO HOLD YOUR HANDS.*

I'm hoping I'll be a wise old bat when I'm nearing the grave – just like Nora. My heart pains for her. I squash my sadness and pull myself together. I need to go to the time of the fire.

*By the time you both read this, you may not remember the time we went through when our house burnt down. You were both very young and seemed to accept it well. In fact, I thought you were more grown-up than I was.*

I wonder if it's wise to tell my kids that that their mother was weak. But bugger it; we're all weak and wimpish most of the time.

*I was quite sad when the house burnt down, because I lost my eighteen years' worth of diaries, all our photographs and, of course, my wedding dress. All the other stuff we lost wasn't important, because it is easily replaceable. In fact, if I lose or break anything from now on, I will mentally throw it into the fire, and say to myself, "Oops ... it's gone! Who cares about material stuff?"*

I would love to have left my diaries to my kids when I die. I don't think I'll ever be able to write a diary again. And I certainly never want to build again! I push on.

*I'm writing this because you may have stored in your subconscious this strange time when Mom became weird when the house burnt down. Unanswered questions seem to raise their heads in our adult lives and may cause some psychological problems. But don't despair! The only reason why I reacted so badly was because I had never dealt with anything that happened to me. The fire was just a spark which caused an electrical fault in my brain, and all the shitty things that happened in the past seemed to tumble down upon me. And trust me, lots of shitty things happen to all of us in life. I hope you only have a few! It's how you deal with them that counts.*

I need to stop dilly-dallying about the psycho-babble and get to the time I abandoned them.

*The fire itself was not a major disaster, but it was the reason I was sent to see a psychologist and, by a comedy of errors, was sent to a hospital and then a rehabilitation clinic. I didn't want to be there, because I had abandoned you.*

I'm hoping that when they read this, they're old enough to understand what a "comedy of errors" is.

*You visited me there and I told you that I was sad and needed rest. You guys were so cool about it! I spent my time resting and revisiting all the things that I hadn't dealt with in my life. These things sneak up on you once in a while, especially if you've always given yourself tomorrow to think about them, like I did. That is foolish!*
*This was a big turning point for me, as you can imagine. And as I write to you now, I'm still feeling rather crappy. But I know that I'll get through this ... because I have you!*

The sun has crept towards the vertical midday line and the cicadas are reaching a crescendo. I throw my pen down and stretch back in my chair.

I should've written a funny poem on the pros and cons of life but, then again, I like to write, and am probably doing the "Fragment (consider revising)" thing. I must get my kids to read Lewis Carroll's poem, "Jabberwocky". It was the only poem that ever made sense to me as a child. It must be because it was full of made-up words, and senseless … like my writing. But, other than Macbeth's "We strut and fret" passage, it was the only poem I could remember and recite in front of the class, even though I pictured my classmates naked to help me along.

I recite the poem to the cicadas in the warm Provencal air:

'Twas brillig, and the slithy toves,
Did gyre and gimble in the wabe …

I can't take the smile off my face as I recite Carroll's poem. And I felt good while I wrote the letter to my kids. The words have exploded from my pen like dynamite. At least I've finally plucked up some energy and found some passion within me. Maybe Lulu's new cocktail has something to do with it. But my heart is still sore … and so is my head. I've completely forgotten about the warnings of alcohol-abstinence while on medication. But it can't be that serious! We're on holiday, and I would rather die than abstain from the alcohol-induced camaraderie … and be a party-pooper.

I feel a Godly presence above me. Stef is here and says, as he breathes his morning coffee-breath over my shoulder, "What are you doing?" He peers over my pages.

I cover them up like a child hiding an exam paper from prying eyes, and say as casually as I can, "Just writing some crap."

"Are you writing a suicide note?"

"Something like that."

We laugh together in the sunshine. At least we can still laugh.

# MARTHA

I'm returning from my evening visit to Mary and galumph up the sandy driveway towards the villa. Having to face the laughter coming from the terrace is making every step harder. I try to walk erect with a spring in my step so that I don't look like the miserable gorilla walking alone in the Congo. Thank heavens for the pretty French dress which swishes around my ankles. I've been washing and wearing it every day and it's faded and lost some of its buttons. But there're so many guests coming and going that no-one would guess that I'm always dressed the same, so I don't care.

I stop short of the terrace and pretend to be pulling a weed from a flowerbed. The thought of putting on a happy-mask for people is making me nauseous. Furthermore, I'm so terribly sad. Stef has gone home.

I curse the drugs I'm on! The only thing that should be written on their instructions should be: IF YOU TAKE THIS STUFF, YOU WILL NEVER WANT SEX AGAIN!

I hate the frigid bitch I've become. And now that he's gone, Stef's become even more sexy and appealing. But as much as I miss and desire him now, my bloody body wouldn't be able to prove it. Even though I was alone when he was here, his absence is like a vacuum. However, the explainable sadness of his departure is overshadowed by the unexplainable sadness in my heart, and I think it's a small consolation.

Time has indeed dragged on. I've been here almost two months instead of the one planned. It's only when I'm with Mary or my kids that time is precious and quick. It's when I'm trying to be the perfect guest and pretending to be fabulous that time is slow. All I'm certain of is that I can't face going home to the ash. Stef has agreed that I should stay longer with the kids. He is the one who has to go home to face hell. I am the one who can hide behind the skirt of her French dress and walk in the French sunshine with an empty head. I feel like a sexless, spoilt brat.

I put on a cheery smile and drag my feet up the steps to the terrace. There's a whole bunch of fresh new guests sipping rosé around the big table. I've already forgotten their names since Manfred introduced us, because I couldn't give a shit who they are or where they're from. All I know is that when you have a beautiful place like this to spend the holidays, friends are plentiful, and family who were once horrible become nice again. The wine is tempting, so I sit down in an empty chair in expectation of some light entertainment and a full cold glass.

As Manfred puts the yummy stuff in front of me, he asks, "Where have you been going each day?"

I'm surprised that it's the first time I'm asked why I've been out twice a day for almost two months, but my desire to fool around with the guests' heads is stronger than my surprise, so I say, "I've been visiting Mary." I don't elaborate, and enjoy the puzzled looks I'm getting from the table guests.

I pull myself together because I'm toying with them and this isn't considerate. I explain: "There's a shrine in the vineyards on the way to the Legion. I visit it each day to talk to Mary." I look at the faces around me and try to analyse which of the guests is religious, or pious, or incredulous. But they're all smiling, which tells me either they're content that I'm sounding spiritual, or they don't speak English.

But Manfred is with me and says, "What do you talk to her about?"

"A lot of stuff. Like thanking Her for Stef and the kids, and asking Her to help me change all the bad luck I've been getting. Oh, and I also ask Her to help me pull myself together." And increase my sex-drive. But I choose not to say it here, however tempting.

Manfred gives me a kind face and says, "That is nice. Did you know that Mary had a sister?"

I shake my head as I quaff my wine. I'm in my catechism exam again and I'm sure to fail, but I try to sound like I know my Bible studies and ask, "Which Mary are you talking about? Mary Magdalene or Mary, Mother of God, the Madonna?"

"Mary Magdalene, the disciple of Jesus. She had a sister called Martha."

I nod to keep him talking. He says, "Martha was always hanging around when Jesus was preaching. While her sister, Mary, was anointing the feet of Jesus, she was the one in the background who was doing the house chores and seeing that the disciples had food and drink. Mary was said to sit at the feet of Jesus, which meant she was accepted as one of His students. Martha was quite annoyed that she was not one of His disciples and was a little jealous of her sister." I picture robed disciples chatting quietly in a small cave like in religious movies on Sunday television.

I want more of this story and Manfred obliges without prompting. "Martha argued with Jesus. She told Him that it was unfair that she had to do all the work and that Mary should help her. Jesus told her that she was too much of a worrier, and that Mary had chosen the better path."

I'm impressed with Manfred's knowledge of the Bible, because he's certainly not a God-fearing man who pushes religion. I admire him for making it his business to research it. All I can offer his story is, "Shoo, that's bloody interesting. I'm sure that must have miffed Martha. It sounds like the Cinderella story, but the characters are swapped around."

Manfred gives me one of his deep Austrian mountain-goat laughs and says, "That is a good way of putting it."

Manfred speaks many languages, like Stef does. He speaks English with a slight Austrian-French accent, but he speaks it as it's meant to be spoken. He says "it is", not "it's" and "the feet of Jesus", not "Jesus' feet". He's always reading posh books by authors like Charles Dickens and Oscar Wilde, and this is probably why he speaks so well.

We're being impolite to the new visitors by having our own conversation, so I gulp down the rest of my wine and say, "I would love to learn more, but I'll leave you to chat to these lovely people and go inside."

"No. Stay a while longer."

Manfred refills my glass as well as the guests', whom I'm sure are getting bored. I don't listen as he chats to them in French, because I'm preoccupied with thoughts about the descendants of Mary and Martha.

I realise that my thumb is in my mouth and I whip it out. I've chewed off a large piece of skin at the cuticle, and it's bleeding. I cup the rest of my fingers around my thumb, and hope that the guests haven't noticed my trance and finger abuse. But my dementia is undetected. No-one's looking at me, other than Manfred. He asks, "Did you cut your finger? It is bleeding."

"Yes, I cut it yesterday and I must've nicked the scab." Shit! I'm lying! Stef would be appalled!

I can't remember if any of the guests has said anything while Manfred and I have been talking. I have a slight suspicion that he's getting as tired of the perpetual entourage as I am, and has enjoyed our thought-provoking conversation more than gossip.

I need to leave them to him now, so I scrape my chair back and say to all, "Bon, je vais a la cuisine pour faire un peu de bouffe pour vous."

I can't believe that I've used the bad French word for food, which hints of slop. But I enjoy their disgusted looks and make my way to the kitchen to cook up a storm with a glass of good red wine … and my troubled mind.

# PLEA TO MARY

"Hi, Mary. How are you today?"

It's early morning and the air is still crisp. Lucky has ducked into the vine-yards to make her morning clever and is sure to be lying at my feet soon, as I stand in front of the shrine. Only one legionnaire van has whizzed past us to take the invalids to Aix.

Lately, it's been difficult to wake up early because, coupled with the vast amount of wine I'm drinking, the many cigarettes I smoke alone at night listening to the owl-calls, and the numerous pills I'm taking, my hangovers are intense and I can't lift my head from my pillow. But today I needed to be here early. I've got something very important to discuss with Mary.

I skip the thank-you bits quickly by saying, "Thank you, thank you, thank you for all the cool things I have."

Her face remains pious, so she must be content that I've thanked Her, albeit in a hurry, so I push on. "Listen, Mary, I've been chatting to Manfred, and he informs me that Mary Magdalene had a sister called Martha. I'm sure You must have met her. She was the one pouring drinks for the guys while Mary was sitting at Your Son's feet."

She squints her eyes at me without moving, and I immediately regret talking about Her family so flippantly, because She's giving me a be-careful-what-you-say look.

But She lowers Her eyes again and allows me to finish my story, like a mother listening to another lame excuse for tardiness from a naughty child. "Look, Mom, I know You know all about Martha, but it's just that Manfred indicated that Martha seemed to have many trials and tribulations in life, while Mary seemed to have no problems at all."

She squints at me again, but I can't back out now because I have to finish what I've started. "Look, I'm leaving tomorrow, and I would have put all of this to You in a much gentler way, but I've got no time for chit-chat because what I have to ask You is urgent."

She raises Her eyebrows and I can almost see Her smile, like only a mother can in the face of such insolence. So I push on: "I want You to do me a favour."

289

She looks surprised, but seems to be allowing me leeway, so I get to the most important thing fast. "I would like You to have a chat to Martha and tell her to let me go."

I bite my lip and give her puppy-eyes, but Her eyes close and I'm left alone.

# FLY AWAY HOME

I smell of aeroplane. I battle to stand upright because the lead in my stomach unbalances me. The flight home with my children was dismal. The wrench of the jet engines, as they propelled me towards the ashes of hell, was difficult to bear. So much so that I was unable to be chipper for my children as they sat beside me in the stinky aeroplane. The only thing I was capable of doing was writing stupid little notes on the state of my mind, on a barf bag.

I prop myself on my children's shoulders as we stand in the entrance hall of the shitty-townhouse in front of a huge bouquet of flowers that Stef has bought to welcome us home. I feel a distinct sense of déjà vu, not one brought about by Lulu's Memory-level Theory, but by the similar way I felt when I last stood here in front of a bouquet I didn't want on my return from a loony-bin I didn't want to go to. Nothing has changed for me. I still feel the same. The pile of ash that once was my home is still two streets away from my physical self, as it was four months ago. It's still alone and wasted, like me.

The only difference is that I now hate my shitty-couch. I don't turn right towards the lounge where it nestles alone without me. Instead I pick up Pooki and climb the stairs without saying anything. The kids are merrily chatting to Stef about their last month's holiday without him, so no guilt for me. All I want to do is fill the bath to the brim and lie in it like a Pasha until I drown …

I'm out of the bath and rub the towel this way and that over my bony shoulder blades as Pooki licks the water from my feet. I've no idea how long I've lain in the water staring at the taps over my feet, and I've no idea what to do with myself after I'm dried. I've no idea what clothes to put on. I've no idea where to go, or what the bloody hell to do with myself. The only sensation I have is the smell of the black sticky ash that clings to my nose-hairs.

I have only enough energy to wrap the towel around my waist and stand here alone until my body decides to do another thing without me.

But I'm not alone …

Someone touches my shoulder. It's a beautiful touch, like the caress of a feather. I should be scared, but I'm not. The touch is the most beautiful thing I've ever felt. A wave of pleasure drifts through me, like an orgasm.

This is not me running down the stairs …

This is a happy girl without a care in the world. This is a happy girl who deserves as much bloody happiness as she can get. This is a happy girl who knows how to build!

This girl is going to get into her car and drive to the stationer to buy a drawing board and some good pencils. This girl is going to work through the night drawing sketch-plans of the most magnificent house in the world. This girl is going to clean away the debris of the fire. This girl is going to design her dream-home and build it on the foundations of the burnt-down one. This girl is going to employ lots of people and make them rich. This girl is going to have concrete between her teeth again while she plays Mozart on the building-site. This girl is going to make everyone laugh. This girl is going to make everyone happy. This is a happy girl, whose touch will turn everything into gold.

Pooki is happy too. She barks behind me as we run down the stairs. I run into Stef at the bottom of the stairs and he's smiling. I hug him and shout into his face, "I'm going to build our home again! From now on you can call me Bob the Builder! I'm off to buy a drawing board. I'll see you later."

He takes my shoulders and shakes his head to catch my eyes. "My love, where do you think you're going like that?"

*Shit!*

I've got the towel around my waist, and I'm naked. He puts his big hands behind my back and draws my breasts into his chest, and we laugh.

My head is tucked under his chin as he says into my wet hair, "I found something for you in the ash. I've been clearing away the debris of the fire, and this was the only thing of yours I found."

His hand is clasped and he opens his palm, like a magician. In it is a tiny gold medallion of the Madonna.

# PHSYCOLOGY ADIEU!

"Hi, Tulula. Thanks for seeing me at such short notice."

"It's great to see you again. You look fabulous. How was your holiday?"

Lulu must have told her I went to France. "Fabulous."

"What would you like to talk about today?"

"Nothing. I don't want to talk about anything. I want to *tell* you something. This is a personal visit, but I still want you to charge me."

She smiles and eases herself into an armchair in front of her desk, the desk with all its little souvenirs and piles of yellow folders strewn across it. She's got what must be my folder closed on her lap. I don't sit down nor does she ask me to, so I say, standing in front of her, "When I was in France, I met the most amazing woman."

"Oh?"

I don't want her to think that *she's* not amazing or that I'm weird, so I choose my words carefully. "You're amazing too, and I don't want you to think I'm weird."

*Shit!*

She opens my folder, which is now an inch thick and filled with the scribbles of Tulula, Dr Shaker, Cranium and Lulu, but I lean over her lap, and shut it.

"We don't need that stupid folder anymore. What I have to tell you goes far beyond its contents." She smiles and lets me take the folder from her, like I am the shrink, and she is the patient.

But I still need her to think that I'm not sounding weird, so I say, "I'm not a weirdo or a Bible-puncher or anything like that. It's just that I found Mary."

"Oh?"

"Yes. There was a shrine in the vineyards that I visited twice a day for two months. I did a lot of talking to the Mary in it."

She shifts her bottom in the armchair. "Oh?"

"I only talked to Her because I was desperate. The medication prescribed for me and my little trip to the hospital and loony-bin did nothing to improve the way I felt … in my *soul*. Are you with me?"

I need her to be with me and she is, because she says, "Yes, I am."

"Anyway, the story continues. When I got home from France, I felt the same as I had before – very crappy." She nods because helping people feeling crappy is her job.

"The first thing I did when I got home was take a bath."

"Oh?"

I need to hurry up with my story because I'm sounding stupid. "When I was drying myself and still feeling crappy, I experienced a miracle."

I leave the miracle in the air until I see her eyebrows go up, and I say, "Mary visited me in my bathroom and touched me, and took my pain away."

She still doesn't say anything, so I say, "I know it was a miracle, because I felt Her caress, and the change in the way I felt was instantaneous. I've done a lot of research and I know that psychiatric medication takes effect on people's minds over time. It's not an instantaneous quick-fix, as you well know. And it certainly *cannot* take the pain from the heart … or the soul."

She nods and I know she's with me, because she asks, "Were you taking your medication as prescribed?"

I feel a tad insulted because I'm not an idiot. I'm a scientist. Furthermore, I had an informative lecture by Lulu on the subject, so I fully respect the chemical impact of psychiatric medication on the brain, and the importance of taking it consistently. So I say, "Yes, I was. In fact I was terrified to miss a dose. But now that I know I don't need it, I'm weaning myself off the stuff." And off alcohol, but I choose not to say it here.

Tulula stands up and, as her face gets closer to mine, I notice tears in her eyes. She hugs me and says into my ear, "No, I don't think you're weird. And yes, I believe you. You're OK girl. You don't need me."

I respect her for her humility. She hasn't shrugged off my story but has embraced it like she's embracing me. *And* she's letting me go. I can't share tears with anyone yet, so I fake a sniff and push her shoulders away from me. "That's all I wanted to tell you. Thanks for listening."

I clutch Mary to make sure She's still safe on the chain around my neck. I'm doing this a lot lately. The symbolism of finding such a tiny gold medallion in such a huge amount of burnt debris hints at alchemy. But this, and the fact that it was a Madonna to boot, is far too powerful and significant for even my tiny brain to grasp. The best I can do is to clutch the small gold disk with the face of Mary as it dangles at my throat. I will wear it forever.

I turn to go and say over my shoulder, "I'm designing our new home. I'm going to build it on the foundations of the burnt one. I've got a lot to do. I've got to go now. Cheers!"

As I close the door, I think I hear her whisper, "Fly away home, little Ladybird …"

# EPILOGUE

I'm standing on my building-site with concrete between my teeth.

It's Mackie's birthday. I can't believe it's already 4 March 2003. It's almost a year since the house burnt down. I'm waiting for the clown to arrive. I'm waiting for my mom, Babs, Gill, Clara, Jen, and the girls who came to the sorry-for-you party. I'm waiting for the kids' friends to arrive to fill this desolate place with joy. I know it's a bit weird to be having Mackie's birthday here, but the weirdness of it delights me.

I'm in dirty jeans and sweaty white T-shirt, and smoking. The stink of burnt plastic is still in the air, but it will soon be replaced by the sweet smell of bricks and mortar. I plonk my bum onto the edge of the concrete foundation slab and gaze at Mackie and Mouse, who are tying balloons onto the pillars of the still-intact gazebo at the far end of the garden. They're happy and excited and playing silly-buggers. I'm glad the gazebo didn't burn down completely, because Stef and his father had built it by hand. Memories of the camaraderie they shared while doing it will always be close. The blazing palm tree where I threw my body is still here. Little green shoots are peeping out of the blackened trunk.

Building work will formally begin tomorrow. I've received the first delivery of concrete bags, river sand, concrete stone and bricks, all paid for by the insurance money. Trixie has managed to get our bond-liability covered and we've got a little cash to spare. She's not such a bad old bat!

I've spent a long time drafting the plans for my new home, because they needed to be perfect. I've designed the entire house around a massive kitchen and can't wait to share my cooking space with my friends and family. I've always dreamt of being an architect and have drafted my plans by hand, and with intense exhilaration. I marvel at my good fortune in having my plans approved so quickly. I took my plans into the Johannesburg City Council yesterday and promptly told the Head of the Planning Department that I was a "burnt-house lady", and that she needed to approve them immediately. She laughed and showed me the backlog of plans awaiting approval but took my hand and walked me to the Roads and Water Departments to give their immediate sign-off. She stamped off my plans with a smile. I bought a bouquet of yellow roses for her and delivered them this morning. What a lucky cow I am … everything is indeed turning to gold.

The labourers are also excited about Mackie's party. But I know they're exhausted. We've spent the last months clearing away the burnt debris from the site and levelling the still-intact surface bed. I have a small building budget, so we've done the clearing painstakingly, by hand. But they're still happy to help with setting out the party tables and preparing for Mackie's birthday. I've erected makeshift accommodation for most of them and they're delighted to be staying here. We're still living in the shitty-townhouse but it's close to the site and it's quick to get here. The only time I sit on the shitty-couch is after a long day's work, when I throw myself onto it for a respite before cooking dinner.

Stef is beside me on the concrete slab. He slides his hand up my back and massages my shoulders. My muscles ache from physical labour and I lean into him. He squeezes the back of my neck and I feel his hot breath in my ear. "You're the tits."

My cellphone screeches and shakes me from my ecstasy. It's Lulu. She asks excitedly, "How's it going, doll?"

I'm impressed that she's called me out of the blue. But then again, she's one of the good ones.

"Great! I'm starting to build my new home tomorrow." I don't elaborate, because guests are arriving and I've got no time to chit-chat.

It appears she doesn't either, and says, "Great, send me a picture when you're finished. Are you taking your medication like a good girl?"

I'm glad she's asked. I clutch my Madonna at my throat and say, "I've stopped taking the bloody stuff! I don't need it. Aren't you proud of me?"

I hear her catch her breath. "Are you mad! Did you not listen to a thing I told you? I need to see you as soon as possible!"

*What the hell?*

# WJEC/Eduqas GCSE
# Drama

# STUDY & REVISION GUIDE

Rachel Knightley

Published in 2020 by Illuminate Publishing Limited, an imprint of Hodder Education, an Hachette UK Company, Carmelite House, 50 Victoria Embankment, London EC4Y 0DZ

Orders: Please visit www.illuminatepublishing.com or email sales@illuminatepublishing.com

British Library Cataloguing-in-Publication Data
A catalogue record of this book is available from the British Library.

ISBN 978-1-912820-27-6

Printed by Printer Trento, Italy

04.22

The publisher's policy is to use papers that are natural, renewable and recyclable products made from wood grown in sustainable forests. The logging and manufacturing processes are expected to conform to the environmental regulations in the country of origin.

Editor: Dawn Booth
Design and layout: Kamae Design
Cover design: EMC Design
Cover photograph: francescoch / iStock

**Author's acknowledgement**
My thanks go to Dr Marianne Izen.

**Text acknowledgements**
p.45 *Random Thoughts in a May Garden* by James Saunders, courtesy the estate of James Saunders, Casarotto Ramsay Theatre Team.

pp.50–51, 70 © Grose, C., Murphy, Anna Maria and Rice, Emma (2005) 'The Red Shoes', in *Kneehigh Anthology Volume 1: Tristan and Yseult Red Shoes, The Wooden Frock, The Bachae*, Oberon Books, an imprint of Bloomsbury Publishing Plc.

pp.52–53 Bertolt Brecht, Der kaukasische Kreidekreis, in: ders., Werke. Große kommentierte
Berliner und Frankfurter Ausgabe, Band 8: Stücke 8.
© Bertolt-Brecht-Erben / Suhrkamp Verlag.

# CONTENTS

# Photo acknowledgements

p.1 franciscoch; p.8 Marko Aliaksandr; p.9 PUSCAU DANIEL; p.11 © Donald Cooper/Photostage; pp.12–13 metamorworks; p.16 (top left) GlebsStock; p.16 (top right) LightField Studios; p.16 (bottom) Alexander Lukatskiy; p.17 (left) ESB Professional; p.17 (right) Arthur Rackham, 'Some British Ballads', public domain; p.18 (top left) Marco Govel; p.18 (top right) Etheireil; p.18 (bottom) Monkey Business Images; p.19 (top) K.Kargona; p.19 (bottom) ASDF_Media; p.20 (top) Crepesoles; p.20 (middle) Yuriy Gorub; p.20 (bottom) Monkey Business Images; p.22 FrameStockFootages; p.23 yurakrasil; p.24 (top to bottom) Billy Bop, Inspired by Maps/Shutterstock.com, aerogondo2, lapandr; p.25 (top to bottom) Sigitas Kondratas, verandah, Susan Quinland-Stringer, SERGEI PRIMAKOV; pp.26–27 JpegPhotographer; p.28 (top) TZIDO SUN; p.28 (bottom) Rawpixel.com; p.29 (top) Martin M303; p.29 (middle) Dmitry Kalinovsky; p.29 (bottom) FamVeld; p.30 (top) Bondart Photography; p.30 (bottom) Philip Vile; p.31 (top) Q Theatre; p.31 (middle) Wharton Center – Own work, CC BY-SA 3.0, https://commons.wikimedia.org/w/index. php?curid=31236286; p.31 © photostage.co.uk; p.32 (top) © Johan Persson /ArenaPal; p.32 (bottom left) © Donald Cooper/Shutterstock; p.32 (bottom right) Courtesy of Alex Marker; p.33 (right) Stackastage; p.33 (left) Padmayogini/ Shutterstock.com; p.34 Kozlik; p.35 Alastair Muir/ Shutterstock; p.36 (top) Ibl/Shutterstock; p.36 (middle) Padmayogini; p.36 (bottom) Kokulina; p.37 (top left) Romolo Tavani; p.37 (top right) Subbotina Anna; p.37 (middle left) Strike Pattern; p.37 (middle middle) andreiuc88; p.37 (middle right) IMG Stock Studio; p.37 (bottom left) Sergey Nivens; p.37 (bottom right) Copter Pixel; p.38 (top left) Andrey Zhorov; p.38 (top right) faak; p.38 (middle bottom) OSABEE p.38 (middle bottom) Tito Wong; p.38 (bottom left) Kozlik; p.38 (bottom right) Stephane Bidouze; p.39 (top) Jstone/ Shutterstock.com; p.39 (bottom) Kizlik; p.40 (top to bottom) FrameStockFootages, Nomad_Soul, Igor Bulgarin, Jonas Petrovas; p.41 Granger/Shutterstock; p.43 (top) Master1305; p.43 (bottom) Daniel M Ernst; p.44 Monkey Business Images; p.47 Pictorial Press Ltd / Alamy Stock Photo; p.49 Public domain; p.50 (top) German Federal Archive/ Creative Commons Attribution-Share Alike 3.0 Germany; p.50 (bottom) Creative Commons Attribution-Share Alike 4.0 Licence; p.52 Roger Utting; p.55 Baal; p.56 (left) Andrii Kobryn; p.56 (middle) Jag_cz; p.56 (right) Paul Wishart; p.57 (top) Monkey Business Images; p.57 (bottom) GNU Free Documentation License; p.58 360b/Shutterstock.com; p.59 Featureflash Photo Agency/Shutterstock.com; p.60 The Trial/ YouTube; p.62 Monkey Business Images; p.64 © Donald Cooper/Photostage; p.65 Geraint Lewis/Alamy Stock Photo; p.66 A. Davidson/Shutterstock; p.67 © Donald Cooper/ Photostage; p.68 (left) sumire8; p.68 (middle) stockcreations; p.68 (right) sruilk; p.69 (top) lineartestpilot; p.69 (bottom) CREATISTA; p.72 (left to right) Michal Vitek, YuriiVD, Sashkin, Roma Borman, vectorfreak, Andrey Burmakin; p.72 (bottom) © leslietravers; p.73 (top) Atstock Productions; p.73 (middle) studiostoks; p.73 (bottom) StanislauV; p.74 Alastair Muir/ Shutterstock; p.75 (top) Katie Mitchell/Creative Commons Attribution-Share Alike 4.0 International license;

p.75 (bottom) Making a Live Cinema Show: The Forbidden Zone; p.77 Donald Cooper/Shutterstock; p.78 (top) Alastair Muir/Shutterstock; p.78 (middle) © Rob Pinney; p.78 (bottom) Alastair Muir/Shutterstock; p.79 (top 3) G-Stock Studio; p.79 (bottom) alchetron.com; p.81 (left) Igor Bulgarin/ Shutterstock.com; p.81 (middle) Marbury; p.81 (right) Fejas; p.83 © Eastfield Primary School; p.84 © Penny Saunders; p.85 (top to bottom) Courtesy of Big Brum, Courtesy of Belgrade Theatre, Ethan Doyle White/Creative Commons Attribution-Share Alike 4.0 International license, © Big Brum TIE 2019; p.86 takayuki; p.89 ESB Professional p.92 (top) Trailer: Baal/Film at Lincoln Center/YouTube; p.92 (middle) Horizon International Images Limited/Alamy Stock Photo; p.92 (bottom) © Donald Cooper/Photostage; p.93 (top) © Maisie Hill; p.93 (bottom) Christian Bertrand/Shutterstock. com; p.94 (top left) Oneinchpunch; p.94 (top middle) TeodorLazarev; p.94 (top right) NinaMalyna; p.94 (bottom left) Mongkolchon Akesin; p.94 (bottom right) Riccardo Mayer; p.96 (top) Jacques Lecoq; p.96 (bottom left) Ann Baldwin; p.96 (bottom middle) Courtesy of mask-maker.com; p.96 (bottom right) Graphic Compressor; p.97 (top) Ververidis Vasilis/Shutterstock.com; p.97 (middle) LILLIAN_GZ; p.97 (bottom left) Billion Photos; p.97 (bottom right) Sergey Nivens; p.99 (top to bottom) John Gomez/Shutterstock.com, Kojoku/Shutterstock.com, © Donald Cooper/Photostage, © Donald Cooper/Photostage, Donald Cooper/Photostage; p.100 (top) Pictorial Press Ltd/Alamy Stock Photo; p.100 (bottom) Roger Utting/Shutterstock.com; p.101 Photo by Johan Persson, © Cameron Mackintosh/ArenaPAL; p.102 (top) EgudinKa; p.102 (middle) buteo/Shutterstock.com; p.103 (top) Public domain; p.103 (bottom left) Kerstin Joensson/AP/Shutterstock; p.103 (bottom middle) Tony Kyriacou/Shutterstock; p.103 (bottom right) Felix Heyder/ EPA/Shutterstock; p.104 Naftalia Louise/Shutterstock.com; p.106 Joseph M. Arseneau/Shutterstock.com; p.107 (top left) wavebreakmedia; p.107 (top right) Artush; p.107 (bottom left) Helenelcg; p.107 (bottom right) Monique Guilbault; p.108 (top left) adrianrodriguezdirector; p.108 (top right) iLpO88; p.108 (middle) Plamen Galabov; p.108 (bottom left) fotandy; p.108 (bottom right) Volodymyr Krasyuk; p.109 (top left) Thomas Andre Fure; p.109 (bottom left) Jose A S Rees; p.109 (right) fizkes; p.110 (top) Public domain; p.110 (bottom) Peter Barritt/Alamy Stock Photo; p.111 Dennis Owusu-Ansah; p.112 (clockwise) Axstokes, Angela Matthews, Hadrian/Shutterstock.com, D.R.3D, Shark_749; p.116 OddySmile Studio; p.124 Iryna Inshyna; p.125 (left) VK Studio; p.125 (right) Alexander Raths; p.126 Monkey Business Images; p.127 gnepphoto; p.131 Brenda Carson; p.132 Mind Pro Studio; p.135 (top) Alastair Muir/Shutterstock; p.135 (bottom) Alastair Muir/Shutterstock; p.136 © The Imaginary Body; p.137 © The Imaginary Body; p.138 Alastair Muir/ Shutterstock; p.139 Alastair Muir/Shutterstock; p.141 (both) Canolfan Peniarth; p.143 (both) © Martin Morley; p.145 Alastair Muir/Shutterstock; p.147 Alastair Muir/Shutterstock; p.148 Billy Goats Scene from HARD TO SWALLOW by Mark Wheeller. Performed by The Gryphon School/Mark Wheeller/ YouTube; p.151 Geraint Lewis/Alamy Stock Photo; p.155 wavebreakmedia

# INTRODUCTION

Your GCSE is made up of three parts:

1 Devising theatre, pages 11–126
2 Performing from a text, pages 127–131
3 Interpreting theatre, pages 132–155

This guide is designed to help you to get the most out of your Drama GCSE. It maps out your course so you know what is expected from you, why you are doing it, and how to do it well. This will help you to ensure that your performance pieces and written work are successful and unique.

# How to use this book

This book has lots of features to help you build your skills and prepare for your assessments:

## FOR YOUR PORTFOLIO

Rehearsals or exercises will give you important evidence that can be included in your portfolio – for example, mind maps, photos, rehearsal notes and annotated sections of script. These For your portfolio boxes will help you to think about some of the things you might include in your portfolio.

## TIP

Hints and advice to help you produce successful work.

 **EXERCISE** 0.0    **ACTIVITY 0.0**

Exercises and activities to develop your skills and knowledge, and help you produce your best work in assessments.

## LINK

Shows where you can find further information on a topic in this guide.

## FIND HELP FOR ...

Shows you where to find additional assistance with key skills.

For 'Devising theatre' and 'Performing from a text' you can choose to be assessed on either performance or design. These icons will help you to identify information and examples specific to the skill you have chosen.

**Key terms**

Key terms are highlighted in **blue** throughout the text and defined in the Glossary on pages 156–157.

**DOWNLOADABLE**

Many of the activities and checklists are available to download – visit the WJEC/Eduqas GCSE Drama Study & Revision Guide page at www. illuminatepublishing.com.

# Assessment Objectives

The Assessment Objectives (AOs) for your course are:

**AO1** Create and develop ideas to communicate meaning for theatrical performance.

**AO2** Apply theatrical skills to realise artistic intentions in live performance.

**AO3** Demonstrate knowledge and understanding of how drama and theatre is developed and performed.

**AO4** Analyse and evaluate your own work and the work of others.

The table below shows how the AOs are covered in your course.

**AO1 AO2 AO3 AO4**
These icons will show you which AOs are covered in each section, and which activities and exercises will particularly help you to develop and practise the skills you need for each AO.

|  | AO1 | AO2 | AO3 | AO4 | Total |
|---|---|---|---|---|---|
| Component/Unit 1 | 20% | 10% | – | 10% | 40% |
| Component/Unit 2 | – | 20% | – | – | 20% |
| Component/Unit 3 | – | – | 30% | 10% | 40% |
| Component/Unit 4 | 20% | 30% | 30% | 20% | 100% |

# Your GCSE

## 1 Devising theatre

You will need to:

- devise a piece of original theatre in response to a **stimulus**, using either the techniques of an influential **theatre practitioner** or the characteristics of a **genre** of drama

- apply theatrical skills and **dramatic devices** to realise artistic intentions through performance or design

- analyse and evaluate your own work.

Assessed through a portfolio of supporting evidence.

Assessed through a 🎭 performance or 👥 design for your devised scene.

Assessed through a written evaluation completed under supervised conditions.

### Using dramatic devices, practitioners and genres

Practitioners such as Constantin Stanislavski and Bertolt Brecht created fundamental tools and lessons for successful drama. You will learn about their techniques and other practitioners who built on their ideas in the chapter on practitioners. Some practitioners work within a specific genre. 'Genre' simply refers to the type, or category, of theatre to which a production belongs. Dramatic devices are visual tools used to communicate a particular impression or effect on an audience.

### 👁 FIND HELP FOR ...

Theatre practitioners on pages 41–82.

Using dramatic devices on pages 17–18.

Choosing a genre on pages 83–105.

**Building your skills**

This revision guide will help you to build the skills you need to pass your GCSE Drama, including:

- how to approach **designing for theatre** (pages 23–40)
- how to place your scenes in a **dramatic structure** (pages 106–116)
- how to structure your **written evaluations** (pages 117–126)
- how to write **reviews** of live theatre performances (page 154).

# 2 Performing from a text

You will participate in a performance from a text. You will select a text, choose extracts and edit them in order to create a performance. You can choose to be assessed on either 🎭 performance or ⚄ design.

# 3 Interpreting theatre

You will study one complete play and be assessed by a written exam. You will need to demonstrate your knowledge and understanding of the play you have studied. You will also need to analyse and evaluate one piece of live theatre viewed during your course.

**Battling stage fright – and 'page fright'!**

Stage fright is something everybody knows about, but it is not unusual to find the written work a bit scary too. Whether you suffer from stage fright or page fright (or even if you do not suffer from either), here are some things you can do to improve your communication skills onstage and on the page.

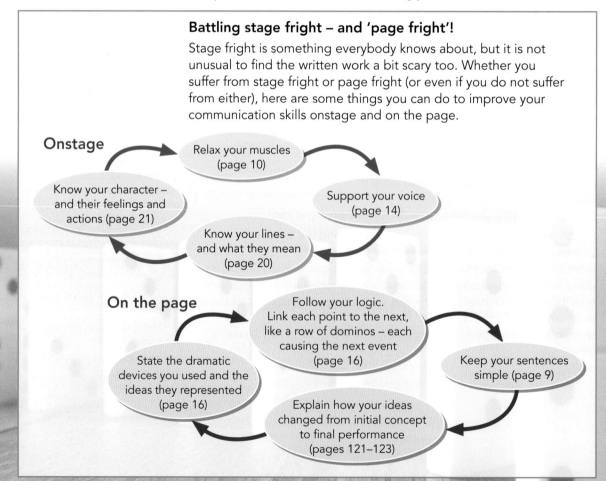

**Onstage**

Relax your muscles (page 10)

Support your voice (page 14)

Know your lines – and what they mean (page 20)

Know your character – and their feelings and actions (page 21)

**On the page**

Follow your logic. Link each point to the next, like a row of dominos – each causing the next event (page 16)

Keep your sentences simple (page 9)

Explain how your ideas changed from initial concept to final performance (pages 121–123)

State the dramatic devices you used and the ideas they represented (page 16)

# Drama watchwords

Whether you are brainstorming ideas, memorising cues and lines, rehearsing or performing, make the most of your ideas, both onstage and on the page, with the following drama watchwords.

## Clarity

It is important to be clear, not only in your speech and the words you choose onstage (**dialogue**) and in your written evaluation but also in the images you use to present your ideas visually to the audience. You need to shape and project your words (diction) for clarity. Remember, natural-looking movement onstage is a lot simpler and bigger than our movement in real life. The events of the plot in your scene need to be clear too – make sure your plot flows logically, with one event causing the next.

Clarity is also important in your written work. You don't need complex sentences, just state as clearly as you can what you chose to do, what you learnt from it and what you would change next time.

## Focus

One of the best ways to help your performance, both onstage and in written work, is what Stanislavski called **concentration of attention**. The more you **focus** on the detail, one thing at a time, the less you will worry about what the audience is thinking, what you look like, who's watching … and that will help you to perform better. Focus on one specific action – or sentence – then move on to the next. As a performer, this allows you to **suspend your disbelief** and make your character **truthful**. It also stops you accidentally looking at the audience, rearranging your clothes, etc.

**LINK**

For more information on Stanislavski, see pages 41–49.

 **FIND HELP FOR …**

Focus exercises and games on pages 44 and 48.

## Imagination

When you are creating a piece, always remember that you are not looking for the one 'right answer' – the trick in creating something new is putting ideas together that have not been put together before. Do not be afraid to use your own ideas and associations when you work with your stimulus and your group. It is very important to try out ideas. write down lines of dialogue from improv circles – also gestures or still images. 'A picture tells a thousand words', so your audience will enjoy interpreting visual images more than having everything explained in words. 'Show, don't tell' your story.

# Relaxation

We all know how unhelpful it is to hear 'keep still' and 'don't fidget', especially if you are nervous – so try giving yourself a list of do's instead of don'ts.

- Do a warm-up before a rehearsal or performance to relax your muscles. Warming up your body and voice is like tuning a musical instrument before a performance: necessary if you want the best performance.

- Do think what your character wants – if you forget a line, remembering what you are trying to achieve in the scene may help you to find it.

- Do keep the scene going – it is better to muddle a line a bit and stay 'in the world of the play' than come out of character to apologise or look at your director or audience.

- Do write a draft of your main points before you start writing an answer. With a plan to follow, you won't need to panic or rush.

**LINK**

For physical and vocal warm-up exercises, see pages 12–14.

# Simplicity

What does your character want? What is your scene about? The more simply you can answer these basic questions, the easier you will find it to select dialogue, dramatic devices, gestures, movement and stage effects to communicate your ideas – and to cut out anything that is not necessary to tell the story.

Simplicity applies to your written work too: straightforward, clear sentences convey your meaning better than anything over-complex or too long. Your audience – or reader – is looking for meaning. If the words help to communicate meaning – great. If not – cut them.

Cut!

# CHAPTER 1 / DEVISING

This chapter will help you to produce:

- a performance or design for your devised scene
- a portfolio of supporting evidence
- a written evaluation.

## What is devising?

**Devising simply means creating (or 'making up') your own piece of theatre.**

Theatre companies work together to devise new theatre from their choice of stimulus, just as you will do. Stimulus for ideas can be any source of inspiration, from political situations and world events to a song, story or painting you love, or a line of dialogue you overhear in the street.

## What do I need to do for my assessment?

**Your group will create, develop and perform a piece of devised theatre.**

The performance will be recorded audio-visually from the audience's point of view.

Your group can have:

- two to five performers
- up to four designers.

Each designer will be responsible for a different design element: **lighting**, **sound**, **set (including props)** or **wardrobe (including make-up)**.

You will be given a selection of stimulus material to help you think of ideas. Your group's devised piece will be based on the work of a theatre practitioner or genre, whose techniques will help you communicate your ideas to your audience in a final performance.

You will each produce a portfolio of evidence showing your devised scene's development.

After your performance, you will each write an evaluation of your contribution to the devised performance, reporting back on the process and results of bringing your devised piece to the stage, including:

- What went well and why?
- What did you learn along the way?
- What would you do differently next time?

*Brief Encounter*, devised and performed by Kneehigh Theatre (see Emma Rice, page 66).

**LINK**

For more information on design elements, see pages 23–40.

**FIND HELP FOR …**

Genres on pages 83–105.

Portfolio of evidence on pages 112–116.

Written evaluation on pages 117–126.

**FOR YOUR PORTFOLIO**

Include your answers to these questions in your portfolio, with visual evidence (diagrams, photographs, discussion notes) of what you tried and why.

# Warm-up exercises

Using effective warm-up exercises will help your voice, body and mind make the most of every rehearsal and performance.

# PHYSICAL WARM-UP

## 1 Find 'neutral position'

Neutral position is standing without holding any unnecessary tension in your body, so your body doesn't suggest any particular emotion. Finding neutral position helps you to build your character effectively, as your body language will be made up from character choices and not your own physical habits.

**TIP**

Keep your eyeline on something straight ahead throughout the warm-up.

## 2 Stand with your feet hip-distance apart

Starting with your feet, consciously relax every muscle in your lower body that you don't need to keep you upright, then work up through your body to the top of your head and down each arm.

**TIP**

Throughout your warm-up, try to use only the muscles you are focusing on at that time. For example, keep your head and neck relaxed and still while stretching your arms.

## 3 Arms

Rotate your hands. Work the rotation through your wrists, then arms and finally shoulders, so you are 'windmilling' your arms in one direction. Then 'windmill' your arms in the opposite direction.

**TIP**

Be clear in your mind what colour the paint on the end of your nose is. The clearer you see it, the better you will do the movement.

## 4 Head and neck

Imagine a blob of paint on the end of your nose. Slowly paint a straight line slowly across your field of vision, from one side to the other, using only your head and neck.

## 5 Shoulders

Roll your shoulders in a circle. Ensure that each circle goes as far back, up, forwards and down as you can. Then reverse the circle.

## 6 Torso and waist

Now bring that rolling stretch from your shoulders into your torso, in whatever direction you like. Continue the rolling stretch down to your waist, in both directions.

## 7 Legs

Move the stretch down to your legs, in any direction you like. Lift one leg and shake it. Make sure your eyes focus on the middle-distance. Now do the same with the other leg.

## 8 Face

Gently massage all the muscles in your face and under your chin, then massage your shoulders slightly harder.

## 9 Whole body

Now shake your whole body, with your throat open on a voiced sound of 'Ahhhhh!'

**TIP**

**Don't be afraid to look silly!**
The more comfortable you are using the whole of your body and your voice in the warm-up, the easier you will find anything you need to do onstage.

**TIP**

As well as your physical focus (eyes on something straight ahead of you), try to keep a mental focus. It could be what your character is thinking about in their first **monologue**, your backstory, your **objective** … Every movement and sound you make during the warm-up will be more comfortable with a mental and physical focus.

13

# VOCAL WARM-UP

## 1 Raspberry chewing gum

Blow a long raspberry, with a hand gesture as if stretching gum from your mouth. If the note goes up, point the gum up. If the note goes down, point it down. Try different lengths and sounds.

## 2 Paintball consonants

With your eyeline straight ahead and a finger on your diaphragm, breathe in then 'shoot' a consonant at the opposite wall as if it is a paintball.

Try these, one at a time:

- Hey
- He
- Ha
- Ho.

Now try a line of these, on one breath:

- Tar Tay Tee Tor Too.

Then try these sound pairs – repeat these sounds as pairs, throwing them like paintballs:

- SS SS, ZZ ZZ, Shh Shh, K K, Wh Wh.

> **TIP**
>
> Think about what your character means for each of your lines and try to get that message across with your vocal tone, diction and facial expression. Experiment with how your face and voice communicate your meaning, even when speaking gibberish.

## 3 Standing snores

Keeping your eyeline at middle-distance, breathe in and release the breath on a long vowel. Then breathe in again and release it on another:

- Ahh
- Ooh
- Ohh.

Now try the same with the vowels of these words:

- Hey
- Ho
- Ha
- He
- Yes
- No.

> **TIP**
>
> Flexible vocal tone and diction will often be the difference between a successful line and an unsuccessful line. See what happens if you try to say the 'One-one was a racehorse' tongue-twister (below) in monotone – it would lack meaning for the audience.

## 4 Vocal flexibility

Try these tongue-twisters:

66 Copper-bottomed coffee pot. 99

66 Whether the weather is cold, whether the weather is hot, we'll weather the weather whatever the weather, whether we like it or not. 99

66 In Hertford, Hereford and Hampshire, hurricanes hardly ever happen. 99

66 One-one was a racehorse, Two-two was one too, One-one won one race, Two-two won one too. 99

# Skills for devising

These skills will help you make the most of the rehearsal process and of working with the members of your group.

## Listen

The best ideas often grow out of other ideas or are ones that you come back to later. During your discussions, listen to everyone and take lots of notes. It is better to have too many ideas than not enough when you begin responding to your stimulus, and it is certainly better to take notes than to struggle to remember great ideas later.

## Try it out

Often, getting an idea 'on its feet', rehearsing (rather than just discussing it) is the best way to discover whether it is right for your piece and what will be needed to make it work. The games on the next pages will help you and your group try out and develop ideas in practical, dramatic ways.

## Play to your strengths

Some actors are great at Physical Theatre, others are great at bringing out the meaning when reading text. Give your group members a chance to shine. You will all find different things more challenging. Make the most of the fact that not everyone has the same strengths by helping each other. Your piece will be stronger for everyone's contribution being different.

## Clear objectives, clear images

It is no good having the most amazing idea in the world if it is not expressed visually and your audience does not understand it. Remember the drama watchwords, 'clarity' and 'simplicity' when writing your piece:

- What is your scene about?
- What key ideas do you need to communicate?
- What are the key images you will use to convey them?
- How can movement, stage design, sound or lighting support them?

Remember, theatre works visually: try to 'show, not tell' whenever possible. Even the most well-written script is only as successful onstage as the actors, director and designers make it.

**ACTIVITY 1.1**

Try out each of the drama watchwords on your scene in class. How does each one make your story clearer?

**LINK**

Read about the drama watchwords on pages 9–10.

**FOR YOUR PORTFOLIO**

Explain what you did for Activity 1.1. Use rehearsal photographs, written explanation or both to help.

# Tools for devising

Dramatic devices are the tools and techniques used in drama to make points and convey meaning. Think of dramatic devices as your drama 'vocabulary'. How many of them do you know already?

**Freeze-frame**
Actors form a still image. Usually showing a significant moment or symbolising something important.

**Dramatic pause**
A hesitation or halt in dialogue, building suspense or showing a character's strong reaction to something.

**Mime**
Performing the story with the body and facial expression only. No words or sounds.

**Choral speaking**
A group speaking together, commenting on or narrating the action of the play.

**Slow motion**
Slowing down a scene to build suspense or examine it closely.

**Flashback**
A character's memory triggers the action of the play to move to a previous time.

**Dramatic devices**

**Cross-cutting**
Scenes move from one part of the stage to another, moving between different places or times in the story.

**Direct address**
A form of narration, when a character inside the story speaks directly to the audience, saying something the other characters cannot hear.

**Thought-tracking**
Characters speaking their private thoughts to the audience aloud.

**Narrator**
A person who tells the story to the audience.

**Monologue**
A long speech by one character within a scene.

**Symbol**
An object standing for an issue or theme.

**Soliloquy**
A long speech by a character alone onstage, sharing private thoughts.

**TIP**

Dramatic devices are ways to help you show – not just tell – what is happening in your plot and what it means. You cannot just rely on how good your lines are – theatre works best when it is visual.

**ACTIVITY 1.2**  AO1 AO2
Pick one of the dramatic devices in this mind map. What moment in your script could you use it for?

DOWNLOADABLE ⬇

# Devising with dramatic devices

## ACTIVITY 1.3 — AO①-AO②

Pick one of the following options to use as your stimulus for a devised scene. What themes, events or characters does it make you think of? Those ideas are the beginning of devising theatre.

Discuss ideas with your group and use up to three dramatic devices from the mind map on page 16 to create a 5-minute scene.

Ready, set, devise!

'Last chance'

'Learning to Fly' – Pink Floyd

'Our greatest glory is not in never falling, but in rising every time we fall'.
– Confucius

I picked the picture of the trees and crows. I want to talk about how humans treat nature. I think the central character might be someone from a town who comes to live in the country …

## ACTIVITY 1.4 — AO①-AO②

To practise using a song as a stimulus, discuss as a group a song you all know and would like to explore as a scene.

### FOR YOUR PORTFOLIO

You can include your material from Activity 1.3 in your portfolio – or, use the same activity on the stimulus material your teacher offers and include that.

### TIP

You don't need to be musical to turn a song you love into theatre. You could even explore the characters and plot you think the song describes and use no music at all.

⬇ DOWNLOADABLE

## ACTIVITY 1.5 ────────────────────────── AO❶ AO❷

Look at the two images below. What story do they in conjure up in your imagination?

Discuss your ideas with your group and develop your own scene.

If you are stuck for inspiration, add one of these two 'atmospheres' to help progress your ideas:

1 *Nostalgic* – looking back to childhood.
2 *Ghostly* – is someone haunted by a memory or an actual ghost?

The old teddy bear made me think of someone looking back at their childhood memories, some time ago. I might even devise a ghost story about the teddy bear's owner …

## FOR YOUR PORTFOLIO

Which was your favourite dramatic device to use? Why did you choose it to help you work with your piece of stimulus? Try drawing or photographing the dramatic device as well as explaining why it was particularly helpful in developing your scene.

# GAMES FOR DEVISING

AO 1
AO 2

DOWNLOADABLE

These games will help you to explore the skills of devising drama. You will come up with lines and use your body and voice to illustrate emotions and ideas. Work together as a group, accepting the ideas of others and offering your own.

## 1 "What's this?"

**A quick-fire game to get ideas and imagination warmed up.**

1 This can be done with any object, for example a pencil.

2 The director (either your teacher or one member of your group) holds up the pencil and asks everyone to observe it closely.

3 Then, the director asks every member of the group, quickly and urgently, 'What's this?'

4 Each member of the group must say something true about the object, for example 'It's pink', 'It's got an eraser on the end', 'It's got a sharp point'.

5 Next, when the director asks 'What's this?' each member of the group must instantly reply with a lie. You can say anything, so long as it is not true, for example 'It's a flamingo!', 'It's a jet engine!', 'It's brown!'

This game is all about **spontaneity** – any hesitation and you are out.

**How does this help me to devise?** This game stops you from overthinking and gets you in the habit of responding authentically and with confidence onstage.

> **TIP**
>
> This game uses Stanislavski's techniques of observation and spontaneity.

## 2 "Yuck ball"

**A great warm-up for Physical Theatre and voice work.**

1 Form a circle. One person in the group is the director. Begin by throwing a mimed ball around the circle.

2 When the ball gets back to the director, they will ask you to throw something disgusting at the imaginary ball in their hands. You can mime flicking snot, throwing dog poo, whatever you can think of!

3 With every bit of snot/slime/dog poo that lands, the mimed ball gets bigger and smellier. You can't drop it. You have to catch it from the person on one side of you and throw it to the person on the other side and you can't talk – all you can say is 'Uuurrrgh!' or 'Yuck!'

**How does this help me to devise?** It makes sure that your body, voice and emotions are working together. It helps you to convey emotions, gestures and tones of voice, so you can 'show, not tell' your audience what your character is feeling and what your scene is about. Because the Yuck ball is invisible, you can only keep its reality for the audience by eye contact and **observation** – keeping it the same shape, etc. as when it was thrown.

**FOR YOUR PORTFOLIO**

Draw an image or describe an idea that came up in one of these games that you could use or develop in your group scene.

# 3 "Eek! Grr! Aagh!"

**A sound-effects and Physical Theatre storytelling game.**

1 Form a circle. One member of the group should be the director. The director turns to the student next to them in the circle and looks that person in the eye, while performing a star jump and saying 'Eek!' That student turns to the person next to them in the circle and copies the action and sound. Repeat, so the 'Eek!' and action is passed around the circle.

2 You can change direction by turning on the person who 'Eeked' you, holding up your hands like claws and saying 'Grrr!' The person next to you should copy the sound and gesture so the 'Grrr!' travels back the way the 'Eek!' has come, until someone challenges the 'Grrr!' by going back to the 'Eek!' You can also throw a sound across the circle, by pointing both arms at the person you want to send it to and saying 'Aagh!' (with fear, as if you are seeing a ghost).

3 Anyone who hesitates is out and sits down in their place in the circle. The more people are out, the more the remaining players have to concentrate.

**How does this help me to devise?** Words are just the surface of a scene. However good the dialogue, what reaches the audience most is how truthful the emotion (shown by your face and voice) is. Any sound – or sound-effect – can be made meaningful.

**TIP**

Try replacing the suggested sounds with ones from ideas of your own, or with individual words, to instantly build a devised text scene.

# 4 "Pickled onions"

**A gibberish game to boost your mime and voice skills.**

1 Stand in a circle, with a large acting space in the middle.

2 Two actors volunteer to go into this 'improvisaton circle'.

3 One actor makes an 'offer' of an idea to begin a scene. For example, Actor 1 might be a child begging an adult to let them go to a party or they might be an adult teaching a child how to cross the road. The clearer and more specific the physical actions, tone of voice and idea in your head, the easier to show in performance.

4 BUT … the only words you can say are 'pickled onions'! Every word must be replaced by this phrase. All the meaning must come from tone of voice, physical movement and facial expression.

**TIP**

Even a sound like a sigh, a cough or a scream should be the phrase 'pickled onions' for the audience to believe in the scene.

**TIP**

Remember, in every drama scene that includes more than one actor, 'offers' are being made and accepted all the time.

**How does this help me to devise?** It encourages you to express your meaning in ways other than words, so that when you say lines you fully inhabit them and bring their meaning to life.

**FOR YOUR PORTFOLIO**

You could use one of these games to develop your scene. If you do this, explain how you have used it, and perhaps take a video of it (you can recreate key moments after the game). This could then be included in your portfolio of evidence.

DOWNLOADABL

## ACTIVITY 1.6 — AO1 AO2

In pairs or small groups, try devising a scene (from information in the script or from your imagination) using just the words 'pickled onions', concentrating on expressing meaning through your face, voice and body.

## Developing your character

Whether you are playing the **protagonist** (main character), **antagonist** (whoever is against them, creating conflict) or a **minor character**, you need to know as much as you can about who you are playing. The more of the following questions you are able to answer, the stronger your performance will be.

### FOR YOUR PORTFOLIO

List the 'Developing your character' questions you used. What new aspects of your character were created?

What's my full name?

How old am I during the play?

How confident do I feel?

What am I hiding?

What am I scared of?

What am I proud of?

Who's the most important person in my life?

When was I happiest?

What do I want?

What am I doing to get it?

### TIP

To develop your character further, try **hot-seating**. Get the rest of your group to ask you questions which you answer in character – a bit like an interview. This is an opportunity to find out about the character's past, background, what they want from the future and what they are doing about it.

> *When you play an old man, look to see where he is young. When you play a young man, look to see where he is old.*

Stanislavski, *My Life in Art*, page 184

### LINK

For more about Stanislavski, inventor of **the System of naturalistic acting**, see pages 41–49.

# Devising: What have I learnt?

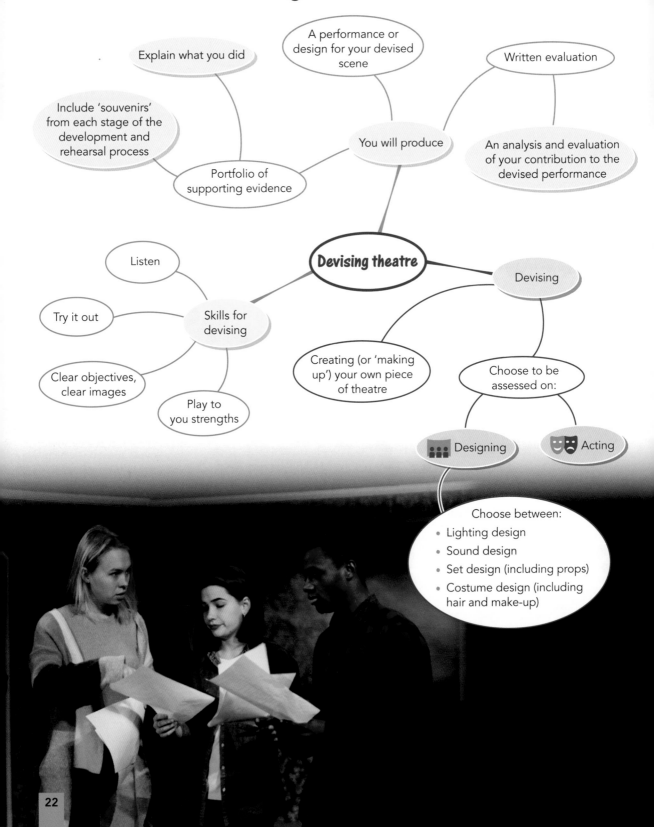

Explain what you did

A performance or design for your devised scene

Written evaluation

Include 'souvenirs' from each stage of the development and rehearsal process

You will produce

An analysis and evaluation of your contribution to the devised performance

Portfolio of supporting evidence

**Devising theatre**

Listen

Skills for devising

Devising

Try it out

Creating (or 'making up') your own piece of theatre

Choose to be assessed on:

Clear objectives, clear images

Play to you strengths

Designing

Acting

Choose between:
- Lighting design
- Sound design
- Set design (including props)
- Costume design (including hair and make-up)

# CHAPTER 2 / DESIGN

This chapter will help you to:
- understand the role of designers
- select an element of design to be examined on
- decide what set, lighting/sound cues or costume/make-up to be examined on.

## Choosing to be a designer

Would you prefer to be assessed on designing for your devised piece rather than acting?

You can choose from any of the following areas of designing for the stage:
- lighting (pages 24–27)
- set, including props (pages 30–34)
- sound (pages 28–29)
- costume, including hair and make-up (pages 35–37).

**TIP**

Each group of actors may have up to four designers, each responsible for a different element of design.

### What do I need to do?

- If you choose lighting or sound design, you will need to include a minimum of five lighting states or sound cues in your design.
- If you choose costume design (including hair and make-up), you will need to produce total costume and make-up for two characters in the devised scene.
- If you choose set design (including props), you will need to provide a set for one group performance, and the set will need to be dressed with the appropriate use of props.

## What does a designer do?

Your design ideas should be guided by the performance text. Everything a designer does must come from this text, whether it is a newly devised script or a published play.

Ask yourself the following questions:

What are the playwright's intentions?

Where and when is the play set?

What practical considerations do I need to think about (e.g. does a phone need to ring onstage)?

What are the most important props?

What are the restrictions of the performance space?

What does the set need to draw attention to?

What does the set need to hide?

Then, discuss with your group how you will use your design to share these ideas with your audience.

# LIGHTING DESIGN
## What does lighting design do?

**Visibility** → Allows the audience to see the stage and action.

**Focus** → Highlights and disguises areas of the stage, to draw the audience's attention towards things the director wants them to see and away from things they should not notice.

**Mood** → Suggests atmosphere and emotions, as well as drawing attention towards people or things.

**Composition** → Lighting the stage design to advantage, giving depth and creating different areas on the stage.

### TIP
The first thing a lighting designer should do is address the questions on page 23. It is very important that a design serves the play, not upstage it. Once you have identified your answers to those questions, it is time to start designing.

## What does lighting design use?
### Types of lantern

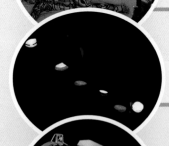

### Practical
In a natural setting, stage lighting must appear to come from standing lamps, chandeliers, etc. on the set.

### Flood
The simplest stage lantern. It is a lamp with a reflector in a box, with no lens. It can be used for skies or cloth backdrops.

### Fresnel
Fresnel, pronounced 'frennel', is a soft-edged spotlight, with more control over beam angle than a flood. It can be used to light an area of the stage or to provide a colour wash to an area of the stage.

## Profile spot

Produces a spot of light with clearly defined edges, which can be gradually softened by adjusting the focus. This makes them very versatile.

## Followspot

A narrow spotlight used to 'follow' a character. It is moved manually by an operator.

## Gel

A thin, coloured sheet of heat-resistant plastic put in a gel frame. It adds colour to the stage floor, profile, etc.

# Intensity/strength

Intensity is how powerful (or strong) a light is. Light becomes more intense not only with the strength of the light but also the angle and distance of the beam, as well as the distance from the area being lit.

# Focus

The way to get your lighting to show the stage space and the story is all in how you focus it. How strong does the beam need to be? Where does it need to be pointing? Quite often, it is necessary to focus and refocus your lighting several times to make sure you get what you want; good lighting, though, is always worth the effort.

**TIP**

Lighting can change certain colours! Remember to check for fluorescence and colour change of costumes and make-up under 'house lights' and stage lights.

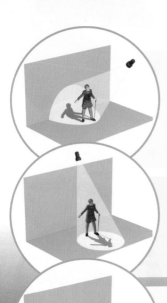

# Angle

### Lit from the front

A 45-degree angle above the actor's head is usual when lighting from the front. However, watch out for shadows. If the light is too close there will be a lot of shadow under the chin. If the subject being lit is a prop or piece of furniture, rather than an actor, the shadow may be even more distracting.

### Lit from the back

Lighting from the back, called backlighting, is used to individualise a subject from the surroundings. This creates a sense of depth and three-dimensionality, distinguishing the person or object from the scenery, set flats or wider space.

### Lit from the side

Lighting from the side is used to highlight movement. It stresses the sides of the subject – face, arms, torso and upper legs – giving a fluid, moving impression.

### Lit from above

Lighting from above is mainly used to wash a whole area of stage and it looks particularly ghostly when focused over an actor.

## Special effects

Strobe lighting (when the light flashes on and off very quickly) gives the effect of jerky movements. Weather, such as rain or lightning, or laser patterns, such as you might see in concerts, are all kinds of special effects.

## Colour

Colours are added through gels (see gel on page 25) and chosen because of the mood or association they create. In naturalistic lighting, colours are chosen to represent the time of day, interior or exterior, as realistically as possible. However, in non-naturalistic theatre, our common associations of colour are used to reflect mood and situation, such as red for danger or green for nature.

**LINK**

For more on colour see pages 34 and 37.

**TIP**

Always work with the power off. Lanterns can cause damage if they fall, so you must always use chains and clamps to attach them securely to lighting bars.

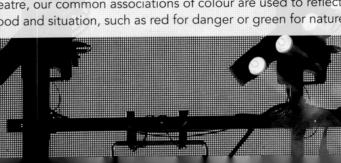

# Gobos

Gobos are metal cut-outs or etchings over glass. They are put in a gobo holder in front of a profile lantern to show a specific shape. They can be used for special effects or to give a particular idea to an audience.

## ACTIVITY 2.1 — AO **1** AO **2**

Draw diagrams of your ideas for your set piece in answer to one or more of the following questions about stage lighting:

- How do different levels of intensity/strength affect the mood of the stage?
- How can you use spotlights to focus the audience's attention in a scene?
- How does changing the angle of a light falling on a performer change the audience's interpretation of the scene?
- What special effects can you include to convey your meaning?
- What are the implications of using different colours?
- How will gobos affect the look and feel of the stage?
- What different types of lantern does your space have?

> **TIP**
>
> You can have a lot of fun with gobos, using them as clouds, foliage, skyscrapers … but do not overuse them. Choose only a few scenes to use gobos or special effects: do not overwhelm the audience with too many special effects or they will lose interest.

**FOR YOUR PORTFOLIO**

You could use the diagrams you create for Activity 2.1 in your portfolio.

# SOUND DESIGN

## What does sound design do?

Sound design is much more than the songs you pick for scene changes and background music. Sound-effects and **soundscapes** can be a subtle and powerful way of creating a sense of location. Sound can also establish the time of day, season, weather, town or countryside, empty room or crowd of people – so it creates mood and atmosphere. It can also give indications about the room the scene takes place in, as much as a set can.

## What does sound design use?

### Music

Choosing the right song or instrumental piece can suggest themes and atmosphere that you want your audience to have in their minds as they watch the performance. It is also a great way of covering scene changes or building atmosphere by underscoring (playing underneath) key moments of tension or importance.

### Sound-effects

On a bare stage, you can create the location of a swamp by the noises of feet in mud; you can create a busy city centre by the noise of cars whizzing by; or you can create extreme cold or heat by the right sound-effects. Your school, college or centre will have lots of recorded sounds, or you can listen to them on the internet or in libraries for inspiration. Remember, you can make your own live sounds as actors inside the scene, or perhaps as a chorus watching and commenting on the action.

### Live sounds

'Live sounds' refers to any sounds that are created as part of the performance. For example, if you mime a character walking through a muddy field, other members of your group could provide the squelches of the mud.

### Recorded sounds

'Recorded sounds' refers to any sound that is not made live by the performers. For example, the same 'squelch' of mud could be provided by selecting a pre-recorded squelch. On an album of sound-effects there are often many sounds you may need – from a wolf howling to a car squealing to a halt.

SQUELCH!

# Volume

Increasing and decreasing the volume – how loud your sounds are – can show the actors moving towards, or away from, a place or object, or can suggest a changing state of emotion. You can see this with how loudly or softly you speak a line – either alone or as a chorus – as well as experimenting with sound-effects by making them louder or quieter.

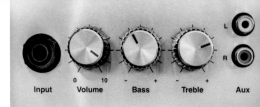

# Reverb/echo

This is a sound or voice bouncing back, as when you hear an echo of your own voice in a cave, church or other large space. You can add the effect to a recording, or even use it in live performances.

# Sound sources, including position on stage

Just like volume and reverb/echo, the positioning of the source for the sound in your performance can make it even more effective. Try placing a speaker under the stage for added threat from below, or hide one behind your prop telephone for added realism. Experiment with lots of speaker positions to find what works best for you and your scene.

# Amplification

If you want to make your actors' voices or particular sound-effects louder or quieter, an amplifier allows you to control how loud or soft your sounds are. Decide on cues (lines or actions) to build the volume and/or reverb so the sound is created when and how you intend.

**TIP**

Don't be afraid to borrow from life! Keep notes from your daily life about the sounds you hear and could either record, or mimic with your voice (live onstage or pre-recorded for a sound cue).

## ACTIVITY 2.2 — AO 1 AO 2

1 See what happens if you try the same dialogue with different sound backgrounds. How does it change the way the audience hears the dialogue? Change the sound background to:

a) a busy road     c) heavy rain

b) an empty café     d) a field in summer.

2 Pick one of the following techniques to explore how underscoring a scene with music or sound affects the drama taking place.

- Use a piano (or a box representing a piano) turned away from the audience. Have one actor mime playing along to a classical piano piece alone onstage.

  Now alter the sound so that the same piece of music is playing but people are talking over it at a party.

- Play out a scene where two people are having an argument. Change the sound to suggest different locations and see how they appear different to an audience. Try the following or suggest your own:

  a) a baby crying     b) a bus or train     c) a pub or bar.

# SET DESIGN (INCLUDING PROPS)

## What does set design do?

Set design can convey the location and time period, and sometimes the themes, of the play that is being performed.

## What does set design use?

Set design communicates meaning through:

- Choice of stage
- Type of set
- Backdrop/**cyclorama**
- Set dressing
- Props

- Furniture
- Colour
- Use of space
- Entrances and exits
- **Sight lines**

## Choice of stage

**Proscenium arch**

A proscenium arch stage has large offstage areas for complex sets and large casts or numerous scene changes. The audience sits in front of the stage, as if looking at a picture frame.

Stage

Apron

Audience

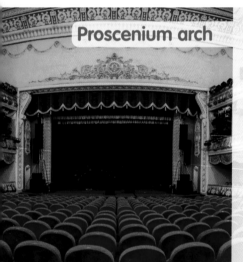

**Theatre in the round**

Theatre in the round, popular for circus and smaller venues, is often square shaped! The audience surrounds the stage. It is intimate and focused, and not reliant on massive scene changes.

Audience

Audience

Stage

Audience

Audience

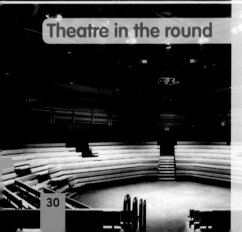

## Traverse

Traverse is a more unusual type of staging. Various scenes can be set up simultaneously, moving easily in time or from location to location. The audience can see others' reactions, as they sit on both sides of the action.

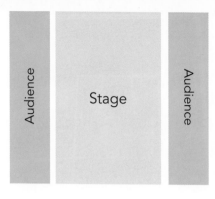

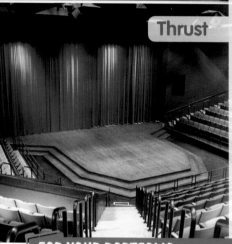

## Thrust

Thrust staging is very popular in modern theatres. Ambitious set designs, and painted flats and backdrops, can be used. There are no curtains to separate the audience, who sit around three sides of the stage, from the play. Large sets or **operational sets** can be used, but these make it difficult to change scene during the play.

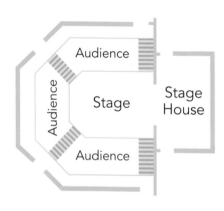

## FOR YOUR PORTFOLIO

Choose a scene from your devised piece and sketch it as it would appear for each different stage layout. What are the strengths and weaknesses for each one? Show how you chose which was the most suitable for your devised piece.

Naturalistic designs are particularly suited to fully naturalistic scripts – and companies with bigger budgets! This production of *Relatively Speaking*, by Alan Ayckbourn, played at the Wyndham's Theatre in London's West End.

# What type of set is most suitable?

The type of set can convey the location and time period, and sometimes the themes, of the play that is being performed.

### Naturalistic sets

If the set is **naturalistic**, it will represent a physical location where the scene takes place.

Naturalistic sets normally contain more detail and often require big budgets. Looking realistic and natural to an audience can be a good thing for some scripts, but the expense cannot always be justified. A set is not as important in making a play seem 'real' as the acting is.

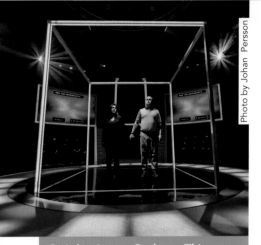

*Photo by Johan Persson*

*Quiz* by James Graham. This set is non-naturalistic as it does not represent a single, literal place. Instead, it places the real-life scenes of the characters' homes and lives in a room that represents a quiz show.

Sir Patrick Stewart and Sir Ian McKellen in *Waiting For Godot* by Samuel Beckett, at the Theatre Royal, Drury Lane in London, with a minimalist set.

### Non-naturalistic sets

If a set is **non-naturalistic**, it might still be very complicated but not represent a literal place.

### Minimalist sets

If a set is minimalist, it can still represent a location but does so with only enough to indicate that place's or room's layout, such as by the use of door frames, a piece of furniture or a prop. Minimalistic sets can convey as much reality by the use of key props or pieces of furniture as naturalistic sets. They are also a good choice for new theatre companies, as the focus becomes the relationships and tensions between the characters without extra money being spent on design. They can create just as much sense of reality as naturalistic sets and can mean a greater focus on the actors. Also, the less naturalistic a set is, the easier it is to represent multiple locations.

### Model box

A good way to make sure your design is giving the director what they want or expect is to build a model box or draw sketches of how the set will look, how bits of it will move, etc. A model box is also useful because it makes you think about how much space you will have for scene changes and how long they will take.

Model box for *Asking Rembrandt*, by Steve Gooch. This artistic design picks up on the themes of the play rather than showing a realistic setting.

*Photo courtesy of Alex Marker.*

## Backdrop/cyclorama

A large curtain or wall that forms the back of the stage, often concave. It can be used to create the illusion of a sky, or distance, beyond the action onstage.

### TIP

The first thing a set designer should do is address the questions on page 23 to identify what is needed in the design.

# Set dressing

The set is usually the first impression the audience has of the production, and the set designer may be able to choose from several types of scenery.

## Flats

Scenery flats are flat pieces of scenery, painted and positioned to represent locations. They can be painted and dressed (set dressing means the pictures, ornaments, etc. that give a sense of place). Alternatively, they can be covered with material.

## Platforms

In theatre, a platform is a stationary, flat surface that actors can perform upon. These are also called rostrum, created with rostra blocks. Differing levels can represent different places, levels of power, or anything you imagine.

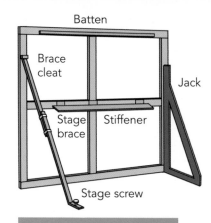

How a flat is constructed.

A rostrum can be used to create different levels.

Before the invention of rostra blocks, theatre practitioners still knew the power of levels. The Globe Theatre was built in the style of theatres that Shakespeare wrote for. The balcony could represent the walls of a town (*King John*), a castle (*Richard II*), the gods looking down on the mortals (*The Tempest*) or even a literal balcony (*Romeo and Juliet*).

Seating rostra refers to the interlocking platforms often used to support seating in a **black-box theatre** (called this because of its versatility; it can be filled or laid out however needed).

## Drapes and curtains

Drapes, particularly black drapes, are often used to mask (hide) backstage areas from the audience. Curtains can also mask areas of the stage, or separate the audience from the stage area before 'curtain up' (the beginning of the play or scene) or 'curtain' (the end of the play or scene). This is also why actors coming on to bow at the end of the performance is called a 'curtain call'.

Drapes and curtains are normally used on a proscenium stage.

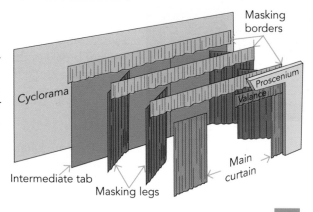

## Props

Props are any objects the actor uses onstage that are not furniture or parts of the set itself. For example, a telephone would be a prop but the table it is placed on would be considered part of the set.

## Furniture

Furniture is anything used on the set that is part of that room and not a movable object. For example, the table a telephone is placed on but not the telephone itself, or a coat stand but not the coat hanging on it.

## Colours

Colours have very basic meanings that we often attribute to them without consciously thinking about it. Red is often associated with danger, white with innocence, green with nature. You can use these associations to create the mood you would like your design to convey, whether that is the set, lighting, costume or make-up.

---

**ACTIVITY 2.3**

1 Write down as many associations as you can for the following colours in 5 minutes:
Black – Red – Green – Blue – Gold.

Some of your ideas may be emotions, such as greed or anger, or they might be concepts, like environmentalism or danger.

2 Think about how you can use colour to suggest themes in your scene.

---

## Use of space

Every designer should think very carefully about how to lay out their set to make best use of the space available. The key is to have enough onstage to give a sense of place and atmosphere, but never to overshadow the action or leave insufficient space for the actors to move about.

## Entrances and exits

Any doorway, vom (short for 'vomitorium' – corridor) or other way actors can get onstage or offstage is an entrance or exit. However, if you are breaking the **fourth wall**, you might want your actors to exit or enter the stage through the audience too, which is not a traditional exit or entrance.

## Sight lines

Sight lines are what the audience is able to see on the stage: make sure that you think about how you place your furniture and actors so what the audience sees is always clear and nothing is blocked from their view.

# COSTUME DESIGN (INCLUDING HAIR AND MAKE-UP)

## What does costume design do?

Like every other aspect of designing for the stage, costume and make-up reflect character and story. When you are working on the design for a character, you need to understand them in the same way an actor does.

Think about the character:

What is their personality like?

Where do they live and work?

Are they wealthy or do they have to cut costs?

What era do they live in?

Is the environment cold or hot?

## What does costume design use?

Choice and use of:

- Materials/fabrics
- Garments
- Hairstyles
- Wigs
- Make-up
- Accessories
- Colour/pattern

### Materials/fabrics

Whether your scene is set in your own era or a previous one, you can use costume to suggest a lot about the character:

- How much money they have.
- How much they work on and care about their appearance.
- What their interests are.

### Garments

You don't need full costume to suggest an era – think about a garment (item of clothing) that immediately shows time and place. For example, a girl or boy with a ponytail and football shirt tells your audience immediately that the play is set in recent times (and what the character's main interest is).

David Suchet as Lady Bracknell in *The Importance of Being Earnest* at the Vaudeville Theatre, London.

You need to know the fashions and technology available in the era your scene is set. Like set and lighting, cost-effective choices are normally the best.

You can look up the styles of different time periods online, and it can be very useful and a lot of fun to look at clips of videos of other productions if you are working from a script.

## Hairstyles

For a short or low-budget piece, keep hairstyles as simple and suggestive as you can. They will very quickly show the character's era and personality.

## Wigs

If you are looking to set your performance in the past, wigs were a common way for society gentry to dress. However, wigs can also be a way of making modern characters look totally different without complex costumes.

## Make-up

If you are looking for a particular era to base your characters in, make sure that you research the style of make-up. Like every element of costume, this can suggest personality and time period. Think about style more than quantity: it is always better to go for a look that is clear and simple and will not take hours to put on. Use make-up to define the eyes and mouth, 'age' your actor if required or show fantasy.

## Accessories

Make sure your choice of jewellery, hats or other accessory items are correct for the time period, social position and personality of your character. In particular, make sure any watches or other accessories were invented at the time your play is set.

# Colour/pattern

Try to keep patterns to a minimum, as they can look fussy and distracting on stage. When choosing colours, think about the meanings your audience will associate with them:

> **TIP**

**Colour and lights**
Be aware of how make-up appears under stage lighting. Foundation that is not specifically made for the stage, for example, can look very yellow under certain stage lights.

> **TIP**

If your play is Brechtian in style, a simple costume item is the best way to represent character. It makes multi-roling easier and helps the audience identify one character from another.

Nature, ecology, good luck, hope

Sunlight, youth, joy, fun

Blood, danger passion, anger

Darkness, death, night, sophistication

Royalty, mystery, wealth, decadence

Peace, innocence, truth, cleanliness

Water, relaxation, calm, sadness

## ACTIVITY 2.4

A01 A02 A03

Discuss the above colours in your groups.
What other colour associations can you list?
How can you use this information in your design?

# Design: What have I learnt?

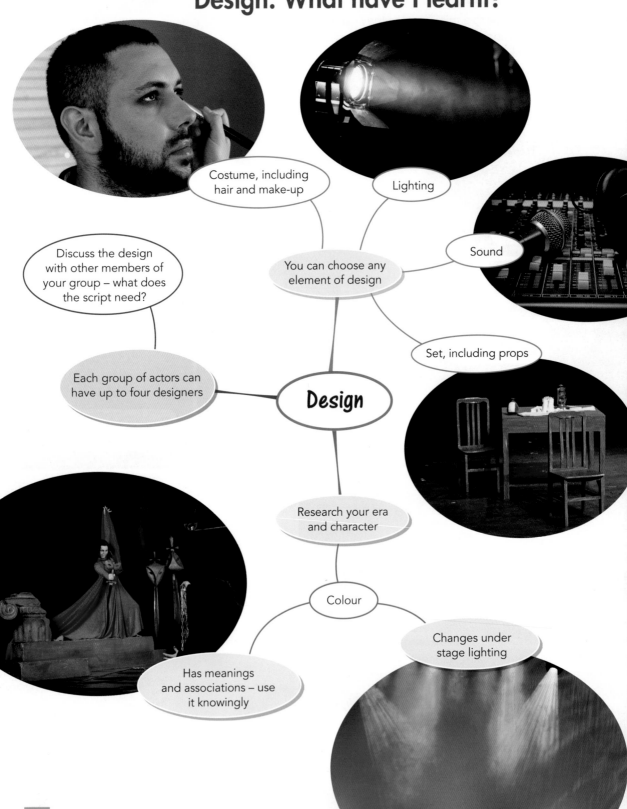

Costume, including hair and make-up

Lighting

Sound

Discuss the design with other members of your group – what does the script need?

You can choose any element of design

Set, including props

Each group of actors can have up to four designers

**Design**

Research your era and character

Colour

Has meanings and associations – use it knowingly

Changes under stage lighting

Here is a mind map of questions for a performer to ask themselves about their scene, followed by similar questions for the designer.

DOWNLOADABLE ⬇

## Performer's mind map

- Relationships between performers and audience
- Performance conventions
- Language/dialogue
- Vocal interpretation of character
- Physical interpretation of character
- Form and style

**Your devised piece**

- Practitioner
- Genre
- Stimulus
- Structure
- Theme/plot

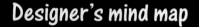

## Designer's mind map

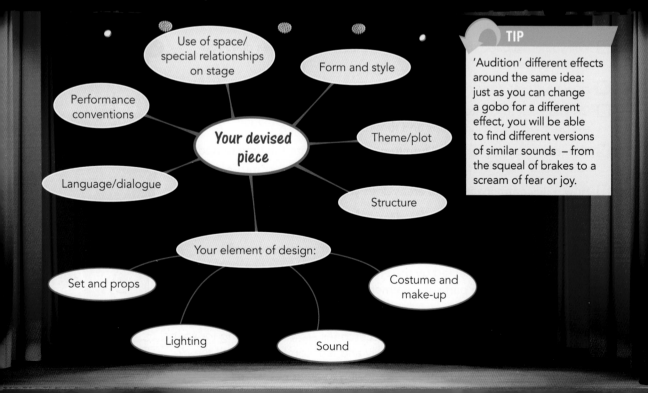

- Use of space/ special relationships on stage
- Form and style
- Performance conventions
- Theme/plot

**Your devised piece**

- Language/dialogue
- Structure

**Your element of design:**

- Set and props
- Costume and make-up
- Lighting
- Sound

# Checklists to help you plan your design

## Lighting design

☐ What colours could suggest your theme?

☐ Do you want the lighting to suggest a particular time of day, season or type of weather?

☐ What gobos, or other special effects, do you need?

☐ What areas of the stage or characters do you need to draw attention to?

☐ What angles do you want to use for your lighting?

## Sound design

☐ How can you use music to suggest your theme?

☐ What sound-effects might help suspense, location, etc.?

☐ What live sounds or recorded sounds might you use in the performance?

☐ How might you use volume, either in recorded music or live sound, to affect mood or communicate messages?

☐ How can you use reverb/echo to create a sense of memory or time passing?

☐ Where will you position your sound sources on the stage? How will this make the best use of amplification without drowning out the action?

## Set design (including props)

☐ What stage configuration will you use? (See pages 30–31.)

☐ Will you use a backdrop or cyclorama? What location or idea does your choice convey?

☐ How much set dressing do you need to convey your location?

☐ Do you want to create a sparse or busy stage? How will the amount of set dressing, including props and furniture, affect this?

☐ How can you use props and furniture to demonstrate the time period of your piece, how rich or poor the characters are, etc.?

☐ How many entrance and exit areas does your stage need?

## Costume design (including hair and make-up)

☐ What materials and fabrics are you choosing for your costumes?

☐ How is your choice affected by the time period, themes or mood of your piece? Are you using particular garments for particular characters? Why?

☐ What hairstyles are appropriate for your characters?

☐ What costumes, wigs, make-up and accessories are you choosing for your actors? Will they be able to move easily and feel comfortable with them?

☐ What colours and patterns are you choosing for your characters?

This chapter will help you to:

- learn about important theatre practitioners and their ideas
- learn key terms and tools associated with their practices
- choose a practitioner to influence your devised piece.

# STANISLAVSKI

## Who was Stanislavski?

Constantin Stanislavski was a Russian actor and director, born in Moscow in 1863. He co-founded the Moscow Art Theatre in 1897 and developed the System, the first formalised training programme for actors. He is often referred to as the father of modern theatre.

Before Stanislavski and his System, actors worked mechanically – using cliched gestures and postures to display emotions. Starring actors would even come out of character to take a series of bows in the middle of a play! Stanislavski changed all this with the fourth wall: an imaginary wall that seals off the world of the play from the audience. It encourages actors to focus on their character's **inner life** and so create **emotional truth** in their performances. This was the beginning of naturalistic acting: instead of unrealistic, generalised performances, Stanislavski's System meant that actors could build three-dimensional characters based on their **emotion memory** which helped them to identify with their characters' feelings.

During his career, Stanislavski wrote many books about acting. In *An Actor Prepares*, he fictionalises himself as the tutor and director, Tortsov, showing student actors how to develop their 'instrument' (the body and mind) in order to act truthfully. After *An Actor Prepares* came *Building a Character* and then *Creating a Role*.

## What did Stanislavski think about theatre?

To Stanislavski, theatre was an opportunity to express life artistically, with the audience 'looking in' on the action as if observing real life. Of course, talking and moving as we do in real life would seem too fast and blurry onstage. Therefore, naturalistic acting involves simplifying gestures and words, so as to appear natural.

## What is the System?

Stanislavski's System, through the techniques described in the following section, helped actors to find inner justification for every action they performed onstage, by adapting and shaping their own thoughts, feelings and memories to those of the characters.

The System covers both **internal characteristics** and **external characteristics**. The actor must develop their character's emotions, inner life, desires and impulses (internal), which lead to truthful physical expression and movement, words, mannerisms and tone of voice (external).

# Stanislavski's techniques

**THE FOURTH WALL**
Imagining the missing 'wall' from the room your play is set in (see page 43).

**FEELING OF TRUTH**
Stanislavskian acting centres on emotions which are truthful – that feel real – to the individual actor. This is achieved by using your 'emotion memory' (see right) and the **magic 'if'** (see page 43).

**EMOTION MEMORY**
Remembering a situation where you felt the emotion your character is feeling and basing your character's feelings on your own.

**THE MAGIC 'IF'**
Asking yourself 'what if' you were in this character's situation, with their memories and emotions. Your brain accepts this magic 'if' but it would never accept being forced to believe that you really were the character.

**MUSCLE MEMORY**
Memory of physical sensation. Actors develop mannerisms and movement for a character, which become habit with rehearsal. Achieved best when supported by warm-ups, muscle relaxation and neutral position (see page 43).

**INTONATION AND PAUSES**
The pitch of the actor's voice and pauses between words or phrases should reflect the character's meaning and emotions.

**CIRCLES OF ATTENTION**
Focusing your attention inside the performance area to create the illusion of solitude (see page 43).

**RESTRAINT AND CONTROL**
Stay in charge of your performance by avoiding forced emotion. Create feelings internally (through the magic 'if', based on your emotion memory and given circumstances) so that your performance grows and you stay in control of the emotion.

**THREE-DIMENSIONAL CHARACTERS**
The **objectives** of your character, the **obstacles** that get in their way and how they are overcome ensures full characterisation (see page 44).

**NATURALISTIC MOVEMENT**
Simplifying gestures and words onstage so that they appear natural.

# The fourth wall

Actors create in their minds the imaginary 'wall' that would complete the room where the scene takes place. This helps them to immerse themselves in the scene and focus on the emotional truth of what is going on.

What if I were in this situation?

# Feeling of truth

An actor playing Hamlet does not know what it is actually like for his dead father to come back as a ghost and tell him to take revenge on his own uncle! However, they do know about fear, love, conflict and all the emotions Hamlet would experience. Use your own emotions and you will be able to infuse your actions and lines with emotional truth. The more specifically you focus on the details of the situation, the more naturally the emotion will come.

# The magic 'if'

The magic 'if' helps you to create a character and get beyond nerves onstage. By asking yourself 'what if?', you are more able to imagine and explore the traits of your character. It also helps the restraint and control of the emotions in your performance, so you do not 'lose yourself' and forget about the audience in a self-indulgent performance.

If I were in this situation, how would I feel?

# Muscle memory

To keep the actor's instrument (their own body and voice) healthy, and get rid of any of the actor's own physical mannerisms or habits so that every gesture is right for the character, learning to relax the muscles through warm-ups are key parts of Stanislavski's System.

# Circles of attention

Stanislavski believed that an actor needed a sense of isolation to support characterisation and avoid unnecessary tension. He described three circles of attention:

The first circle of attention is an actor concentrating on their self. Stanislavski called this 'Solitude in Public'.

The second circle of attention is your character and who they are addressing on stage.

The third circle of attention is the rest of the stage.

**EXERCISE 3.1**

**Actor, objective, obstacle**

This exercise will help you to understand the relationship between your character, their objective (what the character wants) and an obstacle (something preventing them from achieving their objective).

Three volunteers are required (the rest of the group is the audience).

- The **objective** creates a performance in any way the performer likes: do whatever you like to explore the stage and create your own story.

- The **actor** sits on a chair. Their job is to keep looking at the objective, no matter what distractions the obstacle provides.

- The **obstacle**'s role is to make it difficult for the actor to keep focused on the objective. They cannot touch the actor but can distract them or block their view of the objective in any other way. See how creative you can get in distracting the actor.

**What does this teach me about Stanislavski?**

The more you focus on your character's objective (what they want), the more truthfully you will play your scene – and the less you will be distracted from your performance.

This exercise is a lot of fun for everyone, but also reminds you how difficult the actor's job can be. No matter how strong the actor's objective, obstacles in the play and distractions such as mobile phones ringing or people coughing will always be off-putting if the actor lets them. That is why concentration of attention is so important.

# Three-dimensional characters

What are your character's objective in each scene? What is their through-objective, the thing that they want most throughout the play? What do they want out of life? How does that determine their words and actions? What obstacles are in the way of the character achieving their objectives? Make objectives specific to who your character is. Not just 'I want to be happy' but what it is the character thinks would make them happy, e.g. 'I want my dukedom back' (*The Tempest*) or 'I want Phil's approval' (*DNA*).

**ACTIVITY 3.1**

Stanislavski divided scripts into units, based on the character's objectives. A new unit began with a new objective. Identify what your character wants in each unit of your scene. How does each one relate to the character's overall objective?

# What is Method Acting?

More people are more familiar with the term 'Method Acting' than 'the System'. That is because Stanislavski later laid out his techniques as the 'Method of Physical Action', which was followed by many actors and directors around the world – for film as well as theatre. In the USA, working out the physical actions of a character became more popular than the psychological side of Stanislavski's System, so Method Acting is mainly about actions, but still aims to encourage truthful emotion in performance.

After Stanislavski's death, his Method of Physical Action became known in Hollywood as the 'Method' or 'Method Acting'. Stanislavski's system was simplified to seven questions:

1 Who am I?
2 Where am I?
3 When is it?
4 What do I want?
5 Why do I want it?
6 How will I get it?
7 What do I need to overcome?

> **TIP**
>
> These seven questions work for all plots and characters. When devising, even if you have not finished writing your script yet, see if you can develop answers to the questions for your character. If you are working with a text, see if you can answer the questions for the character you are playing.

## EXERCISE 3.2

**1 Stanislavskian 'Huggy Bears'**

This exercise is a version of the party game 'Huggy Bears', with a Stanislavskian twist.

a) Run around the room until the leader of the game shouts 'Huggy Bears' then a number. Get into groups of that number as fast as you can, e.g. 'Huggy Bears two!' means get into groups of two, or 'Huggy Bears three!' means get into groups of three.

b) Then instructions, such as showing an emotion, will be added, for example 'Huggy Bears three – Joy' or 'Huggy Bears – Grief'. (If no number is called, you need to get into pairs. Aim for a different partner each time.) Form a still image, reflecting that emotion. Although the scene requires a freeze-frame, not a full scene, the truer the emotion the clearer the image will be – and the easier you will find it to hold the pose.

**What does this teach me about Stanislavski?**
Emotional truth comes when you identify with your character's feeling and share that feeling without force or exaggeration. You do not need to have experienced the situation to identify with the emotion it causes, but you do have to use your own experience of that emotion to create the character.

**2 Stanislavskian nursery rhymes**

In pairs, choose a nursery rhyme you both know well, such as 'Mary Had a Little Lamb' or 'Three Little Pigs'. Say the nursery rhyme to your partner as if:

- you are sharing juicy gossip
- you are pleading for your life
- you are begging for forgiveness
- you are telling them off.

**What does this teach me about Stanislavski?**
Emotional truth helps you sustain a performance for longer and make it more authentic.

**3 Magic 'if' rehearsed improvs**

In pairs or small groups, use the magic 'if' for one of the following scenarios to inspire a rehearsed improvisation:

- A family comes home to find their house has been burgled. How do they react and what do they do?
- A group of friends are talking in an empty park, when one of them realises their mobile phone is missing. How do they react and what do they do?

**What does this teach me about Stanislavski?**
Placing a character in trouble allows you to learn a lot about them. Different characters will respond to the same situation with different emotions: some with panic, or by being accusatory, others will be calm and efficient, etc.

In the following monologue from *Random Thoughts in a May Garden* by James Saunders, a family photo becomes the vehicle for monologues, showing the private thoughts of the different members of the family.

Ask yourself:

- What is my character feeling that makes them choose these words?
- What thoughts and feelings are they trying to express with their words?
- What thoughts and feelings might they be keeping to themselves, behind the words?

**KATIE.** I think there's a fly on the back of my hand. Walking. I can't look down. I can't even flap my hand or swat it or I shall come out blurred and get the blame for spoiling the photograph. 'Anne sat still, see how still Anne sat, why couldn't you sit still like everyone else?' Well, I can. I don't want to be called Katie fidget whenever they show it to anyone. I can just imagine, how awful. I'd go through the whole of my life with it. The perfect photograph in memory of the wedding of dear Emily – where is she now, why isn't she in the photograph, it's her wedding? – only there in the corner little Katie all blurred. 'What a fidget. Katie fidget, she always was a fidgety child.' I wonder if Georgie will fidget. They've sat Georgie on the other side. He was standing behind me, he put his bony chin on my shoulder-blade and moved it about, it hurt, I told him to get off. I'd have shrugged my shoulders up only I was afraid he'd bite his tongue. That was considerate of me, only I'm afraid nobody will know … I wonder if I'll ever get credit for it, in Heaven, perhaps. And anyway, if he'd cried, I'd have got the blame, because I'm older and should know better. Anne never gets the blame if she upsets me. I'm pig in the middle. One day I shall be grown up. I shall be as old as Anne, and then as old as Emily and get married, and then as old as my mother with children and then as old as Granny Burridge, and then I shall die like Grandad Burridge and Granny Filkins. And Bertie. I'm eleven. Bertie would be thirteen. Anyway I didn't want Georgie's monkey face next to mine, he always looks funny in photographs. Georgie had to go to the other side to balance the picture. I suppose otherwise it would fall over or something. Silly way of putting it, balance, balance is for weight not pictures. He'll probably crack the lens. … Georgie spilt something down his front, I don't know what it was, my mother was ages trying to get it off so that it wouldn't show in the photograph. It would be more typical if it did. I hope this fly shows, but I don't suppose it will. My hands are folded, one on the other as I've been taught. I'm wearing a large hat. I'm looking, looking, looking at the camera. This picture will last forever. But I shall die.

Saunders, *Random Thoughts in a May Garden*, pages 41–42

**EXERCISE 3.3**

1 Read Katie's monologue and consider the emotions and thoughts you would use to create an emotionally truthful performance.

2 In a group, study a school or class photo and discuss what the different students, teachers and other staff members are really thinking behind their smiles. Use some of the emotions you experimented with for Katie, as well as using your emotion memory and imagination to suggest new characters and stories.

3 Write a monologue for your character in the play you are working on, in which the audience learns something about their life and feelings.

**What does this teach me about Stanislavski?**
A character's personality and history should always affect how they speak and what is important to them (their motivation).

# Building a character – Stanislavskian hot-seating

Hot-seating is a bit like an interview – you are asked questions, which you answer in character. This is an opportunity to find out more about your character.

The seven questions in Stanislavski's Method (see page 45) can help you to find the right actions for your character, because they make it clear about what your character wants. You can ask lots of your own questions as well to add even more depth to your character.

When working with a script, it is vital the actor answers the questions from the evidence they find in it:

• What do the stage directions tell you?
• What does your character say about themselves?
• What do others say about them?

**ACTIVITY 3.2**

Try hot-seating your character, then other characters in the play you are working on.

*My Week With Marilyn* (2011) explores the difference between Laurence Olivier's traditional approach to acting and Method Acting in Hollywood, and shows how some established actors struggled with the new techniques.

## EXERCISE 3.4

### 1 Yes/no circle

Stand in a circle as a whole group. The director says 'Yes' to the person next to them, who then says the word to the next person. As the word goes around the circle, listen to how many different things the word seems to mean, depending on how you say it.

At some point, instead of passing on the 'Yes', someone will argue back by saying 'No' to the person who said 'Yes' to them. This changes the direction, sending 'No' around the circle back the way 'Yes' came.

To throw the word to another part of the circle, point both arms at someone and say 'Maybe'. They then have to start a new yes or no in one direction or the other.

**What does this teach me about Stanislavski?** Your objective informs every line you say. For example, if you say 'No!' like you are a parent stopping your child going to a party, it will sound entirely different from if you say 'No!'

like you're listening to your friend tell you a piece of juicy gossip.

### 2 Urgent!

Try to imagine that you are relaxing in bed. It is your first weekend away at university. Suddenly, you get a text message from your family, reminding you they are arriving for a visit in 10 minutes. You look around. The place is a mess! Can you tidy up before they arrive?

Now try to imagine that the last time you saw them you had had a row with a member of your family. How does that affect the performance?

**How does this teach me about Stanislavski?** Your energy level and the intensity of the performance will be based on how clearly you create the circumstances in your head. If you believe in the truth of your words and actions, your emotions will be authentic and your performance will be truthful.

# How do I show Stanislavski's influence on my devised piece?

**Build your character mentally**

Make decisions (based on evidence from the text) about their likes and dislikes, hopes and fears, good and bad points.

**Build your character physically**

Make decisions (based on evidence from the text) about their confidence and status, how they move and talk, and what their mannerisms are.

**Play your objective**

Decide what your character wants, not just 'I want to be happy' but something specific to who they are and what is going on in their life. Use this to inform how you say your lines and the moves you make.

**Act naturalistically**

Using your own emotion memory, base your performance of your character on the feelings you have had in a similar emotional state.

# Stanislavski: What have I learnt?

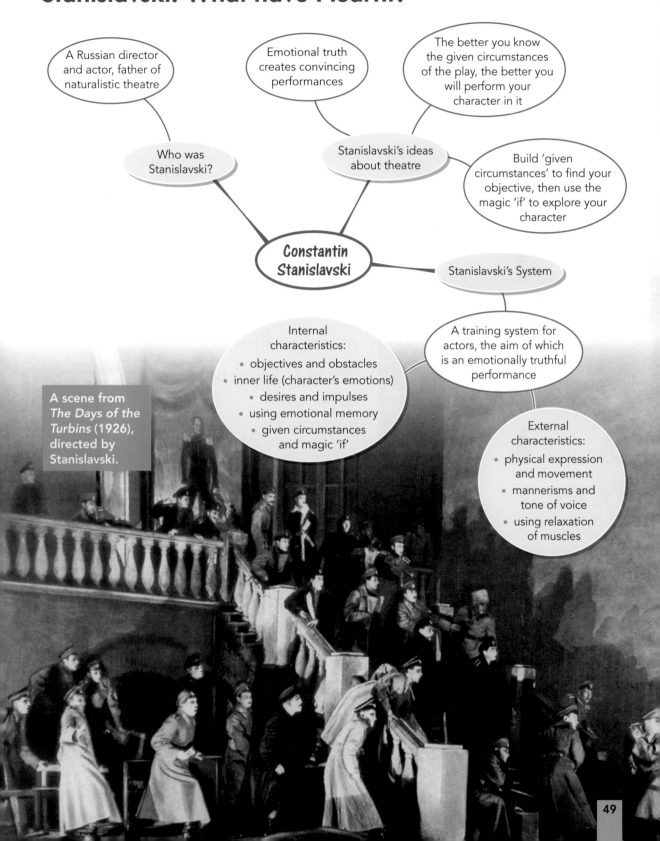

A Russian director and actor, father of naturalistic theatre

Emotional truth creates convincing performances

The better you know the given circumstances of the play, the better you will perform your character in it

Who was Stanislavski?

Stanislavski's ideas about theatre

Build 'given circumstances' to find your objective, then use the magic 'if' to explore your character

**Constantin Stanislavski**

Stanislavski's System

Internal characteristics:
- objectives and obstacles
- inner life (character's emotions)
- desires and impulses
- using emotional memory
- given circumstances and magic 'if'

A training system for actors, the aim of which is an emotionally truthful performance

A scene from *The Days of the Turbins* (1926), directed by Stanislavski.

External characteristics:
- physical expression and movement
- mannerisms and tone of voice
- using relaxation of muscles

49

Elizabeth Cutts playing the title character in *Mother Courage and Her Children*.

# BRECHT

## Who was Brecht?

Bertolt Brecht (1898–1956) was a German playwright, theatre critic, practitioner and director. One of the most influential figures in 20th-century theatre, he believed theatre should be political and issue-based. Where Stanislavski pioneered naturalism and emotional truth, Brecht broke the fourth wall, using placards and direct address to speak directly to the audience. Brecht believed theatre should be didactic: forcing the audience to recognise and resist political and social injustice. Among the best known of his 39 plays are *Baal*, *Fear and Misery of the Third Reich* and *Mother Courage and Her Children*. He left Germany when Hitler came to power in 1933 but returned after World War II. Brecht's theatre company, the Berliner Ensemble, become one of the most famous touring theatre companies in the world. It continues to produce political theatre.

## What is Brechtian theatre?

### Epic theatre

Epic theatre, which is the name often given to Brechtian theatre plays, distances the audience from the play, so they don't become emotionally involved with the characters. Epic theatre is about big issues and it invites the audience to be aware of them in their own lives. This is called **alienation** because it makes the familiar seem strange, making us see things we might otherwise ignore about our world; instead of only becoming emotionally involved in the characters they address the issues.

# Brecht's techniques

**NARRATOR**
The storyteller of the play, who speaks directly to the audience (see pages 52–54).

**MULTI-ROLING**
Actors play a number of roles within the same story.

**DIRECT ADDRESS**
An actor speaks directly to the audience, giving information about their character and situation (see page 52).

**GESTUS**
Combining gesture with facial expression, body language and stance to summarise not only the character's situation but the wider social situation it relates to (see page 54).

**TICKLE AND SLAP**
Lulling the audience into a false sense of security, then hitting them with a shocking event.

**PLACARDS**
Signs or projections that indicate where the scene takes place or other information (see page 55).

**MUSIC AND SONGS**
Characters break into song, often directly addressing the audience (see page 55).

**POLITICAL MESSAGE OR DIDACTICISM**
Educate and inform the audience through the story (see page 55).

**ALIENATION**
Making the familiar strange, as if freshly seen. It involves making the audience respond to the issues rather than immersing themselves emotionally with the characters.

**NO FOURTH WALL**
Brechtian theatre tries to keep the audience aware that it is theatre and that they should be considering more important issues (see page 55).

**EPISODIC STRUCTURE**
Brechtian plays are written as a series of individual episodes, rather than a continuous act. Brechtian plays are in the form of a series of individual episodes, each with its own lesson or point.

The *39 Steps*, adapted from Alfred Hitchcock's film of the thriller by John Buchan, used Brechtian techniques, including stage directions spoken by the characters and a mixture of placards and direct address.

# Direct address

## EXERCISE 3.5

A01 A02

### Unexpected meeting

In pairs, use direct address and placards to help tell the story of an unexpected meeting between two characters. Share each character's private thoughts with the audience, as well as speaking dialogue to each other. How can you use these Brechtian techniques to show the way private feelings contrast with what they say aloud?

### What does this teach me about Brecht?

When actors speak to each other and exist within the world of the play only, that is acting within a fourth wall. Brecht allows characters to 'break' that fourth wall at any time. By breaking the fourth wall, Brechtian theatre lets the actor contrast the character's private thoughts and wishes with their public words and deeds. It can show hidden selflessness, but also hidden cruelty. It's a great source for comedy too.

# Narrator

In Brecht's plays, reported speech was often used, making actors say certain lines in the third person. The narrator, sometimes the same actor who plays the character being described, tells the audience what is being said.

Here is a section of text from *The Caucasian Chalk Circle*, a fascinating play for getting to grips with Brechtian technique.

In this extract, Grusha, who is engaged to marry a solider called Simon when he returns from war, comes across the abandoned baby son of the assassinated governor.

> *Exit with* **IRONSHSIRTS** *through the gateway. Trampling of horses again. Enter* **GRUSHA** *through the doorway looking courteously about her. Clearly she has waited for the* **IRONSHIRTS** *to go. Carrying a bundle, she walks toward the gateway. At the last moment, she turns to see if the* **CHILD** *is still there. Catching sight of the head over the doorway, she screams. Horrified, she picks up her bundle again, and is about to leave when the* **SINGER** *starts to speak. She stands rooted to the spot.*
> SINGER:
>   As she was standing between courtyard and gate,
>   She heard or she thought she heard a low voice calling.
>   The child called to her,
>   Not whining, but calling quite sensibly,
>   Or so it seemed to her,
>   'Woman,' it said, 'help me.'

And it went on, not whining, but saying quite sensibly:

'Know woman, he who hears not a cry for help

But passes by with troubled ears will never hear

The gentle call of a lover nor the blackbird at dawn

Nor the happy sigh of the tired grape-picker as the Angelus rings.'

*She walks a few steps toward the* CHILD *and bends over it.*

Hearing this she went back for one more look at the child:

Only to sit with him for a moment or two,

Only till someone should come,

His mother, or anyone.

*Leaning on a trunk, she sits facing the* CHILD.

Only till she would have to leave, for the danger was too great.

The city was full of flame and crying.

*The light grows dimmer, as though evening and night were coming on.*

Fearful is the seductive power of goodness!

GRUSHA *now settles down to watch over the* CHILD *through the night.*

*Once, she lights a small lamp to look at it. Once, she tucks it in with a coat.*

*From time to time she listens and looks to see whether someone is coming.*

And she sat with the child a long time,

Till evening came, till night came, till dawn came.

She sat too long, too long she saw

The soft breathing, the small clenched fists,

Till toward morning the seduction was complete

And she rose, and bent down and, sighing, took the child

And carried it away.

*She does what the* SINGER *says as he describes it.*

As if it was stolen goods she picked it up.

As if she was a thief she crept away.

Brecht, *The Caucasian Chalk Circle*, pages 28–29

**TIP**

Read the extract and think about narration and Brechtian performance conventions – the extract shares the private thoughts of the character, but also reminds the audience that they are watching a performance.

## ACTIVITY 3.3 — AO1 AO2

Try writing your own speech (soliloquy) of a character's unspoken thoughts. See what happens if you ask a narrator to speak it, with the character silent, as they think it should be read.

Now try the same scene, but with the character speaking those same thoughts. How does the audience see the character differently?

**What does this teach me about Brecht?**

Replacing dialogue with reported speech will make a scene less naturalistic but can be used to convey a lot of information to the audience. Remember, the narrator not only represents the main character's thoughts, but can also share the actions, thoughts and memories of all the characters. You can use narration to show the memories and private thoughts that every character on the stage keeps to themselves.

**EXERCISE 3.6**

**Narrating the action**

Two people are to be 'narrators' and two the 'characters'.

The narrators must talk to the audience, and the characters perform the action being described by the narration. Narrators can use reported speech to tell the characters what to say, as well as the characters' actions. Characters can work in mime at first. But, as the scene develops, you might want to use sound-effects or dialogue too.

**What does this teach me about Brecht?**

Narration such as mime can convey information and emotion in a very visually interesting way.

# Gestus

**EXERCISE 3.7**

1 Imagine a character receiving a message. Choose an action that could be sustained onstage to sum up their situation, which you might choose to be good or bad, for the following messages:

- Exam results – passed or failed?

- Result of a job interview – accepted or rejected?

- A response from someone they have asked out – said yes or no?

**What does this teach me about Brecht?**

It is a great way of exploring 'gestus', where the action of the play represents not only the character's situation but also a wider situation. See if you can spot certain actions that every pair associates with the same theme. That clear image will work for the audience too.

2 As a group, explore the physical difference between:

- clapping at the end of an amazing play and clapping at the end of a boring play

- handing in a test paper on which you knew the answers to all the questions and handing in a test paper on which you didn't know the answers to any of the questions.

**What does this teach me about Brecht?**

A gesture can sum up not only the situation of the character performing it but also a wider social issue.

# Placards

As a group, choose one of the following placards to inspire a scene:

Earlier that morning …

Meanwhile, back home …

In their secret lair …

Midnight is about to strike …

One hour to go …

A storm is brewing …

# Music and songs

Brechtian theatre uses musical interludes to move the action from scene to scene, and to show tension and high emotion. You do not have to be a musician to do this. Try easy sound-effects, such as clicking your tongue like a clock to show the passing of time, or a long 'ahhhhhhh …' from a low pitch to a high pitch to suggest building tension. You can hum or sing simple tunes too, and repeat these during your devised piece to symbolise a character, or show time moving on. Or, you could even have characters participating in a singalong on a car journey or on their way to a concert.

1 Imagine that you are performing to an audience who did not speak the same language as you. Try to create a sound piece to illustrate a specific location or situation. What human, animal and other noises would your audience recognise?

2 Now, try the same location but with a different atmosphere.

   If previously it was tense and busy, make it relaxed this time. If it was funny, make it sad.

*Baal* was Brecht's first play. The film version starred David Bowie who had studied mime under Lindsey Kemp. Bowie used gestus in his characters even when writing songs, playing different characters in his songs the same way as acting in different plays.

# No fourth wall

While Stanislavski's System uses the fourth wall to help the audience and performers suspend their disbelief and immerse themselves in the illusion of the play, Brechtian theatre aims to keep the audience aware of the fact that this is theatre and turn their thoughts to the changes they would like to make in the world, as inspired by the issues the play presents.

# Political message

The focus of Brecht's plays is the situation, not the characters. He saw theatre as a way to create awareness among the public in order to make positive change, both socially and politically. A story that teaches the audience a lesson in this way is didactic.

**TIP**

Unlike Stanislavski's naturalism, Brecht's plays do not call for realistic time-of-day lighting states and realistic sets. Consider what single prop or simple lighting state you might use in your play.

**TIP**

Consider what item of clothing best sums up each character in the scene your group is working on.

# How did Brecht use technical theatre aspects?

Different places and the passing of time were shown with placards.

## Stage

- Bare and basic.
- Technical equipment or scene changes are in full view of the audience.
- Single pieces of furniture stand in for entire locations.

## Lighting

- Stage flooded with bright white light.
- No changes for the time of day or seasons.

## Costume

- Bare and basic.
- Single pieces of costume represent an entire character.

---

**EXERCISE 3.10**

**Brechtian theatre**

There has been a road accident and you are all passers-by who witnessed what happened. Tell the following stories about it:

- What happened to someone who was there.
- Describe everything you saw – using the other actors to create all the characters, sounds and images you say you remember.
- Include gestures, narration, reported speech, dialogue and simple elements of costume to create the scene.

The characters might include:

This is a theatre activity invented by Brecht. It can be done in pairs, small groups, or as a whole class.

 Office worker watching from window  Motorcyclist  Police officer

To Brecht, the most important thing for making the scene successful is for the actors to demonstrate what occurred, recreating it with their bodies, voices and facial expressions to show, not tell, what happened.

Try the same exercise again, but instead of a road accident invent a scene where the actors all witness something and demonstrate it to the audience. It could be:

- a rock concert
- a stray dog running into a school playground.

*The point is that the demonstrator acts the behaviour of the driver or victim or both in such a way that the bystanders are able to form an opinion about the accident.*

Brecht, *Brecht on Theatre*, page 204

## ACTIVITY 3.4

1 In pairs, improvise a scene where two characters have not seen each other for a long time. How might their private thoughts in your direct address to the audience contrast with what they say to each other? For example:

> ACTOR 1: (*To audience*) He was so much older and badly dressed she barely recognised him. (*Turning to other character*) You look great! I'd know you anywhere!

> ACTOR 2: (*To character*) Likewise! I'd know you anywhere! (*To audience*) He desperately tried to remember her name.

2 Below is a picture with several characters, suggesting different viewpoints on the same event.

In a group, write a monologue from the point of view of one character in the picture. Or, write more than one monologue and explore how the perspectives of the different characters vary.

### Using stimulus materials with Brechtian techniques

Choose one of the following quotes and discuss, in your group, what scenario you could perform using the quote as stimulus:

I want to break free.

You've got to go there to come back.

Please believe me.

I'm not the same person I was then.

## ACTIVITY 3.5

Cast someone as the narrator, and use a mixture of dialogue, reported speech, gestures and key items of costume to represent characters. Try to perform the whole of your scenario – everything from warm-up to scene changes – in front of an audience, as a Brechtian production would.

In your group, discuss what is going on in the picture on the right. What do you think the sculptor might mean by it – what issue might it symbolise?

# How do I show Brecht's influence on my devised piece?

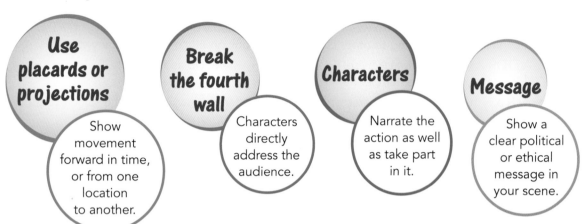

**Use placards or projections**
Show movement forward in time, or from one location to another.

**Break the fourth wall**
Characters directly address the audience.

**Characters**
Narrate the action as well as take part in it.

**Message**
Show a clear political or ethical message in your scene.

# Brecht: What have I learnt?

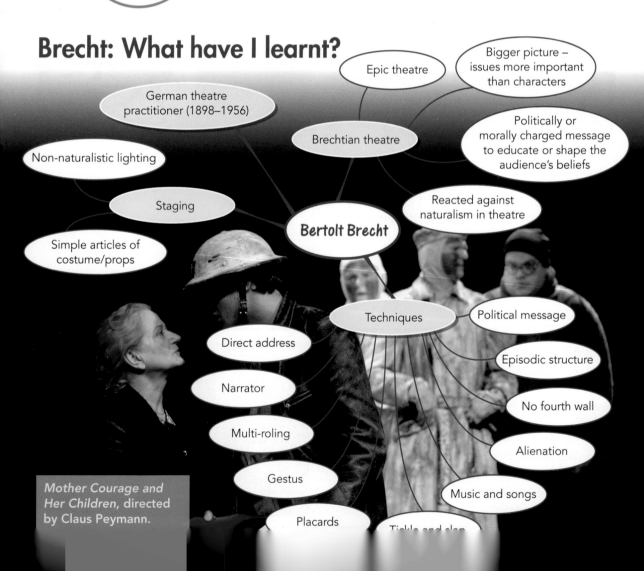

Epic theatre

Bigger picture – issues more important than characters

German theatre practitioner (1898–1956)

Brechtian theatre

Politically or morally charged message to educate or shape the audience's beliefs

Non-naturalistic lighting

Staging

Reacted against naturalism in theatre

Simple articles of costume/props

**Bertolt Brecht**

Techniques

Political message

Direct address

Episodic structure

Narrator

No fourth wall

Multi-roling

Alienation

Gestus

Music and songs

Placards

*Mother Courage and Her Children*, directed by Claus Peymann.

# STEVEN BERKOFF

## Who is Steven Berkoff?

Steven Berkoff (born 1937) is an English character actor, author, playwright and director. His birth name was Leslie Steven Berks, which was changed from Berkowitz when his Jewish Russian family came to England in the 1890s. Berkoff studied drama in London (Webber Douglas) and mime in Paris (L'École Internationale de Théâtre de Jacques Lecoq). He was part of various repertory companies before forming his own company, the London Theatre Group, in 1968.

Berkoff's adaptations of novels and poems have been performed in multiple countries and languages. Among his most famous are Edgar Allan Poe's *The Fall of the House of Usher*, and Franz Kafka's *Metamorphosis* and *The Trial*. He has directed touring productions, including Shakespeare's *Coriolanus* (in which he played the title role) and *Richard II*, and Oscar Wilde's *Salome*. Berkoff has appeared in many films, including *A Clockwork Orange*, *Octopussy*, *Absolute Beginners* and *The Girl With the Dragon Tattoo*. In his eighth decade, he is still acting, writing and directing theatre and film.

> *If I have a trademark style, I suppose it's about physicality, a simplicity of communication both orally and physically. That's very important.*
>
> Steven Berkoff, interviewed by WhatsOnStage (2009)

## What does Berkoff think about theatre?

### Total Theatre

As a director and actor, Berkoff champions **Total Theatre** – rejecting naturalistic sets and scenes in favour of telling the story by using the actors' bodies and facial expressions.

Total Theatre puts the emphasis on physical acting. The bodies of the actors stand in for furniture and props; facial and vocal expression are enhanced beyond naturalistic levels (**stylisation**). Stylised voice, facial expression and movement can also include slow motion and robotic movement. Tableaux, mask and stylised mime are also used.

Total Theatre often makes use of direct address, embracing the fact that this is performance and not real life. However, the enhanced emotions and movements should still be based on a truthful emotion suitable to the story and which the actor understands.

Most of the characters in Berkoff's plays carry great burdens of personal guilt, and suffer from oppression by society or the unfulfilled promise that their lives showed. Berkoff expresses their frustrated emotions physically, in non-naturalistic theatre that still shares very real emotional lives.

> *To make the actors a fundamental part of their environment, to use every actor on that stage to the maximum of their ability and to express something to the utmost of its potential.*
>
> Steven Berkoff, interviewed by WhatsOnStage (2009)

# Berkoff's techniques

**STYLISED MOVEMENT**
Slow motion/robotic movement (see below).

**EXAGGERATED FACIAL EXPRESSIONS**
(see below).

**EXAGGERATED VOCAL WORK**
(see below).

**TABLEAUX**
Still images made by the body of actors to represent a key moment or idea.

**DIRECT ADDRESS**
(see below).

**EXAGGERATED AND STYLISED MIME**
(see page 61).

**MASK**

**MINIMALISM**
(see page 61).

**ENSEMBLE PLAYING**
The cast work together to create the sense of the world of the play using minimal set and props.

---

**TIP**

When working with Total Theatre, or any kind of Physical Theatre, think about 'enhancing' your moves so they stay truthful, rather than 'exaggerating' them.

Berkoff's best-known adaptation is *The Trial* by Franz Kafka. This minimalist set is characteristic of Berkoff.

## Stylised movement (slow motion/robotic)

Berkoff puts the emphasis on Physical Theatre and movement over voice and dialogue. His stories are told in this way. In *East*, Berkoff uses movement so stylised it is described as 'robotic', with the intention of challenging the audience by reminding them of the unreality of the play, making them think about the issues and injustices rather than simply identifying with the individual characters (a Brechtian technique).

## Exaggerated facial expressions

For the same reason, Berkoff uses stylised, enhanced movement, making the audience aware of the character's actions and their impact on the world around them.

### Direct address

Characters inform the audience of their private thoughts and feelings, as well as facts and locations in the play. This is another way of keeping the audience aware that this is all a performance, so they think about the issues in a real-world context and not only about the fate of specific fictional characters.

### Exaggerated vocal work

Berkoff uses stylised, enhanced text, with short phrases, speeches and vocal tones, to convey the full impact of a character's feelings about the situations, characters and world around them.

# Minimalism

Berkoff's sets and style of acting use clear, simple imagery without excessive detail, to indicate character and scenario. Although the actions of Physical Theatre need to be very big, the simplicity of them (both in acting and design) means this is referred to as minimalism.

# Exaggerated and stylised mime

Berkoff uses the actors' bodies and faces to tell the story, with dialogue being less significant to him than the messages conveyed by movement. It's a very clear, straightforward way of staging any scene, too – using the body and its reactions to a busy street can be just as clear a way of representing a street as any set can!

**EXERCISE 3.11**

Pick an emotion from the wheel on the right. With a partner or on your own, create a scene where your tone of voice, facial expression and whole body express that emotion. This is mime – enhancing the expressions and gestures of face and body to express emotion and meaning.

**ACTIVITY 3.6** ─ AO1 AO2

Create a simple storyline that begins with one emotion and changes to another. How does your expression, posture and movement change?

What does this teach me about Berkoff's techniques?

Events and emotions can be conveyed to an audience as clearly and directly through a minimalist approach – enhanced movement, mime and wordless sounds – in a script. Often, more so than dialogue.

## EXERCISE 3.12

### Sound story

Total Theatre is all about using your face, body, voice and imagination.

In your group, see if you can use just sound and no words to tell a story. For example:

Aaaaaaahhhhhhhhh … Splassshhhhh!

It's someone excited to dive into the lake!

No, it's someone scared who's been pushed into the swimming pool!

### What does this teach me about Berkoff's techniques?

Sound can be overlooked, but it can be a really clear way to demonstrate a character's emotional state or the tensions betweentwo characters.

> **TIP**
>
> Physical Theatre creates a sense of place for the audience because the actors are responding to the details in their imagination and memory. Make the pictures in your head as clear and specific as you can, so your feelings will then be clear to the audience.

## EXERCISE 3.13

AO **1** – AO **2** – AO **3**

### Emotion walk

1 Walk around the room as if you were walking along a street you know. Create the situation in your imagination. If you pass someone else, do you ignore them? Glance and look away?

2 What happens if you do something you would not normally do: stare too long, glare at them?
What happens if you stop and look into someone's eyes?

3 What happens if you change your emotion to a stronger one? What if you have just lost your job? Or got your dream job? How do you move differently from other people who are using other emotions?

See if you can both hold on to your own emotion while still taking in the other person's.

### What does this teach me about Berkoff's techniques?

This exercise will build your confidence in physicalising a character. Your stance communicates a lot about your thoughts and feelings, so it is great to be able to experiment with it.

## ACTIVITY 3.7

Mask monologues

In mask, pick one of the following scenes and show it to your group as a silent scene, using some of Berkhoff's techniques:

- Being scared of spiders and finding one in the room.
- Realising there is something smelly in a crowded lift.
- Falling in love with a stranger on the tube.
- A line or monologue you will be performing in your devised scene.

**What does this teach me about Berkoff's techniques?**

You can play truthful and complex feelings in mime – and they can be very funny and very touching.

> **TIP**
>
> Always turn your back to the audience to put on or take off a mask.

# Expressing character's thoughts

Berkoff explores frustration, guilt, unfulfilled promise and individual struggle against society. Often, he does this more through *how* the characters speak rather than what they say. In one scene from his play *Kvetch*, Berkoff shows the private thoughts of three characters who are having dinner together. None of them share their fears with each other but their asides tell the audience what they are really feeling.

## ACTIVITY 3.8

In your group, discuss each of your character's private fears. Try writing a short monologue sharing what they are. How do the characters' fears, seen only by the audience, contrast with the body language and tone of voice the characters show each other?

> **TIP**
>
> Think about emphasis as you read your monologue aloud in your group. How can your use of emphasis change or enhance the meaning?

## ACTIVITY 3.9

On your own or in pairs, rehearse your monologue in Berkoff's style. Remember that Berkoff's scripts are designed for actors to:

1 Use their whole bodies.
2 Use enhanced physical, vocal and facial expressions.
3 Illustrate wider social issues as well as the specific character's private struggles.

**What does this teach me about Berkoff's techniques?**

Repetition and larger-than-life performances mean Total Theatre shows clear themes and characterisation.

> **TIP**
>
> Remember that your performance is still based on truth – think of what you are doing as enhancing, not exaggerating, the characters.

## EXERCISE 3.14

AO1 AO2

Divide the class into two groups. Your teacher will whisper a location to each group, for example a building site, jungle or farm, which you must build as a soundscape, one person's sound at a time, until the entire group is making sounds.

## EXERCISE 3.15

AO1 AO2

One person in your group acts someone waking up in a strange, new place. The rest of the group are the sound-effects and objects in the new place. Remember to use your whole body, whether you are the actor, an object or a sound-effect. How does the atmosphere affect the actor?

Rehearse the scene and think about the following questions:

- What sounds can you hear? How do they make you feel?
- How dark is it here? How does that affect your movement?
- Are you alone? Does it seem like there is anyone else there?
- Do you feel safe or unsafe, excited or afraid? Are you trying to fight panic?

Finally, the actor decides to leave:

- How do they escape?
- What happens in the space after they have gone?

In his 2001 play, *The Secret Love Life of Ophelia*, Berkoff explores Hamlet and Ophelia's deep emotions in their lives before the tragedy that Shakespeare's play tells. This shows his interest in character backstory and behaviour over traditional speeches and the assumptions that theatre-goers might have about the characters.

## ACTIVITY 3.10

AO1 AO2

1 Pick a character whose story you are familiar with and develop their untold story (perhaps one of the characters who is in your set texts). Can you use exaggerated mime to tell a touching story?

Here are two stories that you could use:

- Cinderella: the kitchen years!
- Mummy Bear: family life in a wood, with no telephone or internet.

2 Think about the burdens of guilt or regret your character might carry. Does Mummy Bear regret agreeing to leave the city? Has Baby Bear become more spoilt or angry? Think of a phrase they might repeat, to imply their private feelings about their lives and themselves. What gesture is characteristic of how they move or talk? Mix their words and movements. Move around the other characters in your scene, doing the same thing. How do you relate to each other? Make your way into groups of three or four in character.

Build a mini sound machine, using using repeated sounds or lines of dialogue.

3 Now base a story on this gang or family.

Techniques to explore in your scenes:

Use naturalistic mime

Normal pace

Use exaggerated mime

Sound-effects

Use minimum words

Use repetition

Direct address

# How do I show Berkoff's influence on my devised piece?

**Use stylisation and minimalism**

**Work as an ensemble**

Create a sense of place, conflict and atmosphere using your bodies and expression, with minimal set and props.

**Tableaux, slow-motion and mask**

Clear, larger-than-life movement, set and expression.

**Vocal tone**

The pain and conflict behind the text is more significant than the choice of words in the dialogue.

Some ways to make images tell your story.

# Berkoff: What have I learnt?

*On the Waterfront*, an adaptation directed by Berkoff.

British actor, author, playwright, director and theatre maker – since 1965

**Steven Berkoff**

Mask

Techniques

Ensemble playing

Stylised movement (slow motion/robotic)

Total Theatre

Minimalism

Exaggerated facial expressions

Exaggerated and stylised mime

Exaggerated vocal work

Direct address

Tableaux

# EMMA RICE

## Who is Emma Rice?

Emma Rice (born 1967) is an English actress and director. She studied at Guildhall and then worked with the Gardzienice Theatre Association in Poland. In 1994 she joined Kneehigh Theatre, famous for adapting literature and films using circus tricks, comedy, songs and storytelling. Rice first acted then directed for Kneehigh, before becoming its artistic director. She was then appointed artistic director of the Globe Theatre in 2016 but left after two years because of artistic differences. *Standard Issue Magazine* made her their woman of the year in 2016 for 'fearlessness, leadership, innovation and bravery' (Campbell, 2017).

Rice is now artistic director of Wise Children in Bristol, a theatre company she formed in 2018.

> *I'm always making sure the audience knows what's happening at any given time so they're free to feel or to respond in a personal way.*

Emma Rice interview (Furness, 2016)

---

**ACTIVITY 3.11** _____ AO**1** AO**2**

Kneehigh Theatre uses familiar stories to create new, exciting but recognisable characters and sets. Try drawing an image as you remember it from a fairy tale. Then, using your imagination, think about how you could bring your remembered image to life onstage.

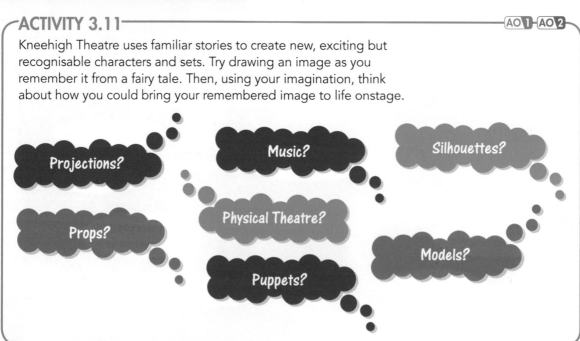

Projections?

Music?

Silhouettes?

Props?

Physical Theatre?

Models?

Puppets?

# What does Emma Rice think about theatre?

## Visual storytelling

Emma Rice's productions mix naturalism, Musical Theatre, circus tricks, gymnastics, comedy, puppetry and Physical Theatre – often within the same scene. She tells stories visually, making the plots easy to follow and the staging attractive and imaginative.

> *I always have – and I always will – call myself a storyteller. We use a number of different elements – acting, music, film, design – to tell the story and we stitch together a great big tapestry of ideas.*

Emma Rice interview (Senter, 2019)

Rice's production of *Knights at the Circus*.

# Rice's techniques

**COMMUNITY THEATRE**
Theatre made by and with a particular community in mind. Both Kneehigh Theatre and Wise Children focus on the importance of theatre for bringing people together through productions that are relevant to their lives. Other community theatres include Playback Theatre Company and SAVVY Theatre Company.

**MIXED PERFORMANCE STYLES**
Mixing the ways in which theatre is presented, for example dance, puppetry and burlesque are all used in *The Red Shoes* (see page 68).

**PHYSICAL THEATRE**
Using the body to convey character and plot, without much or sometimes any use of props and set (see page 68).

**MUSIC/SONGS**
These can move the plot forward or be set pieces that are just enjoyed within the scene (see page 68).

**CIRCUS TRICKS**
Acrobatics, sideshow, puppetry, variety, clowning and magic. Rice uses circus tricks not only as part of the world her characters work in, but also to represent the ups and downs they go through in their lives.

**COMEDY**
Using humour to convey a story or message (see page 68).

**ENSEMBLE WORK**
Creating theatre as a group, working together physically to create location, atmosphere and characters (see page 69).

# Mixed performance styles

Emma Rice mixes styles and methods of theatre, from circus tricks and puppetry to live music, to tell her story. However, the most important thing is always the story she is telling.

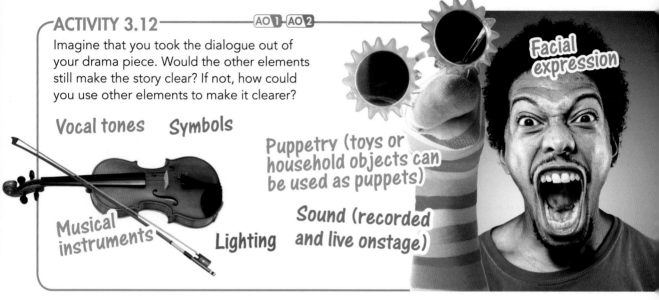

**ACTIVITY 3.12** — AO 1 AO 2

Imagine that you took the dialogue out of your drama piece. Would the other elements still make the story clear? If not, how could you use other elements to make it clearer?

Vocal tones    Symbols

Musical instruments

Puppetry (toys or household objects can be used as puppets)

Lighting    Sound (recorded and live onstage)

Facial expression

# Music/songs

In *Dead Dog in a Suitcase and Other Love Stories*, Emma Rice's previous theatre company, Kneehigh Theatre, uses a violin to represent the small voice of truth in a politically corrupt world. If one of you plays an instrument, or is confident at singing, you could use a musical refrain. Alternatively, you could create your refrain using a sound that can be easily made by banging a certain number of times on a chair, rustling a bag, or something similar that everyone in your group could do.

**ACTIVITY 3.13** — AO 3 AO 4

Explore how you could use your refrain to represent:

1 a theme (justice, freedom, revenge, forgiveness …)

2 a memory (a fire, a favourite moment in childhood, a loss, a betrayal …)

3 an ambition (to find a lost relative, to become president, to repair a relationship …).

# Comedy

Rice believes that theatre should reach an audience visually and joyfully. Comedy plays an important part – in dialogue, in characters' gestures and actions, even in puppetry and dance. Making an audience laugh is often a way of making them understand or empathise with something.

# Physical Theatre

Whether dance and movement sequences are involved, or whether the scene involves naturalistic dialogue, Rice thinks a lot about how each character onstage moves and why – and how their voice and face correspond.

## EXERCISE 3.16

1 Using only your face, body, props, furniture and music, create a scene from a story you know well. You could use a fairy tale, for example:

- 'Red Riding Hood'
- 'Three Little Pigs'
- 'The Boy Who Cried Wolf'.

2 Think about how to establish mood and atmosphere – as well as plot details – visually, including:

- body language
- facial expression
- props
- costume
- music (recorded or live)
- sound-effects (recorded or live)
- lighting.

# Ensemble work

Ensemble is the unified effect of the cast working together, to form a location, or speak in chorus. It emphasises the world of the play, rather than the individual performances.

## The Red Shoes

One of Emma Rice's earliest productions was *The Red Shoes*.

### The premise of *The Red Shoes*

*The Red Shoes* is a folk tale by Hans Christian Andersen.

Karen, a peasant girl, is adopted by a rich, old lady after her mother dies. She grows up vain and spoilt. Before she was adopted, Karen owned a pair of red shoes and her adoptive mother buys her a new pair fit for a princess. Karen is besotted with her red shoes, even wearing them to church. The Old Lady scolds her on her improper behaviour – she must wear black shoes to church. Yet the next Sunday Karen cannot resist wearing her red shoes again. She's about to enter the church when a mysterious old soldier, with a red beard, remarks: 'Oh, what beautiful shoes for dancing.' He taps the sole of each shoe. After church, Karen finds she cannot stop dancing.

The following quote is from the introduction to Kneehigh's script for *The Red Shoes* by Anna Maria Murphy, who wrote poems around which the Andersen fable was woven in this production:

> *Everything in this company's work tells the story: the actors, the set, the music, the costume, the props. A living script grows with Emma and the actors, through devising, improvisation and the poems. Each plays an equal part.*

Grose, Murphy and Rice, page 177

Read the following extract from *The Red Shoes*. Think about how the different elements of the plot from the traditional fairy tale, specially composed poetry and the narration of Lady Lydia work together.

*Four STORYTELLERS enter in grubby vests and pants with suitcases.*

*They wash their feet, put on their shoes and wait.*

*A beautiful 'woman' enters. She is a glamorous and glorious transvestite.*

*Waltz from* Masquerade *by Khachaturian plays.*

LYDIA:
My name is Lydia – Lady Lydia.
I am your host – and hostess. Your fisher of fun.
I welcome you from the deepest darkest depths of my heart to this gorgeous theatre.
Let me lead you through the twisted paths of our tale,
But a word of warning:
for amid the thrills and spills, the twists and the turns, our story has a bite as well.
Let me bait my hook, I'll cast my line, and together we'll see what we might catch.

A-one, a-two, a-one, two, three, four …

*The band plays.*

Oo la la, on commence, let's begin!

Now simmer down, you noisy clapping rabble, for our story has a sombre start.

There was once a girl:

*She chooses one of the STORYTELLERS to play The GIRL.*

*The other STORYTELLERS clothe her.*

Yes, there was once a girl
But not like me.
And she was pretty
And her mother had died.
Yes, her mother had died
Which, in the way of children,
She had not thought possible –
God had lied.
So she was sad
And pretty
Pretty and sad
Pretty sad.

But her shoes (or lack of them)
Let her down,
Which I find often to be the case
(If only folk took more care
Of what they wear).

Grose, Murphy and Rice, *The Red Shoes*, pages 181–182

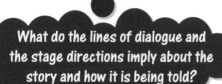

What do the lines of dialogue and the stage directions imply about the story and how it is being told?

How does it seem like a fairy tale? What elements suggest this is a fairy tale for adults and teenagers, rather than children?

Here is an extract of one of the sections of Anna Maria Murphy's poem, which is woven through the script.

LYDIA:
Shoes as red as wounds
That's what I want.
Not an orange hue
Or a vermillion pink
But red red red
Kicking under my bed.

Sensible footwear
Is just too hard to bear.
Shoes as red as desire
That's what I crave.

No glass slippers for me
That turn to skin at the midnight hour
Shoes that bleed
That's what I need.

Soles that with
The Devil have danced
That's what all you girls need!

Grose, Murphy and Rice, *The Red Shoes*, page 185

## ACTIVITY 3.14

Discuss the following in a group:

1 How do you think the poet was inspired by the stimulus of Andersen's story?

2 Could your group consider finding or writing a poem that comments on the story your devised piece tells?

## Symbols and visual storytelling

In Emma Rice's production of *The Red Shoes*, the shoes did not only symbolise simply vanity: '*The Red Shoes* charts the pain of loss, obsession and addiction' (Grose, Murphy, and Rice, 2005, page 87). Therefore, so was the story Rice wanted to tell.

## ACTIVITY 3.15

Choose one of the symbols and one of the themes shown below.

Then, in a group, devise a story using as much visual storytelling as you can.

Symbols

Themes

**Revenge**    **Jealousy**    **Faith**    **Deception**    **Wealth**    **Hope**    **Love**

**What does this teach me about Emma Rice?**

Emma Rice is aware that theatre is a visual medium. Although dialogue is very important, the audience's first impression is what they see. Rice makes sure lots of information comes across about character, plot and conflict through her symbols, music, costume, and the actors' expressions, tricks and body language – as well as through dialogue.

## ACTIVITY 3.16

What object or item of clothing might you use as a symbol in your scene? What would it represent?

**What does this teach me about Emma Rice?**

It is important not to expect the text (your lines) to do all the work for you. How you say a line, and the atmosphere and relationships between characters, tells much of the story. Remember, by the time you say a line, the audience will already 'know' who you are from how you move, speak and react to others.

Kneehigh production of *Rebecca*.

## EXERCISE 3.17

AO 1 – AO 2

### Retelling

1 Pick a folk song or fairy tale from the table below. Retell the words or events of your chosen song or fairy tale to each other as a group.

| Folk song | Fairy tale |
|-----------|-----------|
| 'Greensleeves' | 'Hansel and Gretel' |
| 'The Ash Grove' | 'Robin Hood' |
| 'Scarborough Fair' | 'Three Little Pigs' |
| 'She Moved Through the Fair' | 'Little Red Riding Hood' |

2 Now choose a theme from below. How would you relate your own feelings and experiences about the theme in visual storytelling, as Emma Rice does? What could you use to make soundscapes/sound-effects?

Themes:

Corruption    Greed    Global warming    Poverty

### What does this teach me about Emma Rice?

Emma Rice uses a variety of styles to explore themes and stories that are important to her. This brings familiar stories to life in a totally new way. So, do not be afraid to use a story that lots of people know – you can make it your own and show why it is important to you.

# How do I show Rice's influence on my devised piece?

**Audience involvement**

Encouraging the audience to see themselves as part of the story, thinking about their choices.

**Theatrical styles**

Using a wide variety of theatrical styles, but always keeping the story clear.

**Stories**

Taking traditional stories and making them very modern and relevant.

**Set, lighting and sound**

Suggest a modern world as well as a fairy-tale one, connecting fictional worlds to real worlds.

# Emma Rice: What have I learnt?

The Globe

Kneehigh Theatre

Kneehigh production of *Cymbaline*.

Actor, director, artistic director, born in 1967

Worked at:

Wise Children

Emma Rice

Clear theme and story important – but uses a wide variety of theatrical styles and subject matter

Community theatre

Techniques

Mixed performance styles

Music/songs

Ensemble work

Comedy

Physical Theatre

Circus tricks

# KATIE MITCHELL OBE
## Who is Katie Mitchell?

Katrina Jane Mitchell (born 1964) has directed opera, children's theatre, classical theatre and new writing. Mitchell studied English at Oxford before working at the King's Head Theatre, Paines Plough, The Royal Court Theatre and the Royal Shakespeare Company. She uses Stanislavski's System to work with her actors to build deep, psychologically truthful characters. Mitchell's productions also use technology, including video projections. She is often described as an 'auteur' – a director whose influence is as strong as the author's on the production. An auteur has total creative control over the production and there is a strong visual 'signature' to all the auteur's work.

In 2004, Mitchell directed a series of workshops on Stanislavski and neuroscience at the National Theatre studio. Mitchell was awarded the OBE (Order of the British Empire) in 2009. She began championing 'live cinema' in her productions in 2016. In 2017, she was awarded the President's Medal of the British Academy 'for her work to enhance the presentation of classic and contemporary theatre and opera through innovative new production' (*Alumni News*, 2017).

> " *… from opera to naturalism … installation to multimedia … I think there are no rules about what you can make in theatre.* "

Katie Mitchell on creating *2071*, experimental theatre about climate change, for the Royal Court in 2014 (Brown, 2014)

## What does Katie Mitchell think about theatre?

Mitchell's productions defamiliarise the text, encouraging the audience to step away from preconceptions about the play and see it on its own terms. Her productions have been described as 'distinguished by the intensity of the emotions, the realism of the acting, and the creation of a very distinctive world' (Edwardes, 2007). However, she has also been accused of having been 'wilfully disregarding' of classic texts.

*The Forbidden Zone*, a live cinema show directed by Katie Mitchell.

# Mitchell's techniques

**STANISLAVSKI INFLUENCE**
Stanislavskian method of creating a character (see below).

**USE OF TECHNOLOGY TO ENHANCE THE PERFORMANCE** (see below).

**IMPORTANCE OF NARRATIVE** (see page 77).

**STAGE IMAGERY IMPORTANT** (see page 77).

**PSYCHOLOGY**
Discussing the character's feelings: insecurities, hopes, memories and how all these affect the person they have become (see below).

**DEFAMILIARISATION**
Meeting the text on its own terms and attempting to see beyond common associations or assumptions about it.

## Stanislavskian method of creating a character

Katie Mitchell works very deeply with each actor to develop the inner life of the character, which is reflected in appropriate gestures, vocal inflections and body language. She wants every actor to have a full picture of the world they inhabit 'in which you know where you have just come from, the car you travelled in, how you walked into the room from the front door' (Angus Wright, an actor in her production of *Wastwater* by Simon Stephens at the Royal Court, cited in Higgins, 2016) before they begin rehearsing the scenes in the script.

**LINK**

For more information about Stanislavski, see pages 41–49.

## Use of technology to enhance the performance

Katie Mitchell pioneered the theatre art of 'live cinema', first on an adaptation of Virginia Woolf's *The Waves* and then developed in Duncan Macmillan's *The Forbidden Zone* at the Barbican, which was done with the assistance of video designer Lee Warner. What is happening onstage is projected onto video screens by actors holding film cameras, focusing on the aspects of production, allowing close-ups to focus the audience's attention in the way that cinema does.

## Stage imagery

Katie Mitchell's productions have a strong 'visual signature'. They tend to be suggestive of faded riches, 'shabby-grandiose' interiors (Higgins, 2016) that show the anxiety of passing time. She also uses what she calls 'simultaneity': a set built around the idea of split-screen, so the audience is being asked to watch more than one space at a time, with related scenes being played out in each space to show the pressure on a character from different forces in their lives.

## Importance of narrative

Although Mitchell is criticised for putting her personal style ahead of the text in her productions, she argues that all her production choices are made with the intention of doing justice to the story the author is telling: 'As a director you have a role that is very simple: to say whether it's clear or not. That is the job: to watch in detail and make sure it is precise for the audience, second by second' (Higgins, 2016).

## Psychology

Katie Mitchell's use of deep character psychology is based on Stanislavski's ideas of naturalism. She has used this in all her work – from opera to children's theatre.

## Productions by Katie Mitchell

# CHILDREN'S THEATRE

### *The Cat in the Hat* (2009)

*The Cat in the Hat* was Mitchell's first theatre production for children. It explored the book's theme of order and chaos, using props and costume to create a sense of place (the children's home on a rainy day) and an atmosphere of chaos.

# CLASSICAL THEATRE

## The Seagull (2006)

In her production of this very famous text by Anton Chekhov, Mitchell wanted to defamiliarise it (make the audience see it freshly without any assumptions), so removed all the long monologues that were fashionable in Chekhov's time and introduced 20th-century props to the stage.

# OPERA

## Zauberland (2019)

In October 2019, Mitchell collaborated with the Royal Opera House to create this story of a woman escaping a land at war for a land of peace. It combines 19th-century and specially composed music.

# NEW WRITING

## The City (2008)

The actors each work with Mitchell following Stanislavski's System, creating each character's inner life through script analysis, given circumstances and the magic 'if'.

# Dividing the critics …

In spite of her success in so many genres of theatre, Katie Mitchell has been accused by critics of 'smashing up the classics' – putting her own preferences ahead of the author's intentions.

How will your scene show that you understand the author's intentions, but that you also used ideas inspired by the text that are your own?

I think it's right that a director can take full creative control over their work.

I think it's wrong for a director to put their own preferences ahead of the writer's intentions.

A director's job is to bring out the author's intentions, not just impose their own!

"I'm much more interested in lifelike behaviour than the romantic production of well-spoken language. I'm interested in audiences recognising themselves in the behaviour that they see on stage."
(Mitchell, interviewed by Trueman, 2016)

## ACTIVITY 3.17

As a group, discuss the following question:

What do you think is more important: the author's wishes or the director's vision?

See if you can come up with points for both sides of the argument.

**What does this teach me about Mitchell?**

As an auteur, Katie Mitchell takes total creative control of a production: every aspect from the lighting to the style of acting is recognisable as being her own. This causes a lot of controversy in British theatre, suggesting she puts herself above the wishes of the author.

## ACTIVITY 3.18

1 In a small group, think of an issue that matters to you, or to the world, right now. It could be anything from climate change to school uniform rules or the legal age you can drink alcohol.

- Together, discuss a group of characters for your scene.
- Think about how each character is affected by the issue, and show contrasting views of it.
- Make sure that your characters' views provide opportunities to explore the conflicts of the issue.
- Write backstories for each character, then hot-seat each one.

**What does this teach me about Mitchell?**

Katie Mitchell uses deep character profiling and Stanislavskian acting theory so that every character in her work is three-dimensional.

2 Try playing your scene on a very dark stage. How does the environment affect the way you communicate with each other?

Now try a very bright environment. Does this change how you speak and move?

**What does this teach me about Mitchell?**

Katie Mitchell's productions will prioritise psychological reality over audience visibility – often the stage will be very dark, which is great for atmosphere but means you really have to concentrate to see and understand what is going on.

3 In pairs or small groups, discuss a script you know and love. What are your favourite things about it? If you could set it anywhere you like, or change anything about the characters, what would you alter?

Rehearse 'your' version of the play scene, film scene or TV scene, your way.

**What does this teach me about Mitchell?**

As auteur, a director takes as much power and 'signature' of the script as the writer. As long as you can explain WHY you think your choices are right for the script, you can make any changes you like.

**EXERCISE 3.18** AO 1 AO 2

1 In your group, pick a fairy tale (you could use one shown) and tell it to each other, deciding as a group what you agree are the key events and characters you remember.

'Hansel and Gretel'

'The Gingerbread Man'

'Cinderella'

2 Now, imagine that you are going to turn this fairy tale into another kind of story. Use one of the following three ideas or choose your own:

a) a ghost story

b) an advertisement for your choice of product

c) a reality TV show.

3 Now, try to create a different type of story using the same text.

> We are re-working 'The Gingerbread Man' as a ghost story, based on a child's guilt for eating him!

> We're turning 'Hansel and Gretel' into an advert for camping equipment!

**What does this teach me about Mitchell's techniques?**

You can make a story your own even if you did not write or devise it yourself: decide on visual imagery that interests you, or a particular aspect of the story that you think could stand out more than it does. Then, use clear visual images to communicate it to the audience.

**ACTIVITY 3.19** AO 1 AO 2

Psychology

Fill a page with psychological background for the character you are creating for your devised piece or studying for your text. The more information the better. Remember, there's no wrong answer unless it contradicts information the text has given you.

**What does this teach me about Mitchell's techniques?**

Mitchell uses the techniques of Stanislavski to bring fully rounded characters to life. The more you know about a character, the more confident you will feel about the way you move, think and speak as them onstage.

**TIP**

If you are stuck, look at Stanislavski's seven questions on page 45.

# How do I show Mitchell's influence on my devised piece?

**Explore the psychology of your characters**

Discuss their lives outside the scenes where the audience meets them – what has just happened, where they go after their scenes, where they were and what they were thinking before the scenes started …

**Think about your visual style**

How can you make your set suggest the inner conflicts of the characters?

**Ask your own questions of the text**

How can you show visually the questions the text raised in your mind?

# Katie Mitchell: What have I learnt?

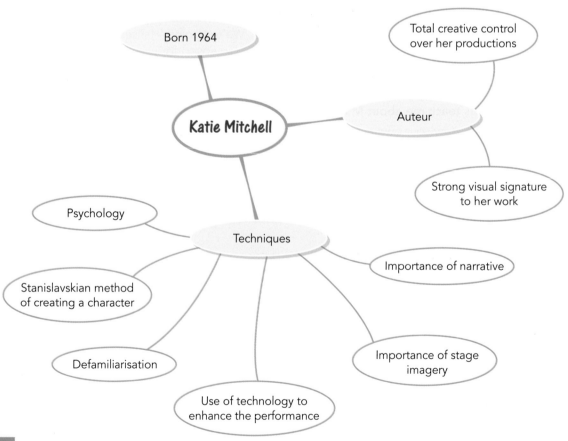

Born 1964

Total creative control over her productions

Katie Mitchell

Auteur

Strong visual signature to her work

Psychology

Techniques

Importance of narrative

Stanislavskian method of creating a character

Defamiliarisation

Importance of stage imagery

Use of technology to enhance the performance

This chapter will help you to:
- learn about theatre genres
- learn key terms and tools associated with each genre
- choose a genre to influence your devised piece.

# THEATRE IN EDUCATION

## What is Theatre in Education?

Theatre in Education (TIE) is theatre created for a particular age group or specific target audience. The aim of Theatre in Education is to educate the audience about a topic, issue or debate – while also entertaining and inspiring them.

TIE can bring stories from history or literature to life: for example, exploring the sensitive issues around contemporary topics such as internet safety or drug use. It uses scripted or partially scripted performances and improvisation, so the audience can interact with the characters and take on roles or communicate with the characters and help them in key decision-making (audience participation).

When Stanislavski was asked about creating theatre for young people, he reportedly said, 'The same as for adults, only better.' That is a good thing to remember when creating TIE!

© Eastfield Primary.

**A Theatre in Education production of *Minotaur* by Big Brum TIE.**

## Features of Theatre in Education

TIE normally has a:

- Clear aim and educational objective
- Small cast (actors multi-roling)
- Script that explores issues from multiple viewpoints
- Low budget
- Portable set design

TIE uses:

- Audience participation or involvement
- Direct address and narration to engage with an audience
- Representational costumes and sets, e.g. simple props to indicate a character
- Facts and figures to educate the audience
- Strong messages or morals

TIE often includes:

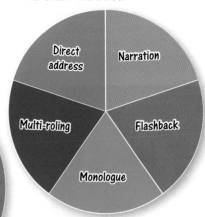

- Direct address
- Narration
- Multi-roling
- Flashback
- Monologue

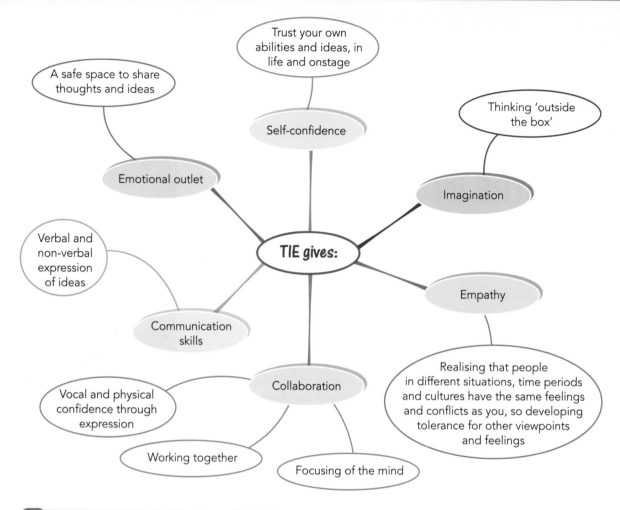

Trust your own
abilities and ideas, in
life and onstage

A safe space to share
thoughts and ideas

Self-confidence

Thinking 'outside
the box'

Emotional outlet

Imagination

Verbal and
non-verbal
expression
of ideas

**TIE gives:**

Empathy

Communication
skills

Vocal and physical
confidence through
expression

Collaboration

Realising that people
in different situations, time periods
and cultures have the same feelings
and conflicts as you, so developing
tolerance for other viewpoints
and feelings

Working together

Focusing of the mind

### LINK

For more on communication
skills, see clarity on page 9
and Physical Theatre on
page 69.

© Penny Saunders.

### How did TIE get start?

A group of actors, teachers and social workers established TIE at the
Belgrade Theatre, Coventry in 1965. It was developed as a free service
to young people in Coventry, and provided an opportunity for them to
explore political, ethical and moral issues in a safe environment.

### TIE isn't just for schools!

On the left is a photograph from *Invisible Bonfires*, devised and
performed by Forkbeard Fantasy. This theatre company is famous for
'crossing the celluloid divide' – timing their use of film onstage so that
they can walk in and out of their own films onto the stage. Forkbeard
Fantasy was awarded a DEFRA Climate Challenge Award to take this
cabaret show on a tour of climate change conferences around the world.
It included live music, puppetry and even a three-dimensional film
sequence for which the audience were issued with their own 3D glasses.

*Invisible Bonfires*, devised and
performed by Forkbeard Fantasy.

# Famous TIE companies

### Big Brum

Founded in 1982 and based in the West Midlands, Big Brum's Theatre in Education programmes tour primary and secondary schools and other educational settings. Big Brum works across all ages, backgrounds and abilities, using theatre and drama to help children and young people make meaning of their lives and the world around them;  learning not what to think but how to think. In 2010 Big Brum was awarded an Action for Children's Arts Members Award. Big Brum is recognised internationally as a leading centre for excellence in arts education.

### The Belgrade Theatre

The target audience of TIE isn't always school-age. At the Belgrade Theatre, Coventry, the theatre where TIE was born, a playwriting course, called 'Critical Mass', is held for people with black and minority ethnic backgrounds, run in partnership with the Drum Arts Centre, Birmingham and the Royal Court Theatre, London.

The Belgrade Theatre's Community and Education Company put on a series of plays called *The Mysteries – In Our Own Words*, a mixture of free and paid-for performances that were put on in unexpected places and highlighted the shared heritage of Christianity, Judaism and Islam.

The original TIE company runs two youth theatre groups with weekly workshops, targeting areas of the city populated by young people who would not otherwise consider or have access to youth theatre.

### The National Trust

The National Trust is not only Europe's largest conservation charity, including maintaining Britain's stately homes and gardens; it also runs an award-winning schools programme led by experienced facilitators and theatre practitioners, with workshops, plays and interactive drama for primary and secondary school children. As Europe's largest conversation charity, it has a wealth of stories and eras to draw on for drama.

Sutton House, a National Trust property which can be hired for performances, musical recitals, plays or as an alternative classroom space.

*Minotaur*, Big Brum production.

© Big Brum TIE 2019.

# What subject can my TIE scene have?

TIE uses drama scenes, games and exercises to encourage its target audience to learn and share experiences, concerns and ideas around a subject. Instead of a traditional classroom environment, TIE lets students develop their knowledge, feelings, thoughts and sensations through exploring multiple sides of an issue.

## What issues affect me and my friends?

Bullying

Friendship

Road safety

History

Literature

Dilemmas

## ACTIVITY 4.1 — A01 A02

Discuss what topic for a TIE play would be good for your place of learning. What topic would you cover for a younger age group?

### TIP

Invite a test audience to a rehearsal – either from a younger year group or a younger sibling at home. Are your phrases too long for them? Any there any words they did not understand? Is what is exciting for you different from what is exciting for them?

# Key questions when creating your TIE scene

**WHO is your target audience?**

Think about the language, attention span, how frightening scenes may appear to different ages – the whole school, teachers, senior school, primary school?

**WHAT is your production about?**

You can choose any topic but it should be something useful or interesting with complex issues such as:
- road safety
- internet safety
- drug and alcohol abuse
- the central character in a book you are studying in literature or history.

**HOW are you going to present your topic?**

Research it as much as possible – what has been written about it already, as well as possibly conducting first-hand interviews to base your monologues and dialogue on.

**WHERE is your production set?**

How are you going to show this economically and inexpensively? Remember, TIE plays tour around different schools and educational establishments, so they need to be easily packed up and moved on, while still giving a clear idea of what and where they are meant to represent.

**WHY did it work and HOW would you change it next time?**

After your production:

DOWNLOADABLE ⊙

Evaluate your production. Discuss with your group what worked and what you would change. You could also use the audience evaluation form that is available online to download.

> *Imagination is more important than knowledge.*
> Albert Einstein, interviewed about his process (Viereck, 1929)

This quote is often used in relation to TIE because TIE is an opportunity for students to problem-solve creatively and make changes to the story.

# Dilemmas and conflict

Drama needs conflict in order to work. Characters involved in conflict have to make decisions and these decisions can change the characters.

Pick one of the following dilemmas to work on in a group. Does the dilemma link to one of the issues mentioned on page 86? If not, what issue would you say it is about?

1 Your new boy-/girlfriend invites you to a party. You have never met their friends before and want to make a good impression. One of their friends offers you drugs. What do you do?

2 You have been talking to a new online friend and they want to meet. What do you do?

3 Your friend tells you they have stolen a magazine from the local shop. What do you do?

Does the dilemma link to one of the issues mentioned on page 86?

> **TIP**
>
> If your TIE scene uses audience participation, you might like to rehearse different endings depending on what your audience thinks the characters should do.

> **TIP**
>
> Political, social, domestic and other situations have inspired successful plays. What political and cultural issues are you hearing about at the moment?

> **TIP**
>
> Try creating a memory that affects the character's judgement – what experience in the past could affect the decision they make in the present?

## EXERCISE 4.1                                    AO**1** AO**2**

Now try these exercises using your chosen dilemma.

1 **Devil's advocate**

   Write a monologue showing the opposite choice or opinion from your own that your character could have. How could you develop this into a scene, or perhaps another character?

2 **Frozen conflict**

   What is the central event or conflict of your devised scene? Can you find a freeze-frame that physically illustrates the moral position of your character and other characters in the play?

3 **Worst-case scenario**

   Think of all the worst decisions the character could make and develop what the consequences of those might be. How can you show the potential consequences in your storyline?

4 **Alternative endings**

   Try out different endings. What do you learn about the characters? What emotions affect the characters' judgements?

> My character knows that what his girlfriend's friend is offering is illegal. He does not want his actions to get his sister, who is a police officer, in trouble.

> My character remembers losing a friendship before and is scared to do anything that might mean losing another one now.

> My character remembers what it was like when her family were struggling for money and she could not have the toys and magazines that her friends did. She considered stealing, although she never did, and this makes her more forgiving.

## ACTIVITY 4.2 — AO 3

**1** Discuss how you can use gestus (see page 54) to show the differing sides of the argument.

Try using freeze-frames to show two opposing characters' or groups' opinions of the issue. How do their feelings, ages and how rich or poor they are, affect your physical performance of them?

**2** Using this technique, make up a scenario of your own, or try one of these:

- One character must persuade the other to do something difficult or scary.
- One character breaks something belonging to the other.
- One character must rescue the other from being trapped in something or being scared by a big spider.

**What does this teach me about TIE?**

Audiences understand visual images much quicker than complex dialogue. Quite often, you can convey very complex emotions to an audience in a simple physical image.

## ACTIVITY 4.3 — AO 1 — AO 2

**1** Pick one of the following dilemmas to explore as a TIE script written by your group:

**a)** At school, you catch your best friend bullying another student. Do you:

- Confront your friend?
- Tell a teacher?
- Pretend you didn't notice?

**b)** At home, you find cigarettes in your brother's or sister's room. Do you:

- Confront your sibling?
- Take the cigarettes?
- Tell your parents?
- Pretend you didn't see them?

**c)** You are about to vote for the first time. Your parents are strong supporters of one party – but you sympathise with another. Do you:

- Follow your instincts?
- Do what your parents do?

**2** Add dramatic devices to bring out your story by using these techniques:

To share the characters' private thoughts as they make up their mind, freeze the scene and let them think privately aloud in a soliloquy, or to another character as a monologue.

Share stage directions or new intentions as direct address. Allow the character to move on using narration.

Is there information about something that happened before the play starts that I need to get across? Try setting one scene in the main character's past, with them remembering it as a flashback.

# How do I show TIE's influence on my devised piece?

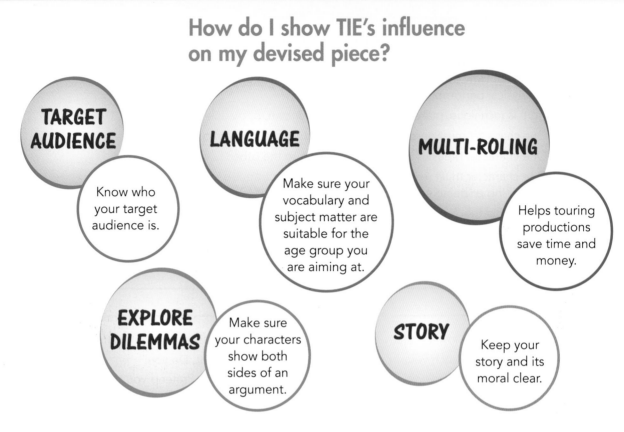

**TARGET AUDIENCE**

Know who your target audience is.

**LANGUAGE**

Make sure your vocabulary and subject matter are suitable for the age group you are aiming at.

**MULTI-ROLING**

Helps touring productions save time and money.

**EXPLORE DILEMMAS**

Make sure your characters show both sides of an argument.

**STORY**

Keep your story and its moral clear.

# Theatre in Education: What have I learnt?

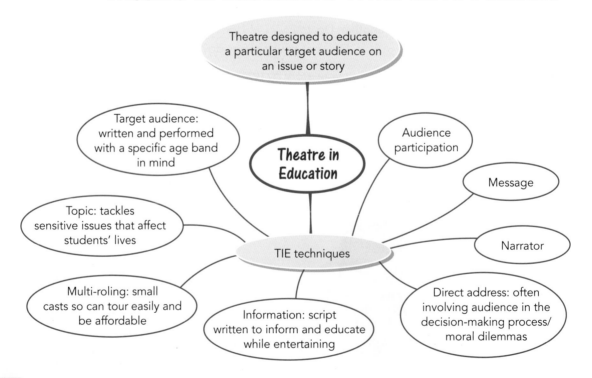

Theatre designed to educate a particular target audience on an issue or story

Target audience: written and performed with a specific age band in mind

**Theatre in Education**

Audience participation

Message

Topic: tackles sensitive issues that affect students' lives

TIE techniques

Narrator

Multi-roling: small casts so can tour easily and be affordable

Information: script written to inform and educate while entertaining

Direct address: often involving audience in the decision-making process/ moral dilemmas

# PHYSICAL THEATRE

## What is Physical Theatre?

Physical Theatre includes any form of theatre where the story is expressed through the use of the body, its movement and positioning. In Physical Theatre, the body does the job not only of the actor but also of the setting, props and even special effects.

## Techniques in Physical Theatre

**ENSEMBLE**

**MOVEMENT**
In any kind of Physical Theatre – from in mime to Total Theatre, dance, physical comedy, music or puppetry – the meaning of the story comes across mainly through the movement of the body (the actor's or the puppet's). The genre's power comes from how expressive the movement is.

**STATUS**
The level of power within a group or situation is shown in body language and facial and vocal expression.

**GESTURE AND BODY LANGUAGE**
The two principal ways of communicating through movement.

**COMMEDIA DELL'ARTE**
Evolved in Italy and was popular in Europe during the 16th and 17th centuries. Troups of actors would perform improvised stories around a number of stock characters, or 'social types', each of whom could be identified easily by a mask and/or costume items that defined them. Among the most famous are Arlecchinno, Pierrot and Harlequin, all clowns with a white mask and baggy white and black clothes, and Pulcinella, who developed into Mr Punch of 'Punch and Judy'.

**MIME**
Voiceless Physical Theatre, where body and face give all the information required to show emotion and situation (see page 92).

**PROXIMITY**
How near or far you are to another actor conveys very powerful messages. For example, if you speak a line or give a gesture in the other actor's face instead of across the stage, or if you deliver a line sitting instead of standing, the meaning and power relationship can appear completely different.

**USE OF MASKS**
Wearing a mask, and concealing your facial expression, draws greater focus to your movement and action. It can also be very freeing, letting you feel less exposed and experiment more with movement (see page 96).

**PHYSICALISING EMOTIONAL STATES**
Stances of the body as well as facial expressions or vocal sounds will immediately suggest particular emotions. Make sure you are aware of – and make use of – the clues your body and voice give to your emotions.

**CIRCUS, VAUDEVILLE AND MASK**

# Examples of Physical Theatre

**Mime**

A still from the film of Bertolt Brecht's *Baal*, starring David Bowie. Bowie was trained by dancer and mime artist Lindsay Kemp, who was very influential in theatre and music. Kemp himself was trained by the mime artist Marcel Marceau.

**Clown**

Probably the most famous mime artist in history is the French actor Marcel Marceau (left). He developed many of his techniques through his Physical Theatre performance as Bip the Clown.

**Total Theatre**

The Total Theatre style grew out of mime, but it rejected the notion of not using the voice in physical performance. Steven Berkoff, seen left in *One Man – Tell Tale Heart*, wanted 'to see how I could bring mime together with the spoken word as its opposite partner, creating the form and structure of the piece' (Berkoff, 1995).

## LINK

For more on Berkoff and Total Theatre, see pages 59–65.

## Theatre in Education

Forkbeard Fantasy (see page 84) and Wise Children (see page 66) both use what Forkbeard calls 'crossing the celluloid divide' – walking in and out of their own films – to tell stories onstage.

### LINK

For more on Theatre in Education, see pages 83–90.

© Maisie Hill.

**A Forkbeard Fantasy production.**

## Commedia dell'Arte

Also known as 'Italian comedy' – comedic theatre by travelling actors originating in 16th-century Italy. They would perform anywhere, from the street to the court, and their stories were easily understood in any language because they used Physical Theatre and mask to show stock characters.

### LINK

For more on Commedia dell'Arte, see page 91.

# Physical Theatre group exercises

**EXERCISE 4.2**

AO 1 – AO 2

**1 What are you doing?**

> **TIP**
>
> Try to use the whole of the acting space inside the circle. This will get you used to thinking about the whole of your acting space, rather than keeping the action stuck in one small part of it.

**a)** Stand in a circle. The first player performs an action in mime, for example digging a hole.

**b)** Player 2 enters the circle, and asks: *What are you doing?*

Player 1 must answer with a lie, for example: *I'm watering the plants.*

**c)** Player 2 must then perform the action Player 1 named.

**d)** Player 3 then asks: *What are you doing?*

and Player 2 must think of another lie: *I'm playing in a rock band.*

*I'm climbing a mountain.*

See how creative you can become with your ideas and your miming.

**What does this teach me about Physical Theatre?**

The clearest messages an audience takes from a scene are what they see, not what they hear. For your dialogue to be fully convincing, your body language has to support it. If not, the audience will believe (or remember) your body more than your words.

## 2 Silent status walk

**a)** Your teacher, or a member of your group, whispers a number between one and five in the ear of every player.

**b)** If the number is high (four or five) you are high status: confident, assured, relaxed.

The lower the number, the lower your status: fearful, lacking in confidence, awkward.

**c)** Begin walking around the room. How does your status affect the way you pass someone else? How does your status make you look at those who pass you?

## 3 Train carriage

**a)** Choose one of the characters pictured above for yourself.

Ask yourself:

- Where are you going?
- Are you anxious or relaxed?
- How high or low is your status?
- What are you thinking about?
- When you pass people, do you nod? Wave? Wink? Maybe you even mutter or shout!

**b)** Now improvise a train scene. Each character should enter the train carriage one at a time. Your teacher or one of your group decides when the train stops at a station and how many characters get on or off.

**d)** After a few minutes, your teacher will clap. Stay in character and try to line up in order of status: high status at one end and low status at the other. If your body language was strong enough, you will be in the correct order.

### What does this teach me about Physical Theatre?

An audience's first impression can tell them a lot about a character before they know even who the character they are watching is or what the scene is going to be about. You, too, will get to know your character by moving around 'in their skin' and feeling 'at home' in their stance.

**c)** What would happen if you create an imaginary rush hour – how does your character react to too many people getting on the train? Or an unexplained delay in a tunnel?

**d)** When you have improvised your train scene, try rehearsing a section of it for performance. What qualities in your characters can you enhance to contrast with each other? How can you use movement to show when the train stops and starts? What sound-effects could you create yourselves to build atmosphere and show location?

### What does this teach me about Physical Theatre?

Rehearsing a scene repeatedly will give you a chance to get used to your character's basic body language, and give you a chance to experiment with the different moods, thoughts and actions they might have. It will also help the whole group get to know each other's characters and explore how they could relate to each other.

> **TIP**
>
> You could also ask everyone in your group to bring a picture and choose from these pictures instead.

**4 Sound machine**

a) One actor walks onto the stage or into the performance space and begins a sound and action on repeat (e.g. bending knees and saying 'Shh').

**Shh**

b) Another actor then comes on with a sound and an action to complement the sound and action of the first actor (e.g. a clap before each 'Shh').

c) One by one, the whole group joins in to build the sound machine.

**What does this teach me about Physical Theatre?**

Working as part of an ensemble is one of the most rewarding things about theatre work. You need to accept the ideas of others, build on them with your own and eventually find a result that nobody could have planned alone. The sound machine is always more than the sum of its parts.

> **TIP**
>
> You could also try choosing in advance what the sound machine does. How can your sounds and actions suggest this? What sort of machine are you?

# Physical Theatre pair exercises

**EXERCISE 4.3**                                              AO**1** AO**2**

1 **'Yes', 'No', 'Maybe'**

Rehearse a scene, using only three words of dialogue – 'Yes', 'No' and 'Maybe' – to convey your meaning.

How clearly can you use physical movement and facial expression to convey meaning and emotion to your audience? Your scene might be:

- an argument
- a marriage proposal
- private gossip.

**What does this teach me about Physical Theatre?**

It takes very little dialogue to convince an audience of the 'reality' of your scene – if you are fully aware of what you want, where you are and what you feel. The audience will get all of that from your physical and vocal expression, so even a very complex story can be 'told' in just 'Yes', 'No' and 'Maybe'.

> **TIP**
>
> The best dialogue leaves the audience to fill in some of the meaning. 'Oh no! She's left me! I can't live without her!' can come across better as a single 'No'. Likewise, 'I'm so happy I got my dream job!' can be expressed as 'Yes!'

2 **Watching**

On an empty stage space, two volunteers lock eyes with each other and maintain eye contact. The object of the exercise is to try to move around the space without looking away from each other. Choose one of the following scenarios before you start:

- predator and prey
- prom queen and reflection.

As you get used to keeping eye contact, try moving towards and away from each other, upstage and downstage, to explore power relationships onstage.

**What does this teach me about Physical Theatre?**

Physical focus onstage is very important, as is trust in your fellow performers. If you keep your focus strong and your movement under control, you will move safely around the stage without ever losing eye contact with your partner.

# Jacques Lecoq

Many of the styles of Physical Theatre we have looked at are influenced by mime artist, director and teacher Jacques Lecoq. Born in 1921, he founded L'École Internationale de Théâtre and taught there from 1956 until his death in 1999.

> *To mime is literally to embody and therefore to understand better. A person who handles bricks all day long reaches a point where he no longer knows what he is handling. It has become an automatic part of his physical life [...] miming is a way of rediscovering a thing with renewed freshness.*

Lecoq, 2000

## Masks

Lecoq's training began with masks, starting with the neutral mask, which was symmetrical and expressionless. He believed that this allowed students be totally open to whatever came on stage and not be limited by past experience or any expression or mannerisms. He would then move them on to expressive masks – half masks – eventually working up to the smallest mask of all: the clown's red nose.

> **TIP**
>
> Remember, the red nose is small, but the courage and command of Physical Theatre required for a clown performance is very big.

Half mask

Neutral mask

The clown's red nose

## Clown

Lecoq believed that to study the clown is to study oneself; no two selves are alike, so no two clown performances will be alike. The principal skills are:

- *le jeu* (playfulness)
- *complicité* (togetherness)
- *disponibilité* (openness).

Clown movement, like mime, generally works through simple movement (the French concept is called *efficace* – efficiency and effectiveness of movement). Lecoq viewed movement as a sort of Zen art of making simple, direct, minimal movements. However, Lecoq also combined mime with vocal expression, finding the most fitting voice for the character as well as the right movement.

### ACTIVITY 4.4

**Night club in mask**

As an ensemble (a group of players working together), practise a scene in mask where everyone is in a night club. Even if you are a small group, you can suggest bodies packed too tightly on the dance floor, or sitting at tables, and see how feelings and intentions are shown in your body language.

### ACTIVITY 4.5

**Inspire a scene**

Choose one of the four images on this page to inspire a Physical Theatre scene.

Use your picture as a stimulus to decide:

- WHERE the scene is set.
- WHAT the characters want.
- WHO the characters are.
- HOW and WHY they move in the space.

# How do I show the influence of Physical Theatre in my devised piece?

Make sure that your body is 'saying' the same thing as your lines.

'Free' your performance by experimenting with mask.

Think about stock characters and body/face positions that you associate with particular emotions.

Be aware of your stance (position of body) and facial expression.

Work as an ensemble to create locations and atmospheres.

# Physical Theatre: What have I learnt?

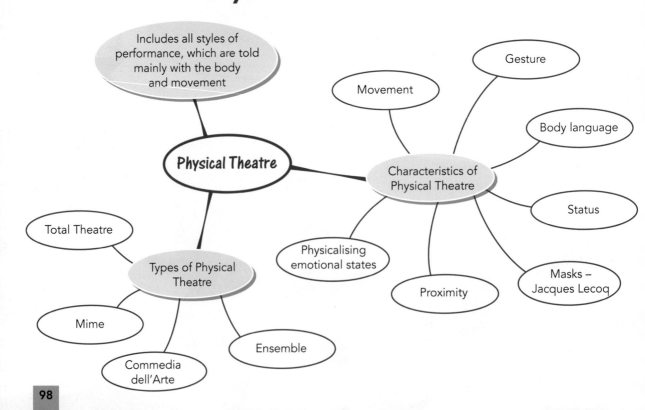

Includes all styles of performance, which are told mainly with the body and movement

Physical Theatre

Characteristics of Physical Theatre

Gesture

Movement

Body language

Status

Physicalising emotional states

Proximity

Masks – Jacques Lecoq

Types of Physical Theatre

Total Theatre

Mime

Commedia dell'Arte

Ensemble

# MUSICAL THEATRE
## What is Musical Theatre?

Musical Theatre is any style of theatre where the story is communicated through music, song and dance.

Some musicals are told entirely in music, song and dance ('sung-through'):

### Les Miserables

Adapted from the novel by French poet and novelist Victor Hugo, by Claude-Michel Schönberg (music), Jean-Marc Natel (original French lyrics) and Herbert Kretzmer (English lyrics), 'Les Mis' (as it is often called) is set in France before the Revolution. It explores social justice and the redemptive power of kindness. With Cameron Mackintosh as producer, its London run from October 1985 makes it the longest-running West End musical.

### Cats

Composed by Andrew Lloyd Webber, based on the book of poems by T. S. Eliot called *Old Possum's Book of Practical Cats*, the musical is told in song and dance, following a tribe of cats, called the Jellicles, who every year at the 'Jellicle Ball' make the 'Jellicle choice': which cat will ascend to the Heavyside Layer and return to a new life? *Cats* was released as a film in 2019.

Other musicals have scattered lines of dialogue, or whole sections of dialogue:

### Company

Written in 1979, with music and lyrics by Stephen Sondheim, famous for writing natural speech rhythms into his musicals. *Company* was among the first musicals to deal with adult themes and relationships, and continued to break new ground in its 2019 London revival. The original production won six Tony Awards and was nominated for 14.

### Waitress

An apparently light comedy, this musical deals with very serious subjects. Jenna Hunterson is a waitress in an abusive relationship with her husband Earl. She sees a pie-cooking competition as her way out and begins to find the strength to change her life. Music and lyrics by Sara Bareilles, *Waitress* was based on the 2007 film of the same name, which was written and directed by Adrienne Shelly, who also co-starred in it.

Another kind of Musical Theatre is the 'jukebox' musical – putting the songs of an artist, band or a group of songs together to create a story:

# Moulin Rouge!

Baz Luhrmann used a collection of 1960s and 1970s rock to tell the story of a young English poet/writer, Christian (Ewan McGregor), who falls in love with Satine (Nicole Kidman), the star of the Moulin Rouge cabaret in Paris, in the film *Moulin Rouge!* The story is told in original dialogue, with songs by T. Rex, David Bowie, Elton John and Madonna. The stage production of this film is due to open in 2021.

# We Will Rock You

Based on the songs of the rock band Queen, in a story by comedian, screenwriter and author Ben Elton, *We Will Rock You* is set in a distant future where everyone dresses, thinks and acts the same, and musical instruments are forbidden, composing is illegal and rock music is unknown. A group of Bohemians struggle to restore free thought, music and fashion to the world.

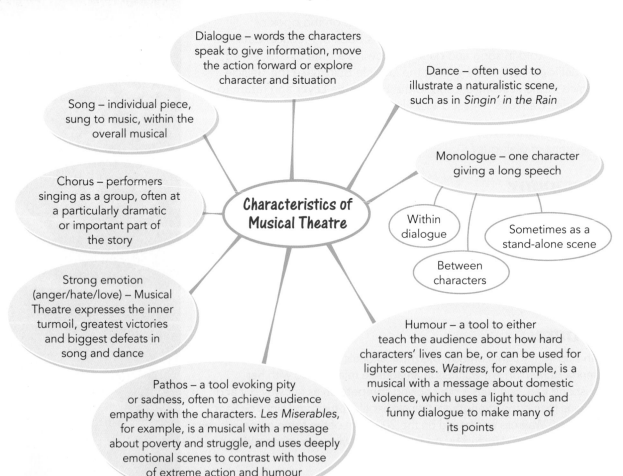

**Characteristics of Musical Theatre**

Dialogue – words the characters speak to give information, move the action forward or explore character and situation

Dance – often used to illustrate a naturalistic scene, such as in *Singin' in the Rain*

Song – individual piece, sung to music, within the overall musical

Monologue – one character giving a long speech

Chorus – performers singing as a group, often at a particularly dramatic or important part of the story

Within dialogue

Sometimes as a stand-alone scene

Between characters

Strong emotion (anger/hate/love) – Musical Theatre expresses the inner turmoil, greatest victories and biggest defeats in song and dance

Humour – a tool to either teach the audience about how hard characters' lives can be, or can be used for lighter scenes. *Waitress*, for example, is a musical with a message about domestic violence, which uses a light touch and funny dialogue to make many of its points

Pathos – a tool evoking pity or sadness, often to achieve audience empathy with the characters. *Les Miserables*, for example, is a musical with a message about poverty and struggle, and uses deeply emotional scenes to contrast with those of extreme action and humour

**TIP**

**High emotion**

If your Musical Theatre piece is not sung-through, the songs should represent moments of high emotion – anger, hate or love. You can find examples of this in the scripts, films or stage shows of *Blood Brothers*, *We Will Rock You*, *Mamma Mia!* and *Moulin Rouge!*

---

**ACTIVITY 4.6**  AO**1** AO**2**

In your group, go through your lines and select a single line of dialogue that best sums up each character and their situation.

- Find a simple note or tune you are comfortable to sing the line to (or speak it, if you prefer not to sing).
- Create a 'round' where each person's line is sung or read in rhythm with each other.

**What does this teach me about Musical Theatre?**

The music is always a reflection of who the characters are and what they are experiencing. Moments of high emotion – which is what songs tend to be – will be based on this.

---

**ACTIVITY 4.7**  AO**1** AO**2**

Choose one of these inspiring quotes from Musical Theatre to inspire a scene:

- 'I've heard it said that people come into our lives for a reason, bringing something we must learn, and we are led to those who help us most to grow.' *Wicked*
- 'Being true to yourself never goes out of style.' *Legally Blonde*
- 'No day but today.' *Rent*

**What does this teach me about Musical Theatre?**

Thinking about the issues behind successful lines from existing musicals will help you to think of ways to bring across your own ideas in punchy, memorable ways.

---

# Does all theatre with music in it count as Musical Theatre?

No! Opera, ballet and dance shows are not Musical Theatre. Sometimes, plays include music but are not Musical Theatre. For example, the West End production of *All About Eve* in 2019 had characters sing songs and play the piano over scene changes. This is not a new idea – Shakespeare often made use of this technique. For example, *Twelfth Night* includes songs the characters sing: both performances by the court jester Feste and shared songs where the characters are drunk and enjoying themselves, as well as music at the celebration at the end.

## Types of songs

The structure of a musical relies on particular types of songs to drive the plot:

### Character songs

These help the audience to learn about the particular character, how they feel and what changes they are trying to make in their lives.

Photograph by Johan Persson.

## Action songs

These move the action forward, in the same way as big events in a novel. Picture a row of dominoes: these are the events of the story. Each event causes the next one.

> **TIP**
>
> When devising Musical Theatre, do not worry about writing songs. The jukebox method is fine. The most important thing is to make it clear how one event leads to the next (think about the dominoes).

## Production songs

The whole ensemble takes part in these, usually at the beginning, significant moments within the plot and the end.

> **TIP**
>
> If you like, you could even choose poems to be your lyrics. Do not forget that T. S. Eliot's poem book *Old Possum's Book of Practical Cats* became the successful musical and film *Cats*.

## ACTIVITY 4.8 — AO 1 – AO 3

1 Try writing lyrics for your own Musical Theatre song. Choose a character from a familiar story and write from their point of view. For example:

a) Red Riding Hood on the path to Grandma's house, before she meets the Big Bad Wolf.

b) The Big Bad Wolf waiting for Red Riding Hood in the wood.

c) Grandma waiting to be rescued from the Wolf.

2 Once you have the lyrics for your song, choose the music of a song or nursery rhyme you know well and see what the effect is of combining the two. You can make a very exciting or sinister effect by combining a nursery rhyme with a scary situation.

## ACTIVITY 4.9 — AO 1 – AO 3

In your group, pick one of the following three songs. Each one tells a story about a character and their feelings:

- 'Next to Me' – Emeli Sandé
- 'I Am a Rock' – Simon and Garfunkel
- 'Ruby Tuesday' – the Rolling Stones.

Listen to the song and tell the story as you understand it, using the following questions:

1 Who is the character?

2 What are their feelings and the events causing the feelings?

3 When did the story take place? In your time, a previous decade or longer ago?

4 Where does the story take place? In your town, your country or somewhere else?

5 Did any of the words they use surprise you? Why? Do they suggest feelings the main character is hiding?

6 How does the story end?

You can now begin developing your story into the plot for a Musical Theatre piece. Think about putting your ideas into monologues and dialogue as well as songs. Perhaps some of the lines in the monologues or dialogue could be sung.

ACTIVITY 4.10 AO 1 AO 3

In a small group, discuss the painting, then devise a scene based on the story the image suggests.

- Use the questions from Activity 4.9 to develop your understanding of the characters in the painting.

- Think about adding dance or movement. What moments, or themes, could the dance or movements show?

## Sources for musicals

Some musicals are inspired by poetry, novels or even rock groups. However, musicals can be inspired by almost anything.

*The Sound of Music* – inspired by the real-life memoirs of Maria von Trapp.

*Romeo and Juliet – the Musical*, inspired by Shakespeare's play.

*Hairspray* – developed from the film produced by John Waters.

ACTIVITY 4.11 AO 1 AO 3

As a group, discuss the films, news stories or public figures that inspire you. Could you base a Musical Theatre scene on these real-life stories?

## ACTIVITY 4.12

AO 1 AO 3

Choose one of the poems below and use the character and plot of the poem to devise a Musical Theatre scene.

- Can you use the events to 'show not tell' the story using dialogue?
- Along with the speaker of the poem, which other characters might have a monologue in your scene?

**In Broken Images by Robert Graves**
He is quick, thinking in clear images;
I am slow, thinking in broken images.

He becomes dull, trusting to his clear images;
I become sharp, mistrusting my broken images.

Trusting his images, he assumes their relevance;
Mistrusting my images, I question their relevance.

Assuming their relevance, he assumes the fact;
Questioning their relevance, I question the fact.

When the fact fails him, he questions his senses;
When the fact fails me, I approve my senses.

He continues quick and dull in his clear images;
I continue slow and sharp in my broken images.

He in a new confusion of his understanding;
I in a new understanding of my confusion.

**I'm Nobody by Emily Dickinson**
I'm nobody! Who are you?
Are you nobody, too?
Then there's a pair of us — don't tell!
They'd banish us, you know.

## ACTIVITY 4.13

AO 1 AO 3

Listen to 'Eleanor Rigby' by The Beatles or 'David Watts' by The Kinks and discuss the characters and setting.

Then use the questions from Activity 4.9 to develop a scene based on these lyrics.

# How do I show the influence of Musical Theatre in my devised piece?

Use singing, live instruments and/or recorded music to enhance moments of high emotion.

Sung-through or featured songs both count as Musical Theatre.

If your group is comfortable with dance, see how you can include it to suggest where your scene is set. Use singing, humming or other voice work to accompany it.

## Musical Theatre: What have I learnt?

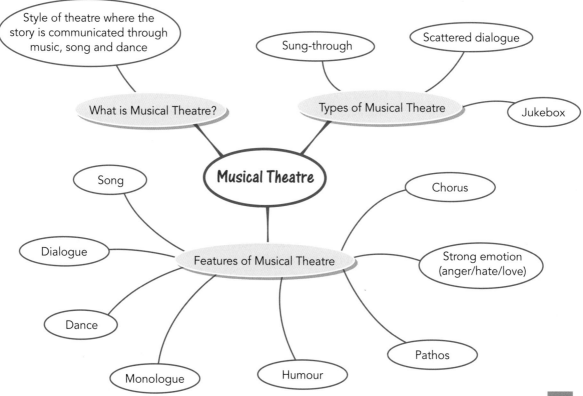

- Style of theatre where the story is communicated through music, song and dance
- Sung-through
- Scattered dialogue
- What is Musical Theatre?
- Types of Musical Theatre
- Jukebox
- Song
- Musical Theatre
- Chorus
- Dialogue
- Features of Musical Theatre
- Strong emotion (anger/hate/love)
- Dance
- Monologue
- Humour
- Pathos

# CHAPTER 5

# STRUCTURING YOUR DEVISED SCENE

## Beginning, middle and end

**Just as a story needs a beginning, middle and end on paper,** so your scene will come across to your audience most successfully if it has key images or events that mark the beginning, middle and end.

**What would happen if you showed the end of the story at the beginning?** *Sunset Boulevard* begins with a dead body being removed from a grand house. The narrator takes the audience back to the beginning to find out how this happened.

**Plot is character and character is plot.** Character arcs, plotting the journey of your characters, make good templates for structure. What's the main event in your story? What made the character do the thing that caused it?

 ## A diagram of your devised piece

- **Make yourself a simple diagram of beginning, middle and end.** Decide what your key image is for the climax, beginning and end. See how much time your key scenes take. This will help you not to crowd your 10 minutes with too much for the audience to take in.
- **Colour code the moods.** Does it begin dark, sinister and slow, then build in suspense? Or does everything seem fine to begin with, then darker feelings creep in?

Also consider the following:

- Could you use choral speaking to represent what society tells the character versus what their conscience (one small voice) tells them?
- Could you use thought-tracking to show the difference between what's being thought and said?
- Could you use different actors to play different ages or aspects of the same character?

 ## Exploring time

You can make your story even more compelling by telling it in a way that is not chronological:

- framing device
- beginning at the end and working back
- flashbacks
- freezing time.

> **TIP**
>
> Make sure that you know what your story is in linear time before you decide the order you will tell it in – this will make your decisions much easier.

# Inspiration for devising

## Quotes

Try keeping a quotes book full of sentences you overhear, and practise letting your mind follow ideas about the characters who say them, and what is going on in their lives.

┌─ACTIVITY 5.1────────────────

1 Use one of the lines on the right to inspire a monologue or scene.

2 Now choose a different line to use as the first line of a scene and explore where you go and who you become.

> First of all, it wasn't my fault …

> I'm assuming this is yours?

> Don't look at me like that!

> We'll laugh about this one day.

## Photographs

┌─ACTIVITY 5.2──────────────── AO❶

Choose one of the following photographs to inspire a scene. Think about your choices and emotions – you may be able to devise two completely different scenes from the same photograph.

A touching family group or a sinister power game?

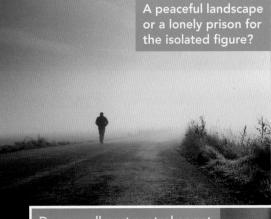

A peaceful landscape or a lonely prison for the isolated figure?

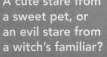

A cute stare from a sweet pet, or an evil stare from a witch's familiar?

Do you call pest control or get the cheese out for this animal?

# Objects

## ACTIVITY 5.3 AO 1

Choose one of the objects on this page to inspire a scene. Why might it represent a happy or unhappy memory to someone?

## Emotions

### ACTIVITY 5.4 — AO 1

Choose one of the following emotions and use it as a prompt for a story. Improvise and discuss it in your group, taking notes of your ideas as you go:

**Jealousy**              **Greed**

        **Revenge**    **Hope**

Who are your characters? Perhaps they are a group of friends. What are the conflicts?

# Monologues

## ACTIVITY 5.5 — AO1 AO2

In groups of four, decide on a group of people who all know each other well. Something happens that causes a conflict, and you get to show four sides of the same fight.

For example, youngest sibling says older one broke the window, oldest sibling says younger one broke the window, parent who says babysitter should have been watching, babysitter who says they can't be everywhere at once.

The result will be four monologues – and the audience can judge who is in the right, or if everyone is in the wrong.

# Scenarios

## ACTIVITY 5.6 — AO1

Design a scenario based on a conflict. If you can't think of one, let yourself be inspired by any of the pictures on this page.

How do they feel about this conflict?

Choose one of the following:

Jealousy  Ambition  Revenge  Hope  Grief

> **TIP**
> Discuss as a group how you can raise the stakes – is something physical being argued over (a will, a necklace, a broken window) that represents something bigger (financial independence, the memory of a dead grandparent, personal responsibility)? Explore the facts the characters agree on and what they might disagree on.

> **TIP**
> Remember that for any idea you have, it could be interesting to reverse the gender or situation.

> **TIP**
> Do not worry if you don't fit all your ideas into your final piece – you can always use them for another story. Nothing is ever wasted.

# Practise devising from stimulus

**1**

> *Never, never, never, never [...] never give in.*
> Winston Churchill

'Across the Universe' by The Beatles

The price of fame

**American Gothic** by Grant Wood (The Art Institute of Chicago).

Working in a group of four or five, devise a piece in response to the stimulus you have chosen from the four shown here.

Make sure that you listen to each other's ideas in the discussions and try out lots of suggestions. Remember, just because it does not sound like it will work in discussion does not mean it won't be different when you get it 'on its feet'.

**2**

> *Youth is wasted on the young.*
> George Bernard Shaw

'American Pie' by Don McLean

The closed door

**Christina's World**, Andrew Wyeth (Museum of Modern Art, New York).

In the same group, choose one of the above stimuli. Devise a piece, using some of the dramatic devises discussed on page 16.

---

**TIP**

You are very likely to find that you already used some of the dramatic devices instinctively when you did exercise 1 (above). Make a note of these, as it will help you later when choosing the practitioner or genre most suited to your ideas and interests.

**FOR YOUR PORTFOLIO**

Which stimulus spoke to you? How did you combine your ideas with those of your group?

# Your performance

Getting to know your character, the world of the play, and the dramatic devices that help you tell your story, will give your performance a stable foundation.

Help yourself further by doing a warm-up before every rehearsal and performance, practising focus within the scene, and doing regular drama exercises and activities with your group so that your stage and group feel comfortable and familiar.

Here are some more exercises to help you build familiarity with your group and the stage.

**FIND HELP FOR …**

Warm-up exercises on pages 12–14.

## EXERCISE 5.1

AO **1** — AO **3**

**1 Missing scene**

Improvise a scene that has been cut from the play. Get to know your character and the other characters even more.

**What does this teach me about performing?**

The more background to your scene you create in your head, the more confident you will feel performing the actual scene onstage.

**2 Context**

Answer the questions in the thought bubbles on the right for your character. Then, write a few thought bubbles of your own and answer those too.

Try doing this again in a group, swapping questions so you can get to know each other's characters, as well as your own, as much as possible.

**What does this teach me about performing?**

Sometimes you might not notice gaps in your knowledge about your character. This exercise is a great way to build awareness of who they are and what they want.

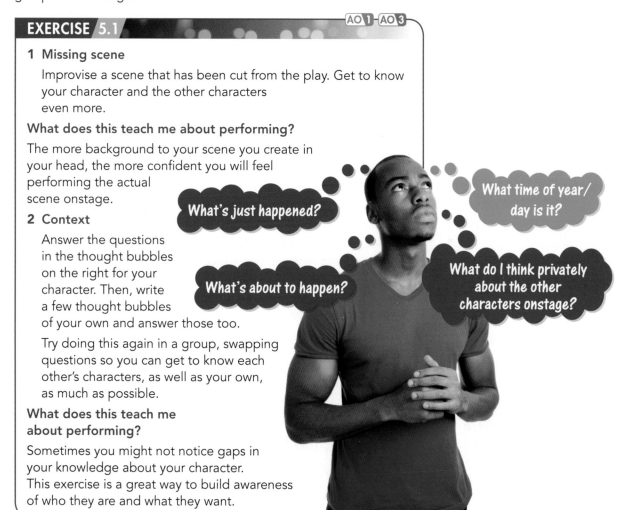

What's just happened?

What's about to happen?

What time of year/ day is it?

What do I think privately about the other characters onstage?

# CHAPTER 6

YOUR PORTFOLIO OF
SUPPORTING EVIDENCE

# What is a portfolio of supporting evidence?

A portfolio of supporting evidence is a collection of evidence showing how your ideas developed through the process of devising your scene. You should include examples to represent the whole process – from your choice of stimulus, through your work with your chosen practitioner or genre, to your final performance.

## What do I need to do?

You need to present visual evidence of your rehearsal process, and provide written explanations (notes) showing the three stages of the rehearsal process:

1 How ideas from your stimulus have been researched, created and developed in response to your choice of stimulus.

2 How ideas from your chosen practitioner or genre have been used to communicate your meaning to the audience.

3 How your ideas have been developed, amended and refined as you developed and rehearsed your piece.

Each section should have a commentary of about 250 words accompanying your visual material. Your portfolio's word count should total no more than 900 words.

Your portfolio can include:

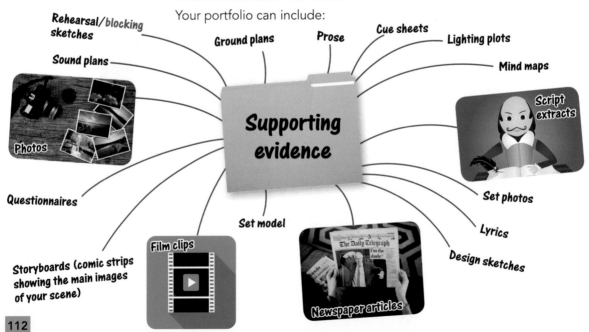

Rehearsal/blocking sketches

Ground plans

Prose

Cue sheets

Lighting plots

Sound plans

Mind maps

Photos

Script extracts

Questionnaires

Set photos

Set model

Lyrics

Film clips

Design sketches

Storyboards (comic strips showing the main images of your scene)

Newspaper articles

Supporting evidence

# ACTIVITY 6.1

## Mind map

Have a look at the headings on the mind map below.
Think about your devised scene and write notes for yourself
(and/or draw diagrams) about your devised scene and how
the headings apply.

When you have completed a mind map for your own scene,
write a short explanation of it.

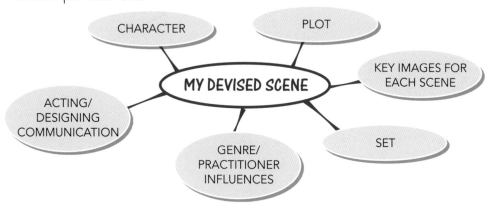

For each of the bubbles on your mind map, add four or five details.

For example:

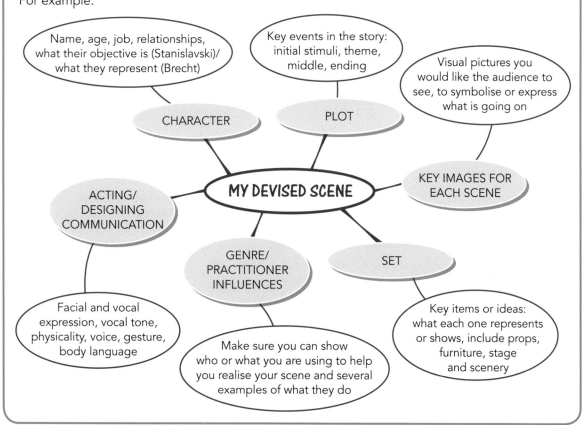

**EXERCISE 6.1**                                          AO 1  AO 3  AO 4

### Ground plans

Compare the ground plans below. Have a look at what changes this group made between their original design and the layout for their final piece. Can you sketch a series of ground plans to show how your stage configuration changed?

**Original design**

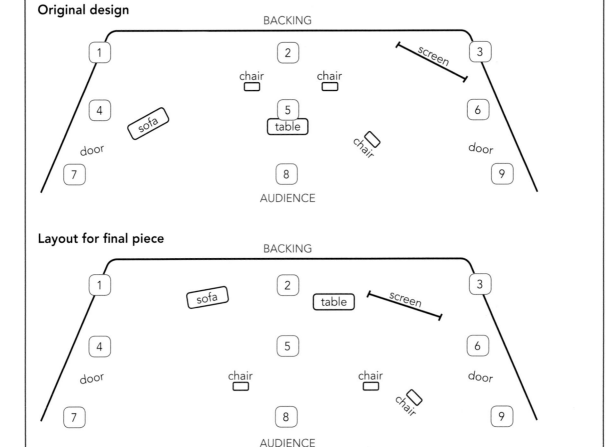

**Layout for final piece**

Key:
1 Upstage right (USR)
2 Upstage centre (USC)
3 Upstage left (USL)
4 Centre stage right (CSR)
5 Centre stage (CS)
6 Centre stage left (CSL)
7 Downstage right (DSR)
8 Downstage centre (DSC)
9 Downstage left (DSL)

> **TIP**
>
> Be specific about why each change occurred. How did it improve sight lines? How did it help the actors move around the stage? Did their blocking show more about their relationships and power struggles?

## Questionnaires

Ahead of your performance, it can be helpful to have an invited audience attend a dress rehearsal and then ask them to complete a questionnaire, similar to the one on the next page.

## Example questionnaire 1

**Group members:** Amerie, Ram, Miles and Jay     **Scene title:** 'Far Apart'

**Describe the plot as it came across to you:** Amerie and Jay used to be best friends, but Amerie joined a new social group and Jay felt left behind. In the end, Jay made new friends but still missed Amerie.

**Describe the characters as they came across to you:** Amerie and Jay were very different: Jay quiet and thoughtful, and Amerie loud and easily distracted. When Miles and Ram played Amerie's friends they were loud and attention-seeking; when they played Jay's friends they were quiet and shy.

**Please comment on what you felt worked best:** I liked the way the lighting showed how Jay felt cut-off and isolated from the other characters. Body language and facial expressions made the atmosphere really tense as well. I liked the way Miles and Ram used multi-roling to play Amerie's new friends, who thought they were really cool, and Jay's friends, who were less confident. It showed how, even though their parts weren't as big as Amerie's and Jay's, they were still clearly really good actors.

**Please comment on anything you did not understand or felt did not work:** I felt like the ending should be clearer. Do they stop being friends completely? It seemed a bit sad and unrealistic to have them totally forget about each other. They could still be friendly but have their own separate groups of friends too.

## Example questionnaire 2

**Group members:** Amerie, Ram, Miles and Jay     **Scene title:** 'Far Apart'

**Describe the plot as it came across to you:** Amerie had dumped her best friend, Jay, to hang out with a new group. Jay felt let down. But in the end Jay realised she had grown out of that friendship.

**Describe the characters as they came across to you:** Miles and Ram play Amerie's loud friends and Jay's quiet friends in turn: a chorus commenting on the action.

**Please comment on what you felt worked best:** I liked the way the friends of both main characters commented on the action, and the whispered sound effects to show the effect gossip could have.

**Please comment on anything you did not understand or felt did not work:** I think the acting should have been more stylised to fit with the lighting. I felt using the lighting as a barrier distracted from the acting too much. If there'd been more, shorter scenes instead of one really long one there might have been more tension.

---

**ACTIVITY 6.2**

If you received the questionnaire answers shown above, what decisions would you make? How would you write them up?

# Portfolio of evidence: What have I learnt?

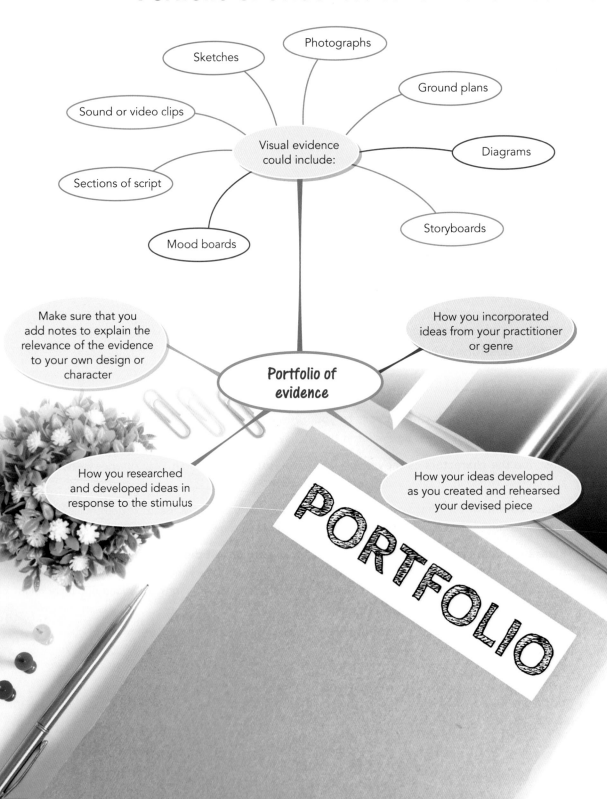

Photographs

Sketches

Ground plans

Sound or video clips

Visual evidence could include:

Diagrams

Sections of script

Storyboards

Mood boards

Make sure that you add notes to explain the relevance of the evidence to your own design or character

How you incorporated ideas from your practitioner or genre

Portfolio of evidence

How you researched and developed ideas in response to the stimulus

How your ideas developed as you created and rehearsed your devised piece

PORTFOLIO

## What is a written evaluation?

AO4

A written evaluation is a report about your own contribution to your devised piece. It explains your ideas, how they developed and how well they worked in front of an audience.

## What do I need to do?

Your written evaluation needs three main ingredients. Analysing and evaluating each of these three will create a good written evaluation:

1  Your interpretation of your character/role (acting) or your realisation of your design in the final performance (design).
2  How your own performance or design skills contributed to the effectiveness of the final performance.
3  Your individual contribution, including how you fulfilled your initial aims and objectives – referring to the practitioner or genre your group chose.

## How long will I have to write my evaluation?

You will have 1 hour and 30 minutes to write your evaluation under exam conditions. However, you are allowed to bring two A4 sheets of bullet pointed notes to help you. The exercises and activities in this section will help you to get the best from your notes and turn them into a good written evaluation in your exam. For help on how to prepare your bullet points, see pages 118–123.

### LINK

If you are battling 'page fright', take a look at the tips on page 8 to ensure your fear does not get in the way of your communication skills.

### EXERCISE 7.1

Discuss the following questions informally as a group:

- In your performance, what came across as you and your group had intended?
- What might you do differently in another performance?

You might find the discussion prompts help you to think of new ideas, as well as helping to clarify the ideas you already have.

Writing your evaluation

## Section 1: Your interpretation of your character/role or your realisation of your design in the final performance.

Start by stating:

- Which skill you chose, 😀😣 acting or ⁞⁞⁞ design, and
- 😀😣 the character you are playing, or
- ⁞⁞⁞ your chosen design option.

> 😀😣 I played Nisha, the former best friend of the main character, 'Polly'. I liked the idea of playing this role because, from Polly's point of view, Nisha is a baddie, having distanced herself since they joined their new school, but I saw it as a chance to use Stanislavskian techniques to explore motivation and understand Nisha's side of the story and her actions. I decided how Nisha's interests had changed since her friendship with Polly: she felt trapped in her old habits and wanted to explore new interests. I thought about how her body language would show how she still misses Polly, but knows they've grown apart and wants Polly to move on too.

 **TIP**

Give examples of performance choices you made, then give the reasons for your choices.

> ⁞⁞⁞ I chose design and wanted to use the space to reflect the theme of isolation. As Polly is our scene's main character, and she is feeling isolated from the other characters, I wanted the design to show how cut off she feels. Initially, I considered dividing the stage as if there was a crack in the floor, cutting Polly off. But when we wrote the line about feeling trapped, I suggested using lighting to suggest a cage Polly was in that only she could see.

## Section 2: How your own performance skills or design skills contributed to the effectiveness of the final performance.

AO 4

In this section you should:

- Describe your individual contribution to the final performance.
- Analyse and evaluate how your skills were used.
- Show how you could tell your choices were effective.
- Give examples from your final performance.
- Explain what worked well and what did not work as well.

🎭 It was a challenge for me playing Polly, as I am used to playing very confident characters. It helped me to imagine that Polly was very confident in the days when she and Nisha were friends, but the feeling of rejection had changed her. I used Stanislavski's magic 'if' to help me work out what could make me feel distrusting and fearful when I used to be confident. As Nisha's rejection of her was something she did not understand, and as she did not know what she had done wrong, Polly mistrusted herself and her actions. Instead of making her body language stereotypically shy, I tried making her movements jerky, and her expression tense and on edge.

In the final duologue between Nisha and Polly, where Polly finds out why Nisha distanced herself, I was aware the contrast between Nisha's confident, slow pace and my character's jerky nervousness helped show how the balance of power had changed. I think my ideas about Polly's movement really contributed to the success of the duologue for this reason. However, from the audience questionnaires we put out in the dress rehearsal, I don't think it was clear enough that in the end Polly understands she has to learn more about who she is and find her own friends and not just rely on her old friendships. I think the visual image of Polly stepping through her cage of light at the end could have been clearer.

🎭 Your character's performance – physically, vocally, mentally, lines – what came across well and what would you change or improve and why?

🎭 It was difficult to decide when the cage of light should be visible, so I had to think of ways for other things to not be distracted by it. In group scenes, we came up with the idea of using a flood of daylight so the cage is less noticeable, such as in the classroom. But when Polly is alone, or when Nisha and her friends are ignoring her, the blue light is clearest.

The part I feel didn't feel worked as well as I would have liked was the final scene. When Polly realises Nisha has been encouraging her to pursue her own friends and interests, we wanted Polly to understand she could do this and feel more powerful. However, that didn't feel like enough on its own for the light to disappear. The sound designer suggested using keys in a lock as Polly stepped out, but the audience questionnaires agreed with me – Polly's motivation wasn't strong enough for the audience to see a big change was happening.

🎭 Your design's performance – what helped the audience understand the concepts, what worked well for the actors, what did not do either of these things and what have you learnt from that?

## Section 3: Your individual contribution, including how you fulfilled your initial aims and objectives – referring to your chosen practitioner or genre.

Make sure that you include:

- A link with the stimulus you chose.
- A link with the practitioner or genre you chose.
- Your individual contribution to fulfilling your group's aims and objectives.
- Audience feedback (if appropriate).

**Individual contribution examples:**

> Link to stimulus material.

• Of the stimuli we were given, we were most interested in the picture of a group of people with one separated from the rest. This gave us the idea of isolation, and what it was like to feel socially isolated from a group …

> Link with practitioner

• 🎭 We enjoyed the experience of using Stanislavski's magic 'if' to develop our characters, asking questions about how we would behave and feel if we were those characters. The questions I asked of my own character included: 'What has made me want to push my friend away?' I found this very helpful in working out why an apparently nasty thing to do had felt like the right thing for Nisha.

> Individual contribution

• 🎭 Each of us chose one of the figures in the image and used their body language as a starting point. From there, we used hot-seating to develop our characters from our magic 'if' questions. One example, which I found particularly helpful, was being asked which of the other characters I admired. This gave me the idea that Nisha would mirror the body language of Eve, the most confident person in the group.

> Individual contribution

• 👥 To illustrate the changing emotional state of the character, I chose colours for the box of light Polly was trapped in. Characters standing outside the box of light showed how isolated she was by her mental state. It also meant that actors had lots of room to move around in.

🎭 Our audience was made up of members of our year group, which was a suitable age bracket for dealing with some of the sensitive issues raised in the play and meant they were able to notice my design and how it affected the play more. It was also useful to have older teenagers in the audience, as we felt this would get the most useful comments on the audience feedback forms, and they were able to comment on how the empty staging and use of light to isolate Polly from the other characters reflected the theme.

Audience feedback

## Tips for writing your evaluation

🎭 Ending the play with a duologue between my character, Nisha, and Polly was an idea that was very important to me. Although it's not a happy ending in the way Polly wanted, it shows both characters have moved on. I could tell from the audience's reaction that this was a moving ending and I am particularly proud of that.

I wanted to show how Nisha's status in the group changed, and used body language to reflect her lessening confidence. I was proud of how different I was able to make her seem from the beginning as her story went on.

**TIP**

Say what you were most proud of.

⚃ Although we don't use spotlights in any other scene, I was pleased with my decision to fade to a spotlight on Polly at the end of the final scene. I intended this to show how it was up to her, now that she had the power to move on with her life however she wanted.

**TIP**

Remember to state which stimulus your group chose, and what ideas it gave you. Did it suggest a theme or a central character? Or was there another starting point?

🎭 The mood of the music made us think of a character who was very lonely, which gave us the theme of isolation.

Music

🎭 We imagine the person who stated the quote was regretting something from the past. We decided this was a story about revenge.

Theme

**TIP**

It's okay to talk about what did not work or was difficult to do. Say what did not work, why it did not work, and how you would do it differently in future.

**TIP**

Evaluate how your ideas contributed to other people's roles as well as your own.

 My character dialogue presented a problem as it was all written in long sentences, and it was difficult to make it sound like natural dialogue instead of an essay. The result of this was the pace of the scene slowed in the dialogue scenes, so it lost its impact. If I were devising dialogue again, I would make the pace and voice better by writing shorter sentences that sound more realistic.

 I was reluctant to give up the idea of the crack in the stage separating Polly and Nisha, but I'm glad to have had the challenge to think how to get the meaning across using a lighting effect. I could tell the audience were really engrossed in the scene where Polly is trapped by this cage of light that none of the other characters can see, and it showed my design really helped the actors express their characters' feelings.

**Acting**

I've always really enjoyed playing confident characters, so Polly was a challenge because she didn't have any confidence left and was so shy. I tried to imagine what it was like not to be able to just go up to people, and show that not by pushing against the cage of light she was trapped in but by walking up to the edge then stepping back, so it was her feelings that were keeping her back and not just the light. I'm really proud of how I was able to show her personality, so the audience understood her feelings and felt sorry for her, and they also were able to understand how the blue light showed how caged in and trapped Polly felt. If I hadn't made Polly so realistic, I don't think her final dialogue with Nisha could have been such a moving end to the scene.

**Set design**

I'm glad that I contributed the idea of using levels in the conversation between my character and her mother, as this gave the set designer the idea of using a platform that could be used in all the scenes.

**Set lighting**

I was glad my idea of using lighting to show the invisible barrier around the main character helped the audience and the actor playing her feel her sense of isolation. The warmer light upstage also showed how she perceived the other characters as happier and I was glad the audience understood that so well.

I was glad my idea of using the single prop of the empty armchair worked to show that, even though the main character was living his life, he was still grieving for his grandmother.

Props

I continued to develop posture and body language to show how shut-off my character felt from the more flexible, faster-moving characters outside the box. I came up with the idea of making her movements slower than everyone else's, as if slightly in slo-mo, and the group came up with the idea that everyone else was slightly sped up. This helped to build the impression of her depression and isolation.

**TIP**

If your idea didn't work at first, make sure you explain how you changed or improved it.

As the actors were experimenting with pace, I came up with the idea of slowing down the background sound so that the school corridor we were imagining came across as slowed down.

Sound design

**EXERCISE 7.2** AO 4

In your group, make a list of how you used the following skills. Try writing sentences about each other's performances or design ideas and how they were used.

Movement    Status    Physical Theatre

Pace    Facial expression    Live sound

Lighting    Voice    Levels

Rhythm    Blocking

## ACTIVITY 7.1 ———————————————— AO 3 AO 4

Sometimes it is easier to talk than write.

1 Turn the following conversation into bullet points.

🎭 I played Polly, she's been best friends with Nisha for years but now they're in a new school and she feels like Nisha's blanking her. The idea came from a picture that was one of the stimulus options, it was a crowd of people with one on the outside. We were like, who are these people from their body language? What unites them as a group and what are the little rivalries in that group? We did loads of Stanislavski exercises to explore who our characters were – magic 'if', given circumstances, emotion memory – got to know their world really well and to link our characters' feelings to our own feelings. Then we hot-seated the characters. This helped me think about how Polly misses Nisha but is doing basically the worst things about it. If anyone else is around she wants Nisha to herself, but Nisha wants to make new friends. I worked loads with my friend who's playing Nisha, so we got a dialogue going where there's loads of subtext because neither of them is saying what's wrong. We split the dialogue into two scenes showing the friendship at the beginning of the play and the end.

> **TIP**
>
> Try recording yourself talking about your devised scene and performance with a friend. Listen to the recording and make bullet points to help you include all the important points in your written evaluation.

2 Read the conversation below and write bullet points to show how this idea changed and evolved during the rehearsal process.

🎭 So we clearly needed the stage to represent the friendship and at first I sketched out ways we could divide the stage so the characters never cross it, but that didn't give the actors much space to move around. So, in the end, I thought how about Polly being trapped in a cage of light and none of the other characters notice, but she can't leave this square of blue, which is what being isolated can feel like.

3 Now, think of an idea that changed during your rehearsal process. Write it in bullet points, and then develop the bullet points into clear sentences.

## EXERCISE 7.3

AO 3  AO 4

Imagine that you are using a messaging app to describe how your performance or design skills contributed to the effectiveness of your final performance.

Now, turn your messages into bullet points.

## ACTIVITY 7.2

AO 3  AO 4

The following questions could be used to help you write your evaluation.

> **What stimulus did you pick and why?**

> **What ideas were communicated clearly?**

> **If you did it again, what would you improve?**

> **How did your character or design communicate your ideas?**

> **What ideas weren't clear enough?**

> I chose the title 'You've Got to Go There to Come Back' by the Stereophonics. It made me think about journeys, not just from one place to another but of a character growing up and looking at things differently.

> My choice of stimulus was the picture of the statue. I was interested in how it could be two people hugging, using each other for support, or two people fighting and pushing against each other.

Write answers to the questions above, then make a bullet list of all the points in your answers – this can be developed into the list you take into your exam.

# Written evaluation: What have I learnt?

1 hour 30 minutes

You can take up to two A4 sides of bullet points in with you

Exam conditions

**Written evaluation**

Give examples of each point

Details, examples, evidence

Refer to your stimulus

Effectiveness of ideas in performance

Refer to your genre or practitioner

Show how you achieved them

Three sections

Give your aims and objectives

Interpretation of character/design

Performance or design skills

Contribution overall

This chapter will help you to produce:

- your performance or design for your group's performance; a visiting examiner will assess this
- an artistic intentions form. This is submitted to help the examiner assess how successfully you have expressed your ideas in your performance.

# What is performing from a text?

Like devising a scene, performing from a text means using your skills to express meaning and ideas onstage. Unlike devising, the meaning and ideas will be those of a published playwright instead of your own.

## What do I need to do?

You will work in groups of up to four actors and up to two designers. You will study two 10-minute extracts from a single performance text.

Your performance or design will be based on the themes, characters, setting or other elements in your scenes.

You will choose whether to be assessed as an actor or a designer:

Each actor must interact with the other performers/the audience for a minimum of 5 minutes.

There can be up to two designers for every group of actors (however, a group of actors does not have to have designers).

Each designer must offer a different design skill (lighting, sound, set or costume).

For your chosen design skill, you must use a minimum of:

- four different lighting states
- four different sound cues
- one set, created for the performance, with appropriate props and set dressing
- one full costume (including hair and make-up) for one character.

**TIP**

You do not have to choose one of the suggested texts from the specification – you can use any suitable text. Use the bullet points to make sure you have chosen a text that provides a good contrast to your Component/Unit 3 text.

# Selecting a text

You need to choose a text that contrasts with your Component/Unit 3 text. This means it needs to have a different:

- **theme** – the texts must explore different concepts or issues
- **playwright** – the texts must be written by different people
- **setting** – the texts must be set in different times and places
- **era** – the texts must have been written at different times.

You can find a list of suggested texts in your GCSE specification.

**TIP**

Very different plays can still share a theme. For example, *1984* and *Two Faces* (both WJEC Unit 3 options) both explore identity and how it can be challenged. Make sure the text you choose for Component/Unit 2 contrasts with your Component/Unit 3 text in all the required areas.

# How do I select passages of text?

It is a good idea to find passages that are not too close together. This will help you to demonstrate an understanding of the play as a whole and not just the beginning, middle or end.

- Choose two 10-minute extracts from the same text.
- Choose enough dialogue from each extract to make the overall story clear.
- Remember you cannot add dialogue or characters that are not written into your extracts.

## ACTIVITY 8.1

As a group, read aloud a scene you are considering using from near the beginning of your text. What questions are being asked? What events or choices are being set up?

## ACTIVITY 8.2

Pick one of the questions or choices your opening scene sets up and work together to find a scene that shows what choice is made or what answer is developed.

# How long should the performance be?

This depends on the number of actors in your group.

- Two actors: 5–10 minutes
- Three actors: 7–12 minutes
- Four actors: 9–14 minutes

# Preparing your performance

You do not need to use the whole 20 minutes of text you have studied. However, you do need to perform enough to show that you have fully understood both extracts. The final performance must be a 'coherent interpretation' of the text.

Here are some examples of how you might divide your extracts for your final performance (coherent interpretation):

| Number of actors | From extract 1 | From extract 2 |
|---|---|---|
| Two | 2 minutes | 3 minutes |
| Three | 5 minutes | 5 minutes |
| Four | Frame scene: 2 minutes; Scene 1: 8 minutes | 3 minutes |

# Outline of artistic intentions

## What do I need to do?

You will need to submit a brief account (approximately 150 words/half a side of A4) outlining your artistic intentions for your performance. Your artistic intentions form will help the examiner to assess how well you have achieved your intended interpretation.

Your artistic intentions should include:

1 How you aim to:

 🎭 interpret your character

 or

2 👥 set the scene based on your understanding of the chosen text.

 How you edited the two 10-minute extracts to create the script of your final performance.

Whether you are an actor or designer, try asking yourself the following questions when thinking about your artistic intentions:

- Are my artistic choices based on the text? What dialogue or stage directions prompted my choices?
- Do I fully understand the lines I am basing my choices on?
- Are my choices being communicated clearly to the audience?

## EXERCISE 8.1

On the next page are two examples of outlines of artistic intention. As a group, discuss how each of these artistic intentions forms gives an indication of what the performance was like.

**TIP**

Your performance can contain monologues, but cannot consist entirely of them.

**TIP**

When you are making cuts, make sure that you keep the most important lines or events. Ensure that anyone who doesn't know the play as well as you can follow the action.

**TIP**

You can download the artistic intentions form you need to complete from the WJEC website.

**TIP**

In your dress rehearsal, give your artistic intentions form to your invited audience. Ask if they can identify the intentions from your performance or design.

| Component/Unit 2 text, playwright and date written | *Too Fast* (National Theatre Connections, 2011) Douglas Maxwell; 2011 | |
|---|---|---|
| Component/Unit 3 text, playwright and date written | *Romeo and Juliet* (1595) Shakespeare; 1590–1595 | |
| Brief account of both extracts | **1** Pages 15–25 | **2** Pages 36–41 |

### Write a brief account of how you aim to interpret your chosen character.

I am playing the role of DD.

My artistic intentions are:

To show DD changing at a key moment: when Laila confronts her about their father. Before, DD is aggressive, bullying the other members of her choir. Afterwards, she listens more and apologises before they go onstage.

To show that DD still wants popularity, but sees better ways to achieve it. I want my body language to show less assertiveness and more awareness of others after her confrontation.

We cut the first scene to show DD is insistent on getting what she wants by force, until Laila confronts her and she learns to cooperate.

The two contrasting scenes are:

- Pages 15–25, when DD lays out her aims for the choir and insults anyone who disagrees with her.
- Pages 36–41, when Laila confronts DD's desperation to get on TV, showing her she needs friendship not fame.

| Chosen design skill: | Set design | |
|---|---|---|
| Component/Unit 2 text, playwright and date written: | *Too Fast* (National Theatre Connections, 2011) Douglas Maxwell; 2011 | |
| Component/Unit 3 text, playwright and date written: | *Romeo and Juliet* (1595) Shakespeare; 1590–1595 | |
| Brief account of both extracts: | **1** Pages 15–25 | **2** Pages 36–41 |

### Write a brief account of how you aim to interpret your chosen extracts/character(s) through design: (you may include additional illustrative material to support your artistic intentions).

I designed the set for *Too Fast*.

My artistic intentions are:

- To show the claustrophobia and fear of the choir waiting for their performance at the funeral. I used cardboard boxes and other abandoned objects to suggest a side-room.
- To show the importance of the key moment in the play, where DD is confronted by her sister Laila. I used the arch window frame to suggest more light coming into the room after their confrontation.
- We edited the first scene to show DD's controlling nature towards the others, telling them what to think and feel. We edited the second scene to show her listening more and apologising to Sean and the others.

The two contrasting scenes are:

- Pages 15–25, DD giving orders of what to do and even think.
- Pages 36–41, Laila showing why DD is behaving badly, and the following conversations and apologies before they go onstage.

# Performing from a text: What have I learnt?

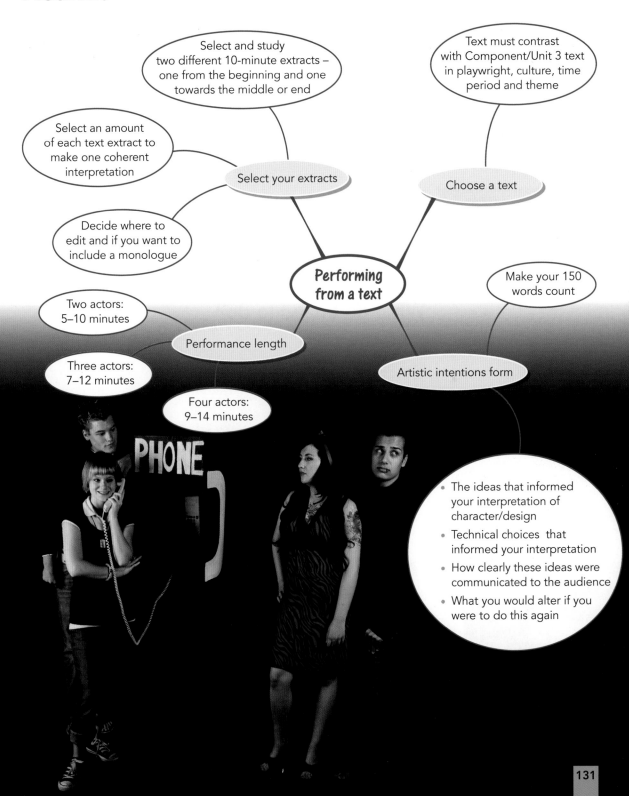

Select and study two different 10-minute extracts – one from the beginning and one towards the middle or end

Text must contrast with Component/Unit 3 text in playwright, culture, time period and theme

Select an amount of each text extract to make one coherent interpretation

Select your extracts

Choose a text

Decide where to edit and if you want to include a monologue

Performing from a text

Make your 150 words count

Two actors: 5–10 minutes

Performance length

Three actors: 7–12 minutes

Artistic intentions form

Four actors: 9–14 minutes

- The ideas that informed your interpretation of character/design
- Technical choices that informed your interpretation
- How clearly these ideas were communicated to the audience
- What you would alter if you were to do this again

## CHAPTER 9 / INTERPRETING THEATRE

This chapter will help you to:

- study one performance text, approaching it as an actor, designer and director
- write an evaluation of a live theatre production.

**TIP**

Make sure you have the copy of your texts prescribed by the exam board.

## What is interpreting theatre?

Interpreting theatre is using your knowledge and understanding of developing drama and theatre for performance. You will demonstrate that knowledge by responding to a performance text and to a live theatre performance.

## What do I need to do?

You will have a written examination of 1 hour and 30 minutes, into which you can bring a clean copy (no annotations) of the text you have studied.

# SECTION A: STUDYING A PERFORMANCE TEXT

The text you study must contrast in theme, be culturally different, from a different time period and by a different author from your performance (Component/Unit 2) text.

---

**ACTIVITY 9.1** ────────────────────────────── AO **3** ─ AO **4**

In your group, discuss the characteristics of your set text, identifying differences between your Component/Unit 2 text and your Component/Unit 3 text.

Think about:

- themes
- genre
- time it was written
- time it is set
- structure
- character

- form and style
- language and dialogue
- stage directions
- social, historical and cultural context, including theatrical conventions of the period
- where the performance text was created.

---

## How the text is constructed and how performances create meaning

Exam questions are based on the features of the text, so the better you know those, the better equipped you are for the exam.

This chapter provides notes on the characteristics of your performance text. Reading these and recognising the characteristics in your texts will help you to understand the performance choices theatre companies make in order to communicate the text's meaning, which will help you to do the same.

In a production, meaning can be interpreted and communicated through:

- performance conventions
- use of performance space and spatial relationships onstage, including the impact of different stages (proscenium arch, theatre in the round, traverse and thrust) on at least one scene
- relationships between performers and audience
- the design of lighting, sound, set (including props) and costume and make-up
- the actor's vocal and physical interpretation of character.

# Set texts

## WJEC

### *Romeo and Juliet* by William Shakespeare

**Written**: 1595.

**Themes**: Love and hate, individual versus society, revenge, death, fate.

**Genre**: Tragedy.

**Structure**: Prologue and five acts.

**Plot summary**

Two important families in Verona – the Montagues and the Capulets – have a long-running, violent feud. Lord Montague's son, Romeo, and Lord Capulet's daughter, Juliet, meet at a party and fall in love. Juliet's cousin, Tybalt, tries to pick a fight with Romeo, who resists, but Tybalt persists and kills Romeo's friend Mercutio; Romeo then slays Tybalt and is banished from Verona. Before Romeo leaves, he and Juliet agree to marry in secret, with the help of their mutual friend and advisor, Friar Laurence. Unaware their daughter is already married, the Capulets betroth her to Paris. Friar Laurence helps her plot the faking of her own death (with the use of a poison that simulates death for a time) to avoid the marriage, but the message of what they are planning does not reach Romeo in time. He discovers Juliet (seemingly dead) and kills himself with poison before Juliet wakes; she discovers him and kills herself with his dagger. Their parents find the bodies of their children and make peace.

**Main characters**:

Romeo, 16-year-old son of the Montagues.

Juliet, nearly 14, daughter of the Capulets.

Mercutio, kinsman of the prince and Romeo's friend.

Benvolio, Romeo's cousin.

Friar Laurence, confessor and friend to both Romeo and Juliet.

Nurse, Juliet's lifelong companion.

Tybalt, Juliet's cousin.

**Form and style**: Poetic in moments of heightened emotion. Prose for more common moments, people and subjects.

**Language and dialogue**: Strong imagery and metaphors relate the characters' emotions to the audience – as do the rude jokes.

**Stage directions**: Minimal. Dialogue conveys character, situation and setting.

**Stage and setting**: The play was written for a simple thrust stage with a balcony and limited backstage areas. However, the minimal stage directions and clear characterisation in the dialogue mean it can be set in any configuration, time or place.

**Social, historical and cultural contexts, including theatrical conventions of the period where the performance text was created**: England was a patriarchal society with outbreaks of violence in the streets. By setting his plays in fictional versions of other countries, Shakespeare is able to comment on his own country's social problems.

The following exercises will help you to explore and demonstrate your knowledge and understanding of how drama and theatre are developed and performed.

## EXERCISE 9.1

AO 3 — AO 4

**1 'Two households, both alike in dignity' (Prologue)**

Have a look at the **Prologue**. If you knew nothing else about *Romeo and Juliet*, and you were a member of Shakespeare's audience seeing this play for the first time, what would you think was going to happen? Note down your ideas and compare them with others in your group.

**2 'Did my heart love till now?'**

Before Romeo meets Juliet, he was in love with someone else. What point do you think Shakespeare was making by having Romeo already displaying the same romantic feelings before he meets Juliet? Note down your ideas and compare them with others in your group.

**3 'Wherefore art thou Romeo?'**

As a group, look at the balcony scene (Act 2, Scene 2).

**A** Discuss these questions:

  **a)** Why does Juliet ask this question, which means 'why must you be Romeo (a Montague)?'

  **b)** How tempted do you think Romeo is to 'deny thy father and refuse thy name' in order to be with Juliet?

  **c)** What do you think would have happened if he did?

  **d)** How does the staging – separation of the characters – help with the meaning of this scene?

**B** Imagine you had a black-box theatre space, so could have any stage format.

Which of the following formats would you use to stage your balcony scene and why?

- Proscenium arch with thrust stage
- Minimalist with elements of contemporary props and costume

**C** Now pick any other scene in the play to see how your format would work for that one too.

## WJEC

### *100* by Christopher Heimann, Neil Monaghan and Diene Petterle

**Written**: 2002.

**Themes**: Memory, identity, life and death.

**Genre**: Physical Theatre.

**Structure**: Continuous, giving a sense of the choice being made in natural time (they have one hour to decide on the memory where they will spend eternity).

**Plot summary**

Four characters find themselves in a mysterious 'void'. They are informed by 'the Guide' that they must choose one memory from their lives in which to spend eternity. The play follows these individual memories. Produced by the Imaginary Body theatre company for the Edinburgh Fringe Festival in 2002, this play won a Fringe First for 'innovation in theatre and outstanding new production' (The Imaginary Body, 2020).

**Characters**: Multi-roling: each actor becomes part of every character's memories.

**Language and dialogue**: Modern.

**Social, historical and cultural contexts, including theatrical conventions of the period where the performance text was created**: Original Physical Theatre work.

**Stage and setting**: The description of the setting is a 'void' with four, apparently randomly placed blocks. Lighting creates selective visibility. In the original production, the actors had only a bamboo stick each.

The following exercises will help you to explore and demonstrate your knowledge and understanding of how drama and theatre are developed and performed.

## EXERCISE 9.2

AO 3 — AO 4

1 As a group, read through Alex's memory scene (pages 16–19). Discuss how you would perform this scene as a Physical Theatre piece.

   **a)** See how much you can do without props, costume or anything else – how much meaning can you convey using only body and voice?

   **b)** If you could use only minimal lighting or sound-effects for this scene, what would be the most helpful way these could be used to convey atmosphere or meaning?

2 Discuss your own 'memory' scene.
How can you make use of the non-naturalistic setting and multi-roling to characterise who and what appears in the memory?

## WJEC

### *1984*, adapted by Robert Icke and Duncan Macmillan from the novel *Nineteen Eighty-Four* by George Orwell

**Written**: Adapted for the stage in 2013. Novel published 1949.

**Themes**: Identity, control, propaganda, technology.

**Characters**: Winston Smith, Julia, O'Brien, Big Brother (never appears but perceived ruler of Oceana), Mr Charrington, Syme, Mrs Parsons, Martin Parsons.

**Plot summary**

Winston Smith tries to resist the oppression of the citizens of Oceania, where the Party scrutinises every human action through the ever-watching Big Brother and individuality is banned. In pursuing a relationship with Julia, and in writing a diary, Winston Smith is a criminal and the state sets out to reform this nonconformist.

**Form and style**: Urgent, aggressive, dystopian (set in a negative/frightening version of the future).

**Language and dialogue**: Written to reflect 'newspeak', the language George Orwell invented in which politicians have removed unwelcome thoughts from the language of the people in order to control them.

**Stage directions**: Need for projections suggests end-on format.

**Social, historical and cultural contexts, including theatrical conventions of the period where the performance text was created**: Orwell's novel was inspired by the 20th century's totalitarian regimes, including Nazi Germany and Soviet Russia. These levels of state control led Orwell to imagine what would happen if machines could watch everyone all the time – both body and mind.

**Stage and setting**: Proscenium arch allows use of projections on the cyclorama wall.

The following exercises will help you to explore and demonstrate your knowledge and understanding of how drama and theatre are developed and performed.

## EXERCISE 9.3

AO 3 — AO 4

**'Big Brother is watching you'**

*1984* imagines a world in which the Thought Police control not only every citizen's actions but their thoughts as well – and, if they fall short, send them to 'Room 101' for punishment by whatever is their deepest fear. Slogans include 'Freedom is slavery' and 'Ignorance is strength'.

a) How would you use Physical Theatre to show that individuality is outlawed? What would a street scene look like? How about behaviour inside the home?

b) Hot-seat each member of your group in turn. Ask them to talk about something they love without showing any emotion for 2 minutes. Is it possible?

c) Mr Charrington is one of the most frightening characters because he appears to be on Winston's side. How could you communicate his personality at the beginning, middle and end of the play? Try using freeze-frames to see how your blocking, staging, facial expressions and body language show the changes emerging.

### LINK

For more on hot-seating, see page 47.

## WJEC

# Two Faces (*Dau Wyneb*) by Manon Steffan Ros

**Written**: 2016, specifically for the GCSE Drama course.

**Themes**: Identity, images, how others see you.

**Characters**: Four actors, multi-rolling: Sam/Ellis, 17 year old/middle-aged.
Helena, their first victim.
Mai (44), Elen's mother and Ellis' lover.
Elen (16), Mai's daughter, subsequent victim.
Fiona (40s), wife of Sam/Ellis and daughter-in-law to Jim.
Jim, elderly father of Sam/Ellis, father-in-law to Fiona.
Matthew (16), Elen's friend.

## Plot summary

Inspired by the social changes created in the wake of the internet, Ros' play explores identity on the internet and how people present a 'better, happier' version of themselves. The play asks if, when we do that, we are lying about who we are. Ellen falls in love online with a stranger she only knows as 'Sam'. In 'hooking' her, he uses a system to make his victims want to meet him, playing to their vanity and playing on their insecurities. The play explores self-identity, and the different sides of self that everyone has, and how this can be manipulated.

**Form and style**: Three scenes. Non-naturalistic. Characters who never meet in reality speak to each other.

**Language and dialogue**: Contemporary – both in speech and in the digital sound-effects that are part of communication (Skype tones, telephone dials).

**Important effects**: Selective visibility, follow-spot.

**Stage directions**: Multiple at first, disappearing as the narrative continues.

**Stage and setting**: The stage needs to be divided into two areas for the play to work (Elen's and Sam's homes), so a proscenium arch formation is recommended.

Proscenium arch or thrust set is helpful as actors sometimes walk in from the audience or walk out of the play into the audience. Use of levels, entering and exiting action.

**Social, historical and cultural contexts, including theatrical conventions of the period when the performance text was created**: 'I have a significant interest in the social changes that have been brought about by the internet. I'm not one of these who thinks that it's all bad, but the way we interact with each other these days is totally different. The play deals with our web-identity, and the way we use the best of our selfies to be posted on Facebook, introducing an enhanced and happier aspect of ourselves to the world. In doing so, are we lying about who we really are?' (Ros, 2016).

These exercises will help you to explore and demonstrate your knowledge and understanding of how drama and theatre are developed and performed.

## EXERCISE 9.4 — AO 3 AO 4

1 **Staging**

   Discuss the effect of the actors leaving the play and entering the audience. What messages does this convey?

2 **Open endings**

   The ending of this play suggests that Sam/Ellis has arranged to meet Elen and Mai.

   a) What do you think is the effect of letting us know this meeting will take place but not including it in the action?

   b) In groups, improvise how the scene might take place.

3 **Technical considerations**

   This is a play with multiple locations and characters. In small groups, discuss how the following aspects could be used to best effect:

   - stage configuration
   - naturalistic or minimalist set design
   - lighting and sound design
   - projections or special effects.

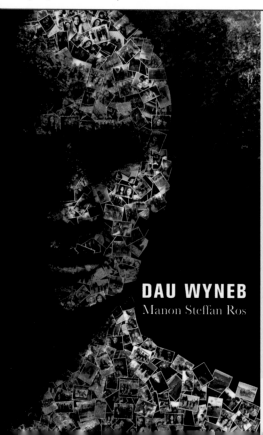

DAU WYNEB
Manon Steffan Ros

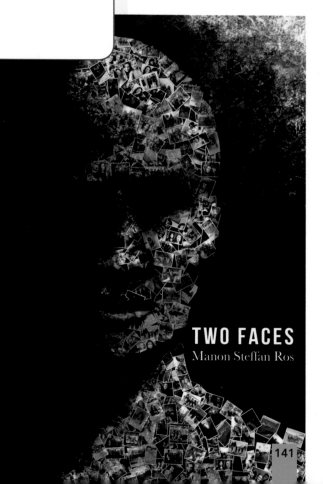

TWO FACES
Manon Steffan Ros

WJEC

## *Shadow of the Sickle (Cysgod y Cryman)*, adapted for the stage by Siôn Eirian from the novel by Islwyn Ffowc Elis

**Written**: Novel published 1953. Staged 2007.

**Themes**: Impact of new ideas and beliefs – personal, political and familial conflict.

**Form and style**: Based on the speech patterns of the area, reflecting the age, education and intentions of the characters.

### Plot summary

A mid-Wales farming community, where individuals and families face great changes in the aftermath of World War II. Harri Vaughan becomes a communist and an atheist who rejects the fiancée he was expected to marry, and rises above his political and personal conflicts to face his father, while quitting university to become a labourer with the local council. As the son of Edward Vaughan, the local landowner, this means political, religious and personal tension. But, in sticking to his principles, Harri finally sees the social change he believes his community needs, when his father loses to Arweinydd Francis as district councillor.

**Genre**: Political.

**Structure**: Episodic. Two acts divided into four scenes each. Various locations.

**Characters**: Multi-roling – 23 characters: Harri Vaughan, Edward Vaughan, Margaret Vaughan, Greta Vaughan.

**Language and dialogue**: Welsh and English translations; contemporary.

**Stage directions**: Multiple locations and episodes.

**Stage and setting**: Bare stage, indicative props and costume. Lighting used for selective visibility.

**Social, historical and cultural contexts, including theatrical conventions of the period when the performance text was created**: Set in a small community in post-war Powys, Wales. While the specifics of communism and farm labour communities may seem dated, the theme of intergenerational conflict over political movements and traditional customs, an individual's beliefs and religious, sexual and political identity versus their parents' traditions remains deeply relevant.

These exercises will help you to explore and demonstrate your knowledge and understanding of how drama and theatre are developed and performed.

## EXERCISE 9.5
AO 3 · AO 4

1 The original best-selling book of *Shadow of the Sickle* was considered an important milestone in the history of the Welsh novel.

Discuss the following questions with your group:

a) What do you think was so striking about Harri Vaughan, the son of a wealthy estate owner and leader of the community, being influenced by Gwylan Thomas and his communist and atheist beliefs?

b) What do you think people were afraid would happen as a result?

c) How does the conflict between Harri and his father represent generational conflict?

d) The sickle is the symbol for communism, but it is also relevant in Harri's community. How do Harri's beliefs become a 'sickle' in another way?

2 **'Your father in law, Harri, coming to keep an eye on you. To see how you can handle a pitchfork after three years in college.'**

Of the minor roles, the farmhand Will James is perhaps the most complex. His racist beliefs and actions and difficult personality cannot be caricatured.

Try hot-seating this character to help you understand the motivation and fears that underlie his personality.

3 Write a dialogue between a parent and a young adult, set in your town today.

a) What issue of identity might they disagree on?

b) Can they accept each other for who they are?

c) What will be the repercussions for each of them if they don't?

Theatr Genedlaethol Cymru production of *Shadow of the Sickle*, directed by Cefin Roberts.

## Eduqas

### *The Tempest* by William Shakespeare

**Written**: 1610–1611.

**Structure**: Nine scenes. The shortest of Shakespeare's plays.

**Themes**: Love, power, illusion, loss, revenge, reconciliation, forgiveness.

**Genre**: Comedy AND romance AND tragedy. A 'problem play' – meaning it does not fit into a specific genre but combines aspects of different ones. Comedy aspects include the happy ending, wedding and dance. Prospero's revenge plot against those who made Miranda and him outcasts belongs to a tragedy.

**Plot summary**

Prospero, rightful Duke of Milan, and his daughter Miranda are exiles on an island somewhere near Italy. In his years of exile, Prospero has learned magic and is master over the island's natives: Ariel, a sprite, and Caliban, a strange wild man somewhat like a human and somewhat like a fish. Prospero summons a storm at sea – a tempest – stranding those who exiled them and separating the company from each other, including King Alonso from his son Ferdinand. Ferdinand falls in love with Miranda and works to win Prospero's favour. There is a final reconciliation, and marriage, and Prospero's dukedom is restored to him. Prospero frees his servant Ariel and everyone sails for home.

**Main characters**:

Prospero, wronged duke of Milan.

Miranda, his daughter.

Ariel, spirit native of the island.

Caliban, native of the island.

Ferdinand, son of Alonso, King of Naples.

**Form and style**: Poetic language, more complex and solemn to reflect the noble status of certain characters. Others speak more plainly and directly.

**Language and dialogue**: Verse form in moments of high emotion. Text follows in iambic pentameter, the natural scansion (rhythm) of speech.

**Stage directions**: Minimal. Freedom to imagine areas of the island on any stage format. However, original stage set would have been limited to thrust, balcony and backstage areas.

**Stage and setting**: Begins on a ship that Prospero sends Ariel to wreck. No one is harmed but all are scared when they are abandoned on the island, as Prospero was. The rest of the play takes place on the island.

**Social, historical and cultural contexts, including theatrical conventions of the period when the performance text was created**: Shakespeare's play was written for a simple stage, with a thrust and balcony. It refers to complex contemporary issues around the old and new worlds, when the country was exploring issues of master and slave, self and other.

The following exercises will help you to explore and demonstrate your knowledge and understanding of how drama and theatre are developed and performed.

## EXERCISE 9.6

AO 3  AO 4

**1 Direction exercise**

'This island's mine, by Sycorax my mother.'

a) Look at Caliban and Prospero's argument in Act 1 Scene 2. Think about what Caliban and Prospero are angry about. What points do they both make?

b) When *The Tempest* was written, Europe had only recently begun to explore the New World. Discuss with your group how thoughts about slavery, and the British Empire, are part of the themes of *The Tempest*.

**2 Costume and make-up exercise**

'This thing of darkness I acknowledge mine.'

Caliban is often called a monster and, in Act 5 Scene 1, a 'plain fish'.

a) What clues does the text give about Caliban's appearance?

b) How would you and your group use costume and make-up to create Caliban's appearance?

**3 Acting exercise**

'We are such stuff as dreams are made on.'

In Act 4 Scene 1, Prospero brings about happy endings for everyone, showing his forgiveness for the plots against him.

Write a monologue from Ariel's, Miranda's or Ferdinand's point of view:

• What is on their mind?

• What have they learnt?

• Who are they talking to?

• How do they imagine the life they are going back to?

## Eduqas

### *The Caucasian Chalk Circle* by Bertolt Brecht

**Written**: 1944.

**Genre**: Political.

**Themes**: Justice, power, class, inequality, motherhood.

**Structure**: 'Play within a play'. Episodic, so not in chronological order. Prologue and five main episodes ('The Noble Child', 'The Flight into the Northern Mountains', 'In the Northern Mountains', 'The Story of the Judge' and 'The Caucasian Chalk Circle').

**Plot summary**

Grusha flees a Caucasian city during a bloody civil war in Georgia, a Russian province, saving Michael, the baby son of Natella, the governor's widow. Years later, Natella tries to claim Michael back from Grusha, who is trapped in a loveless marriage. Grusha wins a legal battle with Natella over Michael when the judge enacts a King Solomon-style test to determine the real mother: placing Michael in a chalk circle, saying that the real mother will be able to pull him out. Grusha does not want to hurt Michael and will not pull the child out, so the judge rules in her favour.

**Main characters**: The Singer (narrating the action), Grusha, Simon, Azdak (the judge), Shauva and Natella Abashwili.

**Form and style**: Brechtian theatre distances the audience, intending to make them examine their world anew. John Willet, Brecht's collaborator and translator, describes gestus as a combination of 'gesture and gist, attitude and point' (Brecht, 1977, page 173): actors were asked to find actions, gestures, movement and intonation that revealed and commented on the wider socio-political level of their scenes.

**Language and dialogue**: Speech, song and dialogue are full of social comment but still realistic.

**Stage directions**: Often spoken, or shown on placards, to indicate changes of place and the movement of time.

**Stage and setting**: Brecht's technique of a floodlit, bare stage reminds the audience they are watching a play, rather than suspending their disbelief, with only simple objects or garments to suggest places and characters. This keeps the audience focused on the issues raised rather than individual characters.

**Social, historical and cultural contexts including theatrical conventions of the period when the performance text was created**: Written by Brecht during his exile in World War II and the only one of his plays to end on a happy note, both for the character and the theme (justice is restored).

> "The songs are an absolutely integral part of the play. I didn't do them separately – there is no break in my mind between the prose and the poetry. By that I mean there's a prosaic quality to the poetry and a poetic quality to the prose that is wonderful to work on. Brecht loves language – he puts such store on the pleasure of the human ear."

Frank McGuiness, who adapted *The Caucasian Chalk Circle* for Unicorn Theatre (Greenwood, 2007, page 21)

The following exercises will help you to explore and demonstrate your knowledge and understanding of how drama and theatre are developed and performed.

## EXERCISE 9.7

AO 3 — AO 4

**1 Discussion exercise**

**'Terrible is the temptation to do good.'**

At the beginning of the play, Grusha, the servant girl, contemplates whether to save the baby Michael and risk her own life in doing so. As Brecht wrote this play during his exile in World War II, this was a question faced by a lot of people in Germany, when helping their fellow citizens could result in death.

What moral issues could you explore in a scene, with a character having to choose between what is easiest for them and what helps someone else?

**2 Music exercise**

**'When the sharks the sharks devour
Little fishes have their hour.'**

Brecht's music, poetry and action all reflected wider socio-political issues. What does the singer mean by the quote above, regarding the characters in the play and the wider situation?

**3 Staging exercise**

**Azdak's judgment**

As a judge, Azdak is as likely to take a bribe from the rich to rule in their favour as he is to show compassion to the poor. Brecht's characters and situations are always political, standing for something bigger than themselves.

How can you stage the symbolism in Azdak's judgment and Grusha's choice, in which she risks losing Michael to avoid harming him?

## Eduqas

### *Hard to Swallow* by Mark Wheeller

**Themes**: Anorexia: stereotypical views, lesser-known risk factors, parental expectations.

**Written**: 1991.

**Genre**: Brechtian elements. Also, Physical Theatre, particularly in 'The Brussels Sprouts Scene'.

**Structure**: Bookended by 'The Three Billy Goats Gruff' scenes: beginning, middle and end.

**Plot summary**

This play is an adaptation of *Catherine: The Story of a Young Girl who Died of Anorexia* by her mother, Maureen Dunbar. It is told mainly through Catherine's own words, as well as her family's, and charts her battle with both her illness itself and what it means for her family. It uses elements of Catherine's diaries and challenges stereotypical views about anorexia.

**Main characters**: Catherine Dunbar, John Dunbar, Maureen Dunbar, Simon Dunbar, Anna Dunbar. 31 characters in all (six male, three female, 22 any gender). The author notes that the play has been performed in the past by an all-female cast.

**Form and style**: The script is taken partly from Catherine's real-life diaries. Some elements are stylised, particularly 'The Three Billy Goats Gruff' scenes.

**Language and dialogue**: Complex issues and characters, difficult and challenging stories.

**Stage directions:** Very detailed. Stylistic and naturalistic scenes interwoven in text.

**Social, historical and cultural context including theatrical conventions of the period when the performance text was created:** Modern period. Challenging stereotypical views that eating disorders are a deliberate cry for attention, rather than a biological reality.

**Stage and setting:** Structured into the three scenes, bookended by the imagery of the fairy tale 'The Three Billy Goats Gruff', who eat the grass in a field until it is gone and then need to overcome obstacles to get to fields further away. The family of goats must work together to cross the bridge, suggesting the need to work together rather than fight or blame each other. This visual reminder comes between the human family scenes.

" *The significance of the Billy goats … I can't remember how they came about but I love nursery rhymes and different ways of looking at them. I remember a book called* Shockheaded Peter *at my uncle's that was for children but it had quite an impact … also those big dogs in the* TinderBox. *I'm a big David Bowie fan … 'Ashes to Ashes', the children's song type thing and love how that little tinkly tune touches something of the child in me … yet it's about something else. It reaches something quite primeval. We had, at one point a Billy goat scene to parallel each scene. In the end the play was too long so I reduced it using the Two Touch technique. This was the result. I liked the idea of surprising the audience. When they came to see a play such as HTS [*Hard to Swallow*] they will have preconceptions of what it's going to be about and I wanted them to be completely thrown off by this opening. 'This isn't what we were expecting!' I wanted them to be thrown into confusion. I didn't want them to be left there (I hate that happening) so, at the end when they have seen the play they will understand the allegory. By inserting the verbatim sections into that scene it elaborates on it and hopefully the links become clear. The audience realise what they have learnt.* "

Mark Wheeller, cited in WJEC (2016)

**The following exercises will help you to explore and demonstrate your knowledge and understanding of how drama and theatre are developed and performed.**

**EXERCISE 9.8** AO3 AO4

**1 Sound exercise**

Stage directions in the play ask the actors to create the sound of a food processor, a human pedal bin, a car horn and the popping of a champagne cork. However, there is also a recorded sound that is very important: a musical box (pages 21, 27, 30, 35 and 45), which on page 27 is said to create 'another worldly atmosphere', changing the mood or rewinding time.

**'Cast make a car … with features such as windscreen, wipers, etc.'**

Choose this (or another) stage direction from the play to inspire a Physical Theatre piece.

**2 Setting exercise**

Mark Wheeller's favourite set for a production of his play was a dining table and chairs, which became everything needed in the play and was a constant reminder of the importance of food and the mealtime ritual.

How could you use furniture to convey family tension?

**3 Titles and issues**

*Hard to Swallow* works so well as a title because it reflects:

a) The physical experience of a person living with an eating disorder.

b) The emotional experience of the family (and wider society) who need to examine their own behaviour and make changes.

As a group, discuss how both these meanings of 'hard to swallow' are reflected in your work. Could the meaning of one of them be brought out more?

Eduqas

## *War Horse* by Nick Stafford

**Written**: Novel written by Michael Morpurgo 1982; adapted for stage 2007.

**Themes**: Courage, loyalty, friendship, conflict, justice, sacrifice.

**Genre**: Adaptation (National Theatre, 2007) of Michael Morpurgo's novel, *War Horse*.

**Structure**: Episodic, placards/projections assist the passing of time and a puppet of the ship crosses the sea when the location changes – dates, places, etc. indicated by projections and puppets.

**Plot summary**

Joey the horse is purchased by Albert's family and trained by Albert. But boy and horse are separated when the war begins and Albert's father sells Joey to help the war effort and get them some money. The action follows Joey's adventures, his friendships with humans and animals alike, and the courage that helps him to survive the war and eventually be reunited with Albert.

**Main characters**: Joey the horse, Major Nicholls, Topthorn the horse, David, the armies of Britain, France and Germany.

**Form and style**: Emotionally charged, minimalist. Conveying historical information through dialogue.

**Language and dialogue**: Accents suggested through text. Naturalistic, minimalist. Silent action shows relationships between humans, animals and each other. Music and songs add to dialogue, character and emotion. Adaptation of swear words and foreign words, so suitable for all ages while being true to voice.

**Stage directions**: Freedom to interpret. Shows intention but leaves room for interpretation.

**Stage and setting**: 1912–1918; World War I. Lifesize animal puppets (originally by Handspring Puppet Company). Audience comes to forget about the puppeteers.

**Social, historical and cultural contexts, including theatrical conventions of the period when the performance text was created**: Familiarity with the historical facts of two world wars; audience sees the realities of war afresh by following the events and sacrifices from the point of view of the animals and young people caught up in it.

The following exercises will help you to explore and demonstrate your knowledge and understanding of how drama and theatre are developed and performed.

## EXERCISE 9.9

AO 3 — AO 4

1 **Directing exercise: Joey with other animals**

In your group, discuss the images that the stage directions call for between Joey and any of the other puppets. Select one of the following scenes:

a) Joey and his mother, Alice, opening of Scene 1.

b) Joey and the goose, opening of Scene 5.

c) Joey and Topthorn, final lines of Scene 8.

2 **Acting exercise**

Read the first two pages of Scene 3, a discussion between Albert, his parents, Rose and Ted, and Joey.

a) What are Albert's parents' worries? How are these communicated indirectly, through subtext (what is implied but not said), dialogue and action?

b) How are Albert's priorities different from his parents'?

c) How do Rose and Ted, Joey and Albert approach each other physically? How could you show humans and animals responding in similar ways?

3 **Direction**

Read the final part of Scene 26, from 'The terrible sound is getting closer' to 'Joey flees'.

Brainstorm in your group how you would interpret the stage directions and lines to bring it to life. You should think about:

• the suggested sound-effects

• the physical actions, including moments of indecision and fear

• the emotions both horses and humans would experience and how their voices, faces and bodies would show this.

## Eduqas

### *DNA* by Dennis Kelly

> *Amongst the darkness of an unnamed wood, a lawless gang are trying to bury a dark secret. The group need someone to take charge, but who can they trust? Who do they follow? While lies spiral and tension mounts, everyday adolescence twists and turns into an anarchic game of survival.*

National Youth Theatre (2018) publicity description

**Themes**: Bullying, belonging, social responsibility, fear, violence, morality, leadership.

**Written**: 2008.

**Genre**: Tragicomedy.

**Structure**: Four acts (14 short scenes).

**Characters**: Eleven characters. Deliberately written so characters can change name and gender (this is specified in the stage directions).

**Plot summary**

A group of teenagers engage in a cover-up, thinking they have killed someone. The cover-up unites them; the tensions and power struggles within the group become a spirit of working together. When they discover they have not killed anyone after all, they find that they are behaving better to each other and gain a greater sense of their own identity.

**Form and style**: Naturalistic speech – subtext comes through what people do not say, leave off saying, and how they cover one emotion with another.

**Language and dialogue**: Modern.

**Stage directions**: Minimal – give key actions and clues to the emotional states of the characters.

**Stage and setting**: Three locations: street, field, wood.

**Social, historical and cultural contexts, including theatrical conventions of the period when the performance text was created**: Dennis Kelly was responding to society's current fears about terrorism when he wrote this play about a teenage gang: 'I began to ask myself whether it was right to sacrifice the individual for the many – this for me is the central question in the play. It's not about bullying or anything like that … What the characters are struggling with in the play itself are questions of how far they should go to protect the group.' Morality in the play becomes centred on what is best for the group, rather than what is morally right.

*" I have deliberately written it so that there are many staging options. Theatre is a very collaborative art-form. Part of my job is to create the circumstances where other people can come in and use their own creativity as much as I've been allowed to use mine … I saw a field a wood and a street as that's where the characters were. "*

Dennis Kelly, cited in WJEC (2020)

**The following exercises will help you to explore and demonstrate your knowledge and understanding of how drama and theatre are developed and performed.**

## EXERCISE 9.10

**1 'Dead?'**

The more you know about your character, the more deeply convincing your performance will be. This is most important when not much is said.

**a)** Read Scene 1 in pairs. Make a list of what we learn about each character and the situation. The following questions will help you:

- Does Jan or Mark have more authority?
- Are there clues that both are panicking, not just one of them?
- What is the effect of ending on a question?

**b)** Now compare this with Jan and Mark's dialogue at the beginning of Scene 4. What has changed? How would you show this in performance?

**2 'What are you thinking?'**

In Scene 2, Leah speaks her monologue to Phil with no verbal responses from him. Try writing a monologue where the other character is silent (N.B. they cannot be dead or asleep).

**3 'Okay. Okay. Okay.'**

In pairs, read Scene 3. In just over two pages, both the characters (Jan and Mark) use simple, often repeated, words and phrases. Notice how the repetition allows the actors to communicate different thoughts with the same, simple words.

**a)** Discuss the subtext (that which they are talking about but do not say). Make sure you know every thought underneath every line.

**b)** Perform the scene again. Note how your speech and actions become more intense and believable when you are clear about what is NOT being said.

# SECTION B: ANALYSING AND EVALUATING LIVE THEATRE

## What do I need to do?

For Section B of the exam, you need to analyse and evaluate one piece of live theatre that you have viewed during your course. This is your opportunity to show your understanding of how meaning is communicated by theatre makers in a professional performance. Think about themes, characters and plots, and how these are communicated onstage.

---

**How to improve your evaluation skills** AO 4

**Read reviews!**

You can read excellent reviews in the *Stage* newspaper – which in a few words say exactly what did and did not work in a production and why.

**Show your working!**

Just like in a maths exam where you would show your working out, a good evaluation needs to provide evidence to back-up your opinion. If something worked well, say how they did it and what the reaction in the audience was. If it went badly, give the same kind of evidence. You should also give a description of the layout of the venue (including limitations on space and sight lines).

**Play or production?**

Make sure you are clear about what is the play (the script itself) and what is the production (the particular interpretation of this production).

---

## Writing an evaluation

In the exam, you may be asked to consider the following aspects:

**Actors:**

- interpretation of character
- character interaction
- vocal skills
- movement skills.

**Designers:**

- creation of mood and atmosphere
- use of performance space
- lighting
- sound
- set and props
- costume and make-up.

**Directors:**

- interpretation and style
- performance conventions
- spatial relationships on stage
- relationship between performer and audience.

**TIP**

Always back-up your statements with details or examples.

**TIP**

Think not only about your individual response but also the response of the audience as a whole.

# INDEX

**Magic 'if'**
The actor's ability to imagine themselves in the circumstances of their character and feel truthful emotions as a consequence.

**Mime**
Performing action, character and emotion without words or sounds. Uses only gestures, expressions and movements.

**Minor character**
A character who is not the primary focus of the story but exists to perform a certain function or present a specific viewpoint in the story.

**Monologue**
A long speech by one character within a scene. When speaking private thoughts, only heard by the audience, it is called a soliloquy.

**Narrator**
Tells the story or gives information directly to the audience.

**Naturalistic**
Performance style intended to give the impression of real life.

**Naturalistic acting**
Acting intended to give the impression of real life (although gestures and diction must be simpler and clearer than in real life to succeed).

**Objective**
What the character wants – the goal of what they say and do in the scene.

**Observation**
Offstage, in addition to using their own memory and imagination, actors depend on their power to observe how others feel, speak or think, and behave in response to the emotion. Onstage, observation is equally important, as the stronger the audience focuses, the deeper your involvement in the scene.

**Obstacle**
What stands in the way of a character's objective – causing dramatic tension and conflict.

**Operational set**
A theatre set with a working part, e.g. a light that is switched on by the actor rather than the lighting operator.

**Protagonist**
Main character, often the hero (or 'goodie').

**Reviews**
A short essay on a theatre production, accessing what decisions have been made in the interpretation of the script by the director and theatre company, and how successful these were.

**Sight lines**
Lines of unobstructed view (sight) between an intended observer and a subject onstage.

**Slow motion**
Action presented slower than natural speed, to build suspense or closely examine something.

**Soliloquy**
A long speech by a character alone onstage, sharing their private thoughts.

**Soundscape**
A collection of sounds created by the actors, recordings or a combination of both, to provide atmosphere and location.

**Spontaneity**
The act of creating, or ability to create, scenes, or make choices without preparation.

**Stimulus (plural stimuli)**
Resource used to inspire or establish the context, focus and purpose of the dramatic topic being presented.

**Stylisation**
Non-naturalistic acting, movement or staging.

**Suspension of disbelief**
The intentional avoidance of critical thinking, allowing performer and audience to invest in the story and issues of the characters and plot.

**Symbol**
An object standing for an issue or theme.

**The System**
Stanislavski's systematic training system for naturalistic acting, based on creating an inner life for the character. He contrasted 'art of experiencing' (truthful acting) with 'art of representation' (mechanical or superficial acting).

**Theatre practitioner**
A creator of theatrical performances, e.g. director, designer or actor.

**Thought-tracking**
Characters speak their private thoughts to the audience aloud.

**Total Theatre**
Theatre in which all elements – music, voice, movement and spectacle – work together. Emphasis on the use of the body to tell the story.

**Truthful acting**
Acting based on re-experiencing authentic emotions, resulting from the combination of the actors' use of their own memories and the given circumstances in the script.

**Written evaluations**
An essay or report giving an argument and providing evidence that justifies the writer's opinion on the subject.

# REFERENCES

*Alumni News* (2017, 5 October) 'Katie Mitchell Wins British Academy Award', Magdalene College, Oxford, https://www.magd.ox.ac.uk/alumni-news/katie-mitchell-wins-british-academy-award/.

Berkoff, Steven (1994) 'Actor', *Steven Berkoff: The Collected Plays Vol. 2*, Faber & Faber.

Brecht, Bertolt (1977) *Brecht on Theatre* (ed. and trans. John Willett), Methuen.

Brecht, Bertolt (2007) *The Caucasian Chalk Circle*, Penguin.

Brown, Griselda Murray (2014, 31 October) 'Katie Mitchell and Carbon-cycle Agitprop', *Financial Times*.

Campbell, Karen (2017) 'Woman of the Year: Emma Rice' *Standard Issue Magazine*, http://standardissuemagazine.com/in-the-news/woman-year-emma-rice/.

Edwardes, Jane (2007, 12 November) 'Katie Mitchell: Interview', *Time Out*, https://www.timeout.com/london/theatre/katie-mitchell-interview.

Furness, Hannah (2016, 25 January) 'Emma Rice: "A Lot of Shakespeare Feels Like Medicine"', the *Telegraph*, https://www.telegraph.co.uk/theatre/actors/emma-rice-a-lot-of-shakespeare-feels-like-medicine/.

Greenwood, Catherine (2007) *The Caucasian Chalk Circle: Teacher Resource Pack*, Unicorn, www.unicorntheatre.com/files/2-Unicorn%20Theatre%20THE%20CAUCASIAN%20CHALK%20CIRCLE%20Teacher%20Resource%20pack.pdf.

Grose, C., Murphy, Anna Maria and Rice, Emma (2005) 'The Red Shoes', in *Kneehigh Anthology Volume 1: Tristan and Yseult Red Shoes, The Wooden Frock, The Bachae*, Oberon Books.

Higgins, Charlotte, (2016, 14 January) 'Katie Mitchell, British Theatre's Queen in Exile', the *Guardian*, https://www.theguardian.com/stage/2016/jan/14/british-theatre-queen-exile-katie-mitchell.

Lecoq, Jacques (2000) *The Moving Body (Le Corps Poetique): Teaching Creative Theatre* (trans. David Bradby), Bloomsbury.

Mahoney, Elisabeth (2010, 3 August) 'The Red Shoes', the *Guardian*, https://www.theguardian.com/stage/2010/aug/03/red-shoes-review.

National Youth Theatre (2018) 'What's On', www.nyt.org.uk/whats-on/dna.

Ros, Manon Steffan (2016, 27 May) 'Urdd Drama Medal Judge, Manon Steffan Ross, to Publish New Drama, *Dau Wyneb*, on the Eisteddford Fields at Flint', University of Wales, https://www.uwtsd.ac.uk/news/press-releases/press-2016/urdd-drama-medal-judge-manon-steffan-ross-to-publish-new-drama-dau-wyneb-on-the-eisteddfod-fields-at-flint.html.

Saunders, James (2002) 'Random Thoughts in a May Garden', *The Methuen Drama Book of Monologues for Young Actors* (ed. Anne Harvey), Methuen.

Senter, Al (2019) 'Interview with Rebecca Director Emma Rice', ATG Tickets, https://www.atgtickets.com/news/interview-with-rebecca-director-emma-rice/.

Stanislavski, C. (2003) *An Actor Prepares*, Bloomsbury Revelations.

The Imaginary Body (2020) *100 – Our Last Play*, http://www.theimaginarybody.co.uk/hundred.html.

Trueman, Matt (2016, 26 February) 'Katie Mitchell: "I was Uncomfortable Coming Back to Work in the UK"', *The Stage*, https://www.thestage.co.uk/features/interviews/2016/katie-mitchell-i-was-uncomfortable-coming-back-to-work-in-the-uk/.

Viereck, Sylvster (1929, 26 October) 'What Life Means to Einstein', *Saturday Evening Post*.

WhatsOnStage (2009, 26 February) 'Steven Berkoff On … *The Waterfront* & the Working Man', https://www.whatsonstage.com/west-end-theatre/news/steven-berkoff-on-the-waterfront-and-the-working-m_17676.html.

WJEC (2016) 'Hard to Swallow, Mark Wheeller, http://resource.download.wjec.co.uk.s3.amazonaws.com/vtc/2015-16/15-16_44/hard%20to%20swallow.pdf.

WJEC (2020) 'DNA by Dennis Kelly, http://resource.download.wjec.co.uk.s3.amazonaws.com/vtc/2015-16/15-16_44/DNA.pdf.

# GLOSSARY OF KEY TERMS

**Alienation**
'Distancing effect', making the familiar strange in order to see issues more clearly.

**Antagonist**
Opposition or enemy of protagonist (main character).

**Black-box theatre**
A flexible performance space, or studio, that can be adapted to different seating configurations.

**Blocking**
The positioning of the actors on the stage so that nothing necessary to the sense of the scene is hidden OR not accepting an offer made by another character (failing to cooperate).

**Choral speaking**
Group of performers speaking together, commenting on or narrating the action of the play.

**Concentration of attention**
When an actor creates a sense of isolation onstage in order to focus on characterisation. The purpose of Stanislavski's 'circles of attention'.

**Cross-cutting**
Two scenes intercut each other, moving between locations and/or periods of time.

**Cyclorama**
Arc-shaped cloth or back of auditorium, stretching behind the stage set, often used to depict the sky.

**Designing for theatre**
Also called 'scenography' when referring to the design of the set. Designing for theatre means creating the pictures of the world in which the actors perform, and can refer to set and props, lighting, sound, costume and make-up.

**Direct address**
A form of narration, when a character breaks the fourth wall by speaking directly to the audience, usually saying something the other characters cannot hear.

**Dramatic devices**
Visual techniques used to communicate meaning to an audience, to emphasise a particular point or moment in the storytelling.

**Dramatic pause**
A hesitation or halt in dialogue, heightening suspense or showing a character's strong reaction to something.

**Emotion memory**
Actor uses a memory of the emotion they think their character would be feeling, to build empathy and involvement and connect with the given circumstances experienced by the character.

**Feeling of truth**
Actor uses own emotions to create an authentic imagined response to the character's circumstances, built on their own emotion memory.

**External characteristics**
Facial and physical features of a character: looks, movement, physical habits.

**Flashback**
A character's memory triggers the action of the play to move to a previous time, recounting a crucial event in the story.

**Focus**
Concentration on the given circumstances of the play, to help the actor give an authentic and unforced performance.

**Fourth wall**
Imaginary wall, separating the world of the play from the audience. Stanislavski encouraged actors to create the details of the wall in their mind as clearly as possible.

**Freeze-frame**
Still image or silent tableau formed by the actors to illustrate a key moment or idea in the script.

**Genre**
Kinds of drama, recognisable through particular conventions attached to each style of performance, e.g. comedy, tragedy, melodrama, tragicomedy.

**Hot-seating**
Character-building strategy in which the actor (in character) sits in front of the rest of the group and is interviewed by them, answering with prior knowledge or developing new details about the character in response to their questions.

**Inner life**
The unique combination of the actor's emotions and memories with their character's given circumstances creates a unique 'inner life', informing the 'external characteristics' of the character.

**Internal characteristics**
The values and emotions of the character that inform the meaning behind their lines, movements and gestures.

# Interpreting theatre: What have I learnt?

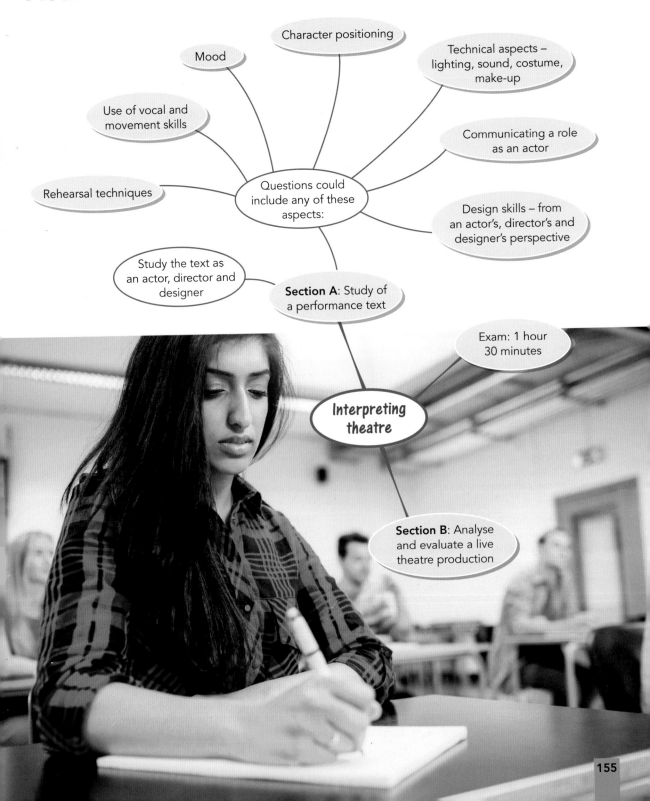

Character positioning

Mood

Technical aspects – lighting, sound, costume, make-up

Use of vocal and movement skills

Communicating a role as an actor

Rehearsal techniques

Questions could include any of these aspects:

Design skills – from an actor's, director's and designer's perspective

Study the text as an actor, director and designer

**Section A**: Study of a performance text

Exam: 1 hour 30 minutes

Interpreting theatre

**Section B**: Analyse and evaluate a live theatre production